Withdrawn

THE Thieves OF Threadneedle Street

THE Thieves OF Threadneedle Street

The Incredible True Story of the American Forgers
Who Nearly Broke the Bank of England

Nicholas Booth

PEGASUS BOOKS
NEW YORK LONDON

For Sarah, my everything

The Thieves of Threadneedle Street

Pegasus Books Ltd
148 West 37th Street, 13th Floor
New York, NY 10018

First Pegasus Books hardcover edition November 2016

ISBN: 978-1-68177-240-0

10 9 8 7 8 6 5 4 3 2 1

Printed in the United States of America
Distributed by W. W. Norton & Company, Inc.

Contents

	Author's Note	7
	Prologue: 'For Lack of a Nail'	8
1	Formidable Rascals	13
2	Strangers, Silk Hats and Salting Wells	35
3	Rogues' Gallery	56
4	The Social Triumphs of a Silver King	77
5	Mistresses of Misfortune	101
6	The Skewering of Colonel Peregrine Madgwick Francis	122
7	The Finer Arts of Forgery	146
8	Hearts and Minds	170
9	Strange Messengers	193
10	Devil to Pay	216
11	Before Your Very Eyes	243
12	Cat and Mouse	268
13	Means of Escape	290
14	The Melancholy of All Things Done	314
	Notes	334
	Acknowledgements	343
	Bibliography and Sources	345
	Index	350

Author's Note

The following narrative is based on several sources. These include official court transcripts, prosecution briefs, witness statements, timelines, detective reports, diaries, letters, telegrams and, of course, contemporary newspaper accounts. Much of this material – especially in the archives of the Bank of England – has never been examined before.

For reasons which will become clear in the text, I have been very careful in using the forgers' own various confessional autobiographies in the narrative which follows, noting their tendencies to exaggerate. Others, writing years after the events, remembered things demonstrably wrongly. More memorable episodes are clearly recalled, but the chronology is invariably incorrect. In other cases, the converse is true.

Wherever possible, I have tried to ensure that the events described were at least verified by more than one source. Given the passage of time, such backup is sometimes impossible to obtain. The more fantastical claims of the forgers, their associates and the detectives who chased them as well as, more obviously, particularly excitable press coverage, cannot be taken at face value. Oddly, a number of the most remarkable stories are confirmed in contemporaneous accounts.

As a result, I have used a standard litmus test: extraordinary claims require extraordinary evidence not least, as one of the witnesses noted towards the end of their trial at the Old Bailey, because the whole of the forgers' conduct was extraordinary.

Prologue

Saturday, 1 March 1873
Cashier's Department, Bank of England, Threadneedle Street,
City of London. 10 a.m.

When he looked at it again, a cold shiver enveloped the deputy chief cashier of the Bank of England. The certificate in his hand was, at face value, a simple piece of paper, a glorified IOU known as a 'bill of exchange' that had been accepted, stamped and its equivalent monetary value long since paid out. To his horror, Frank May had found it was counterfeit.

At first, he thought he had made a mistake. Diligently, he had checked and cross-referenced and come in early on this Saturday to pull the files just to make sure. To his growing dismay, he found he was not wrong. A sense of panic began to engulf him. Throughout his two decades working here, the cashier had never come across anything like this. It did not make any sense. He thought it had to be an oversight, but now, sitting quietly in his office, there could be no doubt. It was an elaborate and almost perfect forgery – and one with terrible consequences.

When he had first come across the bill, he saw there was a date missing. Whoever had accepted it must not have noticed. That in itself was unusual, but then the more he looked into it, the more his suspicions gelled into complete and utter certainty. So, too, were other bills the cause of his growing disquiet. There was a whole slew of forgeries, increasing in value and number over the last few weeks. Most had passed through this building unnoticed and only by accident had he stumbled across this latest one.

Wondering what on earth was behind it all, Frank May decided he had better act before it was all too late – if it wasn't already. Grabbing his hat and coat, the cashier made his way to the bank that had blithely cashed this particular forgery in all good faith. He looked up at the clock in the main entrance. He had better hurry, or else they – whoever the hell they were – would get away with £1 million or more, if they had not already done so.

Bills of exchange represented one of the greater innovations of nineteenth-century finance. They were essentially glorified credit notes sanctioned by reputable merchants who guaranteed them like post-dated cheques. They allowed for the ease and smooth flow of international trade via banks, a Victorian version of wiring money in advance. Today, similar transfers would be carried out electronically in the blink of an eye. Then, in the late Victorian age of steam and telegraph, the preferred method of redeeming such bills was from personal presentation. Providing the bearer was trusted, both he – for it was invariably a male domain – and the bill he presented were accepted at face value. More often than not, the accepting clerk would blithely rubber-stamp them.

The whole system was based on trust. It was a measure of London's financial standing that a simple piece of paper with a reputable banker's signature was as honest and liquid as a banknote. 'A bill on London', as it was known, was every bit as solid as coins and notes of Her Majesty's realm.

In recent years, bankers had been keen to 'discount' them – that is, they would offer real money at a percentage lower than the bills' stated value. They would then recover the full amount from whoever had originally incurred that debt and issued them. That was what Frank May was now attempting to do, essentially balancing his ledger.

Crucially, their acceptance centred on a signature. That was all that was needed to 'endorse' them. In the City of London, the whole process, from acceptance to discounting, was underwritten by the Bank of England, the fulcrum of the most stable financial system in the world. As a result, discount houses had sprung up all over the City. Most were located across the way in Lombard Street, where Mr May was now headed to the Continental Bank at No. 79.

Somebody had clearly subverted the whole process. This particular bill had a date missing. So it was fairly obvious that the 'acceptances' were not genuine. No reputable banker would have allowed it to pass unless they were incompetent, which Mr May very much doubted. That was why he needed to find out more from the bankers who had discounted this specific bill and whether their signature of acceptance was genuine.

'[Those] last seven words give the key to the whole mystery' was how one of the forgers behind it later explained it, a riddle that the deputy chief cashier of the Bank of England was now determined to resolve as he left the building, fearful of what he might find.

It had all started out innocently enough. The evening before, Frank May had been sifting through the day's transactions. It was his job to make sure nothing was amiss. Balancing the books was time consuming, not to say exhausting, but he took pride and care, as he had done for many years. May had been with the bank for years, working with his father for most of them. Both were no-nonsense northerners, tireless recruits from the respectable ranks who took inordinate pride in their work no matter how mind-numbing it might be.

At first, as he went through the post, May came across nothing suspicious. A letter, one of the hundreds received each day, had arrived overnight from Birmingham. It contained a number of acceptances which had already been endorsed at the bank's West End branch in Burlington Gardens. Signed in the name of Frederick Albert Warren, there was nothing particularly disturbing about them. The Bank of England would have a few more weeks to make good the payment, collecting the money in due course.

Yet one of the batch soon caught his attention because of the missed date. 'Strange', he thought. When May looked more closely at the name, he was puzzled. His initial enquiries revealed that they had subsequently been discounted for an American businessman called Charles Johnson Horton at the Continental Bank. He was clearly a very good customer. The files showed he had been doing this for most of the previous month. Frederick Warren held an account at the bank's Western Branch close by Piccadilly Circus and had been sending the bills by registered mail from Birmingham.

That made sense, May thought. The reason they had opened the branch in Burlington Gardens had been to help successful businessmen. No longer would they need to come here into the city every time they wanted to cash a cheque or, in this case, redeem a bill of exchange. But then, as he went through a number of related transactions on the Warren account, May grew increasingly puzzled. There did seem to be an awful number of these bills, growing in value, but there was nothing to suggest they had been used to launder money.

It was late and there was nothing much he could do. Aware of the gathering darkness, he would simply have to wait and make further enquiries in the morning. After a good night's sleep, he might find a better explanation. It might just be some strange, unexpected oversight rather than anything sinister.

Saturday, 1 March 1873
Outside the Bank, Threadneedle Street
10.10 a.m.

It wasn't. Frank May had unearthed incontrovertible proof that something was seriously amiss.

It was not usual for a senior staff member to be in at the weekend, but these were unusual circumstances. Further enquiries revealed that Mr Warren had given no permanent address, provided no references nor any particular credentials in any shape or form. Underlings in the cashier's department were now frantically pulling further files as Mr May left the building and made his way towards the house that had discounted the incomplete bill. There could be no doubt. It wasn't just a one-off. It was nothing less than a systematic attack.

Warren and Horton were either the same person or working in league. The sequence of bills, acceptances and endorsements May had found in the files were proof. A whole series of forgeries had been carried out deliberately and methodically, right here in the heart of the world's greatest financial institution. Frank May could hardly believe it. Who would dare do such a thing?

As he made his way out onto Threadneedle Street, the overcast skies perfectly matched his darkening mood. By his simple reckoning, these Americans had already taken something like £12,000 out of the bank with the forged bills that had arrived from Birmingham the day before. By the end of this Saturday, May would find evidence that the total figure was nudging £100,000. That would be almost £8 million in today's money – in Victorian London, an unimaginable sum to even the richest tycoons, let alone an office worker like himself. Worse, there could be many more fraudulent bills passing through the system which had not yet come due. The full extent of their exposure could take weeks to uncover. It did not bear thinking about.

It was only a fluke that had led him to unravel the scheme. The remarkable enterprise from an ice cool criminal intellect had foundered upon human fallibility. May could hardly explain, let alone comprehend, the enormity of it all. Unless he did something, the cashier realised to his growing horror, vast sums of money could vanish before their very eyes. The banking system depended on trust, and if that was lost, then who knew what might result?

The runes were hardly great for that spring of 1873, the world's economies were plunging headfirst into a recession, later known by historians as the 'long depression'. 'The panic of 1873' has eerie parallels to today. Economies were overheating and it would only take a run on the pound to cause an even greater collapse. That was simply too awful to contemplate.

For Frank May, it was simple. Whoever was behind these frauds had to be stopped. Quickly and determinedly, he walked out onto the street, grim-faced and horrified. In desperation, he looked In every direction. Why, he wondered, could you never find a policeman when you needed one?

1

Formidable Rascals

They laid their plans carefully and performed their work coolly and deliberately. Nor were they hasty or imprudent in carrying out their designs. For months they conducted their operations with a most businesslike caution and they might have eventually succeeded in gaining the coveted millions, had not the first flush of success so unnerved them that they grew careless and made a most foolish and unnecessary error. The manner in which these men worked was as simple as it was ingenious.

Allan Pinkerton, *Thirty Years A Detective*, 1884

Saturday, 1 March 1873
Continental Bank, Lombard Street
Shortly after 10.30 a.m.

Outside it was the kind of spring day reminiscent of winter, a cold front bringing blustery weather and the ceaseless certainty of downpours later in the day. Grim-faced and determined, the deputy chief cashier of the Bank of England crossed Threadneedle Street by the Mansion House and made his way over towards Lombard Street. Frank May still looked ashen faced when, less than 100yds away from the source of his discovery – and in some sense, the scene of the crime – he walked into the Continental Bank with a policeman in tow.

He was barely able to articulate, let alone convey, the full horror of what he had uncovered. Making his way into the office of John Stanton, the manager of the branch, he carried with him the puzzling evidence he had unearthed. They had only been talking for a few moments when Mr Stanton looked up in surprise. 'Talk of the Devil', he thought.

Right before them was the clerk to the character behind the greater fraud. It looked as though he was about to cash another acceptance. They were stunned. The last thing either of them had been expecting was to find one of the Yankee scoundrels in person. With his prematurely balding forehead and droopy moustache, he did not exactly look like an international criminal. The protruding, wary eyes added to a sense of world weariness.

The bank officials both peered out into the gloom of the foyer. 'Is that Mr Horton, or Mr Horton's clerk?' Frank May asked.

'Yes,' the manager replied, 'this is Mr Noyes, Mr Horton's clerk.'

They walked calmly over towards him and politely suggested that Mr May might ask him a few questions. He should, they said, come along with them to a corner office. The American complied. The unsmiling, grave demeanour of the policeman meant he had very little choice. Everything was calm and collected, as though happening upon great forgeries were an everyday occurrence.

Noyes, more regretful than anything, protested his innocence with what seemed well-practised bluster. 'You have no right to take me without a warrant,' he exclaimed. 'Why are you giving me into custody?' Mr May was having none of it. 'I am come from the Bank of England and I give this man in charge of for fraud,' he said to the policeman.

Once inside the manager's office, the American was told that he was going to be held on suspicion of forgery. Noyes looked – and was – genuinely astonished.

A short time later, another policeman joined them to take his details. They would formally book him at the nearest police station. As they prepared to leave, the foyer of the bank had filled with messengers, cashiers, directors of the bank and policemen from nearby stations, summoned by telegraph and courier, to witness what quickly became known as 'The Great Forgeries on the Bank of England'. Soon, the rest of the world would marvel at it too.

The crime, when it was eventually revealed in all its glory, was breathtaking – so complicated, involved and precise, it had clearly taken months to prepare and execute. Nobody would ever quite reconcile its greater ambition with this small, quiet individual with fair hair and a startled demeanour, who kept repeating that he too had been duped and misled for the last few months.

The prisoner – soon entered into the arrest book as 'E. Noyes', which was not his real name – was quickly charged at Bow Lane Police Station. He said very little and repeatedly protested his innocence. Very quickly, the police realised they had stumbled across the outermost edges of a tangled web of intrigue. The obvious starting point was the businessman for whom Noyes said he had been working as a clerk.

As cashiers all over the city started on the paper trail, unearthing all the acceptances and bills related to F.A. Warren or C.J. Horton, the police followed up on where these two characters had redeemed their fraudulent credit. It was dull and painstakingly mind-numbing work but it did, at least, start the evidence trail.

In the days ahead, Scotland Yard interviewed tellers, hoteliers and clerks who had had dealings with Noyes or two other mysterious characters, Horton and Warren. The City of London Police swiftly issued a description of the mysterious Warren. He was tall, perhaps 5ft 10in, with a dark, sallow complexion and black plain hair, a small black moustache and whiskers. He spoke with a strong American accent and seemed to be a Yankee gentleman.

But who was he? Where did he come from? What was his real name? Were, as some of the detectives suspected, Horton and Warren one and the same person? And where on earth had he, or they, disappeared to?

As the detectives looked into it, they found that Warren and/or Horton had assumed a bewildering number and variety of other aliases in all the various business dealings which they were able to trace. In their wake was a paper trail of bogus transactions, false accounting and so many fake identities that their collective minds were boggled.

Those interviewed remembered the smiling, saturnine figure, and the abiding memory was that he seemed impossibly young. For much of his time in London, he had assumed the names of Frederick Warren and Charles Horton. To some, he had also been known as A.H. Wray. To others, he had presented himself as E.A. Yates. Others had known him, and extended him loans and bills of credit, as Captain Bradshaw, A.H. Trafford, H.C. Clark, C.G. Brown, F. Aldrich and W.H. Spaulding.

Several women had known him by the name of Theodore Bingham. But his real name was Austin Biron Bidwell and he was just 27 years of age. His eventful life to date, as one contemporary chronicle later remarked, 'surpassed the imaginations of our famous novelists', and, when eventually apprehended, more than one reporter likened him to the Count of Monte Cristo.

He was truly an 'international man of mystery', perhaps also the world's most accomplished fraudster, which were viewed at the time as a vaguely aristocratic, elite rank of criminals whose ingenuity knew no bounds. Austin Bidwell's singular and peculiar skills – patience, confidence and self-command – represented, in the grudging admiration of one of his later prosecutors, 'a capital instance of misapplied genius'.

His was an extraordinary life that had been informed by astonishing escapades. They had taken place in luxurious hotels, banks, ships and trains. They involved journeys from Frankfurt to Havana, Liverpool to Paris, Brooklyn to Birmingham and Rio to Chicago. As such, the 'Warren forgeries', as they are still known today in official files on both sides of the Atlantic, represent the most audacious heist of the nineteenth century. The scale of their ambition alone justified the hyperbolic claim in a New York tabloid that it was indeed 'the most extraordinary forgery ever tried in any country' and has never since been equalled.

To anyone who ever met him – and in most recent weeks, that had included many of the leading bankers in London, Frankfurt and Paris – it was self-evidently clear how Austin Bidwell got away with it. He had charm, a plausible manner and, as one Chicago newspaper would report, he was 'a smooth, easy talker and a person who was likely to inspire confidence with anyone with whom he talked'.

His was the kind of smile that suggested he was letting you in on the joke too. His dark eyes took in everything and missed nothing. Detectives found that sometimes he had been accompanied by his elder brother, George, though he was rarely introduced as such. George Bidwell was equally confident in having the wit and cunning to talk his way out of any trouble. People remembered him too. His large head was fringed by a fine moustache and beard, the eyes constantly alert for signs of any danger.

Austin and George Bidwell were truly brothers in arms, criminal comrades who had helped each other through many remarkable adventures. In this particular case, they had been aided by a better looking, smoother presence with fair hair and piercing blue eyes and a most impressive beard that, to their perennial amusement, often led to his being mistaken for the Prince of Wales.

George Macdonnell had, for many years, passed himself off as a doctor, even though he had never formally practiced after taking courses in medicine. 'Mac', as he was always known, was conventionally and academically intelligent, a Harvard graduate in medicine, effortlessly superior and fluent in many languages. In the estimation of many who had already tried – and failed – to bring him to justice, he was one of the most slippery conmen in the world.

And soon it became clear that their clerk, Edwin Noyes, whom they called 'Ed', was not, as one newspaper would claim, 'an innocent person in the hands of a scoundrel' – anything but, in fact. His real name was Edwin Noyes Hills, and the others had known him since childhood. This was not the first time they had worked together, but, so far as the forces of law and order were concerned, it would be the last.

'There was a worldwide hue and cry', one newspaper soon reported of the detective work which followed on three continents. It was a manhunt quite unlike any other, which employed the latest technological marvels of steam, photograph and telegraph. 'All the prisoners are well known in New York and the United States' is how Freshfields, the Queen's own solicitors, would later summarise their illustrious careers to date. 'Their life during the last ten years has been one of Forgery and Swindling. During this period they have either as members of the same Gang or with others of the same stamp, defrauded the American public.'

As to why they had travelled to Europe – there were riches galore and fortunes for the brave. 'Finding that America did not offer a sufficiently wide field for their energies or possibly becoming too well known there they changed the scene of their operations to England and the continent of Europe,' the lawyers concluded.

To run them down would require thousands of man-hours. Hundreds of officials became involved. There were chases across rural Ireland, in Scottish cities, across the Atlantic on ships heading towards Manhattan and, most exotic of all, in Cuba, where the most elusive of the quartet would eventually be captured, before escaping and then being recaptured after a dramatic sabre fight with the local police.

Austin Bidwell would become one of the most perfectly elusive criminals in the history of forgery. Working with the others, their greater success stemmed from this wilful confusion in shrouding all their endeavours in mystery. Time and again, they would disappear and reappear assuming other identities, invariably getting away with it, somehow playing the most incredible odds arrayed against them and winning – as they had been from the very beginning of their lives of crime.

Nine Years Earlier – Thursday, 10 March 1864 Cincinnati, Ohio

If the first bullet did not stop him, the second and third surely would. As he crashed to the ground, Austin Bidwell was finally beaten by the forces of law and order, if not the immutable laws of ballistics and mechanics. Along with someone called Frank Kibbe, they had been hiding out in an abandoned house in the middle of nowhere. They were getting ready to have breakfast when they looked up and saw two policemen on horseback riding towards them.

That one was the chief of detectives for the Cincinnati police showed the seriousness of the crimes they had committed, a 'swindle which for its magnitude and daring is seldom excelled', in the words of one contemporary newspaper account. The press had been instrumental in tracking them down. One alert young man, who had read about a pair of swindlers who had abandoned their business leaving behind debts of $10,000, remembered seeing them. Now, on this spring morning, this young fellow had accompanied the policemen, and when Austin Bidwell and his sidekick ran out of the house, he gave chase and shouted for them to stop. When the young man thought the fleeing scoundrel was going for his own revolver, he aimed and fired.

One bullet struck Austin Bidwell on the left leg, another in the small of the back. The third entered his right arm, but amazingly it did not stop him. Austin kept running as fast as he could. A flying tackle by the young man in question brought him to a halt. Austin was not fatally injured for, as another newspaper later reported, the wounds were minimal, 'none, however being dangerous'.

Incarcerated at the 9th Street Jail, he was charged as 'W. Austin Bidwell', the first time that anyone of that name entered the criminal justice system, and certainly not the last.

What the local newspaper aptly termed a 'formidable scheme of rascality' had started the previous December. A sign appeared outside a large building in the mercantile district of Cincinnati advertising 'Bidwell & Co.' at No. 54 East 3rd Street.

Here they worked as commission merchants, obtaining goods on credit and amassing reasonably large bills. At this stage, there was no indication that anything was amiss. They looked and behaved like responsible, respectable businessmen. Their inventory included glassware from Pittsburgh, $750 of linseed oil from Springfield, $1,000 worth of benzine from Cleveland, wines from New York and twenty-one barrels of linseed oil from nearby Columbus.

When the standard three months' notice of credit were up, a chorus of ever more concerned enquiries from creditors grew louder. By the end of February 1864, Mr Bidwell reassured both his suppliers and the owners of the neighbouring shops that all was fine. Indeed, Bidwell & Co. had made it a greater part of their enterprise to get to know all the other traders, not least when, as a local newspaper reported, Mr Bidwell himself became 'particularly attentive to the jewellers, whose temptingly displayed wares adorn 4th Street', on the evening of Monday, 7 March.

Around eight o'clock that evening, Mr Bidwell collected two watches and jewellery worth $1,000 from one store, asking for it to be 'sent round'. In a matter of minutes, he had amassed a total of nearly $3,000 worth of diamonds, watches and other jewellery from other shops. At another of the more salubrious establishments, Mr Bidwell claimed that he and his wife were going to a reception that same evening. He needed some particularly flashy jewellery. 'My wife will most certainly scold if I do not take home to her one of those watches this evening,' he said, twinkling in the spring twilight. This particular jeweller resisted and the mysterious, married Mr Bidwell went off into the night.

So far as the local newspapers later marvelled, his 'success thus far seems most wonderful'. When the police looked into it, they discovered that on the evening of Wednesday of that week any number of wagons and drays had appeared outside Bidwell & Co. All had been loaded with goods and by the time they left seemed heavily laden. At the same time, errand boys were appearing with bills whose issuers were assured they would be paid the next day.

Needless to say, after Mr Bidwell went on his jewellery spree, neither he nor Mr Kibbe ever returned to their place of business. By the weekend, the premises of Bidwell & Co. was surrounded 'by an assemblage of victimized and enraged gentlemen', including the owner of the building who was in arrears for rent. So, too, were the proprietors of Spencer House, one of the more celebrated hotels in the Midwest where presidents had stayed and where, in recent weeks, 'Mr and Mrs Bidwell' had been guests. They now owed a considerable sum for food and lodgings.

The mysterious wife – described as 'a fashionably dressed woman' – had also disappeared off the face of the earth. A reward of $500 for the apprehension of the shopkeepers had been offered. 'We believe that the operations here made known are but a small portion of this accomplished scoundrel and his accomplices,' the *Cincinnati Enquirer* presciently recorded on the Saturday. 'A day or two will doubtless develop circumstances of an equally astonishing character.'

In fact, this would be the prototype for all the Bidwells' subsequent crimes. 'Their first known transactions were what would be classed at the present time under the head of fraudulent bankruptcy,' one account noted in the spring of 1873, 'or in other words, swindling their creditors.' This was their entry into the nefarious world of 'long firm fraud' which would become their speciality. With obvious refinements, it would bring them ever greater riches, culminating in their entry through the portals of the Bank of England a decade later.

'It was new then,' George Bidwell later explained to a reporter, 'and almost anybody by a simple letter could get a wholesaler to ship a lot of goods to him on thirty days' credit or better.' What he did not say was that such letters were fraudulent. Wholesale firms supplied goods on credit against false references and then the goods were sold for cash, invariably at fire sale, 'everything must go' prices. That money – even if it was a fraction of the true worth of the goods – entered their pockets as pure profit. They would do this time and time again, making sure that they would disappear before they were ever caught. Even today, exact details remain immersed in mystery as to what really happened, who did what and when – adding to their lustre and reputation.

Two young men, well dressed and clearly on the run, were highly likely to attract attention even in the boondocks of rural Ohio. And so when a young man called J.G. Foster who lived a good day's ride away due east of the city at the eponymous Foster's Crossing read about the chaos the 'formidable rascals' had left behind, he recalled two such fellows passing by on a wagon the previous day. Foster telegraphed to one of the jewellers who then contacted the police.

Detectives Larry Hazen and Gus Colchear went to investigate. Hazen, routinely described as a legend in law enforcement and vividly recalled as 'a small man, about five feet five or six inches, with black moustache and [very] Irish features', was on the trail. With the young Mr Foster himself, they headed south towards the Ohio River. Another officer, Samuel Bayliss, headed north-west to cut them off at Dayton if they had ventured that far.

But they had not. Hazen and Colchear found the ne'er-do-wells' wagon abandoned, at which point all traces of the pair seemed to disappear into the dirt. Hazen, with his usual aplomb, suggested they follow the railroad. This was the most obvious escape route for anyone on the run who did not know the local terrain particularly well. Within a matter of hours they had headed towards Goshen, roughly 40 miles from Cincinnati, picking up a small posse of citizens to help. They travelled through the night and at about eight o'clock the next morning, they caught up with the pair in an abandoned house about a mile away from the village.

Austin Bidwell was blacking his boots when he saw the officers approaching. Both Austin and Kibbe sped from the back of the house across a field towards a wood. But young Foster, 'being the fleetest of foot', caught up with Austin and, after shooting him and capturing him, bound him with cords so he could not escape.

The detectives then took him to the 9th Street Station House. He was treated by a Dr Ludlow and was waiting to be committed for trial a day or so later. W. Austin Bidwell was charged at the next sitting of the magistrates' court and was fined $1,000 for redress of the swindle. The onlookers were stunned. He was not even held on bail and then promptly disappeared and, as another newspaper reported, 'has never been seen here since'.

It was rumoured he had headed towards Canada – where Kibbe was also believed to have gone – and that was the last the Ohio police heard of either of them ever again. Disappearing was yet another constant in the Bidwell brothers' subsequent career, the wellspring of their criminal invention, and indeed reinvention, in the years ahead.

Who exactly was W. Austin Bidwell? It is an intriguing question because, from this remove, it is impossible to know exactly whether it was Austin or his eldest brother, George Bidwell, who performed this particular crime. Most likely, they worked together, with one hiding in the background helping the other. A nimbus of ambiguity covers many of the Bidwells' earliest criminal deeds, for the evidence was never completely clear. It is significant that in his later 'confessional autobiography' Austin Bidwell conveniently failed to mention this and the following decade's worth of rascality, which left behind in their wake a trail of deceit, lies and intrigue.

Exactly how their life of crime progressed is even murkier, not least because George Bidwell often took the credit for things that his younger brother had carried out. 'I rather insubordinately did the business in the name of Austin Bidwell,' he later lied, about many of his crimes across the United States and Europe. 'Austin was never a principal in any fraud in either of these countries.'

It is more than likely that the elder George pretended to be 'W. Austin Bidwell', for he had already been married for five years at this time. In some newspaper accounts, the character who was arrested in Cincinnati was described as having a wife who was approximately 25 years of age, 'of medium height, light complexion, and, to say the least not plain in personal appearance'.

In some accounts, W. Austin Bidwell also suffered severe injuries after being shot by young Foster. When, in the spring of 1873, both Bidwell brothers came into British custody, further confusion arose because they *both* were severely injured. This had more to do with their recent escapades in Edinburgh and Havana, respectively. In all of their criminal records, it should be noted, there is no mention of injuries sustained while they had earlier been trying to escape.

When news spread in the early spring of 1873 that the Bank of England had been hit, at least one person across the Atlantic had a shrewd idea who might be behind it all. He was a short, stout, heavily bearded man who looked older than his late twenties and was already routinely acknowledged as the greatest detective of the day. Alternately amused and outraged at their audaciousness, he would be responsible for capturing the fraudsters, and, at the back of his mind, he never quite reconciled them with the scope of their ambition.

William Pinkerton, elder son and scion of the famous, eponymous detective agency, had been chasing all of the forgers for the best part of a decade now, a journey through the various dark and disturbing alleyways of American crime. True to his sometimes dour Scottish roots, Pinkerton was rarely given to overstatement or exaggeration. Yet even he acknowledged that this was the most remarkable story of daring forgery and fraud that the world had ever known.

Hyperbole, almost inevitably, attached itself to the Pinkertons. Most famously it came with the claim that they always got their man. It was an exaggeration to say that the Pinkertons tangled 'with every noteworthy wrongdoer of the day', as they also liked to claim, it just seemed like they did. Pinkerton's detectives had already garnered banner headlines for defeating the Reno bank robbers and would, more famously still, in later years chase Jesse James and his gang, Butch Cassidy and the Sundance Kid, as well as Adam Worth, the so-called 'Napoleon of crime', a subject of much more modern hype and wilful misunderstanding.

Sifting fact from fiction, untangling lies from deceit and exaggerations from reality, was difficult in most cases involving fraud and forgery. Latterly, 'Pink' – as he was usually known in London – and his detectives, hired by solicitors acting for the bank in New York, would do the most to disentangle the contradictory evidence and obfuscations. As 'Old A.P.' – Willie's father, the founder of the agency, Allan Pinkerton himself – would write, as cunning criminals they had few equals, 'yet they did what the commonest criminal nearly always does, that is, leave a trail behind upon which a shrewd detective could pile up a mountain of evidence'.

Certainly his son was one of the shrewdest in the world. Employed by Freshfields to go the extra mile, it was thanks to Willie Pinkerton's industry and characteristic doggedness that the thieves of Threadneedle Street would eventually be apprehended. 'When Bill Pinkerton went after a man,' said another ne'er-do-well whom he had arrested, 'he didn't let up until he had got him.'

In the spring of 1873, that man would be Austin Biron Bidwell.

Seven Weeks Later – Wednesday, 16 April 1873
Punto Prison, Havana, Cuba
2 p.m.

Suffering was his most vivid memory of the case. It was so hot that at times Willie Pinkerton thought he might faint from heat exhaustion. Far from being a tropical idyll, the culmination of his chasing Austin Bidwell as far as the tropics had turned into a nightmare. Pink hadn't slept for days, had been haring around in the blistering sunshine and was painfully aware that his quarry was up to his usual tricks. He'd escaped once, the result, the detective was certain, of surefooted trickery that involved bribes, bent officials, sob stories and credulous journalists.

In the couple of weeks he had been here, Pink had done his best to keep in with the Cuban police, knowing full well that they would spring the prisoner if the price was right. 'A Spaniard will sell his soul for money,' he wrote in exasperation. Then there were the local British and American consular officials – the latter believing their prisoner was a fine, upstanding citizen – who were behaving like brats in a kindergarten. They were plotting against each other over exactly in whose custody the prisoner belonged.

Add to that various unscrupulous Cubans, a dodgy Austrian translator, a crooked local lawyer and reporters who were unduly influencing the story, then there was a recipe for a complete mess. Unexpectedly, 'the cause of the imbroglio himself [managed] to solve the problem by disappearing altogether', in the words of a British newspaper report.

The weekend before – on Easter Sunday – Austin Bidwell had been recaptured thanks to Pinkerton's efforts in the face of all these various adversities. Now the prisoner was as well secured as he ever could be, and finally, for the first time, Willie Pinkerton could talk to Austin Bidwell alone.

To look at both of them in the cramped, horrible cell, it was hard to reconcile the fact they were both the same age. Pink's dark, tired eyes met those of his quarry. Even without the heat, Pinkerton tended to perspire, not just from corpulence but also his tendency towards alcoholism. His stout and florid demeanour came from too much drinking in the company of criminals on the fringes of society.

Since he had last dealt with him, Austin Bidwell seemed to have shrunk. His eyes seemed sunken and glassy. His cheeks were hollowed out and his dark, wavy hair was already starting to thin. And he was clearly exhausted from his most recent misadventures.

It was curious, but Pink bore him no ill will nor grudge. Under other circumstances, they might even have become friends – a curious facet to the detective's personality.

'I have made it a feature of my business to know these men and be friendly with them,' he later said of his quarries. Always honest with them, he helped many after their release from prison, and was proud to say many years later 'that only a few of them went back to a life of crime'. Famously, he funded one particular criminal who opened a saloon which subsequently failed. To his chagrin, the owner went back to his formerly recidivist ways.

Pink suspected Austin Bidwell would do the same given half the chance. For now, though, he had the psychological advantage. The prisoner looked broken but remained resolute. It had been, he said, the longest thirty-six hours of his life. 'I will tell you a little of my personal history,' Austin Bidwell said slowly, unwinding a little. And for the next hour or more, he went through how his life in crime had played out.

'I was born in Adrian, Michigan,' he said, which no doubt made the detective smile. That was where Pink's own wife came from. 'There were five brothers and two sisters in the family.' With pride, he went through how accomplished they all were. 'Joe is a lawyer who lives in South Bend, Indiana, John in Black Lake near Grand Rapids. Benson Bidwell, another brother, is a wealthy merchant now doing business in Adrian. George is in England, myself here.'

This much Pink already knew as he had dispatched an 'operative' – as his own staff were known – to Michigan to find out if any of the extended Bidwell clan had been in contact with their illustrious brothers. Though they said they hadn't, Pink had already formed the opinion that they were not exactly trustworthy in this regard.

Austin continued:

When I was quite young my people removed to Grand Rapids where in 1856 my father bought a large amount of real estate which, if he had been able to hold, would now amount to millions. He was then keeping a store under the name of Bidwell and Son. George was then nineteen years of age and a very smart young man and managed the business.

Then came the financial crisis of 1857 when Austin Bidwell had just turned 11 years old. The American economy overheated, many local banks did not honour their notes and commercial credit dried up:

My father, seeing that he was going to be crippled, sent George on east to try and get an extension of this paper. George succeeded in getting time from all parties but two. They insisted on having their money. The result was a failure by which the creditors got 80%.

There was little rancour in his voice, it was far too late for regrets:

Then Joe was at college and Hattie, my eldest sister, was at an academy shortly after my father went insane and the care of the family was left to George and myself. John was married and had a large family of his own to support and the others were at school. We struggled hard to be honest and do right but the tempter came and George embarked on a swindle for a small amount and was successful.

As Pinkerton noted it, the brothers' eyes were opened to a new and easy way of making money to keep the family's head above water. 'We went so deep in that it was impossible to extricate ourselves from the quagmire into which we had fallen,' Austin Bidwell aptly concluded.

Even at this stage, captured and held in a military prison, Austin Bidwell was sure he could get away with it. Three days later, he told Willie Pinkerton he was certain the case would 'fizzle out' in England against anyone but him. 'I am the only one who could be convicted,' he declared matter-of-factly, 'and all the rest will be discharged.'

If that came across as boastfulness, Pink did not care. They had at least formed a bond of trust which would come in useful. 'I have his confidence as thoroughly as a man like myself could get it,' Pink wrote to his brother, Robert, who ran the agency's New York office. Even so, he repeatedly warned the Cuban authorities that Senor Bidwell was a dangerous man.

Not that the great detective was ever quite believed. 'Oh no,' he was constantly informed, 'impossible.' Austin Bidwell would, Pink was certain, try to escape again, possibly en route to the British Isles where he might be sprung. There was no saying what his cronies in the criminal underworld – some of them protected by the New York police – would do. Pink made it quite clear he would chase him no matter what.

'Would your agency attempt to hunt me up and rearrest me in case I went to the US?' Austin asked.

'That's more than I can promise,' Pink replied. 'My father would undoubtedly do so if employed by the bank.'

'I work for money,' Austin said matter-of-factly. 'I would pay more than the Bank of England to be left alone.'

Pink was unmoved. 'We will do nothing for you for all the money you have.'

Austin, despite the hopelessness of the situation, was impressed. 'You are the only detective in America who could and would have done this.'

William Pinkerton would not relax until Austin Bidwell was finally brought to justice in the British Isles. He arrived at the end of May 1873 and so great was the cheering crowd that awaited him at Plymouth Harbour – all eager to see this remarkable fellow in person – that one newspaper reported, 'it was with some difficulty that Bidwell and his escort managed to get a cab.'

The Bidwell brothers always liked to claim they could trace their lineage back to the Saxons. Their forebears, so they also believed, had made an appearance in the Domesday Book. More recent relatives had, they boasted, sailed on the *Mayflower*. Even more recently than that, Austin and George's grandfather had built the family home in Hartford, Connecticut, where their roots had spread deep in the community. Two statues – including one to an eponymous Revolutionary War general, Zebulon – celebrate the family name. 'We are descended from an old and respectable family and for many generations are the first who have been arrested on charge of crime,' George Bidwell would write with characteristic indignation from Newgate Prison.

After the fraudsters' arrival in England in the summer of 1872, George had made a point of visiting an engraver's in Regent Street, then as now, a tony district of the City. There he purchased a seal that he wished to be engraved with the coat of arms of one particular branch of the Bidwells from whom he claimed they were descended. This later caused one newspaper to express thunderous indignation, terming it 'a horrible grotesqueness in [one of the] Bidwells hiring a heraldic engraver to find a coat of arms for him, and causing the cognizance to be emblazoned on vellum'.

Such flashy displays were in stark contrast to the puritanism of their upbringing. Their deeply religious parents seemed suited to an earlier age. According to the Bidwell brothers, their parents had been duped time and time again. This had originally propelled them from prosperity in Connecticut to near penury in Grand Rapids, Michigan. That probably had more to do with their father's lack of business ability, for as George would later remark, 'He was honest, simple hearted and confiding.' Or was he?

When a Pinkerton operative later went to Michigan to find out more, he reported a rather different story. 'The father was a candy maker,' he learned, whose sons 'were raised as candy makers and sellers of peanuts and popcorn, in his business they have generally met with fair success.' They opened other stores and, as was later recorded by detectives, 'Austin, being a boy, assisted and sold the confectionery at the railway station'.

Exactly as Austin had claimed to Willie Pinkerton, when their parents had passed on in the 1860s, reporters also found that the brothers had inherited the family farm in desolate 'scattered peach and buckwheat growing country'. It was a small windfall which they squandered. By the time Pinkerton detectives came across it, the building had deteriorated into an unfinished two-storey house. Their brother, John, and his family lived there, with sister, Harriet, in a rundown, adjacent property. Only too late did detectives realise just how far their siblings would go to help the boys, stranded in a jail many thousands of miles away from home.

Theirs had been a normal existence, typical of the times and their social milieu. Puritanism was deeply engrained within the greater Bidwell family. Austin had not been allowed to play outside with older children. Nor were his brothers and sisters allowed such fripperies as kittens, clocks or even packs of cards. Music and dancing were strictly forbidden.

'My father was proverbial for his honesty,' George Bidwell would note in prison, 'and my mother for self-sacrificing devotion to her family and benevolence to the poor and suffering.' Of himself and his youngest brother, George would claim they were 'honest and our ambition is to occupy an honourable place in the world'.

Yet even with these instincts, the results were lamentable. So far as Austin was concerned, their mother was a gentle soul who regaled them with stories about the shining beacon that would be the afterlife. Enduring a life in poverty here on earth, she repeatedly explained, would allow them to attain heavenly blessings in the hereafter. There was little by way of worldly wisdom imparted to any of their seven children.

'My home life was happy,' Austin would simply record. 'My father had lost his grip on the world, but his faith in the Unseen remained. My mother, caring little for this life, lived in and for the spiritual. To her, heaven was a place as much as the country village where she was born.'

And, in this constant preoccupation with the future, she was no match for the depredations of the present. 'We loved our mother but her soul was too gentle to keep in restraint hot, fiery youths like my brothers and myself,' Austin would add. In his late teens, as Austin later told Willie Pinkerton, George certainly had been the reluctant breadwinner for the whole family. The elder Bidwell brother had then been promptly swindled by a lawyer, or so he claimed. Losing his own first fortune, he became a travelling salesman and was able to bring the family back to Brooklyn, where Austin had started school.

It was here that Austin Bidwell encountered his first scam: the poor standard of teaching. Not only did it not prepare him for life, he subsequently had to learn the hard way the true lessons needed to survive. By the time he was 12, Austin was also selling candy and apples from a small street stand to support the family. By the age of 15, their father was totally dependent on them both and, according to Austin, one day announced, 'My son, I have found a situation for you.'

And with that Austin Bidwell took up employment at a sugar brokerage on South Water Street, so that he could not help from boasting that 'I was soon in the swim'. He was either 15 or 16 (he claimed both) when he started out on Wall Street. 'I had wonderful luck and before I was twenty years old I had a hundred thousand dollars,' he later bragged.

Then that luck mysteriously evaporated. Both brothers liked to make themselves out to be victims of other people's duplicity and greater human venality. Unsurprisingly, a constant theme that permeates Austin Bidwell's writings was that of regret. '[Had] my parents designed me to become a traveller in the "primrose way" they could not have educated me to better purpose,' he wrote.

Today, that reference seems wilfully obscure. The 'primrose way' referred to a life of luxury in this world which led to perdition – a suitably Victorian reaction to hedonism and hubristic overarching. It is a concept with a Shakespearean twist, words which Macbeth himself had uttered, 'The primrose way to the everlasting bonfire,' (*Macbeth*, 2:3), a suitably hellfire and demonic denouement to a life lived on the edge of acceptable behaviour. To better understand this peculiar Victorian viewpoint, a starting point comes from another mention of the primrose way in the play *Hamlet*, where Ophelia says to Laertes, 'Do not, as some ungracious pastors do, show me the steep and thorny way to heaven.' (*Hamlet* 1:3)

There is a certain irony that, in the early 1860s, George Bidwell assumed the role of an ungracious pastor who was taking a very thorny way to heaven. Whenever he needed money, he would use any of a dozen aliases at his disposal or else, as a last resort, assume the role of a Baptist preacher.

There was, at least, some precedent within the family. While their father was a more gracious and genuine pastor, his brother, Joseph, was some sort of travelling preacher. Allan Pinkerton himself would report that one of his operatives had found that when Joseph 'opened his mouth and let the language flow, he called it religion, I call it mockery'. Like his brothers, Joseph too had risen from candy seller to temperance lecturing and street preaching, prosecuting people who sold liquor without licence, threatened by saloon keepers and grocers on a regular basis. 'In fact, I would state that Joseph is like the rest of the Bidwells,' Pinkerton would add, 'an unmitigated scoundrel in every respect.'

It was almost inevitable, perhaps, that in the 1860s George Bidwell appeared with two other brothers as a Baptist preacher 'which his clerical appearance well fitted him'. At various stages, George Bidwell returned home to Michigan in the guise of a preacher, something which prompted a remarkable sermon at the end of April 1873, in South Place Chapel when news of the Bank of England forgeries had carried around the world.

The Revered D. Moncure Conway happened to have been living in Cincinnati where two men had set up a mercantile business and suddenly disappeared 'near fifteen years ago' with $60,000. Thereafter, a new and elegant Baptist preacher 'who by his unctuous and moving sermons' brought in many converts in and around Ohio, despite ugly rumours about his strong resemblance to one of the fraudsters.

The Reverend George Bidwell might not be who he said he was. This, the elders of the church ascribed almost inevitably to the rejection of God's holy works by the Devil. 'He and a brother of his set up then in a business in Michigan and presently vanished carrying away nearly as much money as they had stolen from Cincinnati,' said the Reverend Conway. This accomplice, needless to say, was Austin Bidwell.

His older brother continued around the country for the next decade 'building up the Church with one hand and robbing creditors with the other'. George Bidwell went all over the United States living by his sermons and converting many. 'This was the last known of him until he fell into the hands of English justice, where he now awaits trial for the most stupendous attempt at forgery on the Bank of England known in modern times,' the Reverend Conway continued. 'Under the cloak of piety and preaching this man was able to pursue for years a career of barefaced fraud.'

He ended his sermon with a sad note that many ascribed their faith to the fervid preaching of the Reverend George Bidwell, 'And how many are like him, prowling through the world, wolves in sheep's clothing? How many with glib and unctuous tongues are still enabled by the superstition of the people to use this imposing livery of Heaven to serve the basest purposes?'

⁓

It is hardly surprising, then, that the Devil seemed to loom large throughout the lives of the Bidwell brothers. At a family reunion many years later in Connecticut, Austin and George said they had brought disgrace upon the family name. 'But no,' said another relative, theirs was a greater achievement. One day there would be a third statue erected in their honour in Hartford. 'It will be dedicated to the men who had gone to the Devil and come back again,' he said.

When incarcerated in Cuba, Austin admitted to Willie Pinkerton, 'There is no use playing against the Devil,' when confronted by overwhelming evidence for his complicity in the Bank of England job. Both brothers constantly feared that divine retribution would surely follow. When Austin later talked of his first criminal enterprises in Europe, he confessed, 'I had sold myself to do the Devil's work, and day by day the chain would tighten.'

When that eventually came to constrict him, the younger brother claimed he would be more than equal to the forces of law and order. 'I no longer feared arrest,' he would claim after leaving Great Britain at the start of 1873, 'was confident that never would the hand of human justice be laid on me, but I dimly felt that there was divine justice which would exact retribution.'

For now, legal justice would have to do, and he was a past master at evading the proverbial long arms of the law – as Willie Pinkerton knew only too well. What was most galling for him personally was the fact that the Bidwells had concluded one last long firm fraud, which propelled them on to ever more ambitious scams and schemes. Right under his very nose.

December 1865
Chicago, Illinois

Sometime in 1865, just after the end of the Civil War, a family by the name of Bidwell was renting a house on 18th Street, down by the breakwater on Chicago's shoreline. Two brothers, by the name of George and Biron, along with another man whose name was never ascertained, but whom detectives were pretty certain was George Macdonnell, largely kept themselves to themselves. With good reason, since their sideline – if it could be called that – was selling property which they did not legally own.

In a short while, so he later boasted, George Bidwell had made $160,000 from this secondary business alone. Yet that was nothing compared to their day job. The brothers had also been renting a small office on South Water Street, outside of which the sign 'Bidwell & Co' appeared. While Biron ran the store and expanded it to become a 'commission business', his eldest brother travelled all over Illinois collecting orders for tobacco, cheese, eggs and flour. Anything, in fact, that could be traded and, as always, on credit. The smiling, unassuming Biron, it was always remembered, was present when any goods were delivered – a pleasantly reassuring figure who always seemed to be busy.

His industry, it was later revealed, had more to do with removing all traces of the suppliers (labels and waybills) from the goods that unsuspecting drivers had delivered. These products were then shipped to Canada where they were sold at knockdown prices. Again George Macdonnell, who was born and raised near to Montreal, was the suspected fence for this part of the chain, though the police could never prove it.

As a result, 'Bidwell & Co.' was profitable, though its business model was unique. Nothing was ever invested nor returned. Nobody seemed to buy anything, nor was anything ever paid out. Occasionally, there were complaints from creditors, but the Chicago police never did anything about it. As the debts were usually in the region of, at most, $100, it wasn't worth their time and effort. Debts went unpaid and the brothers did not seem to care. The cops were too busy with other matters, like trying to maintain civil order in a frontier town.

The Windy City in the 1860s was the sort of town where you could not help becoming involved in crime. 'If the Angel Gabriel came to Chicago,' an appalled evangelist remarked at the time, 'he would lose his character.' Though lawlessness characterised much of the contemporary American experience, nowhere was it quite as acute as on the shores of Lake Michigan and the self-styled 'gem of the prairie'. 'Chicago's ecological position as the gateway to the unsettled lands of the west also contributed to its involvement in crime,' notes one professor of modern jurisprudence in the city. It was the start – both figuratively and literally – of the 'Wild West'.

The Bidwells just fit right in. Because Chicago was the last stop in 'civilisation', itinerant travellers often spent a valedictory time in saloons, gambling parlours and brothels before they headed west to make their fortunes. There were so many gamblers in one particular district that it became known as 'Hair Trigger Block' because of the shootings which resulted. One of the more famous saloon owners was Mickey Finn, creator of the eponymous knockout drink which allowed him to rifle unsuspecting drinkers' pockets.

It was unsurprising that Willie Pinkerton learned most of his information about the Chicago underworld in the 'Store', a notorious saloon. It was most likely here – by which time it was too late to do anything – that he first heard about the brothers who were running a long firm fraud down on 18th Street.

By the 1860s, Chicago was an expanding frontier town that was 'now an impressive prairie metropolis whose grain towers and branding steers cast impressive shadows across the land as the mighty gateway to the West', in the estimation of one biographer of Allan Pinkerton. It was here that the patriarch of the formidable detective agency had settled in the early 1850s, disillusioned with political restrictions in his native Scotland.

The son of a Glaswegian policeman, the elder Pinkerton's life story was the strangest of paradoxes. He had been hounded out of his native land as a political agitator. Allan Pinkerton had headed west, not for fame nor fortune like so many others, but to avoid the consequences of his youthful radicalism. In his later years it was hard to reconcile his Chartism – supporting a charter for the earliest ever form of human rights and universal suffrage – with his more reactionary tendencies in becoming a willing tool of power and the industrial elite in his adopted land.

After first settling in Illinois, Pinkerton became a local detective while working as an iron forger. 'In his position as part of the municipal police force of Chicago,' *The New York Times* wrote, by way of his obituary in 1884, 'Mr Pinkerton saw the evil effect of political influence in the thwarting, detection and punishment of crime.' It was an unhappy, frustrating time for the young Scotsman.

At this point in American history, policing across the United States was a patchwork quilt of localised detectives who were either overwhelmed or incompetent. Their sights were never set much higher than the next county line. There was neither a national police force nor any central, federal repository of information. A simple check with records in other cities would have flagged the Bidwells up so much sooner. 'The police authority throughout the country at this time was purely a local matter', is how one academic review succinctly summarises the situation. Unless a crime was committed against the public mails or committed on the high seas, the federal government could not do a thing.

If nature abhorred a vacuum, criminals certainly loved it – and yet, so did Allan Pinkerton. It was into this empty space that the Pinkertons, father and both sons, William and Robert, stepped. In 1852, the independent agency that soon bore their name was formed in Chicago and was an instant success. Their growing number of operatives were kept busy with frauds, murders, counterfeiting and, most of all, policing the rails. The latter had been a classic, intractable problem for local police forces. Once cargo left the cities by rail, nothing could be done to stop raids, smuggling or fraud. And that was where the Pinkertons first stepped into the breach with characteristic dedication.

The railroads have a great deal to do with this story, not just in the Bidwells' home country, but also in their subsequent misadventures all over the world. Increased transportation meant that travel – and trouble – made its way across the country and, indeed, overseas. It is significant that in the late 1860s Chicago had become 'the rail crossroads of the nation', multiplying a hundredfold in extent.

As the lure of riches and gold drew homesteaders westwards, it was the Windy City's own manifest destiny to become the communications hub of its day. Fed by ten railways and with more than thirty ships arriving per day, more than a million bushels of wheat were being deposited at the docks every year for distribution all over the world. In that same decade, Chicago's population tripled, and so did the number of criminals. No wonder highwaymen and train robbers prospered – but so too did the Pinkerton Agency after being asked by the railroad owners to do something about it. Rail thefts and robberies were almost exponential in growth as well as secondary problems like embezzlement by employees. Train conductors invariably abused their powers and so dedicated detectives were tasked by Allan Pinkerton to test their loyalty and honesty.

For that, Pinkerton's 'cinder dicks', as they were known, took to the rails. They were not universally popular, leading to the insulting soubriquets of 'scoundrels', 'jailbirds' and 'thieves to catch thieves'. Allan Pinkerton was oblivious to the brickbats in those febrile years immediately after the end of the Civil War along the shores of Lake Michigan.

This, then, was the background to George Bidwell obtaining $7,000 of tobacco on credit from a merchant in the suburb of Quincy, Illinois, in December 1865. For this, he gave a 'sight draft', which was essentially a credit note that would be redeemed by a bank when presented. This was standard procedure so far as the nods and winks of respectable business were concerned. George Bidwell asked only that the supplier not present the draft in Chicago until ten days had passed. All would be fine, he insisted, smiling his reassurances.

The merchant reluctantly said he would agree to that, but he was more than a little suspicious. There was something about this fellow's hale and hearty manner which grated. To make sure, he decided to call on the Bidwells' store on South Water Street before he cashed it. There was no sign of the brothers when he visited, both then and on several later occasions. Clearly, something was amiss.

So the merchant then went to speak with Captain William Turtle of the Chicago Police Department. Though well established, the Chicago force was hardly a crackerjack operation; it was overwhelmed and invariably incompetent. Turtle was, like Allan Pinkerton, an immigrant from the British Isles, originally from Kent. Where Pinkerton was parsimonious, Turtle enjoyed the good life. His profligacy was a case in this particular point, for he did not seem to want to get his hands dirty. But the trader was insistent – find either the tobacco or the Bidwells. So another detective went in search of the former. The goods were traced to the depot in the Burlington & Quincy rail yard. Chicago's finest then found that the brothers were living in some style on 18th Street. Their house, too, seemed suspiciously quiet.

So one night, the police raided it. Inside, they found George Bidwell, who was about to escape. A revolver pointed at his head persuaded him to stay put. When the detectives examined the property, they were amazed to discover something like $20,000 worth of fine wines and cigars, all of which had been obtained by fraudulent means. And these luxuries – and Captain Turtle's enjoyment of them – seem to have informed what happened next in yet another surreal escapade in the Bidwells' greater genius at elusiveness.

On this occasion, George Bidwell had gone to the front. That would be common to all their subsequent schemes. Using charm, guile and bluster as the 'front man', he would always try to extricate himself as best he could when things went wrong. In this case, that was while George Bidwell was waiting to be carted off for incarceration. Knowing that there would be a delay until the Quincy authorities came for him, George Bidwell told Captain Turtle that he had plenty of money and disliked jail. Could he not stay at a hotel under police guard?

Amazingly, Turtle agreed. Along with two younger detectives, George Bidwell stayed at the luxurious Briggs House for the next three weeks. 'The whole party fared sumptuously,' the local newspaper later reported, 'they had champagne for breakfast and dinner but the board bill remains unpaid to this day.'

On one occasion, George Bidwell chatted about all his various successes to date. He offered £2,500 to Captain Turtle if he would 'step around the corner'. The detective declined. George Bidwell was then escorted to Quincy Jail, where he was due to stand trial. Explaining that he wanted to look his best, he shaved off his whiskers and obtained a new set of clothes.

Then one day, he simply disappeared off the face of the earth. Had the prisoner picked the lock of the cell? Or bribed a warder? As with all stories about the Bidwells around this time, a haze of mystery descends. In some accounts, it was Austin Bidwell who had been arrested and who later pulled a gun on a detective when he went home to visit his brother. In others, it was the other way around: George had visited Austin and sounded the alarm to allow him to escape.

In Cuba, six years later, the younger Bidwell told Willie Pinkerton that it was he who had paid Captain Turtle $2,500 'to compromise an affair and spoke of various clever things in which he and Macdonnell had figured'. The gun, in some other accounts, was provided by a crooked lawyer who might well have been the Bidwells' brother, Joseph. Willie Pinkerton himself later reported to the Bank of England that George Bidwell 'had somehow obtained possession of a loaded pistol which he placed to [the detective's] head and he [being] unarmed was unable to help stop his escape'.

In other words, nobody ever got to the bottom of what had really gone on. So far as the Bidwells were concerned, they expected the same would happen with the 'innocent' who had been captured in London on the first day of March, 1873.

It was around the time of the Quincy escape that Edwin Noyes Hills seems to have first appeared on the scene. 'We had known each other from our schoolboy days, and there was a warm friendship between us,' Austin Bidwell wrote of their friend. 'Our paths in life had been wide apart, but we maintained a frequent correspondence and often met.'

Austin always liked to maintain that Hills really was innocent. It was down to the Pinkertons to find the truth. In a summary for the New York law firm hired to track down the forgers, 'Old A.P.' recorded, 'At the time Austin Bidwell was arrested in this city for his swindling transactions at Quincy, Hills was a partner or agent of Austin Bidwell. Hills has always been connected with the Bidwells in their swindling, being an "outside man".'

Certainly, the bonds of loyalty ran deep into their shared past. After his arrest at the Continental Bank, Noyes would say little about his mysterious 'master', Horton, whose identity he knew perfectly well. Nor, when it was obvious that he was a scoundrel, would he say little about his own career. Neither would Austin Bidwell. When asked about their sidekick in Cuba by Willie Pinkerton, he would not say a word and repeatedly refused to give Hills away.

In his jail cell in Cuba, Austin Bidwell was convinced 'Noyes' (as he called him) would be acquitted. All Austin would do, so he explained to Willie Pinkerton, was state on the record that Noyes was his clerk, that they had had a written agreement and would then add a marvellous twist. 'He swindled me out of £300 which Noyes deposited with me for security.' No doubt he grinned as he said it.

Pink saw through that one straight away. 'You see the dodge he intends to play to get Noyes acquitted,' he would write to his brother in New York and so accordingly forwarded to Freshfields in London to be aware of it when the case came to trial.

A smart man who disappears from the scene of the crime. An outside man who claimed no knowledge of what had gone on. Others who were cut-outs to the greater forgery and then disappeared, using well-rehearsed yet completely baffling escape routes that had been long planned. In these, their earliest endeavours, the thieves of Threadneedle Street learned the basics of assembling a job, refining them as they went along. By the end of the Civil War, young Austin Bidwell was in his early twenties, and already a seasoned professional, like Willie Pinkerton who had served in the cavalry and would become his ultimate nemesis.

What took Austin Bidwell, his brother and their friends from being small-league con artists to international forgers was their subsequent arrival in New York City, where they became willing accomplices to established fraudsters. For public consumption,

Austin Bidwell liked to maintain it was all an inevitable descent into the depredations of temptation which he was powerless to resist. 'If I were inclined to indulge in
reminiscences, what a catalogue could be given of men who had, like myself, drifted
into the "primrose way", he wrote, 'and all, or nearly all, have paid a terrible penalty for
their wrongdoing – none more terrible than myself.'

2

Strangers, Silk Hats and Salting Wells

The history of New York during the years 1867, 1868, 1869, 1870 and down to the middle of 1871 ought to suffuse the cheek of every American citizen with the blush of shame. The State still adhering to the pernicious system of caring for the city, led to a union of corruption in both political parties, and gradually one of these two fell under the domination of an infamous cabal.

The Nether Side of New York, or the Vice, Crime and Poverty of the Great Metropolis by Edward Crapsey, 1872.

Friday, 7 March 1873
Mansion House, Justice Room
Noon

What a difference nearly a week had made. When he had first stood before the bench the previous Saturday, Edwin Noyes Hills had seemed confident though tired. In his subsequent dealings with authorities he was respectful and continued to protest his innocence. He was regretful, yet certain that his local, legal difficulties could easily be cleared up. Described as 'a well-dressed young man of gentlemanly appearance and manners', in one newspaper account, his innocence, he was sure, would soon be established.

Very quickly he became defiant and his condition deteriorated. Today, he was dishevelled and dejected as he walked towards the dock. Indeed, he appeared to have aged. Though he had given his age as 29 years, he had actually just passed his thirty-sixth birthday the month before.

Six days after his original arrest, Hills appeared once more before three unsmiling, bewigged judges in the Justice Room, a small, dark chamber on the ground floor of the official residence of the Lord Mayor of London. His Lordship was now presiding over this second remand hearing where all the proprieties were being observed. The lord mayor's was a uniquely ceremonial role combined with that of chief magistrate for the ancient part of the City in which the financial institutions were based.

Sir Sydney Hedley Waterlow looked thunderous across the darkened court. He was a caricaturist's dream: a small, slightly hunched figure, with a pointed, beaky nose and eyes that narrowed when he was annoyed, as now. Stern and invariably unyielding, he was not one to brook criticism nor be told what to do, especially by the accused's barrister, famously known as 'a champion nuisance of the world'.

Dr Edward Kenealy had gone for the jugular and there was nothing Sir Sydney could do about it. Kenealy was a squat Irish-born advocate whose eccentricities and reck-lessness were well known in and around Gray's Inn, where he was a bencher. Insulting the Lord Mayor of London was all in a day's work for him. What had exercised the fiery Dr Kenealy was that the Saturday before, His Lordship had used his right to draw a veil over the original remand proceedings.

'There are reasons for hearing this case in private,' Sir Sydney had intoned with the full solemnity he could bring to bear. 'Anyone not connected with the case must retire from the court.' And so they had. Their number included clerks, journalists and the usual nosy parkers with nothing better to do. Dr Kenealy now claimed that because of this, Sir Sydney had prejudiced the treatment of his client; the rumours that had resulted, and the very secrecy Sir Sydney had promoted, had worked against Mr Noyes, who had nothing to hide.

So why, Kenealy wanted to know, was Mr Noyes being treated with such con-tempt? 'We are not going to have the inquisition in this country,' he flatly declared. 'I submit that trying a prisoner in camera is a relic of the inquisition.'

Somehow, His Lordship maintained his dignity under such flagrant provocation[1]. Sir Sydney Waterlow simply stated for the record that holding the preliminary hear-ings behind closed doors had better served the wider interests of justice. Discretion was needed and the trial had assuredly not been prejudiced. Despite his spirited bay-oneting by Dr Kenealy, His Lordship did have a point.

With ever more vivid rumours circulating, it had seemed the only way to con-trol the welter of speculation which had spread around the city and beyond. The prisoner himself had said very little apart from monosyllabic replies to pointed questions. Immediately after his arrest, the Governor of the Bank of England him-self, Sir George Lyall, had gone down to see the supposed innocent clerk to offer him immunity. If he would turn Queen's Evidence, he would be paid £1,000 for his trouble. Hills declined, still maintaining that he had been duped by the shady businessman for whom he worked.

And so now in the Justice Room, Dr Kenealy began his opening argument, pointing out that the latest information was even more contradictory. Yes, there was evidence of fraud, but if anything, the seemingly innocent clerk's story held up (much as Austin Bidwell would confidently claim to Willie Pinkerton in Cuba a few days later). The only tangible proof was that there had been frauds on the London & Westminster Bank and Messrs. Rothschild & Son, as well as the Union Bank. This much was now admitted by the clerk who had first stumbled across them the week before. 'I have personally ascertained that they are forgeries,' Frank May testified. 'I have reason to know that all the others are forgeries.'

Their perpetrator was still at large, for Charles Johnson Horton – the man for whom Noyes had worked as a clerk – had disappeared off the face of the earth. How could so complicated a fraud be perpetrated by such a financial Houdini, a forger who had left behind so few clues? Edward Kenealy grandly declared that there was no hint of a conspiracy nor any concrete information that linked Noyes with the greater fraud. His client had simply cashed what he thought were genuine bills at respectable banks for his master. 'Why he should be assumed to have been connected in a forgery I am at a loss to understand.'

As successive witnesses testified, Dr Kenealy also had a point. Cashiers at a couple of banks testified that they recalled Noyes as a chief clerk to Mr Horton, whom they had not seen for some time. Others recalled him in the company of a Mr Warren, who also had not been seen for a while. Most could only vaguely recall him and their descriptions could, Noyes' defence counsel said, refer to anyone.

When it came to the summary, the defence was adamant. There was no evidence against his client, nor was there any concrete proof that Warren and Horton were the same person. In any case, his client had only worked as a clerk for the latter. George Freshfield, acting on behalf of the Crown, asked that Mr Noyes be remanded indefinitely because 'he had been dealing with very large sums of money and asking almost in the character of a principal – certainly in that of an accomplice'. But Noyes' lawyer was incredulous. 'Was it likely, if Horton was about to embark on a gigantic fraud, he would take a perfect stranger into his confidence?' Edward Kenealy asked.

'A perfect stranger' – in all the reams of astonished coverage and excited speculation that followed, that elegant phrase probably got to the nub of the mystery better than anything. Whoever was behind this amazing fraud had indeed achieved some measure of perfection. A perfectly elusive stranger, too, who would dazzle detectives and the waiting public and press with his ingenuity in erasing all traces of their real identity.

'A perfectly executed scheme', as one prosecutor termed it. 'There was no hurry, no unseemly eagerness to reap the fruits of dishonesty,' another newspaper exulted a few days later. 'Everything was done deliberately and upon business like principles,' said another. With forged certificates, which one newspaper would shortly term as 'marvellously perfect'. Except for one tiny, laughable error.

The missed date had, in the grander scheme of things, only derailed the timing of the fraud's greater execution. Despite their forensic following of the evidence trail, the police were no nearer finding their quarry even after the prisoner had offered to help track his mysterious employer. 'I have been directed to do what I have done by Mr Horton, my master,' was one of the few helpful things Noyes had said in his cell, 'and if you will let me out, I think I can find him.'

As regards the equally puzzling F.A. Warren, the prisoner would say nothing at all. And now, as he was remanded once more, the prisoner's eyes were bright with defiance. It was obvious that Edwin Noyes Hills knew more – much more – than he was letting on. Somebody, somewhere, had told him to keep his mouth shut. He had, as George Bidwell later said, played the role of the good soldier who helped to cover up what one newspaper aptly termed, 'one of the most elaborate conspiracies and gigantic frauds which had been held in modern times'.

Without realising it at the time, Sir Sydney Waterlow had personally been defrauded as part of that self-same elaborate forgery. As well as being director of several companies (including railway and a couple of merchant banks), he ran the eponymous printing house that had been started by his father forty years before. Waterlow's now employed 2,000 people down by the city wall. Among its other responsibilities, Sir Sydney's company had the contract to print official government documents.

At the start of 1873 a bombastic German visitor to their Moorgate sub-branch had requested some special vellum-like paper for, what he vaguely termed, commercial purposes. The printers had christened him 'Von', as they never learned his real name. Taken down to the city wall by messenger, this mysterious German had seen Sir Sydney from a distance but neither had engaged the other in conversation. Indeed, he seemed a man of few words, apart from barking a few peremptory orders that he needed the paper in a hurry.

A few days later, this same wretched fellow had returned to take the deep blue paper and paid cash, disappearing off into the winter's afternoon. What Sir Sydney did not realise until much later was that this German was none other than George Bidwell. Not only had he assumed a new identity with consummate ease, he would also cause confusion as to whether it was really he who had visited Waterlow's in the city. With an insouciance that was entirely characteristic, George Bidwell would later boast that he 'had become so used to aliases that their employment had become a matter of indifference'. His ability to think on his feet was his greatest asset. 'Plausible audacious, of extreme quickness of mind in emergencies and of resolute courage,' was how one later chronicler of the case described him.

In the weeks, and indeed months, ahead there was a great deal of speculation as to which of the Bidwell brothers was the prime mover in the Bank of England forgeries. Many assumed that the older George had been a terrible influence on his younger brother. Although George was twelve years Austin's senior, the picture was never entirely clear as to which of them had spearheaded their life of crime.

Fairly quickly, the British authorities had come to the conclusion that the younger Austin was the hidden mastermind. Yet the elder George always liked to maintain otherwise. 'My brother Austin was a fine, steady young man and universally regarded as one likely to fill an honourable position in the world,' he later declared, leading him through what he termed 'the intricate windings of a maze that led to prison'.

At the time he was writing these words, George Bidwell had been released early, while his younger brother was hoping for parole. Straight-faced, George also claimed that he had roped Austin in to the Bank of England business and shielded him from the fact it was not a genuine enterprise. Years later he would write a paean to his brother:

> [Austin] is a young man of most sterling qualities misled:
> Fair seeming tempters swayed
> Who made him think 'twas just to do the same
> As others did it to him – 'twas logic lame
> Which led his striving soul to cover deeps
> With velvet, flowery slopes, then fearful leaps
> Soon pardon him where venging furies are –
> Rumour slew Hope, then handed him to Despair

At times, George Bidwell would unexpectedly wax lyrical about how honest men – of whom he considered himself one – often faced the abyss, blaming others for his misfortunes with a grandiloquence that seems arch, even by his standards.

His misery seems to be genuine, for later in that spring of 1873 George Bidwell would claim that 'no person who has suffered can realise the controlling influence which circumstances even if occasioned by unwarranted misfortunes may have in warping for a time the very best dispositions from the path of rectitude'.

Four Weeks Later – Friday, 4 April 1873
Mansion House, Justice Room
2 p.m.

Certainly, the dark complected, broad-shouldered man who was escorted in and limped painfully slowly across the Justice Room a month later was suffering. Yet he was still trying to maintain that he did not know his co-conspirator, Edwin Noyes Hills, and had refused to give his real name to the authorities who had brought him here for his first remand hearing.

Everyone in court knew perfectly well who he was. George Bidwell was attempting to behave like a stranger who was obviously in a most imperfect condition. And on this cloudy yet occasionally bright spring morning, there was an air of great expectation throughout the court and beyond. His exploits in recent days had been front page news on both sides of the Atlantic.

It might have taken weeks of concerted effort, but the forces of law and order had managed to track him down. In the immediate aftermath of the fraud's discovery, George had what he later called 'a series of most extraordinary adventures' in Ireland, and narrowly escaped arrest on several occasions before being run to ground in Edinburgh two days earlier, after what one amazed onlooker had called 'an exciting chase'.

And now, as he walked in with what seemed agonising pain, George Bidwell could sense that he could play to the crowd on his first remand hearing. 'The Justice Room was more crowded than at any of the previous examinations and continued so throughout the hearing', a newspaper would report the next day. This would be repeated time and again in all subsequent remand hearings. The Mansion House would be full to the rafters. It seemed the whole of the city could not get enough of the forgers' exploits. That included the man himself, despite his injuries. George Bidwell was clearly enjoying the attention.

To those who knew him well – and his friend Ed with whom he was charged was clearly among them – it came as no surprise. What did cause much shocked comment was his tattered and battered state, for George Bidwell normally took great care over his appearance. He was always well dressed and dandified, leading one newspaper to capture it best in the cross-heading 'Handsome rascal'.

Today we might call him 'Gorgeous George', the sort of preening ne'er-do-well who would become lionised and celebrated with reality TV show appearances and double page spreads in *Hello!* magazine. In Victorian England, he struck a rather raffish figure, a good time guy who now seemed to be enjoying himself hugely, even when under lock and key.

Despite his obvious agony, today he had the air of a cat who was about to feast upon a canary. His refusal to give a name, some thought, was typical play-acting for even his arrest in Scotland had managed to be theatrical and, indeed, had 'smacked of the marvellous', according to one newspaper account. While wrestling with his captor, George had grabbed at him with a secret handshake, 'and for the first time, probably', the same newspaper reported, 'Masonry has been the means of effecting a capture'.

As he took his place in the dock, the charges against him were read out by the clerk of the court. Described as a merchant who was not now in business, George Bidwell was allowed to sit out the arraignment because of his injuries. Many wondered how bad, or real, they actually were. His lameness had little to do with the past, but was an obviously useful tool for the present as everyone patiently waited for his lawyer to arrive.

In the immediate aftermath of the discovery of the fraud, one newspaper had presciently remarked it 'must be a bold man who will carry a forged bill to the Bank of England: but the author of these forgeries was equal to the undertaking'. And indeed it was true, for George Bidwell had not just approached the judge's own place of business, but some of the other magistrates too.

Today, as with all the recent hearings, Sir Sydney's baleful presence was augmented by the Governor of the Bank of England as well as two members of the Rothschild family, the banking dynasty which stretched like a seamless robe across the developed world and bankrolled a greater part of it.

To Sir Sydney's immediate left was Sir Anthony de Rothschild – 'Billy' to his family – first son of the baron, whose merchant bank he now also directed. A baronet in his own right, he looked every inch the bluff country squire and 'a very good man' in Queen Victoria's estimation. Next to him was his younger brother, an equally good friend of the Prince of Wales, the rakish and, in private, surprisingly playful Alfred Rothschild. He was the first Jewish director of the Bank of England, but was better known as a man of refinement and impeccable taste. Today, Alfred's large forehead and merry eyes had taken on a more quizzical aspect. Though only dimly aware of it at the time, it had been his curious misfortune to have been defrauded by one of the fraudsters just six weeks before. To his amazement, the Rothschilds' own bank had passed a forged bill of acceptance that would slip through the system unnoticed. 'The whole bill as far as we are concerned, is fictitious,' Alfred would marvel under oath in this same room a few weeks later, 'We know nothing at all of the drawer.'

At this remand hearing, the perpetrator was sitting just 20ft away from him. If George Bidwell's memoirs are to be believed, he was later visited in Newgate by Sir Alfred Rothschild whom he termed a well-built man 'with auburn hair, blue eyes and a rather pleasing expression of countenance', to whom he supposedly said, 'Mr Rothschild, I believe most other men placed in the circumstances would have done much as I have'. That somewhat ridiculous paean to honesty ended badly, the prisoner recalled, as ultimately the visitor saw 'nothing in me worth saving'.

Friday, 4 April 1873
Mansion House, Justice Room
2.15 p.m.

While they waited for George Bidwell's lawyer to arrive, Edwin Noyes Hills' own brief saw a window of opportunity. 'If the bank authorities have any further evidence to adduce against him,' Dr Kenealy declared to the bench, 'the witnesses should be brought at once.' The evidence, he argued, hardly added to the incrimination of his client.

Sir Sydney Waterlow was not one to agree. 'The evidence against the prisoners might affect the new man,' he said, nodding towards the exhausted George Bidwell, 'so he will have to wait.' As Sir Sydney had repeatedly said in earlier hearings, there was clearly 'no hardship until the others involved in the conspiracy could be got together'.

That, as George Bidwell well knew, could take forever. Though the remaining pair of fraudsters had been apprehended, it did not mean anything. George Macdonnell had made it as far as New York, while Austin Bidwell had reached Havana. In both cities, there were unholy arguments going on between the relevant authorities as to the legality of extradition. Both prisoners had taken care to obtain the best legal representation. Would they – as they had been doing for the best part of a decade now – get off on a legal technicality?

From the expression on his face, it was clear that George Bidwell knew something that they didn't. As Willie Pinkerton would later declare to anyone who might care to listen, they would stop at nothing to evade justice, as they had been doing over the past decade.

As the forgeries had been committed in the City of London, it was a function of the English justice system that these first evidentiary hearings had been held at the lord mayor's official residence, almost akin to a grand jury in the prisoners' native land.

Today's hearing, on 4 April with George Bidwell in attendance, was the sixth in sequence and – as with all but the first, when Sir Sydney Waterlow had demanded secrecy – the court was crowded. There would be a further seventeen hearings before His Lordship over the next four months. 'The preliminary proceedings before the lord mayor were long drawn out,' one commentator would dryly remark. In time, George Bidwell would find it all highly amusing too. In the weeks ahead, he reverted to type and seemed to enjoy the court proceedings as though some huge great caper in itself, interrupting whenever he could on many occasions, much to the ire of Sir Sydney Waterlow.

A fortnight later, George Bidwell would stand straight-faced in front of the lord mayor and suggest they should save time and money by delaying their case. It was part of his overarching hubris that he had dismissed his own lawyer and defended himself. On this same matter, Sir Sydney Waterlow addressed the prisoner directly, 'I understand you have expressed a wish for the present to dispense with the attendance of the solicitor who had represented you at the previous examinations?'

'Yes,' George replied, 'he is withdrawn.' And then he explained why. As the whole case would have to be gone into again and again until his brother and Mac were extradited, surely it would be better that no other evidence would be taken until they both arrived here in London? 'I would be willingly so remanded as Your Lordship wishes,' George said. Clearly relishing his words, he added that it would save expense, that was all.

Several of the onlookers wondered if he was being serious. After a great deal of deliberation, Sir Sydney remarked that he could hardly change course. Straight-faced, George Bidwell accepted His Lordship's argument. His theatrics were highly entertaining and many in the courtroom, despite themselves, simply came just to lap it all up; as one newspaper noted, public interest in the case increased rather than diminished as the trial progressed.

It was hardly George Bidwell's debut in a courtroom. For all his cleverness – and many considered him too clever by half – the elder Bidwell brother's ultimate undoing stemmed from taking things too far. He never quite knew when to stop. When he had started his life of crime it had helped that he always looked older than his age. 'At eighteen, I sported a beard and a moustache,' he would recall. Now on the cusp of 40, time had caught up with him. His hair was thinning, his eyes were sunken and the sallowness of his complexion showed how hard his imprisonment had been.

Yet he remained his incorrigible self. Indeed, George Bidwell's industry and stamina had always been remarkable. He later confessed:

> I felt that I possessed energy, perseverance and physical capacity to undergo more hardships and to accomplish more work than most young men. Beside this, I was strictly temperate, and not addicted to any of the vices so common in large cities.

Except, of course, a lifelong addiction to criminality and a devotion to clever schemes that were often breathtaking in their execution, eclipsed only by the barefaced cheek he and the others often employed. '[Their] numerous American friends are not at all astonished to find them implicated in the bank forgeries,' the *Chicago Tribune* had marvelled. They had effortlessly run rings around law enforcement all over the world. If they could have sold sand to the Arabs or snow to the Eskimos, the Bidwells might well have got away with it.

One of their earlier, more curious capers took place when George Bidwell and young Austin sold petroleum in an oil-rich region of Virginia where they undertook a little scam called 'salting wells'. William Pinkerton later explained that this was where 'they bored wells, filled them with Petroleum Oil and then sold them as oil wells'.

While this does sound like one of George Bidwell's more entertaining and fanciful yarns it really did happen, although he does not mention it in his later confessional autobiography. It is a curious omission for an irredeemable show-off who was, at times, clearly more fantasist than outright fabricator. The springboard for George Bidwell's criminal exploits, he always maintained, came from his accidental running-in with fraudsters, crooked lawyers and tricksters who had deceived him at the start of his 'legitimate' business career when he had been supporting the greater

Bidwell family. 'Of my honest struggles, how I was robbed, deceived and duped by those supposed friends,' he later wrote from jail, 'I will not relate now or at a later period of the false adviser and tempter who lays in wait.'

As each of his subsequent businesses failed, he got into ever greater debt trying to cover his existing liabilities. This only made things spectacularly worse. Working on the principle that the only way to beat them was to join them, he began his own career in fraud because he had been the victim of one.

According to his own account in 1863, George Bidwell had invented a steam kettle from which he made several thousand dollars. For this, he decided to move to Toronto, a city that seems to have played an unknown role in his criminal career. There, he opened a factory, sent for his family and in a matter of months made several thousand dollars. With this money he opened a wholesale confectionery business in the Canadian city, but when he then exchanged the local currency into gold he lost out. His profits were redeemed for a fraction of what he supposedly made.

In his account, he went back on the road again, flogging his kettle. On his travels, George happened to meet what he termed 'one of the most skilful swindlers ever known'. This was Frank Kibbe – the same man who later made good his escape with 'W. Austin Bidwell' and who is akin to the Keyser Söze character in *The Usual Suspects*. Kibbe was a criminal chameleon whose own real identity is hard to discern but who was certainly very good at what he did. George Bidwell took an instant dislike to him, feeling he was a coward and braggart. George collected money from one of Kibbe's bad debts. His fast friend then persuaded him to go to Providence, Rhode Island, in the autumn of 1863.

Certainly, the records show that it was there that Kibbe and Bidwell opened a 'swindling' commission house. George maintains he was innocent, thinking it a genuine business, with Kibbe then running off with all the profits. George traced him to Buffalo, New York, where he forced Kibbe to hand him his half of the money. Significantly, George Bidwell does not mention the small matter of the Cincinnati job a couple of months later.

Would he really have carried on working with Kibbe if he had already absconded with their profits? Or was George, as some later thought, pretending to be W. Austin Bidwell and his brother pretending to be Kibbe? Even stranger, George Bidwell later claimed that this version of long firm fraud was never particularly profitable. 'Though we caused merchants to lose goods amounting to hundreds of thousands of dollars, we lost the proceeds of their sale one way and another.' That may well have been, but as Willie Pinkerton later recorded of both Bidwell brothers, 'in this way, they got on for several years, beating everybody'.

While he was also travelling as a preacher in 1864, George Bidwell claims he returned to New York where he came into the orbit of a doctor who called himself Samuel Bolivar. He formed a partnership with this doctor and opened up yet another swindling commercial house, in what was then the state capital of West Virginia, under assumed names.

Who was Bolivar? Again mystery descends for there are no records of such a character, but George Bidwell was spotted in the state capital in the company of his younger brother. 'George and Austin then appeared at Wheeling,' the *Chicago Tribune* later reported. 'Here they again indulged their pastime but being caught were sentenced to jail for one year.'

During the summer of 1864, a suspicious local policeman became interested in what they were up to. The Bidwells had been in contact with another forger and the local detective had intercepted a letter. He soon arrested George, who was then convicted on a charge of conspiracy and spent eight months in West Virginia County Jail, which was, by the standards of the day, a bizarre experience.

'During the greater part of the day, the place was a veritable pandemonium,' George later recalled. 'Laughter, singing, gambling varied with occasional fights, washing and drying of clothes.' While incarcerated, a jailbreak occurred and four prisoners escaped, one of whom was killed by the guards in doing so. George regretted that he had not tried to escape with them.

Sometime in 1865, George Bidwell did succeed in escaping and eventually returned to New York City. 'I had no more to do with forging until some years later,' he then claims. This was nonsense. What really happened was that he and his younger brother, who had been working on Wall Street, just happened to come into contact with a pair of pre-eminent forgers and a counterfeiter who had also been arrested for illegal currency speculation during the Civil War.

If Chicago had been a Wild West town, New York City was nothing short of a criminal Mecca. With its teeming streets and dangerous corners, Gotham, as it soon became known, was the prototypical nineteenth-century metropolis where 'turbulence, poverty, vice and crime', in the vivid phrase of one contemporary chronicler, flourished in the aftermath of the Civil War.

Manhattan became a haven for all sorts of nefarious activity which culminated in the city's greatest ever criminal boom. The Civil War, which had hardly impinged upon New York itself, became the great backdrop to this story. After hostilities ended, the city was flooded with a veritable tsunami of ne'er-do-wells and shysters returning from the fighting. In 1866, the first full year of peace, one Methodist bishop estimated that there were 30,000 thieves among the 800,000 population.

Many soon passed into legend. Among the more extraordinary were 'Hell-Cat Maggie', 'Sadie the Goat' (whose ear was bitten off by the former), 'Eddie the Plague' and 'One-Lung' Curran, all members of gangs who ran amok around the city. Yet none of these characters could compare with the 'commercial and political rascals' who allowed corruption to contaminate the city like a virus. Even today the name 'Tammany Hall' is synonymous with shameless political machinations. At its apex was the 'Tweed Ring', which became the most notorious municipal fraud in history, named for a boss of scarcely imaginable venality who became the undisputed leader of the city.

William Tweed was famously described as being 6ft tall and 300lb of 'jovial swagger'. With the aid of his cronies, Tweed ran the city as his own personal fiefdom. Politicians, police and judiciary were simply for hire: fleecing and rarely protecting the citizens, taking kickbacks and purposefully turning a blind eye to wrongdoing. Austin Bidwell later claimed that he was a pal of Tweed's, as by now he was 'one of the boys about town'. He was, by his own estimation, 'young, hot-headed and fancied that the whole world was my oyster'. In his memoirs, Austin also claims that, along with his criminal associates, he 'bought a silver punch bowl' given by a police superintendent as a wedding present for Tweed's daughter with the proceeds from one particular forgery.

'Scarcely deigning to conceal its rascality from the general view, the Ring prospered and soon became master of the city,' wrote a magazine reporter called Edward Crapsey who became the most colourful chronicler of the times. As a result, the putative New York Police Department (NYPD) was the most corrupt force in history. Much of its greater enterprise concerned the running down of protection money which was then split between the squad and corrupt officials who looked the other way. The police ranks regularly took bribes, rigged elections and turned a blind eye to illegal liquor sales and gin joints all across the city. Crime flourished, and pickpockets, burglars, sneak thieves and confidence tricksters 'became daily more extensive and more enterprising'. In Austin Bidwell's estimation 'the common patrolmen got what blackmail he could on his own account from the unhappy women of the street'.

Yet most of this activity was low level nickel-and-dime stuff. What really opened New Yorkers' eyes to the possibilities of crime was the Rufus Lord case in March 1866. Austin Bidwell described it as 'startling in its ease and magnitude'. Perhaps the first truly professional white-collar job which set the standards for all the later ones, 'this was really the first of many great bond robberies,' Austin added, 'and it struck the popular tag'.

A very wealthy old man called Rufus L. Lord was sitting his office in Exchange Place when a complete stranger walked in and started talking to him. Meanwhile, unbeknownst to him, an accomplice removed bonds worth $1,170,000 from an open safe in another room. When a perpetrator was eventually apprehended, the old man could not recognise him. However, one of the gang who had been involved helped recover some of the bonds to gain a more lenient sentence. Most, it transpired, were in the hands of the ringleader, a former stockbroker and founder of the Hell's Kitchen Gang, 'Dutch' Heinrichs, 'who in his time, has braved the law more than any other', in a later newspaper estimation, and who then absconded to Europe.

As the American economy became more sophisticated, so too did the criminals. They simply aped the professional classes rather than trying to stick them up. Recent historians of the city have concluded, 'With the tremendous expansion in the circulation of easily negotiable paper, greenbacks and federal bonds, and concomitant increases in every day impersonal commercial transactions, a crew of sophisticated counterfeiters, forgers and white-collar con artists sprang into being.'

If nothing else, the Bidwells had impeccable timing. Throughout this story, whenever there was a zeitgeist to dip into, they seemed to be just the right people at exactly the right time. Their arrival in New York coincided with fundamental changes to the American banking system. 'It was then the time of the old boom days,' Austin Bidwell later remarked, 'when money was plenty and speculation brisk.' Before the Civil War robberies were much less lucrative because currency was strictly limited. 'There were absolutely no Government bonds or currency,' Austin Bidwell would later write, 'while the few bonds issued by corporations were not usually made payable to bearer, and therefore, were not negotiable, and were of no use to the robber.'

And then came the fighting which took a million lives. The prosecution of the Civil War had cost $12 billion for the north and $4 billion for the south. To meet its expense, state banks were taxed out of existence and national ones took over. Bonds payable to a bearer were issued from government down to local level and became very popular investments. During the subsequent reconstruction, the rail and telegraph network expanded exponentially.

Vast fortunes were to be made and both brothers wanted to be part of it. 'The great Civil War had but lately ended, and the country was still reeling from the mighty conflict,' Austin Bidwell marvelled. 'The flush times, resultant from the enormous money issue of the Government, kept everything booming.'

And, indeed, Uncle Sam's fiscal faucets had fully opened up, not least because of the introduction of a national currency. Supported by national banks with federal charters, each was now legally required to guarantee a reserve of federal bonds. By the end of the 1860s, there were opportunities galore. 'Patriotism, and profit as well, led banks, corporations and individuals all over the world to invest surplus funds in bonds,' Austin recalled, 'those of the Government being most popular of all.' Not least by international forgers who saw how useful they could be.

So, a whole new breed of criminals defined by their skill and daring entered Manhattan. A new vocabulary was needed to describe both them and their work: 'paper hangers' (cheque forgers), 'stingarees' (cons) and, most important of all, the thieves who would brazenly remove bonds while they were being transported or even held in safes.

'Skinners' represented, in Edward Crapsey's apposite phrasing, 'the rankest growth of that rare roguery which dodges the law at every turn, and is nowhere produced in such perfection as in the financial hotbed of the continent'.

Nowhere was the line between legitimate and illegitimate enterprise more blurred than in the growing financial capital of the country. 'Wall Street has absorbed more of the twisted intellect which delights in trick and device than any other spot of earth,' Crapsey would also note. For the brave, the foolhardy and the speculator, there were vast fortunes to be made. At heart, every great thief was a great gambler, and Austin Bidwell claims he made and lost several fortunes on Wall Street when he was in his late teens. '[Before] I was twenty I was known as the most successful young man on the Stock Exchange,' he later boasted.

To begin with his 'plunges', as he called his own gambling on the stock market, were successful. He lived, so he later claimed, in a handsome suite of rooms at the 5th Avenue Hotel. Around him, the economy was booming. 'The years I speak of were fortunate ones for Wall Street,' Austin recalled.

One result was the rise of robber barons – with names like Cooke, Vanderbilt and Rockefeller – who would propel the stock exchange into overdrive. As with all forms of betting 'stock gambling holds its victims with a fearful power', as another contemporary commentator noted. Certainly, the mania for speculation that occurred after the Civil War meant that Wall Street had become 'a chosen centre from which the worst of swindlers conduct their operations'.

Towards the end of his life, Willie Pinkerton was almost nostalgic for this vanishing breed of gentlemen who were defined by their relative intelligence and sophistication. Where once bank robbers were elegant and educated – 'silk hats', he called them – they had been replaced in the first years of the new century by small-time hoodlums of the 'hobo' or 'yegg' class of degenerates (the latter being a common-or-garden safebreaker who would easily resort to violence). 'The "yeggsman" has taken the place of the "dude" burglar with his silk hat and silk gloves,' Pink later complained.

In the 1860s, the silk hats had been successful because they were helped by the cops in the most important, and certainly most profitable, of scams. 'The Bank Ring' was essentially underwritten by the police where, as one contemporary report had it, there were 'skilled rogues working in collusion with members of the detective service to their mutual profit'. For a 'rake-off' of their plunder, the criminals would be protected by the New York Police Department, a fact of life which would soon be significant so far as the Bidwells were concerned. 'Many a mysterious robbery was perpetrated to which no clue was ever found,' Austin Bidwell wryly noted thanks to this police collusion.

There was also a great deal of mystery as to how Austin himself became involved. In his memoirs, he does not mention any of the earliest jobs he had performed with his brother in West Virginia and Illinois. 'I went into Wall Street in the early sixties,' Austin maintained to a reporter many years later, 'an innocent country boy of sixteen.' All he ever said was that a 'prominent' New York official – 'whom I will not name for that reason,' he later said – gave him some bonds to launder because he was 'a good financier, the right man for the job'. He should simply go to Europe and 'negotiate the sale' of more than $1 million worth of bonds which had been removed from the Ocean Bank in Greenwich Street in June 1869.

The perpetrator had posed as an investment banker who had opened an office next door to the bank. A gang of his heavies then dynamited their way through the stone floor to remove the spoils from the bank's vaults. In his memoirs, Austin Bidwell also implies he was peripherally involved but, though he certainly knew the silk hat behind the Ocean Bank robbery, he was actually in prison when it took place.

Max Shinburn was a German-born master criminal who later fled from the United States but had been a well-known visitor to several NYPD precincts around this time. Well educated, good-looking and highly plausible, his speciality, in the words of a later police chief, 'was taking wax impressions of bank and safe keys' stolen from back offices. According to Robert Pinkerton, he was the greatest bank safe and vault burglar ever known in police history.

Doubtless, as Austin Bidwell later claimed, he met Shinburn, his associates and others like him in gambling houses and the lure of such schemes became too tempting. As he later described it, if they went undetected, 'anything from opening a magnificent bar or hotel in New York to a steam yacht and winter cruises in the tropics and summer nights in the Med' could be the reward. And he became a very willing participant. 'I had taken my first steps in crime,' he later exulted, 'and my success led me to try again.'

The appeal was too much for him to resist. 'I had obligations to meet,' Austin Bidwell said to a reporter many years later, 'and no money for either debts or living. It was then that my first temptation came to me.' In his memoirs, Austin adds that it was at this point that he 'was offered a chance to make $100,000 by selling a large block of stolen bonds'. The greater truth was that the silk hats were not just thick as thieves with the criminal elite, they were 'thicker than fleas on a dog's back', as one policeman described the general criminal milieu at the time.

But before too long, Austin's fortunes changed. 'In truth, I was in the "primrose way" which is ever found a most tormenting and unhappy thoroughfare,' he confessed in his memoirs; though, as the record shows, it did not exactly seem like that at the time.

Unsurprisingly, it was Willie Pinkerton who tied them all together. After their disappearance from Chicago, burgeoning technology helped those who wanted to fight crime. As the telegraph and railroads expanded, so did the reach of the Pinkertons. With his brother Robert appointed in charge of the New York office in late 1865, the Pinkerton National Detective Agency was on hand to record that the Bidwells then arrived in the city shortly thereafter ('which they must have reached about 1867 or 1868'), though the records were never entirely clear. 'Here they became acquainted with [the] prisoners George Macdonnell and E.N. Hills.'

What they really did in those years was simply recorded by Willie Pinkerton. 'They took up all classes of crime. Forgery, swindling by any means of fake agencies; advancing money to persons engaged in robbing banks.' Indeed, the charges were so numerous that it was impossible for him to do justice to them all. 'So ingeniously were their schemes planned and so cleverly was their work executed,' marvelled William Pinkerton, 'that for a long time, they escaped detection.'

By this time, the Pinkertons were flourishing, too. Willie himself was now the head of the Chicago office and the agency's expansion was so quick that their father would write, 'I am overwhelmed with business', in the year after the Civil War ended. In fact, it was those very hostilities which had helped establish the Pinkertons' name.

Old A.P. had become acquainted with several influential people, not least in the form of the legal counsel for the Illinois Central Railroad, Abraham Lincoln, and George Pullman, whose desire to improve rail travel would create a monopoly and great wealth for himself. Powerful connections were made with the business and military elite who were later in charge of the reconstruction. Fairly quickly, it was widely said that nobody was safe from the Pinkertons. They would go to the ends of the earth to run down a suspect and had, most famously, spoiled a plot to kill President Lincoln on the way to his first inauguration. Whether that attempt was genuine – and there were enough who wondered if it wasn't – never became completely clear.

It caused a growing enmity with the NYPD that never abated, not least with the opening of the Pinkertons' New York office in November 1865. The breach with the police department was completed thanks to the Pinkertons knowing perfectly well just how corrupt some policemen were. Allan Pinkerton would later bemoan how detectives had fallen into disrepute 'until the term detective was synonymous with rogue'. If the cops were looking the other way, it would be up to Willie Pinkerton to fill in the breach, his 'success coming from method and thoroughness', in a later appreciation of his life. Thanks to some inspired branding, Willie himself became synonymous with the slightly unsettling symbol carried on their letterheads – the Eye of Providence, all-seeing and pervasive, and, for once, an epithet that was richly deserved.

Somewhere in the festering hothouse of ingenious criminality that was Manhattan, George Bidwell claimed that he 'became intimate with some dangerous operators in Wall Street who played for higher stakes by methods then more easily successful than now'. In his memoirs, he simply says that he was introduced to them by a famous counterfeiter of the Civil War period. 'I trusted in one whom I believed in,' he later explained to a girlfriend in a letter from prison, 'he by false pretences got my notes to a large amount sold then ruined me and paddled me with the ignominy of a fraud of which I was a profitless and innocent dupe.'

In his earlier attempts at running an honest business, George Bidwell claimed that he had used a printer named Winthrop Hilton to create the 'waybills' used to dispatch his stock. The printer asked George if he could extend their collaboration to blank letters of credit, which he says he agreed to with alacrity. By now, the Civil War was raging and the printer realised he could make even more capital out of the Confederacy. According to Hilton, the printer was only ever performing his patriotic duty. Arrested at his printing works, Hilton was accused of printing real southern money – and not fakes – from which he did indeed profit, but was never prosecuted.

The elder Bidwell was supposedly amazed at this kind of enterprise. 'As the art of forgery was then to me a strange one,' he writes, 'I was as much astonished [that] such an operation could be successfully executed.'

One evening, he accompanied Winthrop Hilton to a restaurant where he was introduced to two fast friends from the criminal world. Within minutes, they were plotting together. 'Hilton has made me two books of blank drafts which have the name of a St Louis bank printed in,' one of them said. 'All you have to do is go into Wall Street and buy gold.' And in this way George Bidwell became involved with two of the more famous fraudsters of the period.

In later years, Walter Sheridan and George Wilkes would become equally as infamous as the Bidwells for the ingenuity of their crimes. They, too, were chased by Willie Pinkerton all over the world.

Of the pair, Sheridan would become the most notorious. After drifting into petty crime, he had first been arrested in Chicago where he had planned a bank robbery in 1858. Captured, he was jailed for five years. After release, along with two other robbers they held up a bank in Springfield, Illinois – but did not have to fire their shotguns – and Sheridan was later found with $22,000 about his person by William Pinkerton. This money was used to get him off as he employed the best lawyers.

Thereafter, there were robberies all over the eastern seaboard of the United States, where Pink kept an eye on him but was never able to bring him to justice. In the spring of 1873, when the detective was convinced he was involved in the Bank of England forgeries, Pink learned that Sheridan had recently returned from Europe but had now gone into hiding. Later that same summer when the Bidwells were held in remand, Walter Sheridan and a gang that included George Wilkes began forging railway bonds in earnest in lower Manhattan. Posing as Charles H. Ralston, Sheridan traded on Broadway where he offered bonds at ridiculously low prices and, in the words of a later New York police chief, 'obtained $84,000 in good hard cash. It took months to effect this loan.' When the scam was discovered that autumn, he left for Europe. All was well until 1875 when he returned to the United States where both Pinkerton brothers chased him. Robert Pinkerton finally arrested Sheridan a year later in New York as he arrived in a Pullman train – but that was way in the future.

For now, in the mid- to late 1860s, George Bidwell was also introduced to Sheridan's associate, who was later dubbed 'King of the Forgers' for a scheme that was as equally ambitious as the Bank of England job. George Wilkes, or Henry Wade Wilkes (or sometimes Willis), was widely credited with taking the meticulousness of American forgery overseas in the late 1870s. In the words of another police chief, Wilkes was a key member of 'an international gang [who] made New York, London and Paris in turn their headquarters, and flooded the two continents with their worthless bonds and securities'.

After working for the Erie Railroad Company, Wilkes had become a professional gambler. 'It was in the latter part of 1869 or beginning of 1870 that I was first arrested by the New York police for forgery,' he later confessed. Certainly, by then he had worked with the Bidwells, possibly as early as 1867, though the evidence is unclear. All that George said on the matter was elliptical, namely that 'one step led to another until now I experienced no great repugnance at making the acquaintance of a man who I was informed lived by forgery'.

In later years, both William and, indeed, Allan Pinkerton (who was spending a greater proportion of his time devoted to producing his memoirs with ghost writers as part of his greater promotional activities), were never quite sure that the Bidwells alone were behind the Bank of England forgeries in the spring of 1873. 'My son W.A. Pinkerton', wrote Old A.P. to a firm of New York solicitors using a common yet formal form of address, 'who knows these parties well and the work which they frequent has been very much in the evenings up town, among the people who associate mostly with this class of people.'

If there was anything to know, they would be party to it. Within days, Pink heard that 'an extensive gang of American thieves' had been in London. Their leader, as he recorded for the files, was 'George Wilkes who is said to be one of the most successful forgers in the world'. In London, he had already learned that police had 'followed another noted American forger named Walter Sheridan alias Walter Stuart alias Walter Stanford and many other aliases'.

While working with Sheridan on the forged railway bonds later that same summer, Wilkes fell out with the gang and disappeared in New York City. 'I had saved a large sum of money and for two years did nothing,' Wilkes later claimed. Because he seemed to be lying low in the early part of 1873, it made Pink always wonder if he was somehow implicated in the Bank of England forgeries.

Pink noted in March 1873:

Wilkes is a man who gets up the schemes, writes the drafts but never takes any chances of passing one of them, always having outside people to do that and in this connection, the Bidwells have always been associated with him in the minor work.

A few weeks later when Willie Pinkerton eventually caught up with Austin Bidwell in Cuba, his prisoner repeatedly declared that he did not even like Wilkes. Austin was also vehement that he had not gone to London to meet any associates of Wilkes or his greater gang who later pulled off jobs in Europe. 'He denied all knowledge of George Wilkes,' Pink reported to his brother, 'saying that he knew him and that was all. He denied having met him in Europe yet they stopped at the same hotel in London and in Paris.'

A bank, it had been famously remarked, could be opened by a crowbar and jemmy. For those who were so inclined there were two ways of removing fortunes from sub-terranean vaults. There were the brute force methods that required sledgehammers or dynamite and, as far less successful bank robbers could attest, there was a great deal of luck needed. 'Bank safes are not so easily emptied,' Austin Bidwell would wryly note in his memoirs. He and his associates happened upon a second, ever more auda-cious way of removing money from supposedly impregnable vaults. All they had to do was use a pen. 'I got in with a gang which was beating the banks in Wall Street,' Austin Bidwell later boasted, 'doing an extensive business in forgeries, false checks [sic] and similar transactions.' In this way, the Bidwells joined the silk hats – the gentle-men of crime – who had reached the apex of the criminal aristocracy.

'The insidious craft of the forger, willing the hidden gold from its strongholds with the flourish of a pen or the scratch of a graving tool,' was how one contemporary observer assessed the skill needed. Forgers were the princes of thieves who exhibited a curious mixture of artistic ability and scientific knowledge (particularly chemistry). Altering cheques, or what was better known in the United States as 'raising checks', required 'chemicals which leave no trace of themselves or the former writing upon the paper'. So long as there was no sign of tampering, no questions would be asked.

In addition to high intelligence, a successful forger also needed low cunning. Not only did they need to physically replicate signatures, they needed to gain the trust and confidence of credulous officials to obtain completely real cheques for their nefarious purposes. In time, the more accomplished, like Wilkes and Sheridan, 'out-sourced' all the various tasks needed. There was invariably some sort of backer of the scheme, a middleman who liaised with the forger and the presenter of the cheque, who was at one remove from it.

Certainly, the key to any forgery was sizing up a victim and the extent of his (and rarely her) bank account. Often, it would be necessary to steal cancelled cheques, or a blank one and the ink they used, from the victim. The forger would then practice a signature and a small amount would be made out. Usually, somebody else – a bank sneak or, indeed, the outside man – would then present it to the teller. 'The forger himself never enters the bank and that he has no chance to secure more than this legitimate share of the proceeds of the operation,' Inspector Tommy Byrnes would write. In other words, the mastermind would always have plausible deniability.

Though Austin Bidwell liked to claim that he earned 'a leadership amongst my fellows by originality and carrying out the famous gold forgeries in Wall Street in 1868–1869,' it is a matter of record that at the time, he was actually in the infamous Sing Sing prison upstate. By then the Bidwell brothers had met someone who would perform the actual physical forgery.

Such skilled craftsmen were few and far between. 'Forgers, speaking of them as professionals, are hardly a class, so few are they in number,' wrote the reporter Edward Crapsey. 'They do not exceed twenty-five but it must be remembered that the figures include only the professionals and that the amateur forgers are four or five times as numerous.' A fraudster was only as good as his 'penman' and so the Bidwell brothers hooked up with the most famous forger of them all, a true artisan who had already worked with fraudsters like George Wilkes and Walter Sheridan. As the self-styled 'Terror of Wall Street', he had an even more fearful reputation and, in some estimations, was the key to the forgery on the Bank of England.

George Engels was the kind of German who looked as though he had walked straight in from central casting, a picture of Aryan rectitude, a slim, blue-eyed, blond-haired Prussian who drank heavily, was married to a German girl and had six well-behaved children. His real name was Gottlieb Engels but he was usually known as George Engels.

He was a perfect criminal paradox: well known, but elusive. 'He always remained in the background, prepared the forged papers, cheats etc.,' George Bidwell later wrote, 'leaving to the more foolhardy the risk of presenting them, and the subsequent trial and imprisonment.' Willie Pinkerton – whose estimation of his quarry tended to veer from bonhomie to exasperation – coolly assessed that Engels 'never had a rival among them'. Connected with 'the heaviest forgeries' ever attempted, it was significant to Pink that he was a good friend of his fellow German, Max Shinburn, who was also one of Austin's criminal cronies.

When the Bidwell brothers were just starting out, Engels had already developed a legendary network of characters who identified the marks upon which the frauds were perpetrated. Known as 'ropers in', George Bidwell wrote that these individuals tended to be:

> ... a well-dressed plausible-speaking man who has the faculty of conveying to strangers the idea that he is one of themselves. Engels was the only gambler with whom I ever had anything to do with as I considered it especially dangerous to do any 'crooked business' with the assistance of either gamblers or drunkards.

Already, both traits were apparent in Engels' own character. The seeds of his own and ultimately the Bidwells' destruction were being sown in both his gambling and drinking. By the time they met him, George Engels was depending a little too much on brandy. Yet in the mid-1860s, it was at his feet that the Bidwells learned their art, taking forgery and criminality to another level. New York would be the crucible and Engels, the catalyst.

The German forger could see that the Bidwell brothers were plausible, clever and could easily assume the role of businessmen. 'Confidence-operators exist only because fools and their money can be easily parted,' Crapsey had noted. 'Strictly speaking, they are not thieves but belong rather to the category of swindlers; nor can the majority of those detected in the offence be justly called professionals.' Over the next few years, they worked up a great act.

The Pinks – and indeed, the New York police – became aware that there were 'adroit swindlers' in and around Wall Street at the start of 1867, who obtained small cheques from well-known firms and then copied them with ever greater amounts. These would then be passed on to banks or other businesses. Aware they were being constantly watched, George Macdonnell and Austin Bidwell separated from the rest and went into partnership by themselves. 'After a series of successful forgeries,' Willie later noted, 'Austin Bidwell was arrested in the name of Louis Baker on a charge of passing a forged cheque on [it is believed] the Chatham National Bank for $4,000.' He did two years in Sing Sing prison, less sixty days for 'good conduct'.

Within ten days, according to some sources, George Bidwell was also arrested for a cheque fraud and was actually apprehended inside a Massachusetts bank when he came to present it. Curiously, though both brothers were both incarcerated, they were never together in the same prison in the United States. Significantly, they never mentioned either of these 'stretches' in their memoirs.

By the turn of the new decade, they made a formidable team, forging cheques and carrying out further scams. As a result, immediately before they turned up in England, the thieves of Threadneedle Street, in various combinations, would start out on a grand tour of the United States, which culminated at the end of 1871 when they were all reunited to plan what would have been a financial Armageddon.

'After the release of Macdonnell, George Bidwell and Austin Bidwell from prison they all – accompanied by Engels – went for a tour south through the Western and Southern States,' Willie Pinkerton wrote, in evidence that was presented to the Crown two years later. Throughout the latter part of 1871, they carried out frauds in Chicago, Memphis, New Orleans, Mobile, Alabama and Macon in Georgia. It should have culminated in a whirlwind upon various local banks, with small drafts being altered into major ones and all presented on the same day.

But before they could, they did a very silly thing. They headed to Louisville, Kentucky.

3

Rogues' Gallery

> George Macdonnell was never married, although in his long and varied career, several women have taken his name. He was possessed of great natural advantages, and could be very winning when he chose. Family, education, personal appearance, and great business qualifications were all sacrificed at the bidding of crime, and the malefactor is now suffering the severe penalties of the outraged law.
>
> Allan Pinkerton, *Thirty Years A Detective*, 1884

December 1871
Louisville, Kentucky

His nerves nearly gave him away. The tram had left on time, down Main Street and heading towards 14th, and it was already dark. But, sitting near the front, George Macdonnell knew there was one thing above all others that he should not do. Never go back. If you returned to your lodgings, you could be followed. Your movements could be tracked. Neighbours are nosy. People talk, especially girlfriends. Never push your luck.

It was time to leave. He had enough money to buy a rail ticket and head out of Louisville before they caught up with him again. He sat away from the window, making sure the shadows engulfed him. In the chill of the Kentucky air, George 'Mac' Macdonnell was pondering his next move when he became aware someone had got on. Momentarily, he stiffened. This fellow, whoever he was, was slowly walking up towards him. Within seconds, he had sat down in the next seat.

Mac didn't need to look. He knew perfectly well who it was. Nemesis had arrived in the portly form of the greatest detective in the land. Not only was he aware that George Macdonnell was going to skip bail, he also suspected, true to form, that he would disappear and do it in style, probably taunting them when he was safely some distance away. 'I am going to take you back,' was all the detective said.

'But, my dear sir,' Mac replied in his usual imperious manner, 'you do impose on my good nature.' He turned to beam his most dangerous smile. 'I am a free man until my case is called.'

'Come along,' was all the detective said.

They both soon exited, for George Macdonnell knew he had little choice. Together they walked along the darkened streets to the police station where, once again, he returned to the cells. Later, when it was all over, the portly detective came to regard Mac as the smoothest, shrewdest criminal he had ever met. He would not be alone in his estimation. Many came to view George Macdonnell as the ultimate slippery customer, an extraordinary criminal who was capable of extraordinary behaviour and the execution of the most amazing crimes.

Though Willie Pinkerton could well make the claim of being the greatest detective in the United States, so too could his very good friend Delos Thurman Bligh, chief of the Louisville detectives, who had slipped into the seat next to Mac that December evening. Both were portly pooh-bahs and both were exemplary thief takers. 'D.D.' Bligh, as he normally signed himself, was usually known by another name that scared the living daylights out of criminals all over the Union – 'Yankee' Bligh.

'Don't go to Louisville,' became a familiar lament. 'That Yankee Bligh will nab you sure. He is the toughest fly cop in the country and you can't square him.' Bligh was indeed a native New Yorker transplanted to the Deep South and already, by this time, was a legend in law enforcement. When, fifteen months later, he learned of the Bank of England forgeries, he had a pretty shrewd idea of who was behind it all. 'I had them down for the London job as soon as I heard of it,' he wrote to Willie Pinkerton just eight days after the fraud's discovery.

For Bligh, too, it was a personal vindication. Like his friend, Pinkerton, he had warned the Old Lady of Threadneedle Street about Mac and the Bidwells. It was all the more galling that, if he had had his way in December of 1871, they could have been stopped in their tracks even before they had the chance to begin.

That George Macdonnell had attained bail and then escaped from it was nothing new. Lawyers from the Midwest to both the coasts had learned never to underestimate his ability to wriggle out of things. When arrested by Yankee Bligh, he offered a bribe of $500 to keep his name out of the papers. In the past, larger amounts had been proffered to make the authorities look the other way.

More often than not, he did not have to be so brazen. Detectives would invariably watch in simmering rage as he broke away from the clutches of the law, escaping conviction after conviction. 'He seemed,' Allan Pinkerton later wrote, 'to be perfectly informed of all the technicalities of criminal law, and so adroitly did he manage his affairs that it was impossible to legally convict him.'

By the time Yankee Bligh caught up with him, Mac had spent the best part of the previous decade working up various scams, usually in association with the Bidwells. Like many others – Austin and George included – the Kentucky lawman found himself puzzled as to why. It was not as though fate had ever thrown him a terrible hand. George Macdonnell's background was one of privilege and expensive schooling. If nothing else, such nonchalant wealth and effortless charm added to his credibility. When, on various subsequent occasions, Mac was being investigated by the police, he was invariably living the high life in an expensive hotel suite with a mistress in tow. One newspaper got to the heart of it by describing him as a 'debonair scoundrel'. 'The number of ingenious forgeries, frauds, and illegal adventures which he has had a hand in is very large,' reported another, a conclusion that Willie Pinkerton, Yankee Bligh and others had come to – to their cost – far sooner.

Yankee Bligh's doggedness was entirely characteristic. His life was a story of frontier ruggedness and a kind of manifest destiny in countering criminals in the years when the United States was still a Wild West. Born in Delaware County, New York State, in 1823, Delos Thurman Bligh started out as a brick layer but had wanted to become a fur trader. The meticulousness of the former and the hunting skills required by the latter were put to far better use when he ended up in Louisville. Over 6ft tall, weighing more than 200lb, he was muscular, single-minded and surefooted.

A few years later, when a notorious pickpocket was arrested he provided a particularly vivid portrait. 'Yankee Bligh is a particular genius,' he warned, 'his complexion is sandy, he dressed like a farmer, wears a slang like a horse's bit; he has got an eye like an eagle and a nose like a vulture.' His strength had helped him overpower one of the Younger Gang who had been terrorising the south for years. Yankee would, famously, enrage their leader, Jesse James, who ranted to local newspapers two years after the Bank of England forgeries that it wasn't just he and his gang who carried out major robberies.

A Mexican war veteran, Bligh had been appointed a city watchman in 1846 and eventually, when the Louisville police was formed nine years later, became one of its founding quartet of detectives. Yankee soon became the leader of the pack, an indefatigable chaser of ne'er-do-wells who made his name running down the countless counterfeiters who had flourished at the start of the Civil War.

'Captain Bligh', in the estimation of a local historian, 'sent hundreds of other criminals to the penitentiary and gained a national reputation.' If Yankee Bligh was on your tail, you certainly knew about it. 'He can smell a thief,' the pickpocket had simply warned. 'Fight shy of him.'

In early December 1871, Yankee Bligh became aware of somebody who had swindled another Louisville Bank out of $1,000 with a raised cheque. When Bligh went to investigate, he was most impressed. The cheque's beauty and elegance 'showed the difference between the true criminal artist and the clumsy novice', in the words of a later newspaper account. Bligh made enquiries. His quarry, it soon transpired, was a tall, elegant gentleman with an eastern accent by the name of Swift. He could, it seemed, speak French, Spanish and Italian, and was an accomplished musician and devoted to the arts.

When Bligh caught up with him in a small room downtown, Mr Swift had about him an air of effortless superiority and a grandiloquence all of his own. Eventually, he confessed that he was, indeed, Mr Macdonnell. 'He was a remarkably shrewd, intelligent man,' *The New York Times* later reported, 'and had a wonderful power of talking a great deal without committing himself.'

Yankee marched him off to jail with the suspect's pleas that it was all a cruel mistake ringing in his ears. As ever, Mac soon hired the best lawyers in town, Martin Eljur and W.I. Jackson Jr, whose services did not come cheap. Yet he could easily afford them; as regards surety, telegrams from friends in New York confirmed he was a high wealth individual.

When the case subsequently came to court, Mac played the wounded innocent to a tee. Once again, he was bailed at the ridiculously low figure of $1,000. This was presented straight away and the court ordered his release.

In the meantime, Bligh decided to do something innovative which would have far reaching consequences. He took George Macdonnell's portrait with a camera. When it was later circulated, the photograph showed what another detective report called 'an impossibly handsome man'. Intriguingly, others had already noted his imperfections which tended to be overlooked. There was, for example, a scar on his neck and pimples on his forehead. Although he had only just turned 26 years of age when Bligh caught up with him, Mac's hair was starting to thin despite the luxuriance of his beard.

In the flesh, George Macdonnell was tall and strongly built with a fair complexion. What most people remembered, however, was the faint air of superciliousness which suffused his small blue eyes. They always gave him away. Like George Bidwell, Mac was invariably too clever by half, but sardonic, attractive in his sometimes mysterious roguishness and, in his own mind at least, irresistible to women. Austin Bidwell, for one, was in awe of his abilities. 'Mac's mind was a storehouse of erudition,' he wrote, 'his memory a picture gallery, whose characters were gilded and decorated with many a glowing canvas.'

His learning was genuine. Mac was a Harvard graduate, the scion of a grand Scottish-Irish family, whom he liked to claim were directly related to the ancient kings of Ireland. 'He wore a long, waving dark-brown beard, and his complexion was as fair as a woman's,' Willie Pinkerton's father, Allan, later marvelled. 'His voice was soft and rich, and his powers of conversation were remarkably attractive. He was a brilliant linguist.' In other words, he was a perfectly plausible conman who Yankee Bligh had no difficulty seeing through.

George Macdonnell was held in the 1st Street Police Station to await the arrival of detectives and bankers from all over the Union. Similar frauds had recently been carried out in Chicago, St Louis and other places.

Most interesting was Cincinnati, from where Captain Larry Hazen – who had captured 'W. Austin Bidwell' in the spring of 1864 – was now coming. Ohio was two days' ride away. Just before eight o'clock the next evening, Mr Eljur arrived with a court order. There was, he said, insufficient ground for holding his client. As he and Yankee exchanged words, a telegram arrived from Hazen. He was delayed and would not arrive until the next day. Captain Bligh sensed that fate was turning against him. The lawyer prevailed and both he and his client left, walking out and never looking back. Within half a block, Mac stopped in his tracks. 'I forgot something.'

Eljur was stunned. 'You had better not go back there,' he advised with lawyerly caution.

'But I must,' Mac replied. 'I want to make a little girl, who brought me my food, a present.'

By now, the lawyer was incredulous. 'Let me have your present and I will give it to the child,' suggested Mr Eljur.

'Well that will do,' was the answer. He reached into his pocket. 'Hand her this ten dollar bill with my compliments. Tell her Mr Macdonnell will never forget her kindness. I do love little children. Their honest simplicity charms me.' Whether he was winding the lawyer up, nobody knows. The pair continued on to 4th and Market Streets. There, Mr Eljur left his client who boarded a car for the 14th Street Station. And that cold December evening was when Yankee Bligh took matters into his own hands, nabbing him again and to hell with the consequences.

In these particular capers, Mac was the smart man. Behind him were the Bidwell brothers and George Engels, who acted as the penman or forger, in this, their crime spree of 1871. According to the files, Bligh never actually saw Austin Bidwell but was later able to indict him 'for altering a cheque but got no money'. His elder brother had also recently been released from prison but he, too, was never observed anywhere in Louisville. 'The Bidwells succeeded in making their escape,' was all one newspaper reported.

George Macdonnell also managed to escape. The great irony was that when Hazen finally arrived, he did not recognise him nor were the other bankers and detectives able to pin him down. Yankee Bligh reluctantly had to let him go. Willie Pinkerton later recorded:

He of course forfeited his bail and Bligh then took up the chase and endeavoured to apprehend Macdonnell again, as also the Bidwells with whom, he was then in a position to prove he, [Macdonnell] was connected. They got to New York and the Police there disclaimed all knowledge of them.

George Macdonnell was haughtily confident that he could talk his way out of anything. Whether it was similar blarney or not, Mac claimed that the family on his mother's side were related to the O'Neill Kings of Ireland. After arriving in the British Isles a few months later, he went to visit family in the north of Ireland. He had well-to-do relatives in Brooklyn and Dublin to whom he would always turn when he was in a jam.

Mac's father, a noted lumberman, was well known in the Montreal area and very well-to-do. 'He was born in 1846, near Boston, in a beautiful country villa, the property of his father,' George Bidwell wrote. 'This was surrounded by an evergreen hedge, beyond the limits of which the children were never permitted to stray.'

The desire to escape from such a gilded cage smacks of amateur Freudianism. In an unguarded moment, however, Austin Bidwell told Willie Pinkerton that Mac's parents were so wealthy that their son could have asked for $50,000 and got it straight away. So why did he ever need to become a criminal? It was a question that nobody ever managed to answer completely satisfactorily. Unlike the Bidwells, Mac rarely wrote letters and never seemed to confide in anyone. Was he simply addicted to the danger? Or was it some sort of reaction to the stifling norms of social expectation, an act of the ultimate rebellion?

With nurses, tutors and a good-hearted mother ('a high-minded, noble-hearted woman of a religious character,' George Bidwell noted) Mac certainly had chafed under the unyielding regime of a stern, unsympathetic father ('who required his children to be, like himself, upright and exact in all the relations of life'). George Macdonnell had been destined for greater success. 'At an early age, Mac was sent to Harvard College,' George Bidwell wrote, 'with the understanding that he was to become a physician.'

Though he studied medicine he was never admitted to practice, but he was usually described in court appearances as a physician or doctor, a role he had on several occasions played to perfection. The *Chicago Tribune* later reported that he 'graduated as number one in every class in which he was a student'. In another account, it was claimed that he had also studied in Strasbourg and at Trinity College, Dublin, where he had actually received his MD.

As to how and where the Bidwells originally met Mac, considerable mystery remains. George Bidwell claimed, 'he was a fellow prisoner for a short time in the same cell with an acquaintance of mine' (most likely Walter Sheridan), but there had been sightings of Mac in their company years before. The curious coincidence of his Canadian citizenship suggests that he might well have known the Bidwells as early as 1863 when their first recorded scam in Cincinnati began.

In a confession made to make his readers think that he himself had been the worst influence, George Bidwell claimed that around this time he took the younger man under his wing. 'I told him that I had been engaged in the perpetration of these merchandise frauds long enough to realise the dangers', which was certainly one way of putting it.

∞

Cotton, that hidden, unsettling undercurrent to the prosecution of the Civil War, was the ruin and salvation of George Macdonnell. So far as his family was ever aware, their son had made a fortune in cotton trading, though the reality was he 'by his rascality had amassed a considerable sum of money', in Willie Pinkerton's more honest appreciation.

After settling in New York City, George Macdonnell became a speculator on cotton futures. Though he had little money, Mac often put up everything he had on margins of two or three. If the price of cotton rose, then he would make a fortune. To begin with, he had the luck of his native Irish. And then, when the margins went to pieces, so did he. Facing ruin, Mac engineered a fast buck version of a long firm fraud. He bought a vast amount of cotton on four days' notice. This short-term speculation, he thought, would allow him to negotiate his own debts on the lost margins. Selling it at 'a sacrifice', he could make enough money to live well – certainly, beyond his means.

He could not. His creditors threw him into Ludlow Street Jail, which, as William Pinkerton later noted, was 'a debtors' gaol for civil offences where he remained for a year'. And then Mac 'succeeded in compromising the matter and regain his liberty,' as Pink recorded, probably as a result of family interventions (though in some accounts George Engels was behind it).[2]

Nevertheless, Mac was penniless and immediately after his release in 1866 fate took another curious turn. 'Meantime, his mistress ran away with all his money and jewellery,' the *Tribune* noted, 'he became acquainted with Bidwell.' This would be Austin Bidwell, though as George Bidwell had also suggested, while in jail Mac had become acquainted with George Engels.

George Macdonnell had long since honed another notable ability: to make good friends, invariably on the wrong side of the tracks. In his youth, at Harvard preparatory school, he had also made the acquaintance of the brother of a fellow student who later became a noted minister. He was quiet, unassuming and could turn his hand to anything. His name was Edwin Noyes Hills.

∞

In other words, by the time of George Macdonnell's arrest by Yankee Bligh at the end of 1871, the gang was all there. If there was one thing Willie Pinkerton knew to his cost, there were never any coincidences, particularly in the shady world of forgery.

By now, Pink later observed, the Bidwells, Mac, Hills and George Engels had spent the last few years carrying out swindles either together or in separate couplings. Indeed, one of the first recorded events where they had all worked together had been in 1867 when they descended upon Boston and established a broker's office. They were successful in writing forged cheques and deposit certificates with which they obtained $10,000 from Bowles & Company in the city. 'They also were in the warehouse business and sold at auction all the stock of cotton etc. which they had in their warehouse, belonging to depositors there,' the *Chicago Tribune* later noted.

It was around this time that their activities were enlivened by the addition of another sibling, Michael Macdonnell. When the Bidwells met Mac and his younger brother, they found them 'men of fine education speaking all the foreign languages and thorough Greek and Latin scholars', as Austin told Willie Pinkerton in Cuba. Only later did the forces of law and order come to appreciate how much of a baleful influence George Macdonnell had been upon Mike Macdonnell. Mac was a guiding spirit for the younger man, always in the background and yet at the forefront of his brother's thoughts even when he was in prison.

In the summer of 1868 – when coincidentally, Austin and Mac were both incarcerated in Sing Sing – their brothers carried on regardless. George Bidwell and Mike Macdonnell attempted to remove $5,000 (some accounts say $7,000) out of the Hide & Leather Bank of Boston. It was unsuccessful. Presenting a bogus cheque drawn on a Chicago bank, the officials realised soon enough that it was a forgery. George Bidwell was arrested on sight and sent to prison in Worcester, Massachusetts, for seven years.

After that, attention focuses on the only remaining sibling on the outside. In October 1868, Michael Macdonnell fetched up in Worcester, Massachusetts, using the identity of Hiram Tucker. Here he presented a forged cheque and removed $3,300 from a local bank. Along with a young accomplice, H.B. Conklin, they escaped by stealing a horse and wagon. Bizarrely, they later looked after the horse and returned it to its rightful owner. His elder brother, young Macdonnell later claimed, had been involved in the planning of this scheme from his cell at Sing Sing.

And then a few weeks later, in Elizabeth Town, New Jersey, Tucker and Conklin committed another forgery, this time on the National State Bank. 'The bank lost no money,' wrote one observer, 'the Central Bank, Worcester, alas did.' Michael Macdonnell then ventured to where the Bidwell and Hills families came from. In Hartford, Connecticut, he used the alias of Andrew Stanley to present a forged cheque for $4,500. His young aide Conklin, this time posing as Samuel R. Kellogg, was arrested, tried and convicted.

The younger Macdonnell escaped to California but was later arrested in his native Canada 'and sent for six years to a Connecticut penitentiary', where he was still incarcerated during the immediate aftermath of the Bank of England forgeries. When the elder Macdonnell was later arrested in connection with those crimes, a curious letter was found in his possession. 'It was written in Greek and is evidently from some man in Hartford County Jail,' Freshfields noted, 'He must be an educated rascal.' This was certainly one way of describing his younger brother.

Two years before the Bank of England forgeries, all of them were planning for 'a big thing', nothing less than a fiscal '9/11'. Significantly, Austin Bidwell also later told Pink about 'how they laid their plans for big work which has since electrified America often and this time the whole world'.

A pair of cheques on the Sturtevant Bank for $67 and $41 had been 'double ciphered' to raise them into $6,700 and $4,100. Had they been presented, they would have formed a small part of what the younger Macdonnell later termed a 'gigantic system of forgeries in the United States', when interviewed in prison. Similarly raised cheques would also have been presented, all on the same day, to remove many thousands from unsuspecting institutions across the country. It seemed that George Engels was involved, but he baulked and fled with the arrest of the younger Macdonnell and his accomplice, Conklin.

Conklin (and/or Kellogg) was, needless to say, Edwin Noyes Hills, who was incarcerated from 1869 to 1872, when he was released early thanks to divine intervention (or rather because of his brother, a man of the cloth who had repeatedly interceded on his behalf). The Reverend Charles D. Hills made it his mission to beg the governors of both the state of New Jersey and the prison to vouch for his younger brother. Edwin Noyes Hills was a changed man, possessed of a character of spotless reputation. His brother ended one particular letter with an unusual plea, 'I will keep a supervision over him for the time sentence comes so that society will be as safe as if he were in prison. He will neither be in New Jersey or in New York if pardoned. O let him come to us and he will be saved.'

Amazingly, it worked. Edwin Noyes Hills was released in the spring of 1872. Michael Macdonnell, despite his own older brother's efforts to do the same, was less successful. So young Macdonnell tried to bribe the son of a warder by getting him to deliver a letter in New York City to 'W.W. Bidwell' at the end of 1871. 'These facts go to show the gang is an old one,' the *Boston Post* later recorded, 'and the New York detectives in concealing that fact evidently have some motive for it.'

When the two near contemporaries, Austin Bidwell and George Macdonnell, were released towards the end of 1870 from Sing Sing, they had, according to one newspaper account, 'conceived the idea of going to Europe' as they were flush with cash. Willie Pinkerton later found out that they had both crossed the Atlantic in the company of George Engels and another German forger called James Blosch. Mac, as always, could not help boasting about some of the details when he was held by Yankee Bligh eighteen months later. The chief of Louisville detectives was told, from the horse's mouth, that they had been 'hitting banks in several cities, forged and altered Bills of Exchange'.

It helped that the world's economies were booming. Their arrival in Europe at the turn of the new decade coincided with an unprecedented worldwide economic boom. Wall Street and the City of London were roaring. After the Civil War, the United States were being reunited, with the railway extended to the Pacific.

The imminent Franco-Prussian War consumed vast quantities of cash. Germany's reunification thereafter meant that both victor and loser were ripe for reconstruction. Across the Atlantic, ocean cables were being laid. manufacturing was at an all-time high and, as Austin himself noted, 'stocks of every kind on the boom, the general wealth of the country massing up by leaps and bounds, and every kind of speculative enterprise being launched'.

Money was equally available for those with criminal intent. Government bonds now guaranteed by federal reserves had already become the instruments of choice for determined fraudsters. Unlike gold, bonds were easy to transport; and unlike diamonds, they were easy to fence, especially abroad where their provenance was not checked. 'Bonds issued by our Government and held in Europe, chiefly in Holland and Germany,' Austin Bidwell later wrote, 'were so enormous in volume and passed so freely from hand to hand, that it was easy for a well-dressed business appearing man to sell any quantity.' Though many US Government bonds had been lost to theft in the amount of millions, a certain amount of fraud and wastage was expected. The US Treasury issued warnings to local police forces to make sure they weren't circulated.

Various bankers could testify that stolen bonds, too, were sold in London. Austin Bidwell claimed he had laundered them with the help of the New York police. George Macdonnell also told Bligh that he was responsible for negotiating their sale. With forged letters of introduction and also credit, they succeeded in obtaining upwards of $10,000 from banks in France, Belgium, Holland and Germany. They then made their escape passing through England and Scotland, where they obtained a further £4,000. All four travelled to Dublin and then to Belfast, where they generated fraudulent cheques on the Bank of Belfast (and were later recognised when their mugshots appeared in the press in 1873). Then they did the same in Manchester.

When they were ready to leave for home, they separated as a precaution. Mac shaved off his beard to avoid detection on a New York-bound ship, while Blosch travelled from Glasgow, in Pinkerton's words, 'in the guise of a clergyman and had the impudence to read the service on board and deliver the sermon as a German clergyman'.

Mac boasted that they returned home with a small fortune. So did Austin Bidwell. He later claimed to a New Orleans newspaper:

We made a tour of Ireland and Germany and came back after a ten weeks' trip with $80,000 to our credit. [As] American bonds were sold in millions all over the Continent and were passing freely from hand to hand, as a matter of fact, little or no attention was paid to such circulars.

'[The] mere fact that a man was an American, and had the appearance, dress and manner of a gentleman, they always take it for granted that he must be a gentleman,' Austin Bidwell recalled, viewing his first ever trip to Europe as one of the defining moments of his burgeoning criminal career. So, too, did the forces of law and order. 'Finding that America did not offer a sufficiently wide field for their energies or possibly becoming too well known there, they changed the scene of their operations to England and the continent of Europe,' is how Freshfields explained it. 'Their operations were successful and they returned in the spring of 1872 to what the Americans call "a big thing".'

Curiously, in his memoirs Austin Bidwell is circumspect about these events. After claiming he was put up to it by the New York Police Department, which had obtained $100,000 of stolen bonds through the 'Bank Ring', he describes his arrival in England as a culture shock in what he termed a 'novel and strange' land.

'One May morning I walked into the North Western Railway Station in Liverpool to take the train for London,' he remembered. Taking afternoon tea at the Langham – one of the most luxurious of London hotels, which would become a familiar haunt – he then headed across the Channel to Ostend, via Brussels. Next, he travelled on to Frankfurt, 'that old town I was destined to see so much of during the next few years', where he claimed that he wanted to buy copper mines in Austria for which he would sell his large batch of US bonds. Although stolen and supposedly payable to the bearer, without being asked to prove his identity, he brought one letter 'to serve as an introduction to some of the bankers at Frankfurt'.

In what would have been the last few weeks before the Franco-Prussian War broke out that July, 'all the world went to Wiesbaden to be amused,' Austin would write. He stayed opposite the casino and spent many hours gambling while he steadied himself to hand over the stolen bonds. He remained nervous until they were paid out and then blithely walked over to Rothschild Bank to buy a bill for $80,000 on New York. Without spelling it out, he had expertly fenced the stolen bond into a redeemable bill of exchange.

Immediately thereafter he returned to London, the memory of which always made him feel nostalgic. 'Very many times I journeyed over that route in after years,' Austin recalled, 'but never with so light a heart.' At this point, he would have reached his twenty-fifth birthday and later remarked that 'all the glamour and poetry of life hung around me'. By his own admission, he felt that anything was possible. 'I was young and impressionable,' he said, but more significantly than that, 'I had other people's money to be liberal with.'

Certainly Yankee Bligh was impressed by the scope of their activities when George Macdonnell boasted about them nearly eighteen months later. 'I had several conversations with him about his trip to Europe,' he later noted. 'He is an accomplished thief, a good talker and a fine looking man who dresses well.'

Later, Bligh spoke with a banker in Louisville who had learned about 'three men in the cities of Belfast, Dublin, Leeds and perhaps Cork in the year 1870' who had made vast sums. As he rightly surmised, they were obviously Austin, Mac and Engels. Presciently Yankee Bligh realised that 'they will most likely try them again', after Mac disappeared from view at the end of 1871. '[They] would have done good work here if I had not spoiled it for them and saved the bank some money,' Bligh wrote a few days after the next 'big thing' (the Bank of England forgeries) became worldwide news. 'I know these men were in Europe that year and brought considerable money away with them,' he later warned Scotland Yard, 'and as they are about to try your country again, I thought I would post you and see if you could put them away as they are a dangerous mob.'

That was when he took care to include the photograph he had taken of George Macdonnell. It was a measure of Yankee Bligh's own industry that he had assembled a rogues' gallery of all the villains with whom he tangled. The use of photography promised to revolutionise crime fighting. To date, most police files were based on detective's descriptions that were as vivid as possible, with all the errors of interpretation that might allow. Photographs were reluctantly shared with other departments, which usually had to do with the thorny matter of who got the credit for high-profile captures (or else who kept the money after selling them to newspapers).

As well as sending Mac's picture to Scotland Yard, Yankee Bligh arranged to have one of Austin Bidwell sent from Michigan. Describing them as 'good likenesses', they were clearly a useful tool. Ironically, George Bidwell was not photographed by the American police for another two decades. When one of his girlfriends tried to do that in London in 1873, he went crazy and scolded her. Amazing as it may seem to posterity, George Bidwell's first US police mugshot was taken after he was briefly reunited with his wife in 1887. Despite not having seen sight nor sound of him since the autumn of 1871, she had stood by him. In fact, Mrs Bidwell had a great deal of bearing on what happened to the gang immediately before George Macdonnell's arrest by Yankee Bligh.

Behind every great man is said to be an even greater woman. In the case of George Bidwell, that was the former Martha Anna Brewer, who presents a curious spectre throughout this saga, conveniently trotted out as either alibi or excuse whenever one was needed by her husband. 'His wife is a most respectable woman,' Willie Pinkerton later noted, 'but he has long since deserted her.'

George had at least two children by Martha. By the time of his trial at the Old Bailey, their daughter, Winnie, was about 15 years old, so they had been married for at least that length of time. Their son, Howard, was younger and, in a note from another relative, is described as having become very fat.

According to George's own account, his wife (this 'noble and devoted young lady') was the rock on which his life was based. 'The remarkable prudence she has shown in all affairs of her life and her adherence to me under circumstances which would have irrevocably estranged most women prove that I made a good choice, if she did not,' he wrote in the late 1880s.

If his memoirs are to be believed, George Bidwell says that after moving the family to south Brooklyn, he then worked as a trader for wholesale grocery firms. Business after business failed, and finally in 1861 George opened another confectionery business, this time on Broadway. It failed and he was arrested for having stolen money to pay off his earlier debts. And yet, despite it all, Mrs Bidwell stood by her man, allowing him to buy another business in her name.

The next known failure was in Providence, Rhode Island, in September 1863. Three months later, Bidwell & Company opened their store and Cincinnati and the events where 'W. Austin Bidwell' was shot took place. When George and Martha were married in 1858, George Bidwell maintained he was 26 years old and his wife was nine years younger. If she had posed as W. Austin Bidwell's spouse towards the end of 1863, she would have just turned 21 years.

It might well have been Martha Bidwell, as she was described as 'a woman of flashy dress and morals'. In another account, she had been carrying out frauds all along Pearl Street in the city, independently of her husband. Claiming she worked in the millinery business, Mrs Bidwell wanted to make purchases on 'short time'. She said she had a sick uncle who had just died and left her $10,000, which she would inherit soon.

This Mrs Bidwell obtained hats, furs and '$100 worth of hoop skirts, remarking that she thought she would still need a larger stock room'. Her husband was doing the same with other clothes merchants, so much so that she obtained nearly $3,000 of clothes. Placing credit on Bidwell & Co., she disappeared, and the only evidence she and her husband left behind was a room at the luxurious Spencer House, the bill for which was almost inevitably never paid.

October 1871
Chicago, Illinois

At times, it seemed as if the boys had the fates on their side. In the early autumn of 1871, Austin and Mac briefly returned to Chicago for one of the greater disasters in American history. When, at ten o'clock on the evening of Sunday, 8 October 1871, a small barn burned down after a prolonged, unseasonably dry summer, it led to a galloping conflagration which soon mushroomed into 'a vast ocean of flame'. It quickly consumed everything in its path. Within hours, over 3 square miles, including the business district where the Pinkerton offices were located, were destroyed. 'The very air,' as one survivor put it, 'was full of flame.'

Inevitably, criminals followed the firestorm and removed everything that was left in its wake. Austin and Mac did not have to be quite so obvious. 'The parties were well known in Chicago and vicinity' was a suitable cross-heading with which the local paper later reported what happened next. One of them had already established a real estate office on Madison Street, the other an office above Miller's jewellery store. 'They presented forged letters of introduction at the Cook County National Bank,' the *Chicago Tribune* reported, 'and also at the Second National Bank in Chicago and succeeded in getting considerable money and effecting their escape.'

As a result of the fire, their forgeries were not discovered for another two weeks. By then, they were long gone and subsequently used the after-effects of the fire to another great effect. In fact, Mrs Martha Bidwell now became inextricably linked to the reunion of George Bidwell with his cronies.

In the weeks immediately after the Chicago fire, his friends decided to take precipitate action. Their brother, Joseph – 'the principal man you want to catch', as a later detective report summarised his malign influence – was roped in to petition the governor of the Massachusetts Penitentiary, where George Bidwell was being held. The prisoner should be allowed leniency as his home had been destroyed in the great fire. His wife and children, it was claimed, were homeless.

Once again, the justice system took pity on him. George Bidwell was allowed out early on compassionate grounds. As Willie Pinkerton later lamented, he never went anywhere near Illinois. 'It may also be as well to state that his wife who had lived separate from him for a number of years was not burned out at all as she was living outside the burned district,' Pink later reported to the Bank of England. And within days of being sprung by his friends, he was up to more of his old antics again, a story which was never appreciated at the time, not least with its significance to the forgeries on the Old Lady of Threadneedle Street.

When George Macdonnell had been arrested by Yankee Bligh in downtown Louisville a few weeks later, a large number of letterheads and envelopes for the Ninth and Third National Banks of New York had been found in his possession. In his trunk was further incriminating evidence. This included various inks, pens, erasers and a stamp marked 'G.M.', which would come in useful for forgery. There was also confirmation that he – or most likely, an accomplice – had spent time in New Orleans.

'A large-bound check book of the State National Bank was found,' *The New York Times* reported of other possessions, referring to a financial institution which was located in the same Louisiana city, 'two of the blank checks [*sic*] being signed "Baxter, Bell & Co.", a large firm of cotton factors in New Orleans.' Some of these cheques had been chemically altered ('all the writing had been obliterated except the date and signature') including one payable on a Nashville bank. There were also several strips of cards, each about 1ft long which also bore the name of the above mentioned cotton traders printed in 'bold, black letters'.

Mac later confessed to Yankee Bligh that all would have been used in yet another attempt at a 'big thing' across the Union. A number of small drafts would have been raised in different, distant cities for meagre sums. Then these would have been altered, subsequently raised to larger amounts and presented on the same day – had they not been discovered in his luggage. This would have been the culmination of their plans to date – and possibly, had it been successful, they would not have subsequently crossed the Atlantic to defraud the Bank of England.

Mac and Austin's stop in Chicago had already netted them $12,000. After that, they all went to St Louis and attempted to pass off a cheque for $9,100. A cashier there suspected they were up to something, so they fled. In another account, they went on to Memphis where they bought a genuine draft on the Union Planters' Bank for $4,500 ($5,000, says Willie Pinkerton). Presenting a forged letter of introduction from the Third National Bank in Nashville, the cashier at the Planter's Bank, Mr Reed (in some accounts, Reid) noticed that something was not quite right.

The forgers picked up on this straightaway. As Willie Pinkerton later noted, 'Macdonnell was too sharp for him.' With characteristic chutzpah, Mac walked over to the nearest telegraph office with a pen behind his ear, claiming he was an employee of the bank. 'Has the telegram to Nashville been sent yet?' he asked in an urgent tone. The duty clerk checked through the duty log. 'Yes,' he said, it had. Minutes earlier, a query had been sent to Mr Porterfield, the cashier of the First National Bank in Nashville, concerning the provenance of the draft. 'This was the gentleman whose name was forged to the bogus letter of introduction they had presented,' the *Chicago Tribune* later reported. 'Finding that they were suspected, they all left the city.'

Austin Bidwell next turned up in New Orleans, where another draft of $4,500 was presented at one of the banks there. Though he never mentioned this story in his memoirs, when he came to publicise them in that same city twenty years later, he provided an interesting vignette. 'I spent a part of the winter here,' he said in 1893. 'There was no railway to Mobile. I remember going to that city on a steamer by way of Lake Ponchartrain.'

Willie Pinkerton later determined that Austin Bidwell, and some of the others, had subsequently carried on through Alabama and then Georgia. Taken altogether, they made about $10,000 by committing forgeries in Mobile ($2,000), Macon and Atlanta ($7,000) and Tuscumbia.

At the same time, the cheque which the Memphis bank had refused to pay was then passed on between each of them in turn. In one city, Austin Bidwell endorsed it to George Macdonnell, who then passed it over to a mysterious George Wilson. This gentleman then returned to Memphis and demanded payment with what one newspaper account later described as 'considerable blustering'. George Wilson was, needless to say, George Bidwell. Unless he could explain exactly how he came by this payment, the Memphis Bank would not honour the draft. In one version of the story, George Wilson then advertised that he would sell the draft at a discount.

The bank cashier told his side of the story during a heated exchange carried out in local newspapers. Eventually, the bank paid out. Again, as with Austin Bidwell's reminiscences, there is no mention of this story in George Bidwell's memoirs and considerable mysteries remain. Certainly, when Willie Pinkerton found out that George Bidwell had also been released from prison, he was incandescent. Straightaway, he dispatched one of his operatives to visit Mrs Bidwell at the boarding house she kept at Hibbard Court in Chicago.

Without putting too fine a point on it, Mrs Bidwell was in denial, even though she seemed to be aware that George had been in Kentucky, '[She] did not believe and would not believe that her husband had anything to do with it,' the Pinkerton detective later reported, 'that her husband was no thief and that detectives were the biggest thieves in the world.'

Mrs Bidwell gave the Pinkerton man what is amusingly described as 'a regular spitfire turning over' in the files. According to her, George Bidwell had formerly been a travelling agent for a New York house but declined to identify which one. She did not know where he presently was located though she had received letters from him 'but stated they were neither dated nor postmarked'. Mrs Bidwell then claimed that she knew nothing of George Macdonnell, either. She had never seen him, but she 'had heard of his difficulty in Louisville and of her husband's name being connected with it'.

Martha Bidwell refused to help them track him down. Subterfuge would be needed to find her husband's whereabouts. An undercover operative could either board with her in Hibbard Court or else enlist the help of the local postman. 'One thing is certain – that altho' she may not be living with him and that they are bad friends,' Pink wrote to Yankee Bligh, 'she will not do anything unless properly worked upon to do so.'

Ironically he later learned that, much as George Bidwell had maintained, his wife 'didn't know his real character' when she married him. Despite all the various trials he had subjected her to she 'was an accomplished young lady' of good character about whom Willie Pinkerton said he had never heard a bad thing. Later, Austin Bidwell confessed to Pink that George had sent her $7,000 since the summer of 1872 from their various subsequent travels in Europe.

Most intriguing of all, Pink later found out that Mrs Bidwell admitted having been in Louisville 'after the little girl' which could either be their teenage daughter or perhaps even some unknown progeny from her husband's persistent womanising. There was also an episode where she had thrown him out of her house but detectives were unable to determine precisely when or, indeed, why.

Yankee Bligh was taking no chances. As with the sending of photographs across the Atlantic, he had another trick up his sleeve – following the luggage.

In his hurry to leave Kentucky, George Macdonnell had left behind a trunk, which he did not remove from his lodgings. The chief of detectives ensured that a close eye was kept on it. Within the month, the trunk was shipped by the Adams Express to New York City. Bligh sent the waybill and a description to Robert Pinkerton. 'Find who receives this trunk and where it goes,' he suggested.

The Pinks did that and more. They made sure they had an operative watching the Adams Express office on Broadway. When a person who was clearly not Macdonnell eventually came to collect it, he was then followed. This character was observed taking it to the New York docks, where it was seen being loaded on to a steamer headed for Liverpool. In this way, Bligh and Pink knew that Mac – and presumably others – were headed for Great Britain and would arrive in the spring of April 1872.

Captain Bligh also approached Scotland Yard at about the same time. As well as enclosing photographs he had obtained of Mac and the Bidwells, like any good thief taker he provided a description of the apparel George Macdonnell was most likely to wear – 'a fine light drab cloth overcoat that he bought in Paris that he always wears when riding out which he is fond of'.

Sartorial niceties aside, Bligh was sure that they would strike again. On 17 July 1872, Bligh wrote to his opposite number, whom he called 'the Chief of Police' but was actually the assistant commissioner of the Metropolitan Police, and enclosed photographs of what he termed 'two notorious forgers, cheque receivers' whom he said were now in London. 'They are a genteel mob and smart,' he warned. 'I am certain they will operate through Ireland before they leave and you will hear of them certain,' he added, in later a follow up.

To his regret, the chief of the Louisville detectives had not been able to detain George Macdonnell. Yankee Bligh was certain they would get up to further mischief in the British Isles. 'I am in hopes you may get them down before they leave your city and be able to shadow them until you get them dead to rights,' he concluded in words that came to haunt him in the years ahead.

By the time Bligh's second letter crossed the Atlantic, so had Willie Pinkerton. That autumn, he was visiting his friends at Scotland Yard and the Sûreté (a French police department). As crime had become ever more international in scope and, in particular, forgery and fraud become equally more sophisticated, so had the means of its detection. 'Very few great crimes have occurred in this country in the last twenty years in the detection of which Pinkerton's agency has not had a hand,' *The New York Times* recorded on his father's death in 1884.

There had been the curious incident of the gang of burglars who had stolen $150,000 from the Third National Bank of Baltimore. The case was never officially solved, though Willie knew perfectly well who was behind it all. That October of 1872, he travelled in the wake of the robbers to Europe. By now, the adage that to catch a thief you had to behave like one had started to take its toll on his elder son. Willie Pinkerton was starting to descend into alcoholism. Pink's mixing with the criminal fraternity had led him to become a heavy drinker. Oddly enough, though his father disapproved of the consumption of alcohol and smoking, he grudgingly accepted that to find criminals you had to mix with them. Yet with Willie's extended trips overseas, his father's priggishness went into the stratosphere, not least when he became aware of the extent of his son's expenses in entertaining various detectives. He ordered him home to account for his profligacy.

For once, William Pinkerton ignored him. By now Old A.P. was not as influential, for in the spring of 1869 he had suffered a debilitating stroke. Only through characteristic determination had the 'old man' learned to walk and talk again, reluctantly handing over many of his duties to his sons. Strangely, the Chicago fire seemed to have revitalised him even though most of his original records had been lost. 'I rule my office with an iron hand,' he had once declared, 'I must have my own way of doing things.' And that meant he would brook no criticism nor any deviation from the path of true virtue. As a result, both his sons rarely escaped tongue lashings or their father's ire if things were not done how the old man still wanted them done. Somehow, he and Willie found a way of working together.

In March 1873, after the Bank of England had been hit, Willie Pinkerton got straight into contact with his old friend in Kentucky. Any information that he had gleaned from his long talk into the night with George Macdonnell could be critically important. Yankee replied straight away. 'I thought you would run on them while in Europe,' Bligh wrote on 9 March 1873. 'I had them down for the London job as soon as I heard of it.' Describing them as smart men about which 'very little' was known, Bligh made it his business to contact various banks in Frankfurt as well as New York City (where the fraudster was later arrested).

Bligh's greatest fear was one that others shared too: that, as ever, George Macdonnell would pull a legalistic rabbit out of a hat and avoid prosecution. 'The men who know him in Louisville are confident in their predictions that he will not be convicted if taken back to England,' *The New York Times* reported, 'as he has escaped difficulties and dangers quite as formidable as those that now hem him in.'

Amazingly, that had repeatedly happened in George Macdonnell's last few months in the United States before he left for England in the spring of 1872. The police determined that he had been up to his old tricks and had managed to escape from jail on technicalities. 'They traced his handiwork in half a dozen swindles which were perpetrated on dry goods houses and banking firms,' *The New York Sun* reported of his return to Manhattan, 'but they were baffled in their attempts to catch him in the actual commission of any offense.'

One of his last recorded victims was Daden Frères & Company, a large scale importer of lace, and a well-known business in New York City. Posing as a Mr Edward Johnson, Mac walked into their store in midtown Manhattan one late December morning.

He wanted to buy $2,000 worth of lace. He was, he said, a storekeeper and would send a cheque the next day by cab as he was in a hurry to return to the Midwest. He was, as ever, taken at face value.

Even when he was later arrested on Forsyth Street with the laces in his possession, Mac somehow managed to get off. The authorities were never able to catch him in the act. Subsequently, at the start of 1872 Mac seems to have hidden 'out West' for two or three months. The last he was heard of in the United States was in Portland, Maine, where he stayed for a few weeks. At this point, opinion was later divided in New York as to whether he was rich (the figure of $50,000 was mentioned) or poor.

The Strand, Central London
November 1872

One cold autumn morning later that same year of 1872[3], Willie Pinkerton happened to be walking along the Strand in central London accompanied by one of Scotland Yard's finest. Chief Inspector John Shore, a later head of detectives, would achieve greater notoriety in his replacing Abberline as lead investigator in the saga of Jack the Ripper. Shore would later become the Pinks' official representative in England, an odd choice for a policeman whose whoring and drinking became legendary.

Together they were on the trail of the gang which had robbed the Third National Bank of Baltimore. Their number included Charley Becker and Joseph Chapman, both 'notorious' criminals in Pink's estimation. He had found out from shadowing Chapman's wife that her husband was most likely in Great Britain. Before his own arrival, detectives had learned that there was a 'gang of American thieves' who had opened an office close by the Bank of England and were posing as stockbrokers.

Another Pink operative had shadowed them in case Chapman was among them but did not see him. He also learned from informers that some of the gang had left, 'but the balance of the party were still there'. By the time Willie Pinkerton himself arrived, another informer had told them, 'There will be "big money" in this thing, but I will not touch anything that I do not understand.' That implied it had something to do with forgery.

That November morning, to his amazement Pink spotted a pair of familiar faces at Russell's, the tailors on the Strand. '[I] noticed two men enter the front of the store and recognised them,' he later recalled in an interview. They were Joseph Chapman and Austin Bidwell. After pricing their clothes, he and Shore followed them to some rooms in Piccadilly. When Pink later told this story to the man himself when he was being imprisoned in Cuba, all the colour drained from Austin's face as he had been unaware that he had been spotted. 'Pinkerton, for God's sake why did you not speak to me in England?' he exclaimed. 'I would have given you $50,000 to mind your own affairs and not to do as you have done. You have ruined me and the whole party.'

That the Bank of England had been warned not once but several times is one of the more puzzling aspects of the narrative that follows. Today, there would have been a public enquiry as well as a tsunami of tweets and tabloid calls for resignations. In those more respectful times, the Old Lady of Threadneedle Street hid behind an impenetrable wall of silence.

At Pink's insistence, Shore reported their presence to Freshfields, who not only acted for the Baltimore Bank but the Bank of England. 'It was not thought that these people could accomplish any crimes in England on account of their lack of knowledge of the English banking system,' Willie Pinkerton later lamented.

As a matter of routine, he forwarded pictures of the Bidwells to Scotland Yard as well as the US embassy. The shady characters associated with the Baltimore robbers were clearly up to no good. Given that all of them knew Walter Sheridan and George Wilkes, whom he later learned had been in London, Pink suspected that there was going to be a bigger hit. As a result, Willie Pinkerton also sent a circular to warn most of the banks in the City of London and, most importantly, the Old Lady of Threadneedle Street itself.

'The bank, however, rather pooh-poohed the idea that they could be "done",' William Pinkerton lamented. Like the criminals he was trying to pre-empt, Pink concluded that the bank was indeed run by rank amateurs and pompous officials who could not see how vulnerable their institution might be. It also later emerged that Yankee Bligh's letters to Scotland Yard had been dismissed as the fictions of a 'backwoods sleuthhound'. In one version of the story he was later told, it was only when an official of the bank who had dealt with George Macdonnell happened upon the photograph that Yankee had taken that he shouted, 'That is the man!'

After their subsequent apprehension, the bank acknowledged its debt, sending Yankee a cheque for $50 and a letter of thanks. The detective prized both of them highly, along with a note from Queen Victoria, and had his portrait commissioned by the Bank of England. They remained some of the most treasured items of a career that ended suddenly in the summer of 1890 with heart failure, after which he was widely eulogised as the first ever truly professional chief of police in the United States.

Friday, 29 March 1872
5th Avenue Hotel, New York City

They decided to go out in style. After all their recent trials and tribulations, the thieves of Threadneedle Street wanted to have one final bash before they headed across the Atlantic. Austin Bidwell knew the hotel well and had lived there during the good times. They could not think of a better place to celebrate. A sumptuous meal and champagne in one of the more luxurious suites seemed a suitable place to celebrate and take stock.

Austin Bidwell was now in his mid-twenties, but feeling as though he had aged and weary at times. His brother George was older and not wiser exactly, but more certain than ever of his own powers and cleverness, something he shared with George Macdonnell. Of all of them, Mac never needed any encouragement. Though supposedly lying low, he knew they were going to be making history.

Quieter, and clearly enjoying the drink if not the food, was George Engels who was, as always, preoccupied. Even after all this time, his motives were invariably difficult to discern. For anyone who ever watched them together, it was hard to know whether their forger was their ringleader or the self-effacing technician on whom all their plans revolved. As always, they ended with a toast to the future which began early the next day with their departure on the morning tide aboard a steamer headed for Great Britain. 'We all landed in Liverpool in the highest spirits,' Austin Bidwell would recall, 'and at once took the train for London, enjoying the novelty of everything.'

An opportune piece of pickpocketing on the train to Jersey City had seen an English tourist separated from genuine letters of credit on the Bank of North Wales. They had been bought by Engels from a pickpocket he knew. These could, it was clear, come in very useful when, as George Bidwell later explained, they decided to 'raise the wind' out of European capitalists.

4

The Social Triumphs
of a Silver King

In 1873 it was discovered that the bank had been defrauded of a large sum of money by means of forged bills, which were sent into the Western Branch for discount. The frauds were committed by the exercise of great skill and patience by well-educated men, some of whom could speak several languages, and who might have been benefactors of society if their talents had been turned to good instead of evil account.

Chronicles of the Bank of England, B.B. Turner, 1897

Wednesday, 1 May 1872
Threadneedle Street, City of London

It was yet another glorious moment in time, a vivid memory that would haunt them in all the years to come. 'Boys, you may depend upon it,' Austin Bidwell said, smiling, 'there is the softest spot in the world and we could hit the bank for a million as easy as rolling off a log.'

Right in front of them was the ultimate crime scene, The Old Lady of Threadneedle Street itself, implacable and daunting in the spring sunshine. For a moment, the hustle and bustle all around them ('the human whirlpool in that centre of throbbing life', as he later termed it) was blocked out. Hurrying businessmen and bankers in their top hats and finery rushed past them, before they were gone too, heading back down Lombard Street, and lost to the crowd.

Over the next day or so they became preoccupied by Austin's words. One last job, one final caper that would bring them security, untold riches and, no doubt, infamy for the rest of their lives. A job that would outclass all the other forgeries ever attempted in history. Maybe it was hubris and grasping ambition that blinded them to their folly, but their quest for the ultimate and ultimately elusive criminal chimera would propel them into the history books. Could they really ever get away with it?

The next day, at a roadside inn in the countryside, they were still mulling it over. And then, George Macdonnell, in some estimation the cleverest of them all, got to the heart of the issue. He laid it all out: the appeal of retiring with $100,000 apiece was too great; the Old Lady of Threadneedle Street had more than enough to go round; and then he smiled as he delivered the sucker punch – 'The bank would never miss the money.'

Nobody really knows when the forgers decided to hit the Bank of England. In both their memoirs, the Bidwell brothers offered contradictory evidence. 'What at first was a half jest, an airy theory, rapidly crystallized into a steadfast purpose,' Austin Bidwell later claimed to a reporter. Various investigators, too, could not work out whether they had set out from the States with such an enterprise in mind. 'So far as we can collect, the prisoners had no direct intention at this time of attacking the Bank of England,' Freshfields wrote on the eve of the trial. Yet as they stood outside the bank on that first day of May 1872, their plans had already crystallised.

They had identified a mark whom one of the prosecution would later term 'a perfectly respectable gentleman in Savile Row'. Two weeks earlier, Austin Bidwell had come across his business. It was a tailors whose owner happened to hold his account at the Bank of England's sub-branch in the West End of London. In his memoirs, Austin said he spent the best part of an afternoon watching the magnificent building on Burlington Gardens, behind the Royal Academy of Arts which connected Savile Row to New Bond Street.

Once the London residence of Lord Anglesey, it was a powerful concession to local businesses that they could use the branch if they were recommended. Word of mouth was all that would be required to gain entry. The various depositors were easy to identify as they examined their pocket books once they left the branch. Austin Bidwell then followed at a distance to see where they went. He soon zeroed in on three possible targets: an optician, an import house and a tailors. He chose the latter who, it transpired, had been banking there for the last fifteen years. 'As I had not yet shown up in the previous transactions,' Austin Bidwell recalled, 'I volunteered to go to the front on this.'

Thursday, 18 April 1872
Savile Row, Central London

It had all begun so innocently. Walking down Savile Row in the spring sunshine without an apparent care in the world, Austin Bidwell paused to look through the window of Edward Green & Co. at No. 35. It seemed to be run by a pleasant, unassuming father and son. As such, Edward Hamilton Green was a perfect mark.

When he entered the premises, Bidwell struck the tailor as an American gentleman of considerable wealth. Mr Green later remarked how knowledgeable Frederick Albert Warren appeared to be. As Austin had been involved in cotton futures many years before, he was still well versed in its intricacies. Suave, polished and charming, he made a favourable impression.

Mr Warren appeared to be a 'silver king', someone who had clearly made a fortune across the water thanks to the mining fever that was then at its height. 'I had brought from America with me a Western hat,' Austin recalled, 'and as I had resolved to play the silver king, I wore it when going around with the tradesmen.' It was a neat trick, adding to his image as a rich Yankee with both time and money on his hands. Everybody he subsequently came into contact with that spring clearly believed him.

The forgers' confidence was so great, Austin Bidwell later remarked, that they never even contemplated failure. After all, it was a refinement of everything they had been doing for years now. It was ludicrously easy to put into motion on this spring morning in 1872. 'We laughed then,' Austin Bidwell later lamented, 'but we did not laugh for the next twenty years.'

If there was one thing they had learned to date, it was to take things as slowly as they could, a confidence vividly described by one of the prosecutors as 'a plant of somewhat slow growth'. That way, they could build up their credibility without arousing suspicion and, as the various official files record, it worked remarkably. 'The patience exhibited by these forgers is something wonderful,' the prosecution briefing material would marvel, 'and can alone account for their ultimate success.'

Letters and later detective work subsequently revealed that the gang had taken 'somewhat obscure lodgings' (as a later prosecutor had it) in a little known suburb of London on Wednesday, 10 April 1872, the day after arriving in Liverpool.

The reason they chose this was for the sake of obscurity. If you were an international fraudster planning a caper, it was near perfect. Nobody would ever think of looking for you along that unlovely stretch of the Kingsland Road, which today bisects the digital nirvana of Shoreditch and the urban grime of Hackney. Then better known as Haggerston, it was, by all accounts, Dickensian in the extreme. Its very grime and grimness probably informed their choice of rooms rented out by a widow.

When later interviewed by detectives, Ann Thomas recalled they were surprised by the cleanliness of her house. Two American gentlemen, one fair and one dark, appeared one day out of the blue. They had taken the drawing room floor, a sitting room and a single bedroom. 'We have come on a long journey and would like to make the one bedroom do,' the darker one, Mr Anthony (who was actually George Bidwell), explained. Mr Swift, the fair one, said very little. Mrs Thomas later recalled that he was delicate (this was actually George Macdonnell). They did not want to stay for long, but Mr Anthony assured her they would pay a good rent. They agreed on a shilling a week for the rooms. The terms were that they could leave at any time.

In fact, the two Americans stayed there for little over a week. They breakfasted each day, spending most mornings in their rooms as their landlady took them *The Times*. 'They were writing occasionally together in the room,' Mrs Thomas recalled. 'I did not know what they were or their business.' They did seem to use a lot of ink. They also received the same pair of visitors, either singly or on their own. One was rather more mysterious and well groomed, and had already started to use the name of Frederick Albert Warren.

'There was another person with him,' Mrs Thomas later testified under oath, 'but I never ascertained his name.' This was George Engels, who was using the name Warren K. Siebert. At the outset, as Freshfields later stated, he 'had been chosen to commit the actual forgery', a view shared by others in American law enforcement.

On one of those bright spring days, Mrs Thomas recalled a package coming from a tailors which her little girl took up to the Americans' room. 'It was a parcel for Mr Warren,' she recalled. Then, the following weekend, on Sunday 21 April, all four had dined at 21 Enfield Road. 'I think they remained all night, as there was a rug and some blankets on the sofa,' Mrs Thomas later testified. 'I saw them early in the morning there. A large trunk was packed up on that Monday.' Mr Anthony had stopped 'in doors all day, hard at work' with all the others.

On Tuesday, 22 April, a bracing spring day with showers, Mr Anthony said with regret that he would be leaving. He said he was going to Scotland. When he subsequently left, the American accidentally took a latch-key with him, so Mrs Thomas asked 'the fair gentleman' (whose name of Swift she only heard another of them mention in passing) to ask his friend to return it forthwith. A week later, on 29 April, she received a letter from the Terminus Hotel, London Bridge:

Dear Madam,
In behalf of friends and self, we offer you our sincere thanks for the kindness and attention received during our stay at your house; everything being neat and the cooking superb. Regretting that we are called out of town so soon, we are very truly yours, C.W. Anthony and friends.

Mr Swift had remained for that intervening week.

Towards the end of that time, Mr Warren called and gathered up the things Mr Anthony had left behind: shirts studs, hats, hair restorer and some slippers. 'He left the felt hat,' Mrs Thomas later testified, 'and said he would not take that. The other things he took away. After they all had left, I found three or four ink bottles.'

George Bidwell would not actually visit Scotland for nearly another year, at which point he sent Mrs Thomas a letter, which arrived completely unexpectedly:

Edinburgh, March 14th 1873

Dear Madam
You may remember that I was with you as lodger for a few days last spring and as I am coming to town for a time I wish you to write me by return if you have any room vacant. Either a bedroom or a bed and sitting room will do as I shall be alone and bringing only a portmanteau.

As she was full, Mrs Thomas arranged for him to hire a sitting room and bedroom at a neighbour's on the other side of the road. As she later told the police, the landlady was puzzled why there was no name on the envelope. The return address was given only as the Post Office, Pitt Street, Edinburgh. She thought nothing more of it until a week later when a detective called.

Exactly a year to the day that Mr Anthony had first stayed with her, Mrs Thomas was called as a witness at the Mansion House. She recognised him straightaway. Later that summer, she was deposed again when the case had moved up to the Old Bailey where it was later described by the Lord Chief Justice as 'the most remarkable trial that ever occurred in the annals of England'.

From his air of general distraction, George Bidwell clearly had other things on his mind. Over those eight days that summer, the real story of what they had been doing in those first few days in Europe – and, indeed, subsequent weeks and months – now came to light. All the other people they had duped were under oath and duty-bound to reveal what had actually happened.

Second Day of the Trial – Tuesday, 19 August 1873
City of London
Early Morning

The rumours had been building for months now and today, on yet another gloomy morning in what had been a miserably cold August, the whole of London was agog. There had been endless gossip about these 'Yankee rascals' for months now.

Finally, they were going to stand trial in the most famous law courts in the land. Briefly, they would become the most famous criminals in the world.

All along the busiest thoroughfares which led down from Newgate Prison towards the Old Bailey itself, crowds had formed early. Those expecting to see the prisoners shackled and humiliated would be disappointed. There would be no 'perp' walks, no public humiliation nor any chance for onlookers to shout or cheer them on their way. Out of sight and underground, the prisoners were shielded until the last minute and escorted along the passageway that led directly from Newgate Prison straight to the Central Criminal Court. There was no standing room left in the public gallery as shortly before ten o'clock they were shepherded in by stern policemen in high tunic uniforms.

All four forgers somehow managed to look stylish in their normal daytime attire. Most onlookers were astounded at how young they appeared. They had not said very much. In all their earlier remand hearings – all twenty-three of them – they had often been quiet to the point of taciturnity. Though there had been rumours of turning Queen's Evidence, none of them ever would. It had been a matter of routine at the start of July when Sir Sydney Waterlow, the Lord Mayor of London, had concluded that it was his duty to commit them to the Old Bailey for trial at the next session.

As a merchant in his own right – and one whose family printing businesses had been directly impacted by the fraudsters – he termed the case as 'one of the most complicated to have occurred in the city'. And now, just six weeks later, each of them was being charged with 'offences of the gravest magnitude', evidence for which one of their defence attorneys had aptly summarised 'as most voluminous and very complicated'.

Occasionally, the forgers leaned over the rail of the dock to talk to their individual attorneys or whisper the occasional entreaty among themselves though hindered by the policemen. They did not seem particularly fazed by the proceedings. If anything, they looked more amused than apprehensive.

By this point, George Freshfield and the prosecutors had exhausted every line of enquiry they could. The irony was that at the start of their activities, Austin Bidwell had actually considered their offices in London's West End as a suitable mark but realised that there might be complications. In his later memoirs, he reserved especial scorn for the bank's solicitors. 'Freshfields managed to spend four hundred and fifty thousand dollars of the bank's money in our prosecution,' he later remarked, a sum which in his native United States 'would have ruined reputations'. The only reason they had the book thrown at them was because they had embarrassed the Bank of England by holding 'up to the laughter of the whole world its red-tape idiotic management'.

That the thieves of Threadneedle Street had even made it to the Old Bailey today was an achievement all in itself. The week before strange gossip had been echoing around the highest of legal circles which newspapers began to pick up. 'It is rumoured that an application will be made on behalf of the prisoners to postpone the trial,' the *Daily News* had reported on the Saturday, 'but such a proceeding, it is understood, will be strenuously opposed by the prosecution.'

As always, the rumours were largely true. The day before, the various lawyers involved in the case had faced off against each other in an attempt to do just that. Very quickly they became embroiled in one of those byzantine arguments that only lawyers – particularly in the age of Victoria – seemed to savour. It involved all the minutiae of legal procedures which stemmed from the ballooning in size of the case. In the seven months since the fraud began, and the five and a half since the accidental stumbling upon it, more than 200 witnesses had been found. They had all been interviewed and their statements dutifully recorded, transcribed and notarised.

Police on at least three continents had been involved in finding or attempting to find witnesses to the various crimes and misdemeanours which had supported the greater fraud. Fifty witnesses had already been brought over from the United States. Forty were bank clerks, the rest were hotel staff, chambermaids, waiters, messengers, tellers and cabbies who would shortly appear in procession to present their testimonies. The defence had not, it claimed, had time to prepare.

A further ninety-four witnesses had subsequently been found. Their testimonies had had to be recorded and entered into evidence. Given the sheer volume of banking records, bills and letters, and the need to call foreign witnesses, there would be an unseemly rush. Without putting too fine a point on it, the defence was alleging that the prisoners had been deliberately kept in the dark about this new information.

The judge was having none of it. 'I have arrived at a very clear opinion that I am doing no injustice whatever to the prisoners in requiring that the trial should proceed without delay,' he had concluded the day before. As this was a felony, the jury had not been allowed to separate. As they would for the rest of the trial, they had all stayed in a hotel together the night before. And now, they – as well as all the onlookers who crowded the gallery – would learn where the fraud began in the spring of 1872.

The Right Honourable Hardinge Giffard QC – the future 1st Earl of Halsbury, and later Lord Chancellor in the Marquess of Salisbury's government – looked exactly how a lead prosecutor might in a Victorian melodrama. His gnomic inscrutability fitted well with his vague air of academic distraction as the author of a comprehensive and authoritative encyclopedia on the law (which is still in use today).

Giffard's forensic skills of advocacy were legendary. His reputation came from his mastery of the brief, thanks to his prodigious memory and ability to recall obscure facts and cross-reference minute details. His opening would be nothing less than a tour de force. It took over three hours to complete, a feat that was all the more remarkable for his only occasionally referring to notes. Giffard began:

When I tell you that the charge against the prisoners is in substance that they uttered no less than ninety-four Bills of Exchange, all of which were forged and some of which were upon the finest mercantile houses in the country – when I tell you that the effect of that was to obtain from the Bank of England in the interval between the 21st of January and the 1st of March, a sum considerably exceeding £100,000 you will at once have appreciated that if it is one of those gigantic schemes of fraud, a parallel to which I think might vainly be sought in the criminal jurisprudence of this country.

There had been a ripple of excitement throughout the Central Criminal Court. This palpable sense of amazement was also reflected in subsequent newspaper coverage, where Giffard's elegant phrase became a keynote for the trial.

Today, it would have been an endlessly repeated sound bite on the headline news, or a hashtagged tweet, used and reused until it entered common parlance. At the time, it simply set the tone for the proceedings which would now begin with the entry of the judge into the well of the courtroom.

Tuesday, 19 August 1873
Central Criminal Court, Old Bailey
10 a.m.

Exactly on the hour, His Honour Justice Sir Thomas Dickson Archibald slowly negotiated his way towards his seat, weighed down by his vast expanse of ceremonial garments. Referred to as 'Your Lordship' by everyone in attendance, he was feared and respected in equal measure.

Staring over half-moon spectacles, his jowly, stern demeanour suggested faint dyspepsia and a glowering sense of menace. Knighted at the same time as the crimes he would now have to consider, Judge Archibald was now in his mid-fifties, the lead advocate in the court of common pleas. His accent still carried traces of his early years in Nova Scotia, a deep, booming voice that would brook no contradictions.

His Lordship – as all the lawyers made sure to call him – was a gimlet-eyed stickler for correctness in all things, not least in making sure conventions were followed and rules of evidence strictly adhered to. Looking down from the highest elevation in the court, Sir Thomas took his place in his vast leather chair, his robes pressing down like ballast. Above him the royal coat of arms framed his head like a crown. Directly in front of him, staring up from the floor, was the clerk, Mr Avery, who was charged with handling the vast amount of evidence and its timely injection into the course of the proceedings. The judge nodded towards him and everyone else sat down, apart from the witnesses and the lead prosecutor. The Central Criminal Court was a spectacular setting for a show trial. For the participants and onlookers alike, it was truly a *coup de théâtre*.

Around them were lawyers, clerks, sheriffs, alderman, runners and secretaries all crammed together in the well of the court. The stern faces and dark clothing suggested a solemnity which, at times, contrasted the open-mouthed amazement and anticipation of the crowded public gallery. Out of sight, but hardly out of mind, were the vast quantities of paper and statements which detailed all the remarkable skeins of intrigue that had been carefully and diligently unthreaded. *The Times* had noted:

> They extend over 242 folio pages, including the oral and documentary evidence and make of themselves a thick volume, together with an elaborate index for ready reference. Within living memory there has been no such case for length and importance, heard before any Lord Mayor of London in its preliminary stage, nor one which excited a greater amount of public interest from first to last.[4]

The players of the unfolding drama were now ready – the prisoners, the lawyers and the court officials – and the honour of examining the first witness went to one of the more unassuming silks who had been waiting patiently on the prosecution bench.

Charles Watkin Williams QC was a safe pair of hands, a team player who was happy to accede to others but well known for his dry humour, his clear thinking and his specialised knowledge of financial cases. Like many of the leading barristers of the day, he was also a Member of Parliament (for his native Denbigh). Unusually, Watkin Williams had begun his professional life studying medicine. The medical profession's loss was the legal one's gain, and so, shortly after the hour, Edward Hamilton Green was sworn in so that Mr Watkin Williams could begin his questioning.

'I believe you are a tailor carrying on business in partnership with your son at 35 Saville Row?' he asked.

Edward Green nodded. 'Yes, as a tailors and army clothiers.'

Turning towards the dock, Mr Williams then asked, 'Do you know any of the prisoners at the bar?'

'Yes I do.'

'Which of them do you recognise?'

'I recognise one person of the name of Warren.'

'Will you point him out?'

'The furthest from me.'

Austin Bidwell did not react. It was clear to the jury they knew each other, if not well, then at least with sufficient knowledge to recognise each other in passing. 'That is Austin Bidwell,' Mr Watkin Williams said. 'Any of the others?'

'I recognise the other prisoner next to him.'

'That is George Macdonnell,' prompted Mr Watkin Williams.

'Yes, as Swift.' In his alter ego of Edward Swift, Mac had been party to these opening overtures, the establishing of the bona fides of Frederick Albert Warren.

'You recognise those two?'

'Yes.'

'Do you remember those two prisoners calling upon you on 18 April 1872?'

'I recall them calling on me,' Mr Green said vaguely. 'I believe it was about that time.'

'Did they call alone or with another person?' Watkin Williams asked.

'They called with another person.' This was Engels, who was never mentioned by his real name.

'I believe they called to order some clothes?'

'They did.'

'Is it a practice in your establishment when [a] person order[s] clothes to ask them to sign a book?'

'It is.'

'Have you got your signature book here?'

'I have.' From the bench, Mr Avery, the clerk, handed it over.

'Did the two you have mentioned, Austin Bidwell and Macdonnell, sign their names in that book?'

'They did.'

Now the reasons for all their aliases at Mrs Thomas's became clear, as indeed was the delivery of the package which contained a large quantity of clothes. 'During this time Austin Bidwell and Macdonnell, no doubt for the purpose of enabling them the better to effect their frauds, determined to dress as gentlemen,' Freshfields had noted. 'You will observe that even in these early days they were very careful of preventing themselves from being identified and to cover their retreat.'

In his later writings, George Bidwell maintained that the prosecution made it seem like every shopkeeper 'from whom any of us made purchases' had been defrauded. All throughout his writings, George maintains that there was never any intention of using Mr Green for any purpose beyond his legitimate business. 'Yet the prosecution brought this circumstance in as a link in the alleged long-proposed scheme of fraud,' he claims. He had no idea about the opening of this account nor that he had any prior knowledge that the tailor was a customer at the Western Branch of the Bank of England. He also claimed that over the following summer, he repeatedly told Austin to close the account as they needed the money.

'George Bidwell appears to have been a man of regular habits,' the prosecution maintained. Foremost among them, as we will now see, was telling outrageous lies.

Tuesday, 19 August 1873
Central Criminal Court
10.15 a.m.

After establishing that the Greens had subsequently made a considerable quantity of clothing for Mr Warren, Mr Watkin Williams started a new line of questioning. 'Now on the 4th May did the two prisoners whom you refer to, call again at your home?'

'Yes.'

'They called in a cab, I believe?'

'Yes.'

'Was anybody with him?

'It was Warren Siebert that called and I think there was a third party; but that I will not swear.'

'I believe they tried on the clothes that you had made for them?'

'They did on that occasion.'

His Lordship seemed interested. 'Did you make clothes for them all?' Lord Justice Archibald asked.

'For the prisoners I have named, I did.'

Mr Watkin Williams continued. 'Did you enter into conversation with him on that occasion?'

'On the 4th May, you mean?'

'Yes, when they were trying on the clothes.'

'Yes, we entered into some conversation.'

Patience, clearly, was needed in prompting memories. 'Did they tell you when they were going and where?' Mr Watkin Williams asked.

'Yes, I understood them to say that they were going to visit Ireland,' Mr Green said.

'Did they tell you where?'

'No, they had a cab at the door.'

'Was there any luggage on the cab?'

'Yes.'

'Did they say where they were going to with the cab?'

'They said they were in a hurry to catch a train.'

'Did they say where they were going in that train?'

'I understood them to say that they were going to Ireland – they were going to Birmingham, I think, first and from Birmingham to Liverpool and from Liverpool to Ireland. I think that was what was stated.'

The Tiffany's Robbery
31 October 1867
New York City

Do it in a hurry. And use false names. The oldest tricks in the book, ensuring your mark did not have time to think properly. Both had been the key to one of their earliest and certainly one of their more audacious scams, which, coincidentally, had also involved both Austin Bidwell and George Macdonnell five years earlier. 'The Tiffany's Robbery', as it became known, showed just how ingenious their capers could be. With Austin posing as his valet, Mac pretended that he was a rich Englishman travelling for pleasure in Manhattan by the name of Henry B. Livingston (in some accounts, Livingstone).

It was a role he could play to perfection. He had legitimately rented rooms in the grand residence of a well-known doctor on 5th Avenue, Dr Thomas Barnum (and in some accounts, Barnham). Saying he was disgusted with American hotel life, he explained to the doctor's wife that he and his valet would like to rent the rooms at the front of their house. 'He engaged the parlor and two rooms adjoining at $100 a week,' *The New York Sun* later reported, 'paying for the first week's rent in advance.'

Claiming to be the doctor's son, George Macdonnell repeatedly visited Manhattan's most famous jewellers. In his usual manner, Mac had got to know one of the managing clerks and, as Willie Pinkerton later recorded, 'went in several times and examined diamonds and at last ordered some to be sent to a house on Fifth Avenue.'

At Tiffany's, Mac selected a solitaire ring, a brooch, two diamond ear-drops and two large unset diamonds. Their total value came to nearly $5,000. To his chagrin, Mac realised he did not have enough cash on his person. He would, he said, have to get the money from his father. Along with an eager salesman, they took a carriage to the house on 5th Avenue. The ornate nameplate obviously matched the surname Mac had given.

Once inside, they found an eager-looking valet. 'Clarence,' Mac asked, 'where is father?'

'He has just stepped out,' Austin replied.

'Do you know where he has gone?'

'Yes, I think he has gone around to the building.' Clarence said he would seek out the patriarch on 24th Street. 'The old man is building a new house there,' Mac added for the benefit of the salesman, 'and has gone around to look at it.'

Austin took the waiting carriage and then later returned with a cheque. All three of them – Mac, Austin and the salesman – then went back to Tiffany's. 'On the diamonds being brought there,' William Pinkerton later noted, 'Macdonnell gave a certified cheque for $5,000 which was accepted by the clerk but was found to be a forgery.' Then Mac and Austin disappeared from view. Temporarily, at least.

The break in the case came from the carriage driver who read about the robbery in the press. A New York detective followed George Macdonnell's trail as far as

Portland, Oregon, where, by the time he caught up with him, he had already been jailed in the name of George W. Bradford for yet another forgery, this time involving a cattle swindle. Mac was eventually tried in the Big Apple and was then sent to Sing Sing, in February 1868, for a full term of sentence (three years) and ordered to pay $2,500.

A short while later, Austin Bidwell was arrested and convicted in the name of Louis Baker. He had been passing a number of forged cheques in upstate New York. He too was incarcerated until 1870 in the same prison. Significantly, there is no mention of this and other episodes in his or his brother's memoirs.

Tuesday, 19 August 1873
Central Criminal Court, Old Bailey
10.20 a.m.

The first witness got into a tangle straight away. Throughout the case, the prolixity and profusion of the gang's identities would cause uncommon difficulties. Mr Giffard had noted the day before:

> I think it is absolutely astonishing in the progress of this case to find the enormous variety of aliases that the prisoners, all of them, from time to time adopted, the perfect accuracy with which they preserved their different identities according to the different characters that they assumed for the moment.

To the obvious bemusement of the jury, he went through all forty-one of them, exhorting them not to 'forget the different names by which they have gone'.

This was clearly now too much for Mr Edward Green. 'Did Warren, or Austin Bidwell as we call him now ...' Mr Watkin Williams paused, aware that the tailor already seemed bewildered. He tried a new approach. 'Should you be able to follow me if I call him Austin Bidwell?'

'I would rather you would call him as we have him – Warren,' Green replied.

At this point, His Lordship intervened. 'If you can follow the learned counsel and describe him by the name we know him by here it would be much more convenient for my Note,' Justice Archibald asked, beginning the copious written notes he would make during the trial. Both barrister and witness nodded.

'Should you be confused if I call him Austin Bidwell?'

'Is it George Bidwell or Austin Bidwell?' Mr Green asked, puzzled. 'Austin Bidwell I presume.'

Mr Watkin Williams continued: 'Then I will call him Austin Bidwell. Did he say anything to you about money?'

'He did.'

'Just state what he said.'

'In conversation he said he had some money,' Mr Green said. 'More money than he thought it was prudent for him to leave in his lodgings.' At the time, the tailor had asked, 'Is it of any amount?' It certainly was. It was over £1,000, not an amount that anyone in Victorian London would want to leave lying around. After all, as all four of them could attest with completely straight faces, there were a lot of unscrupulous criminals around.

Saturday, 4 May 1872
Edward Green & Son, No. 35 Savile Row, London
2 p.m.

The impatience was showing on his face. Frederick Albert Warren kept looking at his watch. He was clearly in a great hurry. Much of that urgency came through in his voice, clipped and higher pitched than when he arrived. Time was clearly not a luxury that a silver king could afford, not least with a carriage waiting outside. 'Mr Green we are about going away,' Mr Warren said. 'We have not much time to spare.' He drew his pocket book, smiling ruefully. From where he was stood, the tailor could see it was bulging with large denomination notes. 'I have more money about me than I think I am justified in leaving at my hotel in a drawer,' the American said brightly. 'I think I will get you to take charge of it for me.'

Mr Green was in a dilemma. He obviously did not want to lose the custom of such a cash rich customer. Out of courtesy, Mr Green asked how much money he had. Mr Warren shrugged. 'I guess it would be a thousand or perhaps over two thousand.'

Mr Green's eyes widened. That wasn't just chump change. It was a small fortune. Momentarily, the tailor regained his composure as an elegant solution presented itself. 'That being the case I should not like to take the responsibility of taking your money,' Mr Green said. 'You had better deposit it at the bank.'

Mr Warren pondered this and clearly saw the logic in that. 'Well perhaps it would be as well,' he reluctantly agreed. 'Where do you bank?'

Mr Green smiled with pride. 'At the Bank of England close by,' he said. 'If you like, I will take you down there so you can deposit your money.'

Looking distracted, Mr Warren was grateful. There was never any hint of undue emotion nor excitement. 'Thank you,' was all he said, 'very good.'

Tuesday, 19 August 1873
Central Criminal Court, Old Bailey
10.25 a.m.

The court was all ears. Aware that the tailor had so easily walked into a trap, the judge was amazed. 'You said this to him?' Justice Archibald asked.

'Yes, I did,' Mr Green replied:

He said: 'We have very little time to spare – we are in a hurry to get a cab.' I said 'It will not take long, I can take you down there.' I then accompanied him to the bank, the Western Branch of the Bank of England, where I kept an account and I then saw Mr Fenwick, the sub manager.

The two visitors had entered the building to cross a marbled, parquet floor and then walked up a curved Adam staircase. This was, to use a phrase the American would know, 'high cotton'. After establishing that the manager was absent, Mr Green then explained that he had introduced him 'as an American gentleman and a customer of mine and that he had a certain sum of money that he wished to deposit, something like that'.

'Did you mention his name?'

'I did.'

'As "Warren" I suppose.'

'I think so.'

And that was how easy it was to open an account under a false name in Victorian London. Without anyone realising it at the time, this was the start of Austin Bidwell building up his bona fides. For now, the fraudsters were too clever to take matters any further. Under the guise of Frederick Albert Warren, another prosecutor related Austin Bidwell's comment that he was anxious not to expose his money 'to the perils of fraud'.

'The perils of fraud' – a neat phrase to use when perpetrating one, especially, and exactly as they had hoped, as Mr Green vouched for his suitability even though, as an American police chief noted years later, the tailor 'really knew nothing about him beyond the fact that he was prodigal customer who asked no credit'.

They were off to a flying start.

Tuesday, 19 August 1873
Central Criminal Court, Old Bailey
10.30 a.m.

Now it was time for the first cross-examination led by Austin's barrister, Mr McIntyre, who would try to exploit any vagueness on Mr Green's part about details as well as names, to undermine his credibility, prompting his first question. 'Can you tell me when you first saw Austin Bidwell?' he asked.

'I really cannot without referring,' Mr Green replied. 'It was in April at all events.' He confirmed that he was measured for clothes and tried them on for the first time on 4 May.

'When was the name put in your book: at the time the clothes were ordered as when he came on the 4th of May? Did he write it himself or did one of your men make an entry from his dictation?'

'We made the entry from his dictation.'

Here was a glimmer of hope for the defence. 'Then there is no signature of his in your book?'

'There is a signature.'

'Of his?'

'Yes.'

'Of Austin Bidwell?'

'Yes.'

When Mr McIntyre asked for the book he made reference to something significant. 'Well I do not see any date to any of these entries. Perhaps it is not the custom in your house to have dates put.'

'No.'

'Then you cannot tell me when the signature was written.'

'I cannot.'

The next witness, Edward Elliott Green, simply agreed with his father. He, too, recognised Austin Bidwell and George Macdonnell. 'I was present when they called and ordered clothes,' he said on the stand. Mr Warren and Mr Swift had appeared maybe twenty times at most. Occasionally, they had been with a third person who had given no name nor an address.

Under examination by Mr Giffard, the younger Green was pointedly asked, 'Have you any belief who that third person was?'

'No, I cannot swear to the third person.'

And after a short conversation while the account was opened, the American and the tailor returned to Savile Row, where his two companions, Swift and Seibert, as they were known, had patiently waited for him. As the prosecution had established, their real first names were both George – Macdonnell and Engels, respectively.

Tuesday, 19 August 1873
Central Criminal Court, Old Bailey
10.50 a.m.

Robert Fenwick was a sub-agent at the bank's Western Branch in Burlington Gardens, essentially the under manager of the branch. He well recalled the introduction by Mr Green of the silver king who turned up that Saturday. 'He is an American gentleman, for a short time in this country,' the tailor had said. 'He has a considerable amount of money which he wishes taken care of.'

When Mr Fenwick asked him how he should be described, Mr Warren did not give an answer exactly. Later on, he said he was 'over here on business,' though Mr Fenwick now claimed at the Old Bailey that he could not 'exactly remember the exact words'. 'He said he had acted more as a medium for others than for himself,' Mr Fenwick now recalled on the stand. 'I then said "Shall I describe you as a commission agent" and he said "Yes".'

'Did you enter his description?' the judge asked.

'Yes, in our ledger.'

Frederick Albert Warren certainly looked like he could be trusted with other people's money. Mr Fenwick then recalled him handing over £1,200 – £1,000 in notes, £3 in gold and a draft on the Continental Bank for £197 – to open the account. The sub-manager then gave him a credit slip and handed him a cheque book with fifty cheques in it. These were 'bearer cheques', which were made payable only to the person who cashed them, and this meant that, as the prosecution obviously had later done, they could be traced.

On the stand, Mr Fenwick then related another conversational snippet. 'Should I have more money to pay in,' Mr Warren asked, 'must it come through Mr Green?'

'That is not necessary,' the bank official had replied.

As to where this money had come from, in the run-up to the trial the prosecution had encountered great difficulty establishing its provenance. Three days earlier one of the gang had gone into the Bank of England and exchanged gold for £3,000 in cash. Freshfields was never able to identify which of them it was. Whoever he was, he gave an address as the Clarence Hotel, which in the words of a briefing document the solicitors prepared for the trial was 'nothing more than a small public house, the inhabitants do not or will not identify the prisoners. In fact they are unusually forgetful and stupid.' The forgers were neither.

'It is curious that the prisoners should have chosen this exact time for opening the account,' the prosecutors also noted. A few days before Mr Warren walked through the door, the branch manager, Robert Ruthven Pym, had resigned after twelve and a half years there. He had taken a post with a commercial bank in Cavendish Square. More so than normal, the branch was apprehensive. Mr Pym's former underlings were clearly flustered and, as several onlookers later remarked, seemed much more concerned with keeping in with headquarters, which inevitably meant bringing in more business. And that, as the silver king could attest, also meant they would not ask any difficult questions, which suited him perfectly.

When the fraud had first been discovered, there was a great deal of speculation as to why the forgers had chosen the Western Branch of the Bank of England in the first place. The reasons were simple. This sub-branch was more likely to effect the opening of a simple chequing account than 'head office', as the Old Lady of Threadneedle Street was usually known.

It specialised in a completely different line of business. 'It is intended for the convenience of gentlemen and ladies and West End tradesmen who might find it inconvenient to journey to the City in order to transact their occasional business,' *The Times* had noted three days after the forgery was discovered. In other words, it did not tend to deal with large sums 'and in consequence is less bound by strict regulations in dealing with any business of that nature which [was being] accidentally brought to it'.

More than that, a gentleman's word was enough. There was never any need for proof of identity, hotel registration forms or any request to see any sort of residence permit. Although Mr Warren was obviously an American customer, he was not even asked for his passport. In fact, his nationality acted more as a trump card. Austin Bidwell would later write:

> One great advantage a dishonest man had at that date in Europe, especially an American, was that if he dressed well they considered he must be a gentleman, and if he had money that was a proof of respectability – one they never thought of questioning, nor how he came by it; then, again, it was an article of their creed that all Americans are rich.

They had purposefully chosen its Western Branch so they could enter the grand Old Lady of Threadneedle Street via a back door. The Bank of England was so arrogant, Austin Bidwell later marvelled, that it believed it was invulnerable to fraud. 'They not only believed it themselves,' he wrote, 'but all the world had come to believe it as well.' 'Simple Simons', he termed them. Now in full public view, its officials had learned, to their cost, that the fraudsters had exploited that arrogance to the full.

Tuesday, 19 August 1873
Central Criminal Court, Old Bailey
11 a.m.

Mr McIntyre now took to the stand to defend his client Austin Bidwell. He looked across at Mr Fenwick. 'The address he gave to you first,' he said. 'When he was introduced to you was the Golden Cross. Did he mention any address as well as write it?'

'Yes, he mentioned it and wrote it.'

'Have you got that book with you?'

'I have.'

Mr McIntyre took the 'bank book' and pointed at the relevant section. He passed it back to the clerk of the court and asked, 'Then are these your initials?

'Those are my initials to certify that I saw him write it,' Mr Fenwick agreed.

'At that time did you make any enquiries at the Golden Cross?'

'No.' Mr Fenwick then explained that, although he saw Mr Warren two or three times after that, he never witnessed Austin Bidwell write his signature on the credit slips.

Pointing to the signature of Mr Warren, Mr McIntyre asked, 'Did you see him write that?'

'No, I did not see him write it.'

'Was the only address you had from him the address he gave you – the Golden Cross?'

'The Golden Cross was the only one he gave us.'

Which did at least square the circle so far as detectives were concerned. After his first visit to the tailors, a month before, Austin Bidwell had gone to this five star hotel close by Charing Cross Station. Four days later, Austin checked out, never having slept there. Apart from the occasional, fleeting visits, he would not return there for the next year. Nobody at the Bank of England ever checked that he had ever been in residence there nor did any other institutions anywhere else in the world, especially in France over the next few weeks, something that later solved the riddle of where the gang got their money from to fund the fraud.

Saturday, 4 May 1872
Lyon, France

The same Saturday that Frederick Albert Warren opened his chequing account at the Bank of England, the *procureur* in the city of Lyon had a troubling task to perform. The investigating magistrate had come in especially to issue a '*Signalement Important*'.

What had prompted it was altogether a curious business. Over the last few days, Monsieur Clappier had learned that a gentleman called Walter Roger had perpetrated a financial fraud in this same city, following in the wake of similar forgeries being carried out on banking institutions all over the republic.

Whoever had performed these acts seemed likely to be one and the same person as this Monsieur Roger. As he sat collating the information, the magistrate noted that their perpetrator had spoken with a pronounced accent *Américain*. He had brought with him '*lettres de recommendation*' and '*un fause letter de crédit*' which, in the case of the local Lyon Bank, had been used to remove 60,000 francs.

And now on this Saturday, the *procureur* was going to issue the equivalent of an all-points bulletin to every police force in the country. '*Le monsieur*' was aged between 35 and 40, had thick, dark brown hair with a moustache and sideburns which were joined together in the modern fashion. Various witnesses were at pains to point out that there were no distinguishing features. He had a straight nose, set against grey, sunken eyes. He had a thin face with olive skin. And in every case he wore a black hat with a sand-coloured finish in the style of Flambard.

In other words, he was a rakish fellow, and it was, needless to say, George Bidwell. He had arrived in Bordeaux in the name of W.A. Ross on 25 April, and in his memoirs recalled that he had proceeded at once to the bank where they had lavished every attention upon him. '[They] invited me to dinner and a drive through the city afterward,' he claimed. He had presented a forged cheque for 50,000 francs, which, after a slight delay, was honoured.

The next day he turned up in Marseille, where he arrived at the bank of Brune & Co. in the name of Wellington Best. Worried that word of the Bordeaux fraud might have spread, George was astounded at the courtesy which was extended towards him. He was stunned when the smiling Monsieur Brune himself reappeared with his hands brimming with banknotes. George claimed he nearly fainted from relief.

That came to 62,000 francs and, the next day, he obtained another 60,000 francs in Lyon in the name of Monsieur Roger. Given that he had used so many aliases, it was unclear to the French authorities if he was still in the country or whether he had gone to ground after receiving Clappier's signal from Lyon. The police throughout France were never able to find him.

The French *judiciaire* thought nothing more of this until a year later when, inadvertently, they realised they had in their files the answer to something which had baffled their British counterparts. Why had the forgers left the country even before the grand fraud on the Bank of England had begun?

The simple truth was that once they showed up in England at the start of April, the thieves of Threadneedle Street were badly in need of seed capital. Though they were described in some accounts (their own included) as flush from their recent escapades in New York City, it seems more likely that they had squandered most of their money by the end of the spring.

All of the forgers enjoyed life's little luxuries. To start the greater fraud, they decided upon a trip to the Continent to make some more money. Now, all the ink and industry that had taken place in Mrs Thomas's guest house started to make sense. They had forged letters of credit from the North & South Wales Bank in Liverpool under the assumed names of Ross, Roger, Best and Granville Monk. They committed frauds 'by means of bills drawn against forged letters of credit from a Liverpool bank'. These were the same ones which had been bought from a pickpocket in Jersey City by George Engels who had stayed behind in London.

'They also forged letters of introduction from the Union Bank of London in their favour,' the prosecution later determined. And these various enterprises meant they could perform a rerun of Mac and Austin's trip across Europe two years earlier, but with an additional body to help them. 'It was settled that George should pursue the venture alone in France,' Austin Bidwell recalled, 'while I should go with Mac to Germany.' So, in the last week of April the younger pair went to Berlin, Dresden, Bremen, Hamburg 'and other places', the prosecution found. 'George Bidwell between the same dates went to Bordeaux, Marseille and Lyon.' Over the next six days, they realised nearly £8,000, a sum that, the prosecution suggested, was most likely 'the capital for their further operations'.

On Thursday, 25 April after George Bidwell said goodbye to his brother and Mac at the station at Calais, they waited for a train that would take them eastward to Berlin. Later that same evening as they stood on a bitterly cold platform, both of them were amazed at the beauty of the stars. Austin Bidwell, in his later recollections, was equally astonished by his companion who was only a year older, marvelling at his boundless confidence, elegant speech, logical force and fiery enthusiasm.

Mac was one of those people who could pull a rabbit out of a hat. 'What an honourable future might have been his but for his youthful follies,' Austin would later lament. 'Truly, he could have achieved a wonderful success in any honourable career. Unhappily for him, he, like thousands of our brainiest youth, had entered the "primrose way".' Much of George Macdonnell's confidence and *savoir faire* rubbed off on him.

When they arrived in Berlin, though, Austin was more than a little apprehensive. Acting as a lookout on the Unter den Linden, Mac took a letter of credit for £2,600 forged by Engels into a nearby bank, chosen at random. He seemed to take for ever. When Macdonnell emerged, though, he was all smiles. 'Easy money,' he quipped.

'I don't believe you,' Austin replied.

'It is alright, dear boy, here it is,' Mac added, handing over a bag of notes.

Germany was very different from the country they had first visited a couple of years before. Even though it had been the victor in the Franco-Prussian War, reunification had brought with it a change to the carefree atmosphere they had encountered before the war had broken out.

The pair then travelled on to Munich, Leipzig and Frankfurt, 'the home and still the fortress of the Rothschilds'. After making over £40,000 they made their separate ways, via Brussels and Amsterdam, home to Britain, where Austin pronounced himself excited. 'Our ideas had grown with our successes,' he wrote, '[so] we quickly came to the conclusion that it was part of wisdom, since we were already so far in, to secure $100,000 each.' In other words, to defraud the Bank of England.

On the evening of Monday 29 April, they arrived back in London. Mac got there first and checked into the Terminus Hotel at London Bridge Station and was quickly followed by Austin Bidwell. Shortly after that, there was a knock at their door. It was George Bidwell and there was a boisterous welcome.

In his account of their European adventures, George Bidwell claimed he mailed his spoils back to Engels in London writing '*échantillons du papier*' ('samples of paper') on the envelopes. These notes could be exchanged into gold to insulate themselves should the fraud ever be discovered. The police would then just pounce on the innocent who offered the French money, not the forged letters of credit.

But George Engels had not collected them. 'We were encumbered with a large amount of French paper and a bag of foreign gold which could not be offered safely for exchange in London,' Austin Bidwell recalled. So they needed to launder the money in France. Though never confirmed by the prosecution, Austin Bidwell later claimed that he was dispatched to Paris along with a nervous George Engels, who spent the whole journey by train with a bag of gold under his coat which they successfully sold in Paris. By now the worm of doubt about their forger had surfaced: his drinking had increased and he became ever more erratic. If they did not have a penman, who could they actually rely on?

It would be something that came to preoccupy them in the weeks and months ahead. For now, despite Engels' increasing flakiness, the others continued to discuss their grand plan. Austin Bidwell later claimed:

> Exactly how we were to manipulate the bank we did not know. We were inclined, now we had some fifty thousand dollars capital, to avoid so serious a thing as forgery, but had an idea for one of us to obtain in some way an introduction to the bank and to use all the money of the party to establish a credit.

If Mac and Austin had bonded because they were the same age, so did the two Georges, Macdonnell and Bidwell, mainly because they were both ladies' men who enjoyed the whole process of seduction. Later, there would be reports of roistering in the pubs of south-west London and in taverns in and around St Johns Wood. For now, though, during his first weeks of landing in the country, George Bidwell 'adopted another course', as Freshfields wryly noted, 'and one which he subsequently repeated'.

Just before he left for France, George Bidwell had met a young woman at the same hotel he was staying in at London Bridge Station. This was hardly an innocent encounter; railway stations were noted for their streetwalkers. It seems likely that she, too, was a 'fallen angel', a girl down on her luck, borne out by some of George's observations in the letters he sent to her.

George Bidwell had no sooner met Bessie (or in some accounts, Emily) Hamilton before moving with her to her lodgings in Alfred Terrace, Rotherhithe. There, her landlord was introduced to him. Later, he brought with him two trunks, one large black leather one and another of American cloth which ultimately he gave to her. Though he left for France the next day, he returned there the same night he was reunited with Austin and Mac.

He and Bessie lived together for six weeks 'till about the end of May'. The police later established that, as before, Austin and Mac often visited. When they did, she left them to it. George never said what he did or why he was meeting them, nor did she ever enquire.

Early in the morning of the last Tuesday in May (28th), their domestic bliss evap-orated. George Bidwell told her he was going away to Sierra Leone fearing that he would never return alive. He told her to meet him that night at Euston Square Station. She waited, and he was late, which meant he missed the last train to Liverpool. As a result, he and Bessie stayed at a nearby hotel. Nothing further was elaborated in the official files, though the solicitors reported a tender moment. George gave her a watch and hung it round her neck.

'I would like to give up the life I have been leading,' she said with regret.

His parting words were hardly the salvation she might have expected. 'You had better go home to your relatives and see what you could do.' Yet George Bidwell had already promised to marry Bessie Hamilton and take her back to America. En route to Africa he promised he would write, and the prosecutors subsequently found several letters which charted his progress. The first, from Liverpool, was that he was exhausted and now aboard the *Lusitania*, and then 'at sea' two days later, he wrote a few lines 'to my pet know that I am safe so as far as my journey' which he posted from Bordeaux.

He was proud of the fact he had not been seasick. Though the previous month had been thundery at times, there were no storms reported in the Bay of Biscay. George Bidwell, however, seemed more preoccupied by other matters. 'I don't know why it is but I have very bad presentiments about this trip, perhaps it is only on account of leaving you.' Offering her family and mother best wishes, he said he was headed for Bordeaux and Lisbon. 'I have a dread of going to Africa,' he concluded. 'We shall go at all hazards.'

Bessie Hamilton never heard from him again. Intriguingly Mr Barrett, her landlord, later encountered George Bidwell again walking down the Strand close by where, a few months after that, Willie Pinkerton encountered his brother.

While they had no compunction about dropping their women, they were much less certain what to do about their forger. It was, needless to say, William Pinkerton who got to the heart of what really happened with George Engels. 'It was stated by Austin Bidwell on his apprehension,' the prosecution later noted after Pink reported a con-versation he had had with him in Cuba, 'that Engels was employed to do the forgery involving writing but when it became necessary for him to utter the forged documents his courage failed him and the gang had to pay him off and send him home'.

But there was a far more worrying reason, which had a lot to do with George Bidwell's propensity to pick up women whose respectability was called into ques-tion. It was not as if their forger had not warned them: 'They'll get in the way.' 'They'll blab all your secrets.' But they had not listened, and the seeds for disunity had been sown.

George Engels' warnings became far more urgent when, in time, both Georges Bidwell and Macdonnell became infatuated with other young women. Curiously, though, during these same weeks of the early spring of 1872, it was Austin Bidwell, the quietest of the three, who was, by his own admission, suddenly bowled over. Out of the blue, he declared that he had met the girl of his own dreams whom he wanted to marry as soon as he possibly could.

5

Mistresses of Misfortune

> Your own heart speaks for me with more eloquence than any earthly valour can
> — I know you to possess a generous impulsive soul that would shudder to think
> me capable of being untrue or dishonourable in my love for you.
>
> Austin Bidwell to his soon-to-be fiancée, Jeannie Devereux, 1873

Late Spring 1872
Langham Hotel, Central London

The first time he saw her, she took his breath away. She was young, beautiful and clearly very, very innocent. For once, his desire for her had little to do with using someone for the greater needs of forgery and fraud. Austin Bidwell's feelings were genuine, falling helplessly in love with her there and then.

He would write to her, when almost inevitably the going got rough:

And you dear came into my life a bright and beautiful thing, and by your purity and your truth love so won my heart that to tear you out of it the life would follow 'God works in mysterious ways' it is oh so ardent a hope that in his providences he will let this great happiness be mine.

It was heartily reciprocated. She, too, was clearly looking for something – protection, probably. He could provide her with financial security, rescuing her from the world of genteel poverty from which she saw no escape. The niceties of social convention and their mindless perfunctories did not fool either of them. Their relationship would be, pure and simple, a transaction. If that seemed harsh or stark, it would at least be couched in terms of flattery and the conventions of almost penny dreadful romance.

They would each give the other something they needed. In her case, the sanctity of marriage; in his, insurance as the ultimate human shield. When they eventually married – in circumstances neither of them could ever quite imagine – he would write, 'Until the last minute of my life you will be what you have always been, my first, my last and my only love.' And ultimately, she would become the one true victim of the greater affair.

In all the forgers' accounts of their various deeds and misdemeanours, the name of Jeannie Devereux was missing. It was a serious and significant omission. A naive, beautiful English girl then just 18 years of age, she enchanted everyone she met. Jeannie later became Austin Bidwell's wife after a long, painful and at times protracted seduction. Propelled by an overweening, socially ambitious mother who wanted her eldest daughter to marry well, it was hardly a unique kind of relationship for its time.

From what he termed a 'fine English family', Austin Bidwell, for his part, was attracted to Jeannie Devereux because she was 'a pure-souled woman who thought me an angel of goodness'. Her blessed honesty would make a counterweight to his own duplicity. If he could not quite get away with murder, then he would attempt daylight robbery without her ever realising until it was all too late. Ignorance would be blissful, for in her naivety she never realised what her American beau was really up to.

Austin was careful to insulate her from his various activities, and as a result, the prosecution saw her seduction in terms of the worst kind of opportunism. In a briefing document, Freshfields made it clear that Austin Bidwell's intentions did not seem particularly honourable. Yet he professed 'himself to be desperately in love and proposed marriage on the first day he saw the young lady', the prosecutors noted. There was never any doubt in his contemporaneous letters that Austin Bidwell was utterly captivated by such a luminous presence, a typical blue-eyed, golden-haired Englishwoman who would, as he marvelled, 'give herself to me, in all her youth and beauty'. Waxing lyrical, as was his wont, he foresaw that they would retire to a tropical paradise 'where I could bear my bride, and there, turning over a new leaf, live and die with the respect of all good men mine'.

It was never likely to happen. When it became abundantly clear that he was a career criminal who had used her, the prosecution could only marvel at his marriage, spousal privilege being yet another manifestation of his sly and incorrigible genius. 'Austin Bidwell has thus placed it out of the power of his lady to give evidence against him by marrying her.'

When they met in the early summer of 1872, Jeannie was living in a penurious state with her brother, sister and widowed mother. Her father's Indian Army pension barely covered the rent on their property near to Marble Arch. In recent months, the pension had been overpaid and the matter was in the hands of moneylenders. Relatives had clubbed together to launch her on 'the season', and her mother was on the constant lookout for potential suitors.

At first, the elder Mrs Devereux considered Austin Bidwell a wonderful catch, charmed by his perfect manners and good-humoured nature. Out of such myopia came much misery. 'Her mother was foolish,' Freshfields noted, 'and seemed to have no idea for her daughter beyond marriage.'

On their first meeting, Jeannie Devereux believed him to be 'from one of the best families in America' (as she later told Willie Pinkerton). Her mother had already suggested she marry a rich doctor. So far as the elder Mrs Devereux was concerned, the American would be ideal, not least from the dowry that would inevitably result.

According to William Pinkerton, who later spent a great deal of time with her, Jeannie Devereux was first introduced to Austin Bidwell under the name of Captain Hibbey. It was never explained how or why this alias was used. Jeannie's mother had, it seemed, applied to the editor of the *Matrimonial News*, as a result of which Austin was then formally introduced to her elder daughter in that name, the only alias he ever used in her company. ·

'She was a girl who had just come from school,' the prosecution later noted. Both were hopeless romantics and 'the result was that he did his best to obtain an introduction to her. This was made for himself by sitting next to her at a *table d'hôte* in Calais.'

In another account which Jeannie herself told to Willie Pinkerton, she and her mother met Austin Bidwell at a party organised by a friend of her mother's. According to Jeannie, this lady knew her own son 'was a rather wild young fellow' who had met Austin at the Langham Hotel, the first grand hotel of the era, which enthralled royalty and others from the higher reaches of society. The hostess of this party was indignant that both her son and his friend had been invited. Clearly this lady did not like the cut of Austin Bidwell's jib, though Mrs Devereux did.

As Willie Pinkerton later recorded, 'He became assiduous in his attentions to [Jeannie] and was well dressed, lavish in his expenditures of money.' Many other females at the party were taken with him and his good manners (Mac also became enamoured of her sister, Jenny, but she rejected his advances). 'The woman is not at all smart,' Pink himself would regretfully conclude, 'but a thorough lady in all her actions.' Jeannie was young for her age and so timid that she was greatly upset one snowy winter's afternoon when some boys threw snowballs at her. 'She is very good looking and extremely simple,' Willie Pinkerton later wrote, 'has been very little in society and knows very little of the ways of the world.'

Austin Bidwell swept her off her feet and introduced her to a wonderful new world of glamour, travel and excitement, all lavishly funded by his supposed business activities, for as Pink recorded, she never 'dreamt of the real character of

[Austin], his brother and Macdonnell'. In other words, Jeannie Devereux was yet another perfect mark.

At this point during the late spring of 1872, the Bidwells, Mac and Engels had already opened their account at the Western Branch of the Bank of England and were also flush from their recent trip across the Channel. While Austin Bidwell was flawlessly acting the part of the silver king, he was clearly troubled that he had, at the start, hidden his real identity from Jeannie Devereux as 'Captain Hibbey'. What was later termed a small confession – telling her his real name – had little effect on their relationship. Austin Bidwell also claims that he wanted to tell her what he really did for a living but never had the courage to do so.

Thankfully from his point of view, Jeannie took him at face value. The same could not be said of her mother. This revelation about his alias, the prosecution determined, put the elder Mrs Devereux 'somewhat' on her guard. 'She consulted the editor of the *Matrimonial News* whose fees no doubt remained unpaid and was urged by him to have nothing more to say to him,' Freshfields recorded. Jeannie's mother seems to have taken a fast developing umbrage at Austin's increasing influence.

Increasingly, the elder Devereux's baleful presence cramped their relationship, a situation that Austin described as 'unpleasant and unhappy for her'. Even when he was in London, Austin often had to telegraph or write to Jeannie to arrange secret meetings. The lure of illicit sex added lustre to their relationship. Theirs was a clandestine courtship whose correspondence he did not dare send to the Devereux family home in Marble Arch. He often had to use another address in Bayswater where her younger brother Harry would go to collect them. The surviving letters are also fascinating concerning Austin Bidwell's wealth. 'Above all remember that you will have plenty of money in your pocket,' he advised her when they were due to meet, 'and that makes all the world your slaves and you can never be embarrassed.'

Certainly, Jeannie Devereux had only a dim appreciation of what her suitor actually did for a living or why he travelled so much. For now she blithely accepted that he had business interests all over the world. They had only been seeing each for a few weeks that early summer of 1872 when a letter arrived unexpectedly from overseas. It was all the more exotic for bearing a Rio de Janeiro postmark:

> To my extreme regret, dear Jeannie, I have some news to communicate that I fear may be the reverse or at least that way for I think so much of you that it will give me a certain amount of pleasure to think that you will regret an absence that lasts longer than we first thought.

This trip to South America in the summer of 1872 is an altogether peculiar episode. In the same way that they later claimed they had not wanted to rob the Bank of England, their whole reason for heading to Brazil, the forgers were insistent, had only ever come about because they had concluded it would be too dangerous to defraud the Old Lady of Threadneedle Street. A trip to Rio was a sure-fire way of making money that would allow them to return home to the United States and make a new life.

Termed a 'buccaneering expedition' by Austin Bidwell in his memoirs, their motivation was simple. 'There being no cable in 1872,' he noted, 'and it took, as we ascertained, forty days to send a letter from Rio de Janeiro to Europe and get a reply so that if we executed an operation boldly and well, we might hope for anything.'

Almost inevitably, they were putting a spin on what they were up to. In George Bidwell's estimation, after finishing this job they would not have needed to defraud the Bank of England. They would have crossed South America, then headed up the Pacific coast stopping at all the major ports, until they reached San Francisco and would then take the train to New York 'with at least a million dollars in our possession'.

Their South American expedition also involved the novelty of a curious confession from George Macdonnell, the least likely of any of them to admit to anything, let alone anything criminal, in one of the most public of arenas on the last day of their subsequent trial at the Old Bailey. It was an extraordinary occurrence, even by the standards of the often extraordinary behaviour exhibited by George Macdonnell.

Day Eight – Tuesday, 26 August 1873
Central Criminal Court, Old Bailey
2 p.m.

A sense of hazy oppressiveness hung over the courtroom. It had been a long, exhaustive, yet astonishing trial which was already overrunning. With only one day off to date – the Sabbath – everyone present was looking tired and more than ever so slightly irritable. They should have been done by now. There was a sense that everything had played out. At lunchtime, many of the onlookers had left not to return as everything was overrunning, and that meant they would miss one of the more extraordinary exchanges of the whole trial.

The air of pedestrian procedure suddenly evaporated when George Macdonnell's legal counsel now stood up to address the judge directly. Austin Metcalfe QC was nothing if not professional, despite the sense of wounded inevitability which was playing across his features. In the dock, his client smiled smugly with his usual self-satisfied expression and air of superiority. 'The prisoner whom I represent has a wish to say something to the jury,' Mr Metcalfe paused. 'Perhaps Your Lordship under the circumstances would allow that to be done.'

There was a flurry of excitement. The judge's expression spoke volumes. 'What now?' he seemed to be thinking. 'Very well,' Judge Archibald said with a heavy sigh. 'If they propose to address the jury instead of you they may do so.'

'It will occupy no time,' Mr Metcalfe responded as brightly as he could.

'Then they had better do so,' the judge allowed with little enthusiasm.

And with that, George Macdonnell stood up to address the jury directly. All eyes were on him. He looked splendid and somewhat dashing, clearly enjoying the attention and an unerring faith in his own abilities. This, as several onlookers knew, was when he was at his most dangerous. As he began reading from a few square pieces of paper, everyone in the courtroom listened, hanging on his every word.

'The idea of the prosecution,' Mac gravely intoned, 'which they have endeavoured to enforce on your convictions, is that the original intention with which Austin Bidwell, George Bidwell, and myself came over to this country was to perpetrate this fraud on the Bank of England.' He paused and smiled. 'I think if that idea could be entertained, it would argue for us a knowledge and a prescience something more than men of ordinary ability and attainments could pretend to.'

Arguing that there were so many steps needed to defraud the Old Lady of Threadneedle Street, such a complicated daisy chain of probability was hardly likely. 'When we first came to England it was certainly with no such intention,' Mac continued, managing to keep a straight face. 'Mr Green, of Savile Row has told you that the opening of the account with the Western Branch of the Bank of England was an entire accident, and so it was. That was done on the 4th of May, and on the 28th of May we three left England.' He indicated himself and the two Bidwell brothers.

'We left England without the slightest intention of returning. We were to have gone to South America by Rio as far as San Francisco, and thence back to Rio. Circumstances occurred in Rio to induce us to change our minds, and we came back.' As always, he did not articulate what exactly happened.

Those very same circumstances represented, like this plea in the highest court in the land, George Macdonnell at his finest. Chutzpah beyond belief.

Fourteen Months Earlier – First Week of July, 1872 Rio de Janeiro, South America

So near and yet so far. When Austin Bidwell looked through his field glasses, he was stunned. They had already eluded one detective, but now the chief of police himself and their actual victims were rowing towards them after the forgers had boarded the steamer on which they would make good their escape. 'I recognised the manager of the bank and the Hebrew broker,' Austin later remembered, 'both of whom had been pointed out to me.'

All of the gang's various adventures could be characterised by close shaves and catlike escapes. Yet none were so nail-biting nor Houdini-like as those on this blazing summer morning after, Freshfields noted, they had 'swindled two or three merchants in the Brazils and having done this, they were no doubt obliged to leave the country as rapidly as they had entered it'.

What Austin Bidwell had fervently hoped would have been a 'short cut to fortune' was anything but. He, for one, felt that fate had turned against him. As the rowing boat neared, Austin was certain they would never get away with it. But somehow they did, the most outrageous reversal of fortune they ever survived. Even allowing for some of their exaggerations when they came to tell the story many years later, it was the narrowest of escapes from spectacular failure.

It had all started out so well. After the unseasonably dark bluster of late spring in London, the *Lusitania* had arrived in Rio de Janeiro after three weeks of what Austin Bidwell called a 'pleasant voyage into the tropics'. He and his friends represented, he thought, very much the modern day adventurers, 'mild-mannered, soft-spoken, courteous youngsters'.

Now the mystery of George Bidwell's letters to the unfortunate Bessie Hamilton became clear. Exactly as he had written to her he, along with his brother and Mac, had left Liverpool on 29 May, stopping first at Bordeaux and then Lisbon. But after that, the *Lusitania* headed west, out towards South America. 'We were no better than the pirates of old,' Austin Bidwell later said, 'but, instead of the ancient manner of cruising for gold, we travelled in luxurious style, and the only weapons were pen and paper and unlimited effrontery.'

Given that he rarely recorded his thoughts in writing, it was the uncharacteristically verbose George Macdonnell who was enchanted by 'how pleasant a long voyage with agreeable people can be made'. What struck him most were the moonlit nights as they crossed the tropics. He wrote:

> The whole sky was illuminated with a blaze of soft light which bathed the ship, and sea with a radiance that was perfectly beautiful and the track of the vessel behind us was reflected with a brilliancy that seemed to change the phospho-rescent bubbles into gleaming masses of molten silver.

A few hours before they arrived in Brazil, though, there was a reminder of what awaited them if it all went wrong. The *Lusitania* passed close by the island of Fernando da Noronha, most famously visited a few years before by Charles Darwin. It was a harsh, unforgiving prison to which Brazilians were sent and rarely emerged. Their fellow passengers were none the wiser.

'The steamer was a magnificent vessel,' Mac wrote later, 'and of course during so long a voyage the passengers are becoming very well acquainted with each other.' Though privately finding some of them a little dull, their number included an eccentric chaplain, an army captain and his dogs who were going to hunt for a few months on the pampas, an inveterate champagne drinker ('Come, old fellow, will you toss me for a bottle of fizz?') and a party of English civil engineers, as well as their Swedish boss, Captain Christian Palm.

Certainly, the emphasis had been on having fun wherever they could. That often seemed to involve a musical accompaniment, as there was a piano and other instruments to hand. If George Macdonnell's account is to be believed, they also found time to make another form of sweet music. He wrote in a strangely romantic vein:

> We had dancing every night, and what with that and sitting in some retired spot with a pretty girl to make love to after dancing for an hour or two nibbling refreshments and talking all the nice talk a fellow can think of made I think you believe a very charming and beautiful excursion.

Two passengers, one by the name of Gilmour (in some accounts, Gillmore), the other called Henry Amidown (some accounts have it as Amadown), were the life and soul of the party. Ignoring them but also taking enthusiastic part in the festivities was Gregory Morrison (in some accounts, Morris). He became so popular that he ended up thanking Captain Hammell himself for his courtesy and attention on behalf of the thirty-six passengers in a letter that was written a couple of days before they landed in Rio. It was, to say the least, ridiculously effusive. 'Although favoured with clear skies and soft breezes we cannot perhaps say that you have conducted us safely through "tempest and storms" yet we have not failed to notice and admire the fine discipline maintained in every part of this noble ship,' Mr Morrison wrote. All these prosperous Europeans had such a great time that they carried on drinking at the Hotel d'Europe after they had disembarked together.

They landed on a Wednesday morning, 19 June 1872, in what Mr Amidown later declared was one of the finest harbours in the world. Even though it was only just before the southern hemisphere solstice, there was little sign of winter. The brightness and lushness beckoned them onshore to further fun and games. The newly arrived Mr Amidown went to one party which was held in his honour, as well as a ball. Not to be outdone, Mr Gilmour was also invited to the opera by Captain Palm.

Mr Amidown then explored a dozen different gardens and visited a theatre without an apparent care in the world. But if he was trying to maintain anonymity, he rather spoiled it. A Scotsman called Samuel Robinson later testified at the Old Bailey that he had seen Amidown, Gilmour and Morrison on every day of the voyage. After arriving in Rio, Mr Amidown himself handed him his business card. To his bemusement, it read simply 'Biron Bidwell'.

That the gang had used completely different names on board the ship was hardly a surprise. Mr Gilmour was clearly George Bidwell while Morrison was George Macdonnell, whom Austin described as 'the grand swell of our party'. The fact they had pretended not to know each other was part of a well-rehearsed act. 'From the hour of our [departure], we were outwardly strangers,' Austin Bidwell recorded, 'and during the voyage no one ever suspected that we were anything else.'

After finishing their partying, the three of them all separated and stayed in different hotels. Austin Bidwell joined Captain Palm and his engineers who, as a brief for Freshfields later recorded, 'were going to prospect South America for a railway'. This would provide excellent cover for their various needs, and so impressed were they by Mr Amidown that they made him their secretary and handed him all their money.

This interesting vignette is not recorded in either of the Bidwells' subsequent biographies. '[It] is almost needless for us to say that neither Austin Bidwell nor the money remained long with them,' Freshfields added somewhat tartly. 'The fact is he stole it and took it away with him.'

A great deal of mystery descends over their activities in the Brazilian capital, particularly the extent of which banks they targeted. The Bidwells offered tantalising and, at times, contradictory evidence. The obvious choice for front man was George Macdonnell because of his facility for language and fluency in Portuguese. As Freshfields later determined, documentary evidence revealed most of the forgeries had been written in Macdonnell's hand. 'They there obtained from Messrs. Mauá & Macgregor & Co, £10,000 by means of forged letters of introduction from and credits on the London & Westminster Bank.'

In fact the 'Sociedade Bancária Mauá, MacGregor & Cia', to give it its formal title, had been the banker of choice for expanding the railways across South America since its incorporation twenty years before. As with the rest of the financial world, greed, ambition and wilful stupidity had characterised such railway schemes and the forgers realised that they could play to their own strengths in exploiting such greater gullibility.

This, then, was the background to Austin Bidwell's first letter to his girlfriend on the shortest day of that southern winter. Dated Friday, 21 June 1872, Austin Bidwell twisted not just his intent but also the circumstances. 'On my arrival here I found that the Engineer in Chief of the Railway that I am deeply interested in is about to start over the next route of the proposed road (moving to the Pacific coast) and I at once determined to accompany him,' he blithely informed Jeannie Devereux.

Austin Bidwell had taken care to enclose a map on which he scribbled the route he would be taking on this supposed *Boy's Own* adventure. He would, he said, leave in a special steamer and then trek across the jungle to the Pacific coast by the River Panama:

Believe me, my dear girl that really the only regret I feel in this is that I shall be so long separated from you. I feel that in justice to myself that I should take this trip to reason that you would not understand when I tell you I will return to England before I go home purposely (so as I now know).

Austin Bidwell concluded that he hoped to spend Christmas with her but warned her that he might be away for a full year. Claiming he would be travelling with Captain Palm ('a very good friend of mine'), his trip would be hot and dangerous. 'But you may rest assured dear that I will do all I can to hasten the time when I clasp your dear self in my arms and think that we are not to be separated again.'

At best, the Rio job was only ever seen as a dress rehearsal, a get-rich scheme that was, at worst, a quixotic diversion from trying to break the Bank of England. In the event, it nearly scuppered them.

What they had attempted in Brazil was nothing short of a disaster. Everything that could have gone wrong did go wrong. Worse, it helped create a schism with their penman, and far from giving them confidence to defraud the Old Lady of Threadneedle Street, it pointed out gross deficiencies in their modus operandi.

What the three of them hadn't realised was that their fate had already been sealed in London. George Engels had become more of a liability than a 'master forger' (as the press later called him), managing to misspell words on the various forged certificates they had taken with them. 'By an irony of fortune we carried with us that which was going to balk all our fine schemes,' Austin Bidwell later commented. Their forger, pointedly, had declined to join them.

Whether it was through alcoholism or sheer carelessness, George Engels was sloppy. The London & Westminster Bank had already notified its clients that in future all such letters of credit would have to be signed by both manager and assistant manager. 'Nothing could induce [Engels] to put on both names,' George Bidwell later noted, 'although he might have done it in a few minutes'. Engels refused.

This telling omission did not deter George Macdonnell who was, according to Austin Bidwell, almost champing at the bit so eager was he 'to go to the front' a few hours after arriving in Rio de Janeiro. Their first objective was to cover their expenses. 'This would be paid in Brazilian paper,' Austin later wrote, 'which I would exchange for sovereigns.'

With a gold-tipped cane and a small bag of diamonds, Mac appeared to be a successful businessman when he entered the Mauá Bank. The manager said he would be delighted to exchange their letters of credit. Still posing as Gregory Morrison, Mac said he would call the next day. On that morning (most likely Thursday, 20 June) he was followed at a safe distance by the Bidwell brothers. They waited around the corner, all too aware that Mac was, in Austin's later estimation, 'naked'.

Inside the bank, Mr Morrison was treated suspiciously. One of the clerks noticed that the English sub-manager's name was missing from the letter he brandished. 'This is singular,' he said. 'There is only the name of Mr Bradshaw, the manager.' Claiming it was the London bank's fault, Mac left the premises with what Austin called a look of chagrin and vexation on his face. Back at Mac's hotel, all were aware of the precariousness of their situation. The two younger men were convinced they had been rumbled, but George Bidwell was made of sterner stuff.

It was time for a bold move. 'There are other letters of credit,' George announced, holding another of Engels' forgeries up to the light. He turned to address Mac. 'Take this pen and write in the sub-manager's name.' Handing him a glass of brandy, Macdonnell quickly forged the signature. Such Dutch courage worked, and within an hour he was back at the branch and the manager honoured the request, though the suspicious clerk at the counter was less than impressed.

They had got away with it, barely. 'We presented our letters of credit at the banks and obtained about $75,000 without much trouble,' Austin later breezily remembered to a reporter. The figure was wildly exaggerated for, all told, their total haul was much less than £10,000. But Austin Bidwell's conclusion in that later interview was searingly honest: 'Our greed in trying to raise more nearly cut short our career then.'

Despite the oversight, they did at least now possess sufficient money to cover their expenses in Brazil. Austin Bidwell later claimed he had visited the three largest money brokers in Rio to launder their profits into gold. These sovereigns were stuffed into ten bags, £1,000 each, for which they had to employ porters to move them.

'So we had one big fish landed,' Austin later wrote, 'and confidently counted on several more.' For the next week or more, they all went travelling to the interior. And by the time of their return in the last week of June, they wanted to cash a final pair of forged letters that Engels had prepared, each for the sum of £20,000.

'We expected a nervous day,' Austin later wrote in his memoirs, 'not such a paralysingly nervous one as it proved to be.' They targeted another bank in the capital. When he entered it, Mr Morrison seemed to be delayed there for what seemed like hours. Watching from a park outside, the brothers were convinced something had gone wrong. There also seemed to be a great deal more activity inside the premises. Unable to contain himself, Austin went inside and saw, to his relief, Mac and the manager sitting with what he termed an 'eagle-eyed man' whom the two brothers had seen entering the building.

Here, confusion enters their stories about the stockbroker who was consulted regarding the provenance of the other letters of credit. In Austin's later account he was called Meyers, in George's, Solomons. Whatever his name was, Austin called him 'a sharp young Israelite' who noticed something was wrong on one of Mr Morrison's letters. 'Why, sir, here's the word "indorse" misspelled,' he said. 'Surely the clerks in the London banks know how to spell!'

At that, Mac decided not to push things any further. He stormed off in a huff, saying he would take his business elsewhere and never redeemed that extra £40,000. At this point in Austin Bidwell's account, they noticed someone deliberately shadowing George Macdonnell. 'I followed him,' Austin Bidwell later said, 'and was soon satisfied that he was keeping Mac in view.' While their friend went shopping around the busy streets of the Brazilian capital, the Bidwell brothers followed his tail from a safe distance. 'This set of double hunt was kept up until dusk when Macdonnell returned to his hotel,' Austin wrote, 'unconscious that a moment later his "shadow" entered the place.' They knew they would have a couple of days, at most, until they were found out.

It was now imperative that George Macdonnell leave the country, for he was the only link to the forgeries. As a matter of routine, all passports were held by the authorities. 'When ready to leave the country [the visitor] must take his passport to Police Headquarters and get it right visaed,' Austin recalled, 'at the same time notifying the police of the steamer he proposes to sail on.'

A mail steamer was scheduled to leave the following Tuesday. To avoid detection, they knew that if Mac was to make his escape he would also have to assume a brand new identity. The police had no idea who the actual front man for their scheme was or what he looked like. Only by the forging of a name in a passport would they be able to get away with it – if that forgery, unlike their others to date, would pass muster.

All of them possessed American passports which could be altered. Austin Bidwell says he changed his brother's to the name of Wilson and then amended Mac's passport in his real name to tally with the description of George Bidwell. They would effectively swap identities. (It is significant that the name of 'George Wilson' was one the elder Bidwell had assumed the previous winter on their extended trip around the American south-west.)

Later the same evening, the Bidwell brothers sneaked into their friend's hotel unnoticed by his shadow. George Macdonnell told the brothers that he was going to head to the railway station in the morning with someone he had met in the bar. 'He is going to Sao Paulo by the same train,' he explained, 'and seems a good fellow, for I had a long talk with him.'

When Mac described him, Austin Bidwell was stunned. It was his shadow. 'What in the world can you be thinking of?' Austin exclaimed. Undeterred, Mac booked both himself and his shadow on their trip to the interior. Early the next morning while it was still dark, he entered a reserved compartment, ahead of the detective who had with him a great deal of luggage. In the pre-dawn dark, Mac stepped down onto the tracks, crossed the rails and walked onto an adjoining street. Austin was there to meet him and they both sped away in a carriage. As an additional precaution, they all stayed in a tavern where they had each registered under false names, the sovereigns still separated in their bags and hidden among their luggage.

After lying low, the fraudsters were ready to leave early the following week. They were relieved to find they could board their mail steamer late on the evening before the *Ebro* was due to depart on the early morning tide. It was a beautiful evening and nearly midnight when Mac and the brothers took to their cabin. Austin had spent most of the day hanging around the bank and the police headquarters pretending to wait for his passport. There was no hint that anything had gone wrong.

By daybreak on the Tuesday, they thought they had got away with it. 'The room had been hot and stuffy,' Austin recalled, 'and the noise of stowing cargo had helped to banish sleep.' Mac, as bidden by the Bidwells, remained in his state room. When Austin heard the screws start, he felt he could walk out onto the deck. And so just after seven o'clock that early July morning, he made out a rowing boat in the distance pulling hard astern 'the sight [of which] made my heart give a great thump'.

This was, he later admitted, the tightest bottle he had ever been corked up in. He headed straight back to the cabin. 'Boys, everything is all right,' Austin said as calmly as he could, 'keep perfectly cool.' He had already noticed Lieutenant Barga, the local police chief, in the rowing boat. To his horror, he now saw him walk up to the ship's agent who had been holding the passenger manifest when they had walked onto the ship. As part of their precautions, his brother had made it his business to become friendly with the agent.

Mac, in the meantime, hid under the berth and the brothers piled orange crates in front of him. George sat on a camp stool minding his own business. 'How do you do, Mr Wilson,' the agent said somewhat apologetically when he walked in with Lieutenant Barga. The chief of police merely nodded and they departed. Moments later, George Macdonnell, in Austin's words, 'half-roasted came from behind the bags of oranges'. Ten minutes before departure, the Bidwells also left so that Mac, in Austin's recollection, could speed 'northward ho! with Wilson's passport'.

In his later relating of what had happened at sea, George Macdonnell told them there had been one heart-stopping moment. As the *Ebro* passed the prison island of Fernando da Noronha, its sheer desolation made him shiver with fright. Worse, 200 miles out, the ship's engines broke down. For the best part of an hour, Mac thought he would be doomed to return to Rio, where imprisonment would have been inevitable. With just under £10,000 in gold sovereigns about his person, he could hardly claim he was an innocent holidaymaker. More likely, he would be recognised as Gregory Morrison and fate would turn against him.

'How slight a thing may change the whole future life of a man.' So later noted George Bidwell about George Engel's obstinacy, but it could equally have applied to the predicament George Macdonnell found himself in adrift in the Atlantic. Thankfully the engines of the *Ebro* were fixed and Mac returned to Europe[5] to take Engels' place as he was 'a skilful penman' in George Bidwell's estimation.

According to his memoirs, George Bidwell claims that their trip to Brazil was hardly a failure. They had, he said, made $40,000 in gold. In the rather more accurate account of Freshfields, it was much less than the £10,000 they had bartered from the Maúa Bank.

Those bags of sovereigns made George Macdonnell extremely paranoid on his own return. According to George Bidwell, he stayed in his state room aboard the *Ebro*, never venturing out to take meals or walks on the deck 'for fear it may be stolen'. He wanted to get rid of their spoils at the earliest opportunity. 'As the gold was too heavy a load to lug about,' Mac later explained by letter, 'and likely to attract attention, I went to an English firm of brokers doing business in Lisbon and purchased Portuguese stocks.'

When he returned to London, George Macdonnell – using the name 'Harry', a pseudonym he often used – wrote to someone in New York identified only as 'Friend Phil'.[6] For once, he was uncharacteristically honest. '[The] business upon which I have travelled several thousand miles has been a lamentable failure,' he noted, 'but luckily the matter is not so bad as it might be.' The experience, he claimed, of that failure 'will I am sure be successful'.

Intriguingly, Austin Bidwell had come to the opposite conclusion about their jaunt to Rio. In the future, he later wrote, 'if success did come, the success would in the end prove a failure'. That difference spoke volumes about their characters, for as Freshfields later noted, it was the 'great caution he compelled his associates to use and which they neglected as they became more prosperous'.

The Bidwells had made their own way home a few days later. First, they had altered Mac's real passport to fit George Bidwell's description. Then they travelled across the pampas to take a French steamer from Montevideo to Marseilles. The brothers took care to destroy any incriminating evidence in their possession.

For once, there were no particular adventures at sea, and the brothers returned to Europe with their tails very much between their legs. It was 17 August before the Bidwells reached Marseille. Straight away, they telegraphed Mac care of Bowles Brothers, a branch of an American bank at Charing Cross on the Strand. 'Just arrived well. Poor success in shipments. Shall we meet you in London or Paris? Telegraph or write Hotel Bristol, Paris. Austin.'

It seems likely that George Macdonnell never received this communication, as he had been visiting friends and relatives in Ireland for the first half of the month. The police later determined he was in Fleetwood on the Lancashire coast on 16 August, where he probably had landed by steamer from across the Irish Sea. By the 21st, the prosecution determined, he had been occupying 'room No. 14 at the Queen's Hotel, Manchester'.

Two days earlier, the brothers had sent another more urgent telegram from Paris: 'Meet us here if convenient.' As it was obvious their friend was not yet in London, the brothers returned and stayed at the luxurious Langham Hotel. Two days later, Mac turned up, and the prosecution determined that the two Georges met up every day for the next week and went out together, doubtless roistering during this first week of their return.

It was a cause of much puzzlement that Austin Bidwell was never settled for very long at any one particular hotel. '[His] movements are not so easily traced,' the prosecution later recorded. 'He was, as we have said, exceedingly shifty and never stayed long at any one place. Sometimes he had as many as three lodgings in occupation at once, never stopping any length of time at any one.'

That late summer of 1872, he had one objective above all else. To renew his acquaintance with Jeannie Devereux. Within days of returning home, they were seeing each other again and, ironically, with the very thing in mind that had brought them together originally – matrimony.

Despite her mother's serious misgivings, by now Jeannie 'had made up her mind to marry', as the prosecution noted. 'Either clandestinely or openly she frequently saw and corresponded with Austin Bidwell,' Freshfields also concluded. Whenever she could sneak away from her mother, Jeannie Devereux spent time with her beau as she was never quite sure how long he would be around for.

If business was hardly thriving that August, then other affairs of the heart soon would be. In what might be termed 'amorous activities', George Bidwell was never one to be outdone. The elder Bidwell was a serial adulterer whose dedication to chasing women went far beyond the depredations of the *droit de seigneur* which was then common.

Some time that third week of August, George Bidwell once again picked up a young girl, this time on Regent Street. Very quickly, he grandly declared he was madly in love with her, was going to take her away from it all, and for once, genuinely seemed to mean it. Her name was Helen Ethel Vernon, whom he usually called 'Nellie' and sometimes 'Ethel'. 'She is a girl of but limited education and of no position,' the prosecution later determined, 'the daughter of a second rate veterinary surgeon and has evidently been acquainted with the ballet if she has not danced herself.'

Almost inevitably, Nellie was young, beautiful and fell for him straightaway for reasons which were depressingly familiar. 'As far as we can recollect,' Freshfields would discover, 'she had a quarrel with her relations, ran away from home and as a matter of course went on the town.'

'Went on the town'. Without spelling it out, what this meant was that the authorities knew perfectly well that Nellie Vernon was a glorified streetwalker. The mention of Regent Street was significant as it was a notorious hangout for prostitutes in Victorian London as, indeed, were railway stations at one of which George Bidwell had met his previous inamorata. Nellie Vernon was just one of the innumerable 'fallen souls' who participated in the 'circulating harlotry' round the streets of London.

The Victorians had a peculiar prurience towards prostitution, regarded as one of the greater social ills of the time, which was regularly accompanied by thunderous condemnations. By the 1870s, though the moral panic about prostitution had abated somewhat, their number were estimated at anywhere from a few thousand to hundreds of thousands.

Though a woman reigned at the very apex of society, Victorian London was still very much a man's world. Females were still generally disparaged and dismissed throughout a male-dominated society. 'Women were regarded as the weaker sex, physically and mentally,' one economic historian has written of the prevalent attitudes at this time, 'unfitted for full involvement in the world.' When Queen Victoria herself lamented on the marriage of her daughter in 1859 that her fellow gender was 'born for man's pleasure and amusement', she was expressing a widely held view.

There was also a great deal of hypocrisy in society, when supposedly 'respectable' men were regular and unapologetic users of the services of 'disreputable' women. Many waifs and strays had worked as servants and then drifted into transitory 'sexual commerce' after being dismissed or having become pregnant by the very men they were working for. Some of these 'dollymops', as they were often known, supplemented their earnings as dressmakers and milliners. 'The best of a series of unattractive alternatives,' as one assiduous reviewer of the subject has stated, it was 'difficult to distinguish what may have been a traditional bartering of goods in exchange for sexual favours'.

It is fairly obvious that George Bidwell would have been aware how Nellie Vernon was making her living. George always prided himself on his abilities at seduction, not least in finding glamorous women who were excited by his faint aura of mystery, his raffishness and, of course, the money. Certainly, the women with whom the forgers came into contact in London were from the higher echelons of society.

'I first saw Mr George Bidwell and Mr Austin Bidwell at Covent Garden Theatre, London, in the beginning of September last,' Nellie later explained on the stand (though this was clearly wrong: they had already met by then). 'George Bidwell was with me at the theatre, and the other two came in and were introduced to me there while we were in a private box.'

Whatever the reality of their meeting, they formed a great bond. Nellie Vernon and George Bidwell started walking out with an abandon that was entirely characteristic. There was no shame in their relationship and they were playful together in public. Within days, he began writing her a flood of billets-doux, usually concerning their social arrangements. In one, George says he 'will be with my little sweetheart at the hour named 4 p.m. this afternoon and trust to find her as sweet and blooming as she has remained in my thoughts'. 'How are you today?' he asks in another. 'Has our darling survived the dissipations *de la soir*?' he teases. Another note refers to their going to the theatre together, briskly informing her that his carriage would arrive fifteen minutes before the performance started.

Prostitute or not, social conventions remained rigidly in force. Nellie Vernon never invited gentleman callers to her lodgings at 11 Dukes Road, near to Euston Station. According to her landlords who were later interviewed by police, she never entertained anyone there. So far as they were concerned, their lodger lived quietly and respectably.

When they started seeing each other, significantly, Nellie possessed no jewellery. That would change very quickly as George Bidwell had a curious interest in what might be termed 'Victorian bling'. On his first day back in London, he went to a jeweller's where he bought a walking stick. The tip was set with gold and diamonds. The fact it was inscribed 'G.M. – from George and Austin' would play a curious role in their subsequent apprehension by the forces of law and order. 'It was found on Macdonnell when he was apprehended in America,' the prosecution later noted.

In a pub on Long Acre four days later on 24 August, George Bidwell made the acquaintance of a jeweller called Benjamin Nathan and bought the first of several pieces from him. As he had little money on his person, the jeweller agreed to meet the American at the Terminus Hotel at 1 p.m. (even though he seems to have been staying in the more luxurious Langham). George paid him with Bank of England notes. Austin and Mac were in attendance taking coffee. The money was genuine, though the alias he gave, Charles Warren, was not.

One of the pieces of jewellery he purchased was 'peculiar enough in its own way', a bracelet which he later gave to Nellie Vernon. In his usual breezy manner, he told her it had originally been his mother's and 'had been in the family for two hundred years'.

By now, the problems with George Engels[7] were terminal and would have a serious impact on the timing of the greater forgery upon the Bank of England. Whether it was wisdom after the event, but both the Bidwell brothers reckoned their forger had lost his bottle. Discussing the matter with Willie Pinkerton in Cuba a year later, Austin Bidwell suggested another reason. 'He talks too much to detectives,' he claimed.

But according to Engels, the shoe was very much on the other foot. George Bidwell's burgeoning relationship with Nellie Vernon was the cause. Unless he gave her up, it was claimed by a later New York chief of detectives, their penman had threatened to cut off business relations with them. 'Engels became frightened when informed that the women knew all about the scheme,' Inspector Tommy Byrnes later noted, 'and with his share of the plunder, disappeared.'

In another version of the story, Walter Sheridan – whom Willie Pinkerton always thought was involved – also claimed he fought shy of these 'disreputable women' and wanted nothing more to do with the greater fraud for exactly the same reason. In yet another account, the police were 'morally certain that Engels was the real leader of the plot against the Bank of England,' another newspaper would claim, 'but they confess their inability to legally connect him with it'.

As to when Engels had actually left Great Britain, there are equally conflicting accounts. 'Upon my arrival in England I wrote to our German friend and gave him particulars,' Mac had written to 'friend Phil'. This implies George Engels had already left England by the end of August 1872. Yet the police were never able to confirm this and Austin Bidwell later informed Willie Pinkerton that 'our German friend' had returned to New York almost straight away after their return from South America. In another account it was as late as November, after which time Engels opened up a gambling house in Manhattan. Six weeks later, he then supposedly disappeared.

In fact, Pink determined that Engels did not arrive in the United States until January 1873 under circumstances which made the detective even more suspicious about what had really gone on. 'His confederates have become afraid of him,' the detective noted. 'They had some words and Engels was given $10,000 in gold to keep him quiet.' When quizzed in Cuba, Austin Bidwell later claimed that in spite of their good treatment of their forger, Engels had obviously blabbed their details in both London and New York. 'I need hardly tell you that it is not the case,' Pink confessed to his brother, 'but I did not tell Bidwell so.'

Thereafter, George Engels continued on his travels around the world and remained in contact with Austin Bidwell even when he was subsequently incarcerated. The irony is that, given that the Bidwells and Mac were jailed 'as a warning to prevent forgers from coming into Europe', it singularly failed. George Engels continued his forgeries which culminated in a spectacular that had been planned by George Wilkes. Later described by Inspector Tommy Byrnes as 'one of the most extraordinary chapters of crime', it was yet another 'big thing' which would have seen a great many banks swindled all over the Continent at the end of the decade.

Central to its execution was George Engels who, in the summer of 1879, settled in London with his family and, according to several accounts, lived like a prince. He was, however, subsequently arrested on the first day of 1881 in Italy, suspected of planning to issue vast amounts of 'forged mercantile paper' in support of this greater forgery. After the usual legalistic run-around, he was successfully extradited back to the United States. The forger died five years later after a lingering illness where, one contemporary chronicle makes clear, he had become 'an impoverished man in spite of the large sums he had made during his career'.

In George Bidwell's estimation, George Engels was a coward to the last, having squandered $1 million or more, and 'died prematurely, leaving his family destitute'.

In that same last week of August 1872, George Bidwell moved into Nelson's Portland Hotel in the West End of London. The manageress, Kate English, remembered him when later questioned by detectives. She recalled that he told her he had been previously staying at the Langham on his own. A couple of days later he asked her a pointed question. 'Could you tell me of somewhere quiet,' he asked, 'a watering place that I might go for a day or two?'

'Eastbourne,' she replied without hesitation. The Victorians regarded the south coast, with its villas and genteel charm, as the very acme of sophistication. The more well-to-do would often venture there to take in the sea air. Thanks to the London, Brighton and South Coast Railways, so would George and Nellie over the upcoming August Bank Holiday weekend.

'The train leaves Victoria at 6.30 p.m. for Eastbourne and I shall be there waiting to help you out of the cab,' George informed her in yet another note. Though undated, it was presumably written early on the morning of the last Friday in August when detectives determined they had left for the south coast. They went on their own and it was here where they consummated their relationship. The lovebirds came back on the Sunday, the first day of the new month.

Within a day, the letters continued. George Bidwell hoped she was as refreshed as he was after their recent holiday. 'Nellie's George', as he describes himself, 'woke this morning from pleasant dreams of somebody, I shan't tell you who it is and I know it would make you ever and ever so bad.'

That same Monday morning, George informed Nellie that 'his friends' would break-fast with him at 11 a.m. – the thieves of Threadneedle Street had quite a lot to discuss. After staying in England for a few more days, George Bidwell suddenly told Kate English that he was leaving. She should forward on any letters that came for him to Paris, as well as any others addressed to his brother or Mac. 'He left with me a letter for Mr Hills,' Miss English later testified, 'but he did not say when Hills would be likely to arrive.'

The letter to 'Friend Phil' suggested it would be imminent. 'I hope to see you towards the middle of November,' Mac had written, implying the greater fraud would be done by then. Enclosing $400, he then made an altogether more curious claim. Mac said he had wanted to either send a draft bill or dollars – 'It is with considerable difficulty that a person can procure Greenbacks here at all,' he complained. He ended with a horribly ironic statement; he was worried about their 'safety from the infernal thieves in the New York Post Office. I shall register the letters.'

Bizarrely, in all their later writings, the forgers tried to downplay that they had wanted to 'hit' the Bank of England that same autumn. Certainly, that was exactly what George Macdonnell later claimed on the stand. 'There is no doubt at all the intention was to close the account with the Bank of England because it was of no use,' he concluded on the last day of their trial. 'But when we came back to England it was of considerable use and advantage to us to cash any documents that might come in our possession.'

Austin Bidwell, too, claimed that he had been to the Western Branch of the Bank of England the week before he sailed for Brazil. He had, he maintained, told Mr Fenwick that he was going to St Petersburg and wanted to close his account. 'He begged me not to do so,' Austin wrote of the under manager, 'said many flattering things to me, and urged that it would be convenient to have an open account in London.'

The only problem with these claims is the more reliable testimony of Robert Fenwick, who was under oath. Though the balance of Mr Warren's account was low (which normally prompted a closure) by the end of May 1872, Mr Fenwick had no recollection of such a conversation. 'I will swear that he did not speak to me about closing his account during last year, nor did I advise him not to close it,' he had said on the stand. 'I never remember his speaking to me about closing it.'

In other words, the forgers had no intention of clearing the account. Far from it, for when Frederick Albert Warren returned to the Western Branch in early September, he told officials that he was going to be spending more time abroad. Which, ironically, was true. Over the next three months, Austin and the two Georges would, in Willie Pinkerton's later estimation, journey 'backwards and forwards between England and the Continent'. Certainly, the most significant development so far as Nellie Vernon was concerned came when they shortly headed across the English Channel.

Second Week of September 1872
Trouville, Normandy, France

It could have been a scene painted by Claude Renoir. A young, beautiful woman, picking sea shells, watched intently by her older beau, smiling in the sunshine, happy and content, both determined to enjoy themselves. The summer was over but they would have this wonderful holiday together. There were the casinos, where they spent much of their time, and the associated glitz and glamour. There were the fantastic hotels as well as the marvellous meals they feasted upon. More than anything, they would have time to themselves. Alone, away from the others. That was what she really wanted. Now she had her man, she did not want to share him with anyone. But, as she would find to her increasing annoyance, she would have to, for sometimes business – and his brother – held a far greater sway.

For now, all seemed to be well. It was yet another glorious memory, a snapshot in time before the recriminations, the fights and the shadows of deceit consumed them both. On the endlessly sunny beaches of Normandy, Nellie Vernon had no idea that everything was not as it seemed. And for his part, George Bidwell was completely smitten with her, in all her delightful beauty and the foolishness of youth. She was more than just a passing distraction.

If their relationship had caused the break with their penman, it did not matter. They had money, some measure of security and now, after the tribulations of the early summer, they could plan ahead. Later, as the daylight faded, they returned hand in hand to their hotel, where Nellie, for all her neediness and youthfulness, had the pleasure of seeing something she wanted more than anything in the world. There, written in ink in the registration book, the names she had never dared hope she would see so soon after their meeting the month before – 'Mr & Mrs George Bidwell'.

As the summer turned to autumn, there was a sense of make or break. 'In all nearly five months had elapsed since Green had introduced me to the Old Lady whose impregnable vaults we had now at last determined to loot,' Austin later claimed. 'That in itself was a favourable circumstance, as it would give me a chance to flourish in a grandly indefinite way.'

After the recent failures in Brazil, the forgers had regained their composure, secure in the fact that, far from George Engels' fears, their women were not just useful protection but provided them with a cover for their activities. And, now, as they began the next stage of the fraud, they were confident of their ultimate success, for they had already secured a human sacrifice.

6

The Skewering of Colonel Peregrine Madgwick Francis

> How Austin Bidwell conceived the scheme and with the aid of his associates carried it almost through, I don't profess to understand. It was a capital instance of misapplied genius; one feels inclined to reiterate the old formula of the Judges in passing sentence on clever tricksters, and say that if he had only bent his talents in the direction of honest work, he might have obtained legitimate fame; as it was he only obtained the distinction of a place in the list of great criminals.
>
> Sir Harry Poland, counsel for the prosecution, recalling the events of 'the trial of the century' (*Seventy-Two Years at the Bar*, 1924)

Wednesday, 3 September 1872
Western Branch, Bank of England, Burlington Gardens,
London

The American gentleman who walked into the branch on this gloomy September morning was clearly tanned, fit and well-to-do. He was greeted by the manager, who was effusive, reassuring and, so far as Austin Bidwell was concerned, hopelessly out of his depth. As soon as he shook his hand, he knew. They would have no problems defrauding the Bank of England. 'Entering the bank, I sent in my card,' Austin Bidwell later recalled after having walked in through the ornate portico, 'by a liveried flunkey, and was immediately ushered into the manager's parlor.'

Finally, he could relax. In his guise as Frederick Albert Warren he certainly looked the part, but the surroundings helped too. The branch was more like a gentleman's club, rich in mahogany and gold, and its opulence was matched by his effortless superiority. As with all high net worth customers, Mr Warren was offered a sherry and biscuit. Though he did not say anything about it to the newly appointed manager, Mr Warren had obviously been travelling. He was polite, restrained and well mannered. Fascinating, too, for as he discussed his future plans, it struck the manager that Pullman carriages, like the visitor, were an American byword for luxury and efficiency.

When it was all over, blame would attach itself to this same fellow, the splendidly named Peregrine Madgwick Francis. He had been a colonel in the Royal Engineers, working in the Raj before returning to England to begin a solid, if until this point unspectacular, career on the lower rungs of the banking establishments. Several observers wondered if that was why he had been played so effectively. He was simply no match for Austin Bidwell's cunning and guile. The astute American had reported as much when he went back outside, where George Macdonnell and his brother were waiting. The message was simple, 'Our way to the vaults of the bank was wide open.'

Day Two – Tuesday, 19 August 1873
Central Criminal Court, Old Bailey
11 a.m.

Harry Bodkin Poland, a dapper, squat adornment to all the most important trials brought by HM Treasury over the previous eight years, was a well-known and, more to the point, well-liked figure in legal circles. Admired for his scrupulous fairness as well as his lucidity and forcefulness, his was a methodical and understated style.

The 44-year-old Harry Poland always ensured he had a meticulous mastery of the facts. He had been called to the bar in 1851 and would remain there for seventy-two years, an achievement which provided him with the title of his autobiographical memories (he died just a year short of a century). Engaged by the Crown in the more important cases of the day, it is said that he came up with the defence of kleptomania and also refused to accept a high court judgeship.

'Mr Poland's fame rests chiefly upon his achievements as a criminal lawyer,' noted one later profile. Such greatness would be needed, thanks to the sheer volume and size of the transactions in this great fraud. Reducing them into something digestible would play to Harry Poland's strengths, which were very much on display during this day in court: clear headedness, a firm grasp of the details 'and the most untiring and marvellous industry'.

Now, as he stood up, Poland's face was a mask of concentration. On this grey summer morning his greater task was to show just how plausible Austin Bidwell could be, as his first witness took to the stand. In the preceding hour, on this second day of the trial, the tailor Edward Green and the colonel's colleague Robert Fenwick had shown how easy it was to open a bank account with the Bank of England. Now the prosecution would show the jury how that account had been flooded with fraudulent money. Far from being more than a little dull, it was soon, against all expectations, riveting.

Possibly he never saw it coming, or perhaps, given his military background, he was only doing his duty and covering for his superiors. But when Colonel Peregrine Francis walked slowly to the stand and was sworn in just after eleven o'clock, he had little idea about what was going to hit him.

After recalling that he had been on annual leave for Frederick Albert Warren's first few visits, Harry Poland prompted Colonel Francis to recall the stranger who had walked into his office just under a year previously. 'Who was that person?' he asked.

The colonel looked towards the bar. 'The furthest from me,' he said. Austin Bidwell remained impassive, the faintest smile playing across his lips. 'He bought some Portuguese bonds,' the colonel continued, 'and asked me to take care of them for him.' These were genuine bonds purchased two days earlier from Jay Cooke & Company in London.

'Were they of the face value of £8,000, not the market value?' They were what the colonel called 'the nominal value'.[8] This was the amount an issuer would buy them for after they had been redeemed by a customer. Such a transaction allowed for any interest accrued. Mr Fenwick, who had previously dealt with him, brought the American into the colonel's office and introduced him as Mr Warren. 'Did he sit down in your room?'

'Yes.'

'And did you have some consultation with him?'

'Yes.'

'And in the course of conversation about the bonds what did he say about himself?'

'He told me generally what he had come over to England for.'

'What was that?' Harry Poland wanted to know.

'That he had come over to introduce sundry American inventions, first and foremost among which was the sleeping cars and some other inventions, but that was the principal one. He did speak about a steam brake and I asked him some particulars about it, which he declined to tell me as it was a secret.'

As before, Mr Warren had explained that he wanted the rail cars to run on the line between the French and Austrian capitals to transport visitors to the forthcoming Grand Exhibition in Vienna. Intended by the Habsburg dynasty to show off its power and splendour, when the exhibition eventually opened in May 1873, it had been an abject failure and suffered calamity after calamity.[9] But when he talked about it with Colonel Francis, it seemed a sure-fire investment hit.

The subject of international travel now prompted further questions from Harry Poland. 'What more was said?' he asked.

'That he hoped afterwards to introduce a company for the same purpose into England and that then he hoped to have a good account at the branch,' Francis explained, 'but I understood him to say at that time he was simply working this foreign line to introduce them on this foreign line.'

'Working to introduce them on to this foreign line?'

'Yes.'

The judge looked across. 'From Paris to Vienna?' he asked.

'Yes.'

Mr Poland continued. 'Did he say at all where he was working?'

'He said that he was going to work at Birmingham.'

'Was anything more said about Birmingham then?'

'I don't think there was anything more said about Birmingham at that time.'

'Was that the substance?' Poland wanted to clarify.

'That was the substance of the conversation.'

'Do you know what countryman he is?'

'An American.'

Again, the judge was intrigued as to what exactly had been discussed. 'He told you that he had come over from America?'

'Yes, and there was no doubt about that.'

'The cars are American cars are they?'

'Yes, sleeping cars.'

Little more needed to be said at the time. Like all the best cons, Mr Warren's claims were driven by the purest sliver of plausibility. It was a curious coincidence that, in February 1873, when forged bills were coming thick and fast from Mr Warren in Birmingham, George Pullman himself had addressed shareholders of the Midland Railway in the same city to celebrate the signing of an agreement which would introduce the 'vestibule' Pullman carriages in Great Britain. In other words, the news added to the forgers' credibility. In all their endeavours, the Bidwells followed the zeitgeist. Indeed, Mr Warren clearly seemed to know what he was talking about and Colonel Francis recalled a telling detail from their exchange about railway carriages. 'No country,' his visitor had added, 'in the future will be able to do without them.'

No country could also do without bills of exchange which formed the basis for the fraud that now fell upon the Bank of England. Despite its complicated nature, their central role was fairly easy to comprehend.

Bills of exchange had essentially modernised the money market by smoothing the passage of international trade. Though they had been used since antiquity to transfer money between countries, when traders had used them as notes for consignments of goods, and to allow for time and travel, payment would usually come due in three months' time. They were the bitcoins of the steam age, treated as legal tender and whose very issue and provenance was largely unregulated. This same unquestioned acceptance would essentially drive the fraud forward. As such, they were glorified IOUs and, once the provenance of a customer had been established, their use was open to abuse. The system assumed that only 'unimpeachable' bills would be presented. It was always said an old bill broker could 'smell' if a bill was not genuine.

The Bank of England would invariably discount them as the lender of last resort, essentially propping up the system as a whole ('its semi-permanent position of some-times recalcitrant long stop,' as one recent chronicler has put it). In other words, the buck stopped right here at the entrance to the Old Lady of Threadneedle Street.

There was little sense that crime was behind Frederick Albert Warren's transac-tions in the autumn of 1872. Harry Poland gently guided Peregrine Francis through them, occasionally referring to the 'the bank book', the account ledger which was propped up in front of him. The colonel was clearly embarrassed at the facility with which he had eased the greatest ever fraud in recorded history. On his very first day of their dealings, Mr Warren had blithely filled up a form for the acceptance of the Portuguese bonds. He had signed it in the colonel's presence. In essence, it was a voucher which allowed him to receive and hold these bonds on his account. The next day, he had returned and bought £4,000 worth of the same securities.

'This constituted a portion of the prisoners' capital with which they were to work their account,' Freshfields noted at the start of the trial. Mr Warren was clear that he wanted the whole of them sold, fixing a limit to their sale price ('41¾ I think it is'). Again, Colonel Francis wrote out the request and Mr Warren signed it in his presence.

'Did anything pass between you on that occasion?' Poland asked.

'Nothing particular, I think.'

For the rest of the autumn, Mr Warren sent in genuine bills from his travels around the Continent 'from which they were to forge the signatures of the various parties to the bills,' the prosecution recorded.

'Again and again, I went to the Continent repeating the operations until at last my credit at the bank was solid as a rock and we were ready to reap our harvest,' Austin Bidwell would later record. As a result, financiers in France, Germany, Austria, Holland, Belgium and Portugal would soon become victims. So, too, would the state banks of Russia and Turkey in London.

Nobody ever checked his real identity. Nobody thought he was not genuine, espe-cially Peregrine Francis. 'I did not see him at all times he came into the bank,' the colonel recalled. 'It was not necessary.' By his later reckoning, Mr Warren came in 'sev-enteen or eighteen times', and 'perhaps I may have seen him seven or eight times.'

It was the exception to the rule that began with Frederick Albert Warren's next visit in person to Colonel Francis. In the boastful phrase of Austin Bidwell, it started the wheel turning for, as he later noted, 'it only needed the mastering of a few details to cause the bank to grind out a few millions of its dearly prized gold'.

On Halloween, Mr Warren bought two bills for £500 each, which were due on 3 February. 'He asked me whether I would discount these bills for him,' the colonel recalled. 'I said I must inquire about them first and see. I took them down to the City and got permission to discount them for him.'

Normally, the Old Lady of Threadneedle Street would not deal with anybody who had walked in off the street. Customers were usually only well known to the bank. But as with the opening of his account, the usual checks were not carried out. 'Head office' in Threadneedle Street agreed to discount them. The bank's high-ups, like the colonel, had no reason to suspect their customer in Mayfair who in the weeks that followed was slowly building up his capital.

Colonel Francis did not see Mr Warren personally to inform him that there had been no problems. He did not need to because, as the prosecution would note, 'the case from the 4th May to the 29th November is [one] of perfect regularity'.

Colonel Francis had occasion to remember that same last Friday in November when Mr Warren appeared again. There would, the American said, be further transactions. 'He might ask us to discount a few more bills of the same character,' the colonel now explained on the stand.

'He said he might?' the judge asked, seeking clarification.

'Yes.' And, indeed, Mr Warren did. When Colonel Francis next saw him in person it was Monday of Christmas week, 23 December 1872. The American informed him that he was going to Birmingham to attend to business about his workshops. 'He would send us a few bills of the same stamp as those we had had from Birmingham,' the colonel recalled. Which, again, he did. The bank received a letter from him on 30 December, which contained ten bills amounting to £4,307 4s 6d. 'They were all genuine bills and were all paid at maturity,' one newspaper reported.

As the New Year of 1873 dawned, the balance on Mr Warren's account was £3,600. Colonel Francis came to regard Frederick Albert Warren as a good customer with access to private capital. 'He represented himself as a commission agent,' Colonel Francis had previously testified, 'and in my own mind I thought these bills showed that he was well supported by friends abroad.' The bank manager had no idea how he came by these bills, they were self-evidently genuine and that was all that mattered.

At the start of the New Year, as a matter of routine Austin applied for and was issued with a new cheque book, which the prosecution anticipated might imply negligence, for he had yet to use the old one. As the brief for Mr Poland stated, they 'were cheques made payable to "order" and not "bearer" and this is sufficient answer if any answer were necessary.' What they did not spell out was a fatal flaw in the bank's supposed systems of security: anybody could cash them with no questions asked. Once started, they could not be stopped.

The next steps would be equally effortless. 'At that time it was not the custom of the bank to send acceptances offered for discount,' a later police chief remarked about the case, 'to the acceptors for verification of signatures. Upon the lack of this precaution, the gigantic forgery scheme of Austin Bidwell and his confederates was founded.' With Colonel Francis' final audience with Mr Warren, the next phase of the operation could begin.

Friday, 17 January 1873
Western Branch, Bank of England, Burlington Gardens, London

The weather was terrible. It was a cold, dark day in London, even by the usual standards of this bitingly harsh and horrible winter. The New Year had been unyieldingly wild and windy, with gales and heavy rain lashing the country, and the Frederick Albert Warren who walked (though, painfully limped would have been a more accurate description) into Colonel Peregrine Francis's comfortable office reflected that. He was evidently relieved to be inside and for the chance to sit down.

Indeed, he looked quite unlike any of his earlier appearances. It was the same fellow, no doubt, a point that the colonel was sure to make in virtually all of his later testimonies. But herein lay the rub. From this point onwards other Warrens – a tortuous complexity of them – would make appearances in London and other cities all over the Continent as well.

But this was the same man, and the colonel was amazed how ill Frederick Albert Warren looked. His face was badly bruised, his eyes looked swollen and he was clearly in agony. As he was escorted into the room by Mr Fenwick, a patina of almost oriental politeness suffused their conversation. No reference was made to his injuries when, a short while later, Mr Warren brandished one particular bill with a flourish. 'There,' he said in an almost offhand way, 'I suppose that is good enough for you.'

Both officials saw that it was a bill of exchange drawn on Rothschilds in Paris, the very byword for financial probity. 'Would you discount it for me?' Mr Warren asked. The colonel acceded simply because it looked genuine. Once again, the American mentioned Pullman carriages. 'I hope to see sleeping cars introduced shortly abroad,' Warren said, 'so that an English tourist might use them on going to the Exhibition at Vienna.' He also mentioned a patent brake and also a signal light for placing in front of the engines, the kind of innovations which were reluctantly added refinements for the appalling rail safety records of the time.

Mr Warren explained that he had the choice of three different factories in Birmingham. 'I am going there at once,' he said, clearly oblivious to his injuries. 'I hope to commence business by the first of February.' As that was only two weeks away, no wonder he was in such a hurry.

Austin Bidwell's recollection of these same events had a great deal more exaggeration. There was, however, a basic kernel of truth: the bank did not have a clue what on earth was being unleashed. In his later recollection, he asked the colonel if forgery was possible. He was emphatically informed that it was not.

'Why impossible?' he replied. 'Other banks get hit sometimes, and why not the Bank of England?'

The manager visibly bristled. 'Our wise forefathers have bequeathed us a system which is perfect.'

Austin Bidwell merely twinkled in response. As he was leaving, Colonel Francis finally asked him how he had come by his injuries. 'I had a bad fall from a horse,' he said, not providing any further information as to when and where. After that, his valued customer disappeared into the cold, wintry gloom. 'I do not think he was even at the bank after that day,' the colonel later recalled on the stand. 'I never saw him.'

That Rothschild bills was behind his injuries. The whole ghastly business all stemmed from what Austin Bidwell called 'a supreme test' of their skills. It came from his brother's insistence that they needed to give their forgeries the imprimatur of respectability.

George Bidwell was adamant that his younger brother should 'go to Paris and get a bill on London from Rothschild drawn to the order of F.A. Warren direct'. Citing it 'a pretty nervy thing to do', they knew they would have to pass muster with the most famous financial institution in Europe. Targeting Rothschilds was, to say the least, the ultimate act of chutzpah at best, and complete and utter folly at worst.

'We tried to talk George out of this notion,' Austin said of him and Mac. But his brother was insistent and so, against his better judgement, Austin Bidwell reluctantly volunteered to go to the French capital. It was an enterprise that damned near killed him.

There had been little sense of impending doom when, on the freezing Sunday evening before, 12 January 1873, Austin Bidwell had taken the regular ferry train from Dover and then connected to the late mail train from Calais to Paris. Just after 2.30 a.m. local time, close to the town of Marquise, about 10 miles south of the coast, there was a terrible accident.[10]

The train crashed. The engine, tender and luggage van derailed and at least two carriages were mangled. There were several fatalities, including those of the driver and stoker. One *graisseur* (oilman) and four passengers were slightly wounded. Among them was Austin Bidwell. He was thrown around like a mouse in a cage. Though he later claimed his own injuries were 'trifling', for once he was underplaying things. He became jammed within some wreckage and was also wounded by splinters and glass all over his face that came dangerously close to his eyes. Taken away on a stretcher, he recovered quickly though he was still traumatised and suffered 'a nervous shock which took some weeks to wear off'. For quite some time he still had a painful leg and running sores from where his ribs had been cracked.

The aftermath provided him with a golden opportunity to gain sympathy, but for now Austin Bidwell was anxious to get to the French capital. At 6.30 a.m., the train and mails continued on to Paris. Obviously looking the worse for wear, Austin later maintained that he went straight to the bank, but it was more likely to have been the next day. With plasters on his forehead and limping badly, he took a carriage to Rothschilds on rue Lafitte – more akin, he thought, to a nobleman's palace on an open courtyard – where Baron Alphonse himself received him.

It helped that the baron was a director of the railway company whose train had crashed. Austin Bidwell was certain the old man felt guilty and seemed to feel personally responsible. 'This was not a usual transaction or one which Messrs Rothschild should have entered into with a stranger,' Freshfields later concluded, 'but Messrs Rothschild ever activated by the kindest motives. But for the accident it is probable that Austin Bidwell might have asked for the bill in vain.'

Despite his injuries, Austin Bidwell returned across the Channel in triumph. In his memoirs, he says he had successfully played what he called his 'trump card' on the Rothschilds, sending a telegram to London: 'The Egyptians all passed over the Red Sea, but the Hebrews are drowned herein.' If this was ever sent, it was never found.

Perhaps it was significant that the first person Austin Bidwell went to see after his return to London that second week of January was George Macdonnell at the Coburg Hotel, a gothic yet salubrious establishment (now known as the Connaught) in the West End of London. When Austin walked in, his friend was horrified. 'Mac, I have had a most miraculous escape from instant death,' Austin said after taking a whisky. Not only was he covered in bandages and plasters, he could only walk with the help of a gold-topped cane. All the colour had drained from his face, and he was clearly in considerable pain.

On the last day of the trial, Mac recalled how his friend's accident had bonded them even closer. He grandly declared:

Austin Bidwell had probably as narrow an escape from instant death and being smashed to pieces as any man ever had. On arriving in London he was in such a condition that it was almost impossible for him to move. He was helped from the station to the hotel where I was then stopping, and visited by a physician (Dr Coulson), who told him he was in very great danger of being paralyzed for life, that his spine was affected.

Both of them claimed that the accident had forced Austin Bidwell to take stock. 'He told me that it was his intention to utterly withdraw from anything connected with this or any other similar matter,' Mac later lied on the stand.

'It took a day or two to make sure that the acceptance of Messrs Rothschild was properly copied and engraved,' the prosecution later noted. By the Friday of that week, Austin was sufficiently recovered to take a carriage to Piccadilly with his friend. 'I went with him as far as the door,' Mac later testified, 'and afterwards helped him back to my quarters.'

He would only stay in the country for a few more days. This would be his last ever visit to Colonel Francis's office. There was more play-acting, and the prosecution noted, 'he almost seemed to be wearied with the difficulties which the Bank of England interposed in his way to prevent him discounting and their apparent excess of caution'.

It later transpired that he had wanted more, much more. 'There is no doubt that Warren, in asking for a £20,000 bill asked for a great deal more than he expected to get,' Freshfields concluded. 'He was accordingly cut down and had to be satisfied with a bill for £4,500 which we have no doubt was equally satisfactory to him.' Up to this point, and including this Rothschilds one, all the bills were genuine.

So far as the Bank of England ever knew, Mr Warren subsequently carried out the rest of his business by mail with greater frequency than before. They did not realise what he was up to until it was far too late. 'From that date,' Colonel Francis had already noted at the Mansion House, 'the account suddenly grew to vast proportions.'

If his arrival at Colonel Francis' office at the start of the previous September had seen the start of one strand of the scam, Austin Bidwell's departure from London at the start of 1873 signalled its successful conclusion. With Frederick Albert Warren now out of the country, by definition all the subsequent bills arriving in later January and February in his name were obviously forged. They were forwarded to the Bank of England from Birmingham, which George Bidwell repeatedly visited in the guise of Warren. There, he introduced himself to various landowners as a businessman looking for a place to build a factory. In case they attracted too much attention locally, George made sure that he was never watched when he went to collect the correspondence with the Western Branch.

It was, as Austin Bidwell would later remark, an anxious time for his friends. Amazingly, nothing went wrong. 'Everything smiled upon them,' Austin later noted. As remarkable as it may seem to posterity, in the weeks ahead nobody checked on his provenance or even those of the bills coming in the post. 'In these days of the telephone and telegraph,' an American police chief would later remark, 'this precaution will involve only a slight delay, if the application is authorized, and the cost of this reference will not be grudged by any honest applicant.'

Simple checking would have unearthed the scam straightaway. As it was, Colonel Francis did not suspect a thing about all the 'perfectly regular bills' which turned up in the post. 'I looked upon them in the same light as the others,' Colonel Francis had already testified at the Mansion House. Their significance was spelled out by the prosecution in their briefing document. 'From this point,' Freshfields had concluded, 'the Bank of England was practically at the mercy of the forgers.'

Tuesday, 19 August 1873
Central Criminal Court, Old Bailey
12 p.m.

On the stand, Peregrine Francis now consulted his records and read from them where necessary. The Wednesday after his final audience with Mr Warren (22 January 1873), Colonel Francis received the first registered letter in the post from Birmingham. It also contained three bills, two for £1,000 and one for £2,250, purportedly drawn by H.C. Streeter, another alias used by George Bidwell. It was accepted 'payable three months after date' by the London & Westminster Bank.

And now, back in the Central Criminal Court, this first bill – the one for which the indictment had been issued – was read out, igniting a great deal of interest when it was entered into court as evidence. 'Do you pledge yourself that that letter is in Warren's handwriting?' Mr Poland asked.

The colonel looked uncomfortable. 'I do not undertake to say that.'

At this point, the judge wanted clarification. 'What is the signature?' His Lordship asked.

Colonel Francis stared hard at the letter that was handed to him by the clerk of the court. 'The signature to this letter now I look at with the knowledge I have now – I do not think this is Warren's signature.'

There was an echoing silence in the Central Criminal Court. 'Is it an imitation of it?' Mr Poland asked.

'It is an imitation of it, I should say,' Colonel Francis agreed.

'And at that time did you take it as Warren's signature?'

'I did at the time,' he said carefully, 'having no suspicion.'

'And the endorsement on the bills?'

'The endorsement on the bills I should say are an imitation of his. There are certain little characteristics wanting.'

'At the time did you take them as his endorsement?'

'At the time I took them as his endorsement.'

⚬⚬⚬

There was a buzz in the court. Had the colonel really meant what he appeared to have said? That far from being certain all along, he had harboured doubts? That the

Old Lady of Threadneedle Street had evidence for the fraud six weeks before it was actually discovered? And that they had not done anything about it? For the defence, it opened a great window of opportunity.

The bank – in the form of Colonel Francis – had essentially admitted gross negligence. Austin Bidwell himself was genuinely amazed that such a conservative institution had asked him for no personal or credit references, nor any addresses of his business or residence. 'Had I related my story to any banker in America I would have been told that I had escaped from a lunatic asylum,' he later remarked.

So why had the colonel discounted them? George Bidwell had a simple and engaging theory. As he was new to the job, Peregrine Francis was eager to drum up business. It was not naivety which had informed the colonel's looking the other way, but toadying to his bosses, 'to increase the business as much as possible in order to make a grand showing at the head office'.

After Austin Bidwell's departure, the false bills came thick and fast. On 25 January, £9,350 had been placed into the Warren account thanks to bills which carried forged acceptances from Rothschilds, Blydenstein's, Suse & Sibeth and the International Bank of Hamburg. All were similar to genuine ones which had been endorsed before. Colonel Francis discounted them without question. Throughout February 1873, the rate accelerated.

On the third of that month eleven bills were received, all similar in appearance to bills that had previously passed muster. In his covering note from Birmingham, Mr Warren explained that he did 'not find myself yet able for the journey, still suffering greatly from my fall or rather its effects; but I hope to see you before long. Please direct as last, as I am staying with a friend a short distance out of town.'

The enclosed amounted to £11,072 18s 6d. 'I discounted them and put the bills to his account in the same way as before,' Colonel Francis explained on the stand.

'What do you say as to the letter?' Mr Poland asked.

'The signature to the letter is very bad indeed. It is not so good as many of the others – not so like the signature.'

'Does it purport to be an imitation?'

'Yes, I passed it at the time as his signature, but I say – looking at it now in my present experience – that it is a bad imitation.'

Again, a wave of astonishment passed through the court. 'What do you say to the signature on the bills?'

• 'That is a better imitation than the letter,' the colonel said, 'if it is an imitation.'

'Do you believe the signature on the bills to be Warren's or not?'

'Well there is an indecision about them which makes them very doubtful but I passed them at the time.'

Judge Archibald wanted to double check something. 'Was this a registered letter?' he asked.

'Yes, all the letters were registered that came from Birmingham.'

It got worse. On 4 February the next letter came with acceptances from Rothschilds, the Bank of Belgium and Holland, the Anglo-Austrian Bank and the International Bank of Hamburg and London, Blydenstein's and Baring Brothers. All were highly regarded financial institutions whose provenance would hardly be suspect. Yet one particular bill in that batch, Colonel Francis now admitted, had caught his attention. It had been drawn by a banker in Rio de Janeiro on the Hamburg account.

The prosecution noted in its briefing document:

> This is a bill for £2,500 described in the body of the bill as twenty-five hundred pounds, and it was to use a technical American phrase 'raised' by the Prisoner Macdonnell from Twenty-Five pounds, its original amount, to that of £2,500. For the original amount, namely £25, the bill is genuine as are also the signatures. The Ink has been discharged with acids and the Body of the Bill carefully filled in with Ink of the same colour.

In other words, as Mr Poland now acknowledged, it was forged. 'It is a bill which has been altered from £25 to £2,500,' he now said, to astonishment in the court.

'The acceptance is genuine?'

'Yes, to the bill for £25.'

'That was refused payment?' Mr Poland asked.

'It was refused beyond £25.'

'You find it acknowledged as a bill for £25?'

'For £25.'

A pause. 'Are all the others returned as forgeries?'

'Yes.' Crucially, that had been after the discovery of the fraud, just four weeks later, on the first day of March.

There were times when the colonel looked distinctly ill at ease. Perhaps he had a suspicion that he would be held up to ridicule, 'blamed in some quarters for having been too confiding and for not making sufficient inquiries about his new customers', as one chronicler of the bank's activities later put it. Yet Colonel Francis had been ordered and diligent. He acknowledged receipt of each batch of bills by letter and addressed them to 'F.A. Warren, Post Office, Birmingham'. On 10 February, he received two bills amounting to £4,642 19s 4d. Three days later, on 13 February, there were fourteen further bills totalling £14,696 16s 2d.

Mr Warren mentioned 'that I am gradually but slowly recovering,' in passing a covering note, 'and also am succeeding thus far in matters of business to my wish.' With the dispatch of the subsequent bills, there was no further mention of illness.

On 21 February, there were sixteen bills, worth £14,686 15s 4d. On 25th, another sixteen bills worth £19,253 10s 3d. And then the last, dated 27 February, two dozen bills, worth £26,265. As these arrived at around the same time as the balloon went up, the judge wanted to know more. 'On what day did you credit the account with that?' he asked.

'On 28 February.'

These bills prompted the discovery of the greater fraud itself that same Friday evening when Frank May came across them in Threadneedle Street. By then, there was nothing that could be done. All the earlier, fraudulent bills had already been discounted. But were there others in the pipeline?

That was what Austin Bidwell would boast to Willie Pinkerton just two weeks later. 'The English bankers don't know how badly they are going to be hit,' he boasted, implying that there were a great number of other forgeries in the system that had yet to be discovered. In the event, there were not, and the fearful rumours – that the whole banking system had fallen victim – were false.

Further embarrassment for Colonel Francis came with the cancelled cheques connected to Frederick Albert Warren's account. There had been fifty of them in each of the two passbooks which had been issued to Mr Warren. All had been used up before Austin Bidwell had left for Paris but, as the prosecution established, 'the signatures to the whole of these are written in the same ink with the pen and they are all blotted so that the ink is faint and it is quite clear that they were signed at one and the same time'. It was a significant observation. 'This, of course, gets over the question of the handwriting and the imitation of the signature.'

In fact, the bodies of the cheques on the Bank of England were filled in by George Bidwell, and all were now shown in court. 'There are eleven here,' Colonel Francis later explained, 'they are all out of the second cheque-book.' Their provenance now prompted Austin Bidwell's defence lawyer to make doubly certain.

'Before they are read I should like to ask a question or two,' Mr McIntyre said. The judge agreed. 'You say the signature of the cheques are all Warren's?'

'Yes,' Colonel Francis answered.

'And the filling up of his cheques is not?'

'Will you let me look at them again,' the colonel replied, before quickly scanning the entry in the book. 'I can't say that the filling up of this is his writing, but the signature I have no doubt about.'

Mr McIntyre looked across at him. 'You had no doubt about those other signatures which are not his?'

'At the time I passed them,' Colonel Francis replied. The court was suddenly very quiet.

'Why do you say that those are his?' Mr McIntyre asked.

'Because I have studied it a good deal and I know all the peculiarities of his signature now.'

Mr McIntyre tried a different approach. 'How many times have you seen him write?'

'Three times.'

'Did you see him write more than his signature?'

'No,' the colonel replied, 'on those occasions the forms were filled up by somebody else and signed by him.'

'Are they the only times you have seen him write his signature?'

'They are the only times I think I have seen him write.'

Mr McIntyre weighed this statement up. 'And it is from that that you judge?'

'And from our signature book also which was signed in the presence of Mr Fenwick.'

At this point, Justice Archibald intervened. 'Does your cashier refer to the signature book before paying cheques?'

'If the cashier has any doubt about it.' The only problem was, no cashiers throughout the city had any such suspicions either, about any of these forged bills at all.

To summarise, Mr Poland then asked Colonel Francis a pointed question. 'The total amount of money drawn out after 22 January when the first lot of forged bills came in was £100,405 7s 5d.'

Colonel Francis, only too aware of the vastness of the fraud, replied simply, 'Yes.'

'The total of the bills returned as forged is £102,217 19s 7d.'[11]

'Yes.'

By now, it was lunchtime and several of the jurors were visibly wilting. Though it was cool for August, there was an oppressive humidity pressing down from the rainy skies. Small wonder that when one of the jurors asked if they could be allowed out – literally – for air Justice Archibald said he would do what he could to help them all.

Tuesday, 19 August 1873
Central Criminal Court, Old Bailey
2 p.m.

After lunch, Colonel Francis was recalled to the stand, well aware that things would get worse still. The defence now used the colonel's earlier admissions to hammer home the point that the bank was grossly negligent. If Peregrine Francis had known as early as January that there were suspected forgeries, what had possessed him to keep paying out the money?

Mr Warren's defence lawyer would now try to portray him as a bumbling fool ill-suited to the modern world of finance and went in for the kill straightaway.[12] 'Have you in the books of your bank the addresses of your customers?' he asked.

'Yes.'

'Of every instance?'

'Of every instance.'

'When was your attention first called to the account of Mr Warren?'

Colonel Francis admitted that he had not looked at it on his return from leave because it was 'an ordinary drawing account', with what some noticed was a defiance in his voice.

'The address was the Golden Cross Hotel was it not?'

Colonel Francis smiled. 'But an ordinary account would not be allowed to be over-drawn and it would not matter what the address was.'

Mr McIntyre was not happy. 'That is not an answer to my question. The only address you had of his was the Golden Cross Hotel?'

'Quite so.'

'Was there a description of him in your book?'

'Simply at the head of the ledger is a commission agent, Golden Cross Hotel. You will find it in the ledger.'

'That is so in the ledger, is it? "Commission agent, Golden Cross Hotel"?'

'Yes.'

'Did you ever make any enquiries at the Golden Cross Hotel about him?'

'Certainly not.'

'Quite so' and 'Certainly not': stock responses from a shocked – or at least, embar-rassed – official trying to save face, as George Bidwell later described it. '[On] being pressed on these points,' he wrote about the bank authorities, 'they had "forgotten" or could only say "to the best of their belief" and so on.' It was a stance that did not fool anybody.

Colonel Francis then went over all the payments until the end of the year. Colonel Francis reiterated that all the bills received before 21 January were genuine and paid at maturity.

'I suppose you acknowledged every batch of bills?' McIntyre asked.

'The bills were acknowledged.'

Mr McIntyre continued. 'I may take it up to the 21st of January, you wrote them to the Post Office, Birmingham?'

'Yes.'

'Has the Bank of England a branch bank at Birmingham?'

'Yes.'

Now the matter of inconsistencies would be raised once more. After reading Mr Warren's letter from 28 December 1872, Colonel Francis acknowledged that he had not received another until 21 January, which he was now holding in his hands.

'Now I ask you to look at the bodies of these letters,' Mr McIntyre asked. 'Did it not strike you when you received that letter of the 21st January that the body of it was very different to the body of that of the 28th December?'

The colonel stood his ground. 'It did not strike me certainly.'

'Does it now?' Mr McIntyre said, his haughty *froideur* seeping through the court. 'I am taking the body of the letter. Does it strike you as being very different?'

'It is somewhat different,' the colonel allowed.

'Somewhat – is it not very different?'

There was an eerie silence in court. 'There are some differences.'

Mr McIntyre paused. 'You say it did not strike you at the time?'

'No,' the colonel said, 'it did not strike me at the time.'

'In the other letters that came with the other bills from the 21st of January to the 28th of February did not they strike you as being different from the letter that you had first from him on the 28th of December?' Colonel Francis was clearly reluctant to admit his liabilities. 'There is a general similarity between them all which without suspicion being excited would not attract attention?' McIntyre continued.

It certainly attracted Lord Justice Archibald's attention. 'That is in all the letters after the 21st January?'

'After the 21st of January,' Mr McIntyre confirmed. Turning to the witness, he went for the kill. 'You know at first you swore positively to all these letters being in the handwriting of Warren?'

'I believed them to be so at the time.'

'When did you change your opinion?'

'Of course, since that I have studied his handwriting a good deal.'

Mr McIntyre was not happy. 'When did you change your opinion?'

'I cannot say exactly when, but after a process of study was Mr Chabôt called in?' (This was the most famous handwriting expert in the land, who had yet to appear as an expert witness in the Old Bailey, though he had done so at the Mansion House two months previously.)

'I do not know anything about Mr Chabôt,' the colonel said. 'I have only seen Mr Chabôt to speak to him quite lately.'

'I do not want to know about your speaking to him,' Mr McIntyre said. 'Were those documents submitted to Mr Chabôt?'

'I dare say they were.'

'Don't you know it?'

'No, I do not.'

At this point, the judge interrupted. 'Unless suspicion was aroused you think there was a similarity to prevent your noticing the difference?' he asked the witness.

'Yes, I did not notice any particular difference.' The colonel's relief was palpable, and the faintest glimmer of a smile played across several onlookers in the crowded courtroom.

In Victorian England, there was one man synonymous with the serious investigation of handwriting. Charles Chabôt was a lithographer of Huguenot descent who lived and worked in Red Lion Square close by Holborn Station. His expertise and professionalism ensured that he became the expert witness of choice in many of the famous trials of the era where, as the *Dictionary of National Biography* puts it, 'his testimony practically determined the decisions'. This included the concurrent case of the Tichborne claimant which, after many years of involved wrangling over the right to an identity, continued to rumble through the courts, as well as the Junius one – a century old riddle concerning the identity of an anonymous letter writer – on which the lithographer himself had written a book in 1871.

'I have made handwriting my study for many years,' Mr Chabôt had said at the Mansion House on 27 June. He had 'examined all these documents alleged to be in the writing of Austin Bidwell' and found them to be genuine. In his opinion, they were in the same handwriting as the signatures in the books of the Bank of England, the ones at the tailor's, the Continental Bank and the particular bill of the indictment, that of 21 January, the first one of many which had been posted from Birmingham.

Although Mr Chabôt admitted that he had never seen any of the forgers actually write, he had based his judgement upon all the documents that the various witnesses said Austin Bidwell had signed. 'I have examined the admitted handwriting till I have become fully acquainted with it,' he would conclude, 'and then I compare that with the handwriting in dispute.'

What was the real proof that the prisoners had actually committed the forgeries? What is today known as the 'discipline of questioned documents' was in its infancy. Expertise came from the forensic examination of shapes, slopes, spaces and pen pressure, noting similarities between specific letters on the page.

When Charles Chabôt was examined in the Central Criminal Court a week hence, one of the defence attorneys, Mr Ribton, who was acting for Edwin Noyes Hills, attempted to goad him. As ever, his words were couched in the oleaginous flattery expected in the highest court in the land. 'In the course of your long and valuable life,' Ribton began, 'I believe you have made some mistakes about writing.'

After further provocations over the fact that he had been wrong in one particular case involving a will ('I have never admitted that it was not a forgery,' Chabôt acknowledged) he pointed out that this particular case had yet to be settled.

'We all know you are conscientious man,' Ribton continued, 'but the most conscientious men sometimes make mistakes.'

Mr Chabôt did not rise to the bait. He merely added that he was cautious, and pointed out that whenever similar cases had been tried again his verdicts had always been secured.

'Always?' Ribton asked.

'Always,' came the defiant reply.

Tuesday, 19 August 1873
Central Criminal Court, Old Bailey
3 p.m.

The contrast was striking. When Mr McIntyre came to consider the two letters of 28 December and 21 January – the last genuine one and the first forged one – it was evident that the former appeared to have been written in a much larger and freer hand. 'Certainly,' Colonel Francis acknowledged, '[it] is much more cramped.' The signatures, too, looked larger in the January letter.

'Now I ask you, with the knowledge that you now have, don't you believe the body of the letter is not in the handwriting of Warren?' Mr McIntyre asked. 'Take your present knowledge. Take that letter now and with your present knowledge will you say that the body of that letter is not in the handwriting of Warren?'

Colonel Francis held it awkwardly in his hand. 'I believe it may not be,' he said slowly, 'but I think the signature is.'

'Stop a moment!' Mr McIntyre implored. His words resounded powerfully. All was quiet in the courtroom. 'I will come to the signature presently. Does the signature appear to be written with the same ink and at the same time?'

'It looks like it.'

'I may take it, may I, as your opinion that the signature was written at the same time as the rest of the letter.'

'I do not say that at all.' A pin could have dropped at this point.

Once again, the judge intervened. 'I understand you to say that you think the signature is Warren's?' he asked the colonel.

'Yes, but I say the colour of the ink is very much like the colour of the ink in the writing,' Francis replied. 'It looks pretty much the same colour.'

Biding his time, Mr McIntyre continued. 'Does it appear from the position it holds with respect to the rest of the letter as if that and the last line of the letter had been written at the same time?'

'It is a very natural position.'

'And is it not stiff writing like the body of the letter, larger but stiff writing?'

'No.'

'Do you mean to say it is not a stiff signature?'

'No.'

'Well I do not understand you. Do you say it is not a stiff signature?'

'I do not consider it as a stiff signature.' The colonel clearly was going to stand his ground.

'Is it as free a signature as this, in the other letter?'

'I think so, quite – look at the two R's.'

Mr McIntyre could not have cared less about such details. He was more interested in getting an admission from the witness that he had changed his mind. 'You know that you have been examined several times upon this matter?' he asked.

'Not upon these two.'

'But generally upon the handwriting. Was it after your last examination that you changed your opinion as to these other letters being in the handwriting of Warren?'

'I do not know.'

'Is that so?' The courtroom was on a knife edge.

'I do not know what time the last examination was about handwriting,' the colonel stated.

'Was it when you found that Warren was not in this country at the time these letters were written from Birmingham that you changed your opinion about it?'

'I do not know.'

Though the forgers liked to claim that they had hit the ground running, in one of the first bills they had forged – for £1,000 drawn on the London & Westminster Bank which George Bidwell had sent from Birmingham dated 21 January – there was what Colonel Francis termed a 'peculiarity' in the stamp of the London & Westminster Bank. 'Here is a "B", the colonel said looking directly at it, 'and the word "bank" is not finished.'

'Is that a peculiarity?'

'Yes.'

'Did not that lead you to make enquiries into the genuineness of the document?' Mr McIntyre said slowly.

The colonel shrugged. 'Or that might easily have escaped finishing the stamp,' he replied.

'You did not notice that at the time then?' McIntyre countered.

'Yes I did.'

'Did you make any enquiry at that time?'

'I made enquiries to this extent that all the bills, for a very considerable period, were shown to the headquarters previously to being discounted.'

'Do you mean that you sent them on to your bank?'

'I either took them or sent them down to the head office to know whether I should discount them, before they were discounted.'

It was not as if headquarters had been any more perspicacious. Throughout the month of February, none of Colonel Francis's superiors in Threadneedle Street had objected to his making such large discounts to this particular customer.

'Every fortnight a statement of discount business was sent to the chief office,' the colonel explained.

Yet there had been another near miss which nobody at the bank had picked up on. Colonel Francis had referred to this amazing oversight as a 'hitch' in his earlier testimony at the Mansion House. It concerned one or two of the endorsements on bills which were dated 25 January 1873 and 21 February 1873 for £3,400 and £4,500 respectively. 'The payee's name was not the same on the latter,' Colonel Francis had noted.

These inconsistencies had nothing to do with the solvency of the customer. They were of a certain class of bills which he had been instructed by Threadneedle Street not to discount. They were passed, but around this time the colonel said he was 'looking out anxiously to learn the address of the works in Birmingham'. He had no information about the London offices of any company connected 'to the sleeping cars or as to who the promoters were' or who was backing the scheme.

Tuesday, 19 August 1873
Central Criminal Court, Old Bailey
3.45 p.m.

Mr McIntyre now moved on to the way in which the forged bills were being paid out despite these various concerns. 'You see you are discounting to a very great extent,' he said.

'Yes.'

'From the 21st of January till the 28th of February, you were discounting to upwards of £100,000.'

'Yes.'

'For a man whose only address was Post Office, Birmingham. That is so, is it not?'

'Yes, quite so.'

'Have you any more of that sort of thing in your bank?'

'No.'

'It is not a gradual increase you see, it is a complete [influx] of bills, was it not, after the 21st of January?'

'Yes, they came in very sharp.'

'Very sharp indeed,' which could also now describe Mr McIntyre's tone.

'Yes.'

'Well, did not that make you think that you ought to enquire about the gentleman who had only an address at the Post Office at Birmingham?'

'All these bills were submitted to Headquarters and his address also.'

'Now that is the way they did business at Headquarters.' The court resounded with laughter, though the colonel did not seem to find it funny.

'The bills were of a very first-rate class and I supposed stood on their own merits,' was all he said to maintain his own dignity.

Though Colonel Francis was ridiculed in the court, headquarters did not repay him in kind. At the half-yearly general court of the proprietors (a sort of six month summary of how things were going), which had taken place on 13 March 1873, just days after the forgery had first been discovered, the Governor of the Bank of England himself made a surprising statement. 'I may state, with regard to Colonel Francis, our agent at the Western Branch,' George Lyall said in his only ever public reference to the case, 'during his period of service that gentleman has given great satisfaction.' Through the extraordinary ingenuity in the manufacture of 'those bills', as Lyall termed them, 'he had involved the bank in a serious loss, I cannot see that any blame is to be attached to his conduct'.

George Bidwell, for one, was hardly surprised. The Old Lady of Threadneedle Street would always find ways to save face. 'After all,' he later wrote, '[the bank] had succeeded in "proving" that we had been working on and preparing the scheme during more than a year before the possibility of such a fraud had entered our heads.'

If, as the forgers maintained, their attack on the bank was a last minute thing, then a shorter sentence would result. 'At the trial the prosecution slurred over this and every other fact which would tend to show that the "Great Bank Forgery" was not a long planned scheme,' George Bidwell wrote, knowing perfectly well that the converse was true.

Just before 5 p.m. that Tuesday, Colonel Francis left the stand looking as though he had been put through a shredder. If there was any consolation, he was not alone.

'Additional formal proof of the forged bills was then given and occupied a considerable time,' *The Daily Telegraph* reported the next day. And it was true. During the final hour of the second day's proceedings, a succession of six witnesses came in, all of whom told essentially the same story: that the endorsements on the bills of exchange were genuine. All were lost in the sheer volume of transactions which were routinely carried out.

'We have many thousands of these bills in the course of a month, and that was so last year,' said one clerk from the London & Westminster Bank in Lothbury. 'We gave no authority to anyone to sign our names.' And that authority reached the very dynasty whose imprimatur George Bidwell had insisted upon using.

When at four o'clock that Tuesday afternoon Alfred de Rothschild took to the stand, there was even greater amazement. Not only was he a director of the Bank of England, but Alfred de Rothschild had already sat in judgement at many of the first few hearings of the earlier parts of the trial at the Mansion House. 'It is a forgery,' he had already said there, when examining one particular bill that had been endorsed by his own institution.

'The stamp is an imitation of the stamp we use for acceptances. The whole bill as far as we are concerned, is fictitious. We know nothing at all of the drawer.'

On the stand today, he was even more certain about the particular bill for £4,500 that had nearly killed Austin Bidwell. 'It purports to be in the writing of Sir Antony De Rothschild but it is a forgery and the others are all forgeries,' Sir Alfred concluded. The prisoners had the pleasure of knowing that Austin's suffering in the train crash had been worth it. The forgeries on these particular bills were only detected, Sir Alfred explained under cross-examination, because they were 'not written in the peculiar ink which is specially used by the firm as one of the means of checkmating that description of fraud'. Most onlookers in the court, as elsewhere, were stunned. If a Rothschild could be fooled, what chance did anyone else have?

A week later – Tuesday, 26 August 1873
Central Criminal Court, Old Bailey
7.40 p.m.

In several estimations, Austin Bidwell had not taken the proceedings too seriously. 'An unseemly levity' was how one newspaper put it, but the smile had long since been wiped from his face when Judge Archibald prepared to hand down their sentence. At the last possible moment, the prisoner showed some genuine contrition for his actions when they were each in turn allowed to make a personal statement.

When Austin Bidwell stood up, his face was glum with despair. As he spoke, he folded his arms and one reporter noted 'a very slight flush comes across his pallid face, and a strange light gleams from his coal black eyes'. Now, with darkness descending the prisoner became, in turns, wistful, contrite and, as far as anyone could tell, genuinely sorry. On the stand, Austin Bidwell seemed to be echoing the walrus in *Alice in Wonderland*. He could, he said, talk of many things about his youth, of the opportunities turned down and talents wasted on a life of crime. 'I do not choose to do so now, but I wish to take advantage of the only opportunity that I will ever have to repair a wrong that I have done to a gentleman now in this court.'

Austin Bidwell then looked straight into the eyes of the man who, a week earlier, had been pulled apart in this same room. 'I allude to Colonel Francis,' he explained in case anyone was in doubt. It was an electric, yet oddly poignant, moment for both of them:

> I quite understand and appreciate very well the sentiment that he must enter-tain for me, but I hope that in the course of years as the edge of his resentment wears away he will give me credit for being sincerely sorry for the wrong that I have done him.
>
> I know that considerable comment has been made upon his lack of dis-cretion or lack of caution, but speaking from my experience of the world

which is limited, but which is rather great for a young man, and my knowledge of men and businessmen – speaking from that knowledge, I assert that any man in London – I care not how able he might have been, had he been placed in Colonel Francis' position would have been deceived in the same way.

It was Austin Bidwell's peculiar genius to make his apology sound like a boast, too. But he did look genuinely ashamed as he drew to his conclusion. 'This is the only explanation I can ever make to that gentleman,' he said, 'and I assure him I am sincerely sorry for what I have done to him.'

And with that, he sat down again, waiting to hear what his sentence would be, knowing full well, as he later acknowledged, 'fate, providence, call it what you will, seldom fails to upset wrongdoing, making it rocky for the wrongdoer'.

7

The Finer Arts of Forgery

> My dear M
> I am more sorry than I can tell to hear that you are suffering so much. Of course, you know that you have my ardent sympathies and best wishes for a speedy restoration to your heretofore blooming health. This episode will in future years serve to point a moral and adorn a tail. Well adorned it certainly has not been in perfect good taste for beauty unadorned when in the language of your favourite poet Longfellow:
>
> 'From such afflictions are
> Swollen peckers not of paradise.'
>
> Letter to George Macdonnell from Austin Bidwell, sent while ill in
> Vienna in October 1872.

Wednesday, 4 December 1872
Paternoster Row, London

It seemed as though the whole of the city was covered in water. Great Britain had been battered by squally rain, gales and floods for days and now, as he trudged through the soaking gloom, the American who would shortly introduce himself as F.W. Warren could not even make out St Paul's Cathedral just a few hundred yards away. Discordant noises more than compensated for the murk, growing louder as he negotiated his way through the mud and puddles.

The roar of printing and foundries echoed all around. Paternoster Row was host to a thriving community of engravers and stationers who sold books, creeds, graces

– and paternosters. The street's very name derived from the penitent figures who made their way to St Paul's and uttered the Lord's Prayer. Now, as the American made his way along, he smiled grimly to himself. 'Lead us not into temptation,' he thought, accompanied by a storm of appropriately biblical proportions.

At random, he entered the cramped and dingy workshop at No. 21, where he was met by a gentle giant of a man who looked at him quizzically, oddly oblivious to the noise all around. The American's nerves tightened. Had he made the right choice?

A forger has to know exactly how to forge. Though usually presumed to derive from the noun 'forge' (a place associated with metalwork), its origins actually stem from the French verb *forger* (to 'falsify') and refers to the singular art of creating counterfeit documents. Ironically, the thieves of Threadneedle Street would now need specialised metals and forges to engrave and then print the false bills of exchange they would shortly unleash upon unsuspecting bankers.

Counterfeit documents have a long, and some might say noble, heritage. 'As soon as an honest man learned how to write in the old days,' noted one police chief, 'he found to his sorrow that a rascal was able to use a stylus or some other lettering tool as well as himself.' But as the technology improved, so did the expertise required. The same police chief added:

> Only artists of the foremost professional study are engaged in the preparation of the plates for printing this paper, and the lettering, scroll work, figure drawing and all the other embellishments are purposely so elaborate and artful that their exact imitation and reproduction are undertakings of great and constantly increasing difficulty.

Such artistry was obviously beyond them, so the forgers had come up with a characteristically bold solution – get genuine artisans to do the work.

Forging a bill of exchange was akin to assembling a jigsaw, its essential elements, plates, scrolls and engravings, fitting together to form an exact replica. The fraudsters simply broke these tasks up into their constituent components. 'George Bidwell appears to have taken this department of the partnership,' the prosecution noted, 'and to have made it his business to go to different printers and stationers to order the different parts of the bills which he wanted for use.'

Despite the terrible weather, he had driven around the city in a cab for two or three days before he came across the narrow street in which, as another earlier visitor had termed it, 'the publishing trade is carried on in dingy houses'. And so it was on the first Wednesday of December, George Bidwell entered one particular establishment where he soon realised all his worries were unfounded. This first engraver would have severe problems communicating with anyone, let alone the police. James Dalton was completely deaf and almost dumb. 'The prisoner communicated with me on slips of paper when he came,' Mr Dalton's interpreter later explained on the stand at the Mansion House. 'Sometimes with a pencil and sometimes with a pen.'

Mr Warren returned in the New Year – he made twenty visits in all – and gave Mr Dalton several pieces of paper from which he should print. The visitor was at pains to make him understand the German lettering. Dalton cut a great many dates and numbers, running through the sequence of a month. Like others in Paternoster Row, he had no idea what they were intended for but gained the impression that his visitor was a German businessman. This notion was reinforced later when he explained he wanted the words 'London & Westminster Bank' and some Dutch lettering engraved.

In particular, Dalton had kept one piece of paper as he did not understand the words '*Ich will hald mehr haben*', which meant 'I will have more soon'.

In fact, his visitor already had many more soon. The fraudsters had spent most of the previous couple of months journeying 'backwards between England and the Continent', in the prosecution's later assessment. They had not attempted anything criminal for nearly two months, the cause of much puzzlement at the time. In all their later writings, the Bidwell brothers were at their most elliptical about what they had been doing.

'We finally concluded to go to Paris and Vienna, for a time,' is all that George Bidwell says in his memoirs. Austin Bidwell also drew a conveniently opaque curtain. 'Again and again I went to the Continent,' is all he says. 'I probably travelled 10,000 miles over the Continent in my bill buying expeditions to Paris, Amsterdam, Frankfurt and Vienna.'

What they had really been doing was probing, looking for weaknesses in financial systems while obtaining as many genuine bills as possible to copy 'and whether any fraud could be committed with them,' as the prosecutors later speculated. All throughout this time, they were still sending genuine bills to Colonel Francis in London 'which were to be discounted with the Bank of England so as to test the bank before attempting to discount forgeries'.

Now, as 1872 drew to a close, they had obtained genuine bills from financial institutions across France, Germany, Austria, Holland, Belgium and Portugal which they would shortly copy. The state banks of Russia and Turkey in London would also become victims. To generate exact replicas, all the accoutrements of bills of exchange had to be perfectly copied.

Mr Dalton was not alone in providing inadvertent help. Several others in Paternoster Row recalled just such a natty gentleman visiting them early that December. For George Bidwell, his visits also carried considerable risks. If any of the printers or engravers became suspicious they would obviously alert the police who might set a trap. So he decided to limit his exposure. He would systematically move from engraver to wood cutter to printer, in each case waiting a day or two before moving on to the next establishment. Word of mouth recommendations would be enough, not least when it became clear that many printers only knew of their near neighbours by name or reputation. They did not seem to meet and gossip. 'The result proved that I made no mistake in my selections,' George Bidwell later exulted, 'as the work was quickly done and no suspicions as to its real object transpired.'

The experiences of the printers in Paternoster Row were all roughly similar. Although in the estimation of one later press report, their subsequent Old Bailey testimonies 'were most technical and uninteresting', there was one extraordinary and almost surreal exchange which went largely unnoticed at the time. It went to the heart of the prosecution's case – and, paradoxically, exposed one of its greater weaknesses. Which of the forgers was it who had visited the printers?

Day Seven – Monday, 25 August 1873
Central Criminal Court, Old Bailey
10.15 a.m.

It was only just after ten o'clock and already weariness pervaded the whole of the courtroom. It was a humid, slow morning with thunderstorms rumbling in the distance. Despite the bright sunshine, everyone seemed exhausted. Both jurors and witnesses were finding it hard to concentrate. And that, as the prosecution knew only too well, worked against them when now, a week after the proceedings had begun, a 'die sinker and stamp cutter' as William Mitchell described himself, recalled his first meeting George Bidwell the previous winter.

The prisoner had ordered an endorsement stamp – now produced in court – on which Mr Mitchell recognised the words 'Sub-country man' and 'Secret' had been written. The court stirred at the mention of the latter. 'Do you recognise any impression upon that?' Mr Watkin Williams asked.

Holding it in his hand, Mr Mitchell did not. 'The impression upon this paper is rather heavier than the one on the bill,' he said, 'and I do not recognise it as being the same stamp.'

There was a pause and then a surprising statement came from Douglas Straight QC, acting for the defence. He looked slightly embarrassed. 'George Bidwell wishes to cross-examine the witness as Mr Besley, his counsel, is not here.'

'Allow the prisoner himself to cross-examine!' the judge exclaimed.

'Yes, My Lord.'

'Very well,' His Lordship slowly intoned with weary resignation, 'cross-examine.'

And so, to the amazement of the courtroom, George Bidwell stepped up to the plate.

For those who knew him, it was nothing out of the ordinary. George Bidwell's arrogance was born out of necessity. In his memoirs, he says his original plan at this stage of the fraud had been to stay in the background 'contriving and giving directions, leaving others to carry them out'. This was so much hogwash, as today's evidence in court would show.

He also claims he sent George Macdonnell across the Channel to obtain some wooden blocks from which they could print false bills. Mac, he says, returned saying, 'There are no wood engravers in Paris.' This was palpable nonsense. There were plenty of wood engravers in the French capital and the timing was wrong. Mac did not reach Paris until the New Year and never went near any printers.

What George Bidwell was really trying to do was sow confusion. If he could raise doubt about who exactly had visited the various printing establishments, he could expose a serious flaw in the prosecution's case, a crucial, and central mystery with the events which followed during his repeated visits to Paternoster Row in the run-up to Christmas 1872.

Monday, 25 August 1873
Central Criminal Court, Old Bailey
10.20 a.m.

The court was all ears as George Bidwell addressed William Mitchell. For many it would be a surprise to hear what one newspaper called his 'strong Yankee accent'. On the stand, Mr Mitchell waited and looked bemused as the prisoner leaned forward. 'How do you know that the impression upon that bill is from the stamp by you?'

The engraver smiled. 'Because I kept an impression of the one which I cut for you which I forwarded to Messrs Freshfield, and there I compared the impression of your stamp with the one on the bill and found it to be the same.'

George nodded gravely. 'How do you recognise the man you say you gave the stamp to as being me?'

Mr Mitchell was amazed. 'By what means did I recognise you?' he repeated. 'By the usual means – I should be stupid if I did not recognise you afterwards, especially if I looked at the man two or three times as I did you.'

There were one or two chuckles of amusement. George remained unflustered. 'Did he have the same appearance as I have now?'

'No.'

'What is the difference?' he asked.

'He had no whiskers and he had a moustache which was curled at each end in the French style.'

If fraud was, as was invariably reckoned, a crime with no victims, it was often equally difficult to pin down the perpetrators. In this particular case, mistaken identities and reasonable doubt were curious bedfellows. Both were intertwined, presenting a continual handicap to the prosecution. 'As the forged bills were all sent by mail,' Austin Bidwell aptly summarised, 'it was necessary to convict us by circumstantial evidence.'

Confusion was rife across Europe and also in Great Britain as to exactly who carried out this part of the 'fraud machine'. Much of the actual mechanics of forgery took place away from prying eyes. The uncertainties ushered in by flawed identification provided the thieves of Threadneedle Street with the barest glimmer of hope in their defence.

Monday, 25 August 1873
Central Criminal Court, Old Bailey
11.15 a.m.

William Cheshire was another engraver in Paternoster Row who encountered George Bidwell several times between December 1872 and February 1873. The visitor to his workshop never offered a name but seemed to be German and was probably a printer. Among his colleagues they christened him 'Von'.

'He gave the names of several towns and wished them done in some fancy kind of lettering,' Mr Cheshire now said under oath. Amsterdam, Lubeck, Bremen, Hamburg and Zurich were all mentioned. The forgers had obtained genuine bills of exchange from banks in those cities. The prosecution now patiently went through a number of bills on which Mr Cheshire recognised his stamps had been used. When asked about one bill in particular dated 11 February 1873 and drawn on the London & Westminster Bank (on which 'Secret' was shorthand for secretary), Mr Cheshire was adamant that the block had been engraved by him and him alone.

'Could not any engraver do one exactly like it?' George asked.

'Certainly,' he allowed, 'but I think it would be possible to detect the difference in some little particular or other.'

Perhaps the most unusual part of this exchange came when George Bidwell asked the engraver to confirm that he had first seen him 'downstairs' at the Mansion House. 'Was I brought up into your presence in order to take off my hat?' the prisoner now asked.

'You were.'

'There were no other persons present,' George continued. 'No other person except the officer who brought me up?'

'No.'

'I would like to have you state that at the time you did fail to recognise me as the person with whom you had done the business?'

'No, I recognised you directly,' Mr Cheshire continued. 'My only remark was that you looked very ill, which you did at that time.' This had been towards the end of June when his remand had clearly been taking its toll.

George Bidwell continued: 'Did I look different from the person that you saw?'

'You were different,' the witness acknowledged. 'You had been unshaven for some days; but I recognised you in a moment.'

'Was my dress the same?'

'Not at all.'

'Was my hat the same?'

'No.'

George thought he had an opening. 'My personal appearance was entirely different from the man you saw?'

'Your personal appearance was the same; your dress and surroundings were different.'

Throughout the autumn of 1872, George Bidwell had not looked very well at all. Illnesses both small and large had been a constant handicap for all the forgers over those last few months in Europe. Though only alluded to in their various trials, illnesses had a significant impact on the timing of the overall scheme of forgery.

When 'Mr and Mrs Bidwell' had stayed in Trouville that September, both had been under the weather. George Bidwell had been suffering from a heavy cold, while it was never stated on the record what had been ailing Nellie Vernon. She returned to London, the circumstances of which her boyfriend was soon touchingly concerned. 'Take the best of care of yourself my darling and I wish to see you fat and happy,' he wrote. 'I beg you not to permit a moment's gloom or despondency to delay your recovery.'

George's own cold was one of the annoyingly persistent varieties that he could not seem to shake. 'I have been so poorly myself you would have had a poor time with me here,' he assured her. After only a few days of separation, George Bidwell was waiting for 'the happy moment that shall bring my sweet little one into my arms'.

Soon, he assured her, he would be off on his travels. While recuperating in Paris, he had teased her, 'Can you be true to me and not hear from me for a fortnight?' As ever, he provided little explanation as to what he was doing. 'I may not be able to write to you for some time, perhaps not until you see me,' George wrote from Munich at the end of September. 'I am very miserable with that cold but oh all be alright soon.'

In fact, it got much worse, portending darker, more serious illnesses which delayed the start of the scheme. With Nellie Vernon, though, George Bidwell always remained as upbeat as he had been on the golden beaches of Normandy. 'You know that I should do anything reasonable to please you,' he declared and 'cannot but express my love and admiration at the delivery, good judgement and consideration which you, my darling, have shown.'

Five days after his encounter with Mr Dalton, George Bidwell made his way in the driving rain to No. 56 Paternoster Row to order an electroplate from George Boule Challoner who worked at a well-known printers called Nelson & Co. The American gave no name nor address and paid two shillings on account. When Challoner came to recollect the circumstances, Harry Poland prompted, 'And did he ask you for some printing ink?'

'For a small portion of printing ink,' Mr Challoner agreed.

'Did you supply him with any?'

'A little.'

In reality, George Bidwell did not need that much ink. On his travels around Europe, he had taken care to buy various inks to make any foreign signatures appear genuine. The others laughed at him for carrying it all around with him, as well as blank bills of exchange, which he had also purchased 'out of curiosity'. They were in French, German, Italian, Dutch, Russian, Turkish and Arabic. He had also, he claimed, obtained 'a great number of the endorsements, stamps and signatures of leading firms on the Continent and London.'

Mr Challoner had a vivid recollection of the exact words George wanted for the 'indorsement' on one particular bill:

'*Fur uns an die ordre die*'
'*Herr*'
'*Werth*'
'*Hamburg*'

These were subsequently engraved and transferred to the plate. The word '*fur*' Challoner thought must be wrong, so he substituted an 'n' for the 'r'. The word 'fun' appeared in all subsequent endorsements printed from Mr Challoner's original. The customer did not seem to notice and did not return to his premises until the New Year.

As with most of the other engravers in Paternoster Row, William Cheshire would recall on the stand that his visitor came 'perhaps twice in the week and perhaps not for a fortnight'. Mr Cheshire saw him probably half a dozen times.

To dispel any lingering uncertainties, Hardinge Giffard posed a pointed question. 'Have you the slightest doubt that he is the man?' he asked.

'Not the slightest.'

When he subsequently went to visit Challoner, George Bidwell gave the name of J.R. Nelson. During a conversation about lithography, he mentioned another printer's where he had given the name Brooks. On the stand, George Bidwell tried to exploit the doubt with George Challoner. 'Do you think it probable that a man would go to you and give you the name of Nelson and give the name of a near neighbour who it was liable that he might meet in your house?'

The judge was clearly irritated. 'That is a matter for the jury,' Justice Archibald stated.

'I am asking his opinion,' George Bidwell said smoothly.

The printer showed he could give as good as he got. 'I can only state the fact and facts are stubborn things,' he said, refusing to be browbeaten.

The facts were helped by the forgers' various correspondences with their girlfriends. 'Letter writing appears to have been one of the besetting sins of these forgers,' the prosecution would observe, adding later that they 'were great writers, George Bidwell especially'.

His letters to Nellie Vernon were invaluable in building up a chronology of their criss-crossing of the Continent. From this, the prosecution could obtain strict legal proof to tie everything together. Pinkerton detectives, police officials and Freshfields solicitors had meticulously traced the various transactions and aliases the gang had used to build up an evidence trail. They had interviewed receptionists, waiters, chambermaids and even traced fellow guests where they could help reconstruct the most accurate picture of their time in Europe.

On 4 October 1872, George Bidwell had written to Nellie Vernon from Dresden where he had arrived that same morning, 'I leave here in an hour and have only time to write a few lines', and refers to having received a letter from her which she had sent to Munich. His next stop would be Hanover, from where he hoped 'money from Frankfurt reached you all right'. The next day he added, 'I am now quite well and waiting with the greatest patience – a picture of impatience you would say – to see me until the moment that shall bring my sweet little one into my arms.'

Describing the journey across Germany, he struck a strangely introspective chord:

What a beautiful country I have passed through, through the historic lands these pleasant fields and smiling valleys where all now seems peaceful content yet in times past how often has the surge of battle, the shrieks of pain, the cries of women, children and old men driven homeless from their hearths.

However obliquely, George Bidwell was referring to the after-effects of the Franco-Prussian War, which would have a more immediate effect on their own fortunes – literally – with the replacement of various thalers, kreutzers and guilders with the mark. Some time later, George Bidwell claims that he could not buy anything to eat on a train journey. 'This was before the new Prussian coinage had displaced the wretched system previously in vogue,' he added, 'by which each petty state manufactured its own circulating medium.'

As he travelled through Germany, George Bidwell found that each state was still using their own different currencies. None would exchange any other currency. This probably explains his next communication with Nellie. 'I enclose a £5 note which is all I could find of English paper here,' he wrote from Frankfurt on 13 October, 'and I am not sure that I can telegraph money as I thought.' Enclosing some German money, 'which you can use after arriving at the frontier of Germany', he said that she should also be able to exchange it in Calais for a half sovereign of gold.

On 21 October 1872, George Bidwell was in Hamburg from where he wrote to Nellie that he was 'passing this evening with a friend at the Casino which is a very a grand affair'. This was his younger brother who had arrived from Frankfurt the day before. The gaming tables, George wrote, were crowded: 'I saw many beautiful young girls with heaps of gold lying before them upon the table and winning or losing a hundred or two pounds with the greatest indifference.' In the files, there is reference to a German girl who became friendly with Austin, but nothing more was ever said about this.

The imminent arrival of Nellie Vernon had buoyed George Bidwell's spirits. From Wiesbaden on 26 October he had written to her that there were 'one or two matters of business to be decided' which would alter his movements. Claiming he did not know what his plans would be, 'as the money market on the Continent is in such an unusual state', all he asked is that she come to Rotterdam in a few days' time.

Nellie should buy a first class ticket to Harwich, then take an overnight steamer to the Dutch port, 'arriving early the next morning after leaving London', and as he did not know any hotels there, he would send her a dispatch as to how they should meet up. 'Please consider this a hasty business letter,' he concluded.

Three days later he informed her that he would be starting for Rotterdam the next day and would be staying close to the port. 'Do not trouble about your luggage,' he wrote, 'but come direct to the hotel in the morning when I shall have rooms engaged for myself and wife and the luggage can be taken care of after.' It was clear what he had in mind, for the money he had sent, would 'last you until you reach somebody's arms and then will get such an awful hug ('go away peaches, you've lost your taste')'.

In all their later writings, both Bidwell brothers often confused dates and times, sometimes deliberately so. If they were trying to hide their identities, then they were doing exactly the same when later trying to explain their motives. It suited all of them, especially the two Georges, to portray their European trip in the autumn of 1872 as proof they had no grand plan to defraud the Bank of England. With their arrival in the Netherlands at the start of November, they claimed they were thinking of giving it all up, half-heartedly carrying out what George Bidwell termed 'one more operation which was to be the very last'.

The reality was very different. Holland was the springboard for the rest of the fraud, thanks to an unexpected fillip. After landing in Rotterdam on the first of the month, Nellie Vernon later recalled that 'we both stayed a week or ten days at Haarlem'. They were in constant contact with George Macdonnell in the Dutch capital as they were only 'distant half an hour by rail from Amsterdam'.

In his memoirs, George Bidwell says that 'difficulties arose' when he tried to pass some letters of credit with his passport as surety. In Rotterdam, he says he visited bankers almost at random who refused to deal with him. Using the name H.E. Gilbert, he swiftly made the acquaintance of what he referred to as his 'Hebrew' banker. The conversation with Simon Louis Pinto was stilted, taking place in broken English and German. Mr Gilbert, he recalled, wanted to discount some bills from Frankfurt which had been purchased five days earlier by Austin Bidwell. Mr Pinto declined to discount them. 'It is very difficult to obtain anything of the sort,' he explained, 'as they are very dear in Amsterdam, that sort of bill.'

There were, however, some bills on Hamburg in the market which had become available the day before. Possibly, Mr Pinto said, he might be able to obtain them – and did. 'I saw George Bidwell four or five, or perhaps six, times,' the broker later recalled. On his first visit, Mr Gilbert had said in passing that he was 'living with a friend in the country'. All throughout their subsequent dealings, Mr Pinto got the impression that the American 'had some business connected with the railway works or railway'.

On 22 November, the broker received a letter by post from him and then 'afterwards received other letters from him from London'. Over the next two months H.E. Gilbert sent him 10,545 guilders' worth of money, which were inserted among four letters. The unsuspecting Mr Pinto had no idea that many of these later bills used fraudulent acceptances. Once again, the forgers were taking things slowly.

Freshfields later summarised:

> During the last fortnight of the prisoners' stay on the Continent, the prisoners had commenced work in earnest. They had been buying the bills which were to form the models from which the forged bills were to be taken. They bought a considerable number, some of which they have used for actual forging and some for comparison with forged bills.

During the first week of November, George Macdonnell briefly returned to London where he had personally cashed a bill drawn by Baron Schey in Vienna at Barings Bank. It was nothing less than an epiphany. Mac said on the final day of the Old Bailey trial:

> In America, when bills are presented at a bank for discount, when acceptances are presented, it is the custom to send the acceptances round to the persons accepting to be what is technically called 'initialled', in order that their validity

and genuineness may be certified. I found that was not the case here, and the result of that discovery is that I am standing before you today.

Calling it 'a great discovery', straight-faced he then claimed this proved that only then could they even contemplate the greater fraud. 'That was the first moment at which anything of the kind entered my mind,' he lied.

When they all subsequently met up in Amsterdam on 8 November, they knew exactly what this discovery meant. 'Instead of paying the amount by check or gold or notes, as I expected,' Mac explained, 'the cashier stamped on the face "Payable at the London & Westminster Bank" and endorsed it.' If they forged bills of exchange, they could obtain as much money as they liked. Bank tellers would simply rubber-stamp the bills. So long as they bore the acceptance of a reputable firm, they would be cashed without question. If the fraudulent bill looked the part – in other words, if it was forged with sufficient accuracy – it would be redeemed without question. For that, they now needed the printers and engravers in Paternoster Row.

The swindle would only ever become apparent when the bill fell due, which could be many weeks in the future. It was breathtaking in its simplicity, for as one commentator later wrote, 'It may sound fantastic that great financial institutions should neglect so obvious a business precaution'.

The way for the greater fraud was open, so a week later they returned to London. On Thursday, 14 November, George and Nellie crossed from Rotterdam to Harwich, taking the train and carriage to Victoria Station, near to where they stayed at the Alexandra Hotel. They remained there for the next three nights and were joined by George Macdonnell, who stayed in another room.

Throughout the trial at the Old Bailey, George Macdonnell did not seem particularly fazed by the proceedings. Though very little ever seemed to derail his confidence, earlier that autumn even he had not been immune to what Hardinge Giffard had aptly termed 'one of those accidents which all sometimes disturb schemes'.

While he had been in Vienna – where he bought the bill which he later presented to Barings – he was, as he later said on the stand, 'taken very seriously ill and returned to England for the benefit of medical advice'. Both he and the other George had picked up a form of malaria from their trip to South America, most likely when hiding away from his shadow in various fleapits of hotels. Even a year later, his sallow complexion, occasional sweats and his sporadic need to use crutches showed how ill he continued to be.

After arriving in Vienna towards the end of September, 1872, Mac had been bedridden for three weeks while he was staying at the Grand Hotel. 'During that period he was visited there by George Bidwell, Austin Bidwell and perhaps Engels,' the prosecution determined. 'They all from time to time accepted and went about their business amusing themselves and preparing for their winter campaign.'

If George Bidwell's memoirs are to be believed, that involved nightly visits to the opera. He also claims that he looked after his seriously ill friend with a medical technique that was all the rage. 'I nursed him for two or three weeks and during that time gave him several powerful shots from my battery,' George Bidwell recalled, 'which nearly raised him out of bed, if they did not cure him.'

When Mac started to recover, George Bidwell then promptly fell ill, 'prostrated and confined to my room for a whole week'. If the other George did indeed look after Mac, who was laid low for weeks, he only did it for a few days because in between he was travelling around Germany. Significantly, they were both noted together by a servant at the Rheinscher Kaiser Hotel in Vienna. 'I saw them in October last,' Anna Shmech recalled at the Old Bailey. 'Macdonnell then appeared to be very ill and used crutches.'

On 19 October, Mac was helped aboard a train when he left Vienna. Thereafter he travelled to Frankfurt where his health improved, but then, when he joined the others in Holland the certainties evaporated. Exactly what George Macdonnell had been up to would cause the prosecution no end of problems when, as they simply noted in their pre-trial briefing, 'one of the prisoners called on a money changer at Rotterdam'.

Thursday, 14 November 1872
Rotterdam, The Netherlands

The heavily bearded American who walked into what its owners termed a private bank – though it was, in reality, a glorified money changers – did not exactly look in the best of health. It was a cold, unsettled day, and he was clearly suffering. Despite the windy weather, the visitor was wrapped up well. Despite his obvious ill health, he was breezily confident.

Frederick Warren, as he introduced himself, was pleasant and knew exactly what he wanted. Addressing Johannes de Waal, who ran the establishment with his father, he said, 'I want to purchase one or more bills on the London & Westminster Bank for about £600'. Mr De Waal's face fell.

'London & Westminster Bank bills are difficult to get,' the Dutchman explained, 'more than other banks.' Mr De Waal did his best to mollify the customer. He would do his best to get them. Blydenstein & Company, he explained, were the only brokers in Rotterdam entitled to draw on the London & Westminster Bank and 'charged high' for doing so. Mr Warren did not seem to mind and handed over 7,435 guilders ('which is £622 3s,' Mr De Waal's translator later explained on the stand). 'When you get them,' Mr Warren concluded, 'send them to my hotel.'

This particular incarnation of Frederick Albert Warren was symptomatic of a much greater problem for the prosecution. Over the next few weeks, he had an amazing ability to be everywhere, and nowhere, all at the same time.

Everywhere and nowhere. If not the heart of this particular operation, George Macdonnell was, in several estimations, the systematic, cool-headed brain. Although ultimately the instrument of overarching hubris upon which the great forgeries foundered, paradoxically the Bidwells were utterly dependent on Mac's skills, both as a penman but also in his very elusiveness.

Hiding his real identity formed a useful plank in all their defences, and so it would prove with this visit to the money changers in Rotterdam. The prosecution would note:

> The above transaction taking place in the name of F.A. Warren one would be almost inclined to assume that Austin Bidwell was the person who had so called on Mr De Waal. Mr De Waal, however has been in England since the announcement of the criminal proceedings and he has seen all the prisoners at the Mansion House.

His visitor, De Waal recalled, was fair haired and smooth talking and, much to his chagrin, Mr De Waal was unable to positively identify him. He believed his visitor was George Macdonnell, but he wasn't sure. At the end of his subsequent cross-examination, Hardinge Giffard stood up and tried to banish any lingering uncertainty. 'Have you any doubt whether the man second from this side is the man who dealt with you?'

'No doubt.'

Certainly, all the documents that were signed by this particular Mr Warren bore Mac's handwriting. But confusion came with the receipt of the purchase of that first bill from Blydenstein's, in the form of a card which had been returned to Mr De Waal. When the prosecution came to ask the Dutch moneylender about it, there was a surprising exchange with Mr Watkin Williams in the Old Bailey. 'Where is the card?' he asked. There was an embarrassed pause. 'I have torn it up,' Mr De Waal confessed.

The Dutchman did not hear from Mr Warren again until 24 January, when he enclosed a bill signed by a W.J. Spaulding, which Mr De Waal sent to another bill broker. None of them realised at the time that this was the first of many fraudulent bills of exchange, based on the real ones they had obtained in all their European travels.

The same day (Tuesday, 19 November 1872) that Mr Warren acknowledged receipt of the Blydenstein's bill in French, George and 'Mrs Bidwell', aka Nellie Vernon, checked in to Ford's Hotel in Manchester Street. Staff recalled they came with a great deal of luggage 'and remained there till 1 January 1873, when he went with Ellen Vernon to lodgings at 87 Upper Gloucester Place'. From this quarter, there was little to report. 'During the month of November, the life of the prisoner George Bidwell and Helen Vernon at Ford's Hotel appears to have been without incident,' the prosecution noted.

Austin Bidwell's whereabouts were, as ever, more difficult to ascertain. An interesting contributory factor was how much Nellie Vernon had started to resent his presence. '[He cannot] be said ever to have settled himself in any one place', was how the prosecution neatly put it. Occasionally, Austin and Mac both called on 'Mr & Mrs Bidwell' at Ford's. Significantly, the two brothers saw little of each other as Nellie Vernon clearly did not enjoy his company. George Macdonnell visited more frequently, as he was staying in Weymouth Street, 'within five minutes' walk', at the Alexandra Hotel. This proximity eased the start of the laborious process of copying all the genuine bills of exchange which they had obtained on their travels.

At the outset, they took care to target one particular and pre-eminent printers in the city, as a result of which just before the Old Bailey trial began, the prosecution had named 'Macdonnell as the person who ordered the plates'. That statement would create a serious hole in their case, not least for the unfortunate owner of the printers in front of whom they had been paraded on several occasions already over the summer of 1873.

Friday, 13 June 1873
Mansion House, Justice Room

Sir Sydney Waterlow was never one for introspection. Soul-searching was an anathema to such a steely martinet who was often imperious, abrupt and used to getting his own way. But when, at the end of his life, he came to recall his time as Lord Mayor of London, he uttered an uncharacteristic note of caution. 'The position of Chief Magistrate is a supremely difficult one,' Sir Sydney told his biographer, 'and no man who relied solely upon himself has, I think, ever satisfied the public or passed through his year of office pleasantly and profitably.' As lord mayor, he had sat in the Mansion House Justice Room 'for some three hours or more daily to administer the law', as his biographer put it.

The case which had rumbled on through the spring and early summer of 1873 was a case in point. It had presented Sir Sydney with a considerable personal conundrum concerning which of the forgers had visited his own family's printing works down by the city wall. In the same way that they had targeted a pre-eminent bank like the Rothschilds', it was inevitable that the thieves of Threadneedle Street would identify Waterlows as a mark. If there was one thing which Sir Sydney genuinely knew about, it was printing. Of French Walloon descent, his family had ink running through their veins. Sir Sydney's father had started a small stationery business in Birchin Lane in 1836. Over the subsequent decade, his five sons, including Sydney, joined him as they came of age.

Their first great commercial success was *Bankers'* magazine and a large share of railway timetable printing and stationery. His involvement with various railways provided

Austin Biron Bidwell, photographed by the police, who believed he masterminded the fraud. *(Courtesy of the Bank of England Archive F5/22)*

George Bidwell, Austin's eldest brother, a baleful influence whose life of crime began earlier than previously known. *(Courtesy of the Bank of England Archive F5/22)*

Edwin Noyes Hills, the patsy and supposed innocent, who, until his dying day, claimed he was not aware of the plot. *(Courtesy of the Bank of England Archive F5/22)*

George Macdonnell, the smartest of the gang, with the 'fine, light, drab cloth overcoat that he bought in Paris'.

The most famous criminals in the land, as they appeared in *The Penny Illustrated News*, at the time of their last Mansion House trial. *(Courtesy of the Bank of England Archive F5/22)*

Helen Ethel Vernon, better known as Nellie, girlfriend of George Bidwell, whose innocence was brought into question by the authorities. *(Courtesy of the Bank of England Archive F5/22)*

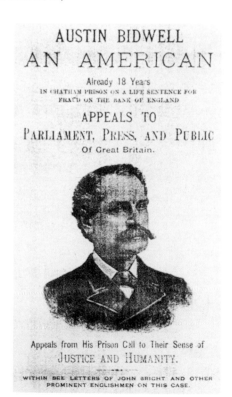

An older Austin, impeccably turned out even after the harsh rigours of imprisonment. *(TNA HO 144 20568)*

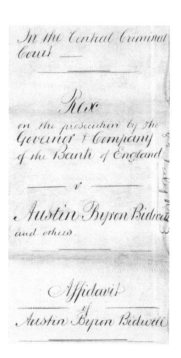

One of the many thousands of court documents in the 'most extraordinary trial' with one of the many alternate spellings of Austin's second name. *(TNA HO 144 20568)*

THE CRUSADER.

Published Monthly by
THE GEORGE BIDWELL PUB. CO.
HARTFORD, CONN.

SALUTATORY.

In making its bow to the Press and Public THE CRUSADER gives as a reason for existence that the Gambling Power has reached amazing dimensions within the past dozen years, and there is no special newspaper devoted to the cause of its annihilation. This Power has obtained political influence

but their business is destructive. That business I must fight. These may rest assured I shall fight fairly, and it is to be hoped, effectively.

To the Press, as leader in all things—as moulder of opinions, I am under special and eternal obligation for their generous reception and fair treatment during my lectures and introduction of my book, "Forging His Own Chains," throughout the country.

To the many editors, merchants, bankers, clergymen and other professional gentlemen whom I have met and who have so cordially taken me by the hand, given me

MISSION OF THE CRUSADER.

THE CRUSADER'S mission is to arouse the honest community to a full realization of the rapid growth of the desolating Gambling Power —of the necessity of stopping and finally crushing this and its less brainy but deadly co-worker, the Rum Power—so that these shall be prevented from obtaining entire political supremacy.

To secure the success of this movement every lover of his country, every one who wishes to aid in putting an end to this wholesale destruction of our fel-

multitudinous satellites of the Rum and Gambling powers.

Even if the fighters are fully posted regarding the actual power of these monsters, they number about one for every hundred engaged in the work of ruin.

Try to realize their advantage and encourage us who are engaged in this momentous battle by enlisting your friends to aid the cause as they are able.

As stated above the other side have millions fleeced from their dupes, while we must depend on contributions, subscriptions and advertisements for the necessary

To show that crime never paid, the Bidwell brothers spent their final years publishing warnings to others in their own magazine. *(TNA HO 144 20568)*

BIDWELLS
National Crusader

FOR OFFICE AND HOUSEHOLD

❀ - HONESTY - SOBRIETY - ❀ ❀ ❀ CONTENTMENT - HAPPINESS ❀

FIRST YEAR.   HARTFORD, JANUARY, 1894.   { SUBSCRIPTION $2.00 PER YEAR. { SINGLE COPIES, 20 CENTS.

Bidwells National Crusader.

ISSUED EVERY MONTH BY THE BIDWELL PUBLISHING COMPANY, AT HARTFORD, CONN.

Entered at the Post Office at Hartford as Second Class Mail Matter.

SOLD BY SUBSCRIPTION ONLY.

One Year $2.00
Six Months 1.25

(Postage Prepaid.)

Liberal Commission Allowed Club Agents. Sample Copies Sent Free.

ANNOUNCEMENT.

By harsh experience, by the sacrifice of thirty-four years of our lives, into which were crowded the tortures of mind and body indescribable, out from the crucible test of public opinion, with character established, manhood restored and the good-will and encouragement of our fellow-men, justifies the assumption that we may be the humble means of exerting an influence for good from the rostrum and in the field of journalism. "Forging His Own Chains" having met with such universal favor is assurance that our efforts may not be in vain.

Crime in any guise or the direct and indirect causes which lead to the committal of the same, will be handled without fear, but will be pre-

A second edition of *The Crusader*, that the Bidwells sold as they lectured about their experiences to audiences across the United States. *(TNA HO 144 20568)*

The paper trail continued for years, including this missive from the Bank of England to their American solicitors concerning pleas to release the prisoners. (HO 144 20568)

Bank of England.—E.C.

2 April 1891.

Sir,

I am directed by the Deputy Governor of the Bank, in the absence of the Governor, to acknowledge the receipt of your letter of the 31st ultimo, No.20568 C/54, enclosing a copy of a despatch from the Consul General of New York, dated the 20th February last, and also of a Petition from the Board of Pardons of Connecticut, in which they urge the remission of the sentence passed upon Austin Byron Bidwell for forgery.

In this petition it is stated that "Deeming the punishment sufficient, the Bank Authorities have written to the Honorable Robert Lincoln, U. S. Minister to the Court of St James, that his release will not be opposed by them";- and you ask that Mr Matthews may be furnished with a copy of the letter in which this opinion was conveyed to Mr Lincoln.

The only communication to Mr Lincoln on this subject was a letter written by Mr Lidderdale, the Governor, on the 9th August 1889, of which I enclose a copy. This letter clearly states the ground which the Bank have always held in regard to the appeals for remission of sentence which have been made on the part of Austin Bidwell and his confederates, and from it you will observe,

iency or otherwise of the punishment which these men have under-gone, the Governors feel that the question should be left entirely

to

eigh Pemberton, Esq.,

£10,000   London July 10th 1872

The Bank of England

Pay to— Albert C Hubbell — or order

Ten Thousand Pounds in — sterling

F. A. Warren

A facsimile of a Warren credit note from the summer of 1872, one of many hundreds that were later assembled into a damning chain of evidence.

St James Place, as it appeared in 1873, where the staff at the private hotel at No. 17 were alerted by George Macdonnell's odd behaviour.

A clean-shaven Austin Bidwell at the time of the last Mansion House hearing where he and his brother's pleas led to an explosive denouement.

BOTH THE BIDWELLS DEAD.

Men Who Swindled the Bank of England End in Want.

SAN FRANCISCO, Cal., March 26.— George Bidwell, the elder of the two brothers whose swindle of the Bank of England made such a sensation, died here this morning in a lodging house. He was taken with pneumonia a week after the recent death of his brother, and his constitution proved unequal to the ordeal.

He died in want, and the body of his brother is yet unburied, although it has been three weeks dead. The Bidwells came West several months ago to engage in mining.

Where once the Bidwells garnered front-page news, in the spring of 1899 their passing received only a few polite references.

At the Old Bailey, George Macdonnell leans forward to speak to his attorney, with Austin Bidwell to his right and George to the left. Hills is at far right in this picture.

Duke's Road close to Euston where Nellie Vernon lived, and saw all her hopes and dreams disappear at the station nearby.

George Bidwell in his later years, careworn and exhausted by his imprisonment, yet still dandified.

WILLIAM A. PINKERTON

Willie Pinkerton, who chased the Bidwells all over the world and, in the estimation of Austin, was the greatest detective in America.

Hardinge Giffard QC, lead prosecutor, whose opening statement lasted three hours without reference to notes.

The Gold Weighing Room, at the heart of the Bank of England, where George Macdonnell openly laundered money as the final phases of the fraud began.

Standing outside the bank on 1 May 1872, Austin called it 'the softest spot in the world' and stated that they could 'hit the bank for a million as easy as rolling off a log'.

Sir Sydney with much of his later personal fortune. The firm expanded with several premises, not least the large printing works down by the London Wall. An active philanthropist, politician and all round Victorian do-gooder, his company attracted many customers from around the country and overseas too.

So it had been on the first Wednesday the previous December when the prosecution noted that George Macdonnell had called 'on Messrs Waterlow & Sons and buys bills forms in the name of F.W. Warren'. That unequivocal certainty was something the forgers' defence lawyers would exploit to the full for the good reason Mac hadn't – or so George Bidwell claimed. 'I went to the printing and stationery establishment of Sir Sydney Waterlow,' he said in his memoirs. Even more curious, a couple of employees also swore before their master, the lord mayor, 'on our examination that Macdonnell was the man – he having light hair and blue eyes, my hair being black – and Mac and I sitting beside each other in full view of the witnesses'.

Wednesday, 4 December 1872
Waterlow Stationers, Birchin Lane, City of London

When F.W. Warren came into the store, he clearly knew what he wanted. He was a brisk, confident American who simply asked to look at printing patterns – in this case, for bills of exchange – and examined two books of samples. He quickly looked them over and asked if the standard templates could be altered, specifically removing both the oval picture in one and the name of Waterlows in all the others.

'It is always the custom to have a sketch made before the plate is engraved,' clerk Thomas Lyell explained.

'Very well,' Mr Warren said. After examining such a sketch, he could then decide on which colours he might require. The customer wanted 500 of the two together as soon as they could be printed up. Mr Warren had given his address as Cannon Street Hotel. When asked for a reference or a deposit, he chose the latter, paying in cash.

'The sketch will be ready in two days,' Lyell added. He wrote down 'Warren, £2' in his work book, adding that the forms would be printed in 'about ten days'. After that, Mr Lyell saw him leave the shop and subsequently had no more dealings with him. However, his colleague James Mowat, a general assistant, did. The American called three more times before the bills were finally ready in the week before Christmas. 'We had printed two hundred and thirty copies from each of the two patterns in various coloured inks at his request,' Mowat later recalled at the Mansion House. When the papers were handed over, Mr Warren asked for the original plates. They were not available at Birchin Lane so Mowat called for a messenger who took the American with him to the London Wall printing works. There he collected the plates and, if George Bidwell's own testimony is to be believed, it was there he saw Sir Sydney in the distance, an occurrence of which the lord mayor had no memory at all.

There is an old statement that nobody lies like an eyewitness. In this case it rang true, for here was a potentially damaging case of mistaken identity. The Waterlows staff who had dealt with F.W. Warren were convinced he was really George Macdonnell. Yet as the prosecution lamented in their briefing papers, 'both George Bidwell and Macdonnell say that the identification is a mistake and that it was in fact George Bidwell who did the work.'

The lawyers were never quite sure. Neither Georges could ever be truly believed. While it would do George Bidwell no harm to be identified as F.W. Warren, it would, however, 'injure Macdonnell seriously to have him brought into the Commercial part of the transaction'.

What made it worse was that when James Mowat was further deposed, far from clearing the matter up, he seemed even more confused. 'To the best of my belief, the prisoner Macdonnell is the man,' said the Waterlow's assistant at the next remand hearing eight days later. 'I am positive the prisoner George Macdonnell is the person who gave me the order. He was wearing a moustache then also and had a top coat on.'

It was significant that when the case came to the Old Bailey, neither Lyell nor Mowat were called as witnesses. The prosecution was not taking any chances. That was why, on the third day of the subsequent trial, they made sure there was no ambiguity about the identity of a well-dressed character who suddenly showed up at the country's main passenger port to begin another entwined strand of the fraud. Claiming that he was in a hurry to leave for London, he was, he said, just 'a traveller from America' and, as ever, such an unseemly rush would work in his favour.

Friday, 6 December 1872
Liverpool, England

Everywhere and nowhere.[13] It is fitting that in the words of a song written by perhaps the city's most famous sons, a 'Nowhere Man' should make a brief trip to Liverpool at the start of December 1872. Often called the United States of Europe, the thriving port was the engine room for Great Britain's Empire and exports. Something like two-fifths of the world's trade passed through its docks, with an estimated 5,000 vessels arriving and disembarking each year. It had also, as a result, gained a certain notoriety. 'Liverpool is the most murderous, drunken and disorderly town in England', an American newspaper correspondent had written a few years earlier, 'and Manchester the most dishonest.'

But what to make of the bearded fellow who clearly knew both those cities, had committed crimes in all of them and who, on the wet and cold afternoon of the first Friday in December, walked into a teeming Liverpool bank and claimed (as usual) to be in a great hurry. The mystery is further compounded because there is no mention of this visit to Liverpool in the prosecution's briefing document. Nor was there any evidence that George Macdonnell had ever stayed at what was known as 'England's Waiting Room', the Adelphi Hotel – the most pre-eminent establishment famed for its turtle soup – or any other less salubrious hotels.

Mac's visit to Liverpool was significant. The fraudsters needed to obtain home-grown bills of exchange to copy so they could leaven the mix of forgeries they would shortly present in London. Liverpool's relative distance meant that it would also take some time for any checking up on their provenance.

It was on the third day of the trial at the Old Bailey that the first Liverpudlian witness, Edward Wilson Gates, a partner in the bank of Wilson, Gates & Company, was asked about this American visitor who had wanted to invest £2,000 or £3,000 in bills. 'He desired what we call first-class paper,' Mr Gates said. 'I showed him some bills in my bill box.'

When Austin Metcalfe QC asked exactly who it was he had seen that day, the bank manager said he was morally certain it was George Macdonnell. 'Morally certain?' Metcalfe asked, feigning surprise.

'Yes,' Gates reiterated, 'that means that I was certain.'

Later, Hardinge Giffard re-examined the Liverpudlian to be absolutely sure. 'When you first saw him in the dock had you any doubt he was the man who dealt with you for the bills,' he asked of Mac's appearance at the Mansion House.

'Not the slightest doubt.'

'Have you any doubt now?' Giffard pressed.

'Not the slightest doubt.'

Once again, this was reported even more explicitly in the next day's *The Times* – 'He had no doubt that Macdonnell was the man.'

Neither did William Anderson, a clerk to Richardson, Spence & Co., merchants and agents for several large American houses, have any doubt. The visitor had appeared earlier that same Friday, and Mr Anderson recalled his bearded appearance.

'He has a beard now?' Mr Metcalfe prompted.

'Yes, and he had one then.'

Just to be on the safe side, Giffard pressed the point once more. 'Have you any doubt?' Giffard subsequently asked of the prisoner's identity.

'I have no doubt,' Mr Anderson replied.

That too was the testimony of the clerk who had escorted Mac round the corner to Mr Gates' bank. Edward Coupland happened to have overheard the American asking Mr Anderson for bills, 'which is a thing I never heard before in our office,' he said on the stand. Coupland then walked with Mac the 'two hundred or three hundred yards' to Gates' bank. 'I was talking to him on the way,' he said. 'I have not the least doubt he is the man.'

He reiterated this same point when re-examined by Hardinge Giffard. 'Had you any doubt about him?' the prosecutor prompted.

'Not in the least,' the witness said, 'I knew him as soon as he came up.'

Austin Bidwell was, as the prosecution later noted, the most peripatetic of the forgers. Unlike his brother, Austin rarely sent letters, and even then only ever seemed to write to Jeannie Devereux, but as Freshfields also noted, he did 'not appear to have been a pleasant correspondent and certainly was not a very agreeable company with strangers'.

An interesting vignette came from a waiter at Ford's Hotel, who one day recalled a pair of visitors arriving to see Mr and Mrs Bidwell towards the end of their stay. Already, Charles Guyot had registered something curious about Mr Bidwell. 'I gave him an American newspaper and he told me he was no American,' the sceptical waiter later testified, 'but a Briton.'

On this later occasion, one of the visitors held a parcel, while the other was carrying a candle and some sealing wax. Though they never said what they were doing, the pair wanted to gain access to the Bidwells' room. Mr Guyot refused. When he noticed a likeness between one of them and the guest, he relented a little. 'Are you George Bidwell's brother?' he asked.

'I am,' Austin said. The waiter apologised and immediately let them into the room. 'It is alright,' Austin added magnanimously, 'you are acting under the same principle as we are.' This, the prosecution speculated, was extreme caution, which explains what happened next.

Conmen had to be consistent, and not just confident. If you looked the part and did not draw attention to yourself, then you would be fine.

So far as bankers in the city were ever aware, the thieves of Threadneedle Street were always solvent. If they drew heavily from their account in Mayfair, they would replace the money with genuine drafts or cash from bills drawn on reputable firms like Rothschilds. Nobody sounded an alarm because there was nothing to cause anxiety. 'A man's bank account is a sort of index to his whole business,' a teller of some great experience later told an American police chief about how forgers were often caught out, 'It shows with whom he is dealing, what are the sources of his income, and when and how he makes his payments.' Bank accounts provided a snapshot 'concerning his financial affairs'.

Now the forgers needed to open another account into which the proceeds from the fraudulent bills would eventually be paid. It provided insulation, for if all went well the two would never be connected with the greater fraud. So on the afternoon of the first Monday in December 1872, Austin Bidwell removed £1,250 from the Warren account at the Bank of England. He took a cab over to the city, alighted at 79 Lombard Street, and walked up the steps of the Continental Bank to start this next, concurrent part of the fraud.

Monday, 2 December 1872
Continental Bank, No. 79 Lombard Street, City of London
2 p.m.

Charles Johnson Horton was typical of the Americans you often saw around at that time: tall, thin, confident and bristling with bonhomie. 'I'd like to open an account with you,' was all he said. John Thomas Stanton, the bank manager, agreed, taking both his words and identity at face value. Again, there was nothing unusual about this, as there were a lot of Americans looking for safer places to store their money. Two weeks earlier, Bowles Brothers, the London arm of an American banking house often used by tourists from the United States, had gone bankrupt with liabilities of up to £500,000. Mr Stanton's visitor smiled ruefully after claiming that he had banked there.

'Thankfully,' Mr Horton said with obvious relief, 'I closed my account.' Explaining that he had removed a sum of about £7,500 just in time, Mr Stanton agreed to open his customer a current account with alacrity. He did not ask for any references. It was clear that he might lose this gentleman's business to a competitor. The manager got the impression that the account would not be particularly active, 'more of a deposit account,' he later explained under oath, because Mr Horton had asked about rates of interest.

The American handed over £1,250 in notes, and with the exception of one £100 note, all were later traced. Mr Stanton then handed him a cheque book and they were in business. It was as simple as that.

When they later came to examine the circumstances, the prosecution was amazed. 'The prisoner Austin Bidwell thus found how easy it was to discount good Bills but he used his wisdom with discretion,' Freshfields wrote. 'He made as much as he could of the Capital although a considerable portion of it must then have been locked up.'

The next day, Mr Horton called again and paid in two cheques of Mr Warren's for a total of £235 10s. On 5 December, he paid in a Warren cheque for £95 2s, and on that same day, he drew out £1,000 in cash. No suspicions were aired. Nobody raised an alarm. The fraudsters could issue a sigh of relief. They were in.

That same Monday, George Bidwell sent a telegraph from Victoria Station:

Edwin Hills
Clarendon Hotel
New York

Come Wednesday's steamer without fail.
Answer Spaulding, Langham Hotel.

Tuesday, 17 December 1872
Liverpool Docks
3 p.m.

Certainly, there was never any question about the identity nor the motives of the American who stepped off the White Star ship *Atlantic* at Liverpool docks on this gloomy December afternoon. He had been staying in berth 58 and had a saloon ticket in his pocket.

En route, he wanted to obtain an upgrade to a separate room which he had happened to have seen was empty. The ship's purser, William Guest Barrett, pointed out that it was actually full of wash-hand stands and looking glasses. So the passenger ended up sharing a cabin with a Colonel Steele.

Occasionally, they needed to come up for air as the Atlantic swells and storms took their toll. So Mr Barrett took pity on him and let him into the saloon if he was feeling unwell. It was for these reasons that the purser had reason to remember him. They had spoken every day during the transatlantic voyage, which had begun ten days previously. 'I frequently had occasion to speak to him on board,' Mr Barrett said, 'and addressed him as Mr Hills.' He recalled his name (he used his full given name of Edwin Noyes Hills both in person and on the ticket) and it stuck in his memory. It was a standard joke among all the steamer crews that Yanks always had too much luggage. But this fellow was different. 'He had no luggage excepting a small bag and he never volunteered any information respecting himself,' Mr Barrett later recalled.

Would an honest man respond to a telegram summons from a friend who used a false name? Edwin Noyes Hills certainly did, for he was hardly an innocent abroad whose presence in Great Britain, the prosecution noted, 'was more than ever necessary'.

By the time he reached London the next day everything was set for the greater fraud to begin. The forgers had now obtained genuine European and, after the trip to Liverpool, home-grown bills of exchange. They now had another bank account into which they could pour all their ill-gained profits. 'The Prisoner

Austin Bidwell had thus supplied the Banking Accounts and some of the Models for the Forgeries to be perpetrated,' the prosecution noted, 'George Bidwell had supplied others of the forms and the printing Blocks and Macdonnell the paper, also some of the Bill Models.'

And now, the fourth member of the gang could take his place alongside them. Edwin Noyes Hills would assume the role of the fall guy 'who might drag the chestnuts out of the fire while [the others] remained in comparative obscurity', in the colourful phrase of George Dilnot, the first chronicler of the case, who actually interviewed Hills many years later.

Wednesday, 18 December 1872
No. 16 Ivy Lane, Paternoster Row, London

George Bidwell had had a lot on his mind that Christmas. A week earlier, he had gone to yet another engraver and printer in Paternoster Row. Thomas Straker greeted him in welcome. As noted earlier, he said he was recommended by Nelson's, where Mr Challoner was a partner, so Mr Straker took notice.

This would be the first of many visits, and strangely, Mr Straker did not actually ask him his name. Nor did the printer ever ask him for an address; the visitor never told him, nor did he ever say outright what his business was. On this visit, he presented a pair of copper plates which had blank bill forms engraved upon them. 'Do you do copper plates?' he asked

'Yes,' Mr Straker replied.

When he handed them over, they seemed new. The American smiled. One plate had the figure '1', the other the word 'first'. Both plates should, he insisted, look the same. He wanted the word put on the numbered plate and vice versa so 'in the process of printing reversing the figure and word by transfer'. Mr Straker got it straightaway. 'What would you do five hundred for?' Mr Brooks asked.

'Fifteen shillings,' Mr Straker replied.

'Could you try to do them before Christmas?' he asked. The printer demurred. 'Try and get them done before Christmas,' the American implored. 'I'll give you five shillings extra.'

Mr Straker said he would endeavour to do so and, as he later testified, 'continued to do business with George Bidwell till about the end of February'. At some point, he said his name was Brooks and Mr Straker took him at face value. 'Nothing caused the slightest suspicion in my mind while the work was going on,' he said.

The urgency was understandable, for now in the final days of 1872 everything came together. The gang was all here and so were all the elements required to forge copies of bills of exchange. To their amazement, they had not been that difficult to forge. In consequence, they could now set the greater fraud in motion.

Friday, 27 December 1872
Grosvenor Hotel, London

There was something satisfying in holding the genuine articles in their hands and comparing them to the forgeries. Austin Bidwell would always vividly recall his reaction to examining the fruits of their labour, 'for it was upon the imitation of just such acceptances that our whole plan was based'. It seemed apt that they were ensconced in a suite at what Austin later termed 'a swell hotel'.

As with all American visitors, he found the cuisine a little difficult to take, 'so we resolved to sleep at the Grosvenor,' he wrote, 'but to avoid the apple tart'. They would often congregate at a nearby restaurant, where on this evening, they treated their latest recruit to 'a little dinner given in his honor'. There, according to Austin's memoirs, they told him of their plot and 'he was astounded'.

Austin Bidwell had checked in at the Grosvenor at the start of December as Captain Bradshaw. A chambermaid recalled him saying that he had a friend coming, and a few days later a Colonel Mapelson duly arrived. This was George Macdonnell, and for a few days they shared a large room.

Then Captain Bradshaw said he had another friend coming, and when this fellow had duly arrived he gave the name Brooks and stayed for a few days. This was Edwin Hills and it was just after Christmas.

A further mystery concerning Edwin Noyes Hills' whereabouts hung over his first few days in the capital. The prosecution was never able to determine exactly where he had stayed. It did appear that he had checked into the Grosvenor under the name of the Reverend T.T. Hills. 'Where he went afterwards has not yet been discovered,' Freshfields would write, 'although we have advertised in the papers for the information.'

The next day would see the dispatch of the first forged bill based on one George Macdonnell had obtained in Liverpool at Gates' bank. As quickly as they obtained genuine bills, they would crank out forgeries, 'only leaving out the date until such time as we should be ready to put them in for discount'. If they passed muster, the way to the greater fraud was open. If they did not, the forgers could be arrested forthwith.

Ultimately, the culmination of their plans depended on whether the accepting banks would verify the genuineness of the signatures of the forged bills. 'This is always done in America,' Austin Bidwell noted, 'and had this very requisite precaution been used by the Bank of England our plan would have been fruitless and we should have been a few thousand pounds out of pocket.'

As remarkable as it seems to posterity, the acceptances were not checked. Bills of exchange bearing the acceptance of reputable companies were taken at face value and discounted without further inquiry. The fact they were forgeries would not be discovered until the bills fell due. 'It may sound fantastic that great financial institutions should neglect so obvious a business precaution,' one commentator noted. 'But more than one criminal history has shown that banks are blindly simple in some directions.'

But so too were lovelorn Americans many miles from home, whose need for female company would coincide with the greatest dangers they now faced at the culmination of their grand scheme upon the Old Lady of Threadneedle Street.

8

Hearts and Minds

> The briefest and truest way of describing Lombard Street is to say that it is by far the greatest combination of economical power and economical delicacy that the world has ever seen. Of the greatness of the power there will be no doubt. Money is economical power. Everyone is aware that England is the greatest moneyed country in the world; everyone admits that it has much more immediately disposable and ready cash than any other country. But very few persons are aware how much greater the ready balance the floating loan-fund which can be lent to anyone or for any purposes in England than it is anywhere in the world.
>
> Walter Bagehot, *Lombard Street*, written in 1873 as the events described here unfolded.

Christmas Day, 1872
Ford's Hotel, Central London

She knew she should have said no and stopped it while she had the chance. When she later heard about Austin's train crash, Nellie Vernon was grimly reminded of Christmas Day. That was exactly what their yuletide celebrations had been like. George Bidwell had been in a characteristically expansive mood. He wanted what he had termed a 'ladies evening'. Nellie's heart sank. She knew exactly what that would mean. His brother and their friend. For dinner. Again. She knew what was expected of her.

No doubt, George was thinking mostly of his younger brother, towards whom she had developed a terrible antipathy. She no longer had any illusions about Austin Bidwell, how out of kilter he had become. Introducing him to female company was always going to end badly. As for the other George, Mac, as they called him, he was more palatable but an inveterate show-off and at times his arrogance grated.

Against her better judgement, though, she had acquiesced. Nellie knew a pair of ballet girls from their days in Covent Garden. She suspected the boys might like them. Most men would fall for their delicate beauty – petite creatures, who were hardly as naive as they made out. Birds of a feather, you might say. As detectives later ascertained, Nellie seemed ashamed of them, a cause of great puzzlement at the time. 'She had always in the main held herself aloof from her old associates,' the prosecution would later surmise, 'and had tried to suggest she was a person of some position superior to that which she then occupied.'

Nellie often told people she was the daughter, or sometimes governess, of a medical man, but was in fact 'the daughter of a very second class Veterinary Surgeon'. Nevertheless, she looked down on the ballet girls she had invited over for Christmas lunch. 'One of them was kept by a clerk at the St James Restaurant,' Freshfields later noted. 'The other is on the town.' No further comment was necessary.

In the immediate run-up to Christmas, Nellie Vernon had gone to the West End to buy presents. George Bidwell had already opened an account at Arundell's, a hosiers on Bond Street. She returned with silk neck-wrappers for the boys and two small boxes with gloves for the girls. 'Her own present was a small keyless watch which George Bidwell purchased for her', the prosecution later determined, adding that it had come from a high-end jewellers in Leicester Square 'costing £8 10s'.

When Nellie examined the neckties, she saw that various initials were monogrammed on them. She was puzzled that there were four in total, the last one having the initials E.H. on them. 'George Bidwell told me that Austin, Macdonnell, and a friend of theirs would come to dine with us on Christmas Day,' she later recalled under oath. On 25 December 1872, that minor mystery was solved when she was introduced to a Mr Howe from Liverpool. 'I did not know what he was or what his business was, or where he was staying or the name of the hotel,' Nellie Vernon later said.

She warmed to him straightaway. He was different to the others, gentle, polite and courteous, which is more than could be said for Austin and Mac. Their behaviour on Christmas Day had been outrageous. That Wednesday, the dancers did not turn up until after dinner, which meant that their soirée did not actually break up until one o'clock in the morning. By then, they had all had too much to drink. The result, in the prosecution's later estimation, was that Austin and Mac 'wanted to be on more intimate terms with the young ladies'. It had been their turn to be disgusted, as the dancers refused to say anything more to them.

'Hills did not take any part in these proceedings,' the prosecutors noted. 'On the contrary, he appears to have been a quiet man keeping a great deal to himself.'

The others, who invariably fancied themselves as ladies' men, often laughed at his diffidence, 'but in a perfectly friendly way', as the prosecution termed it.

As it was late, the girls stayed overnight in another room at the hotel. They then had breakfast with George and Nellie, who had no further contact with them ever again. When they were subsequently traced, she denied all knowledge of knowing who they were. 'It was only by chance that we happened to find out who they were,' the prosecution later tabled, adding nothing further to resolve this mystery.

Similar chances revealed who exactly the fourth man really was. In the middle of March, Nellie Vernon was reintroduced to him at the Mansion House where he was being held on remand. There followed what the prosecution called a 'curious incident'. Down in the cells, Nellie greeted him 'much to his surprise and disgust, as Mr Howe of Liverpool'. He was not quite as innocent as he was trying to make out. 'He imagined at the time he was doing his part well and passing off as Noyes,' the prosecution noted, 'the clerk of C.J. Horton who had the account at the Continental Bank.'

In other words, the game was up so far as Edwin Noyes Hills was concerned.

Whether the drunkenness on Christmas Day was the breaking point is unknown, but immediately afterwards Nellie made it clear that she wanted little else to do with George's younger brother. 'Austin Bidwell was no favourite of Helen Vernon,' the prosecution commented. 'She says he tried to get her away from George Bidwell to himself, a story which we do not believe – his story is that he tried to keep his brother from women who he saw must prove a source of insecurity but without effect. This is more probable.'

Several others felt sorry for Austin Bidwell, but they were not half as sorry as he felt for himself over what the prosecution termed his 'private affairs'. Freshfields noted:

> During the previous month his affairs had been very much deranged by his attempts to induce the young lady whom he ultimately married to elope with him. At first we believe he was desirous of treating her as his mistress but when he found that she would not agree he determined on marrying her.

The prosecution, never ones to waste an opportunity to demolish his character, came up with a suitably damning description: 'A man of irregular mind.'

Austin Bidwell was hoping for a reversal of fortune so far as his relationship with Jeannie Devereux was concerned. He had, in the words of the prosecution, 'been making himself as agreeable as circumstances would permit to Miss Jeannie and consequently disagreeable to his future mother-in-law.' What little respect the elder Devereux had ever exhibited towards her daughter's suitor had evaporated. There was no longer any trust between them. Certainly, Jeannie's mother thought it a grave mistake that she had ever introduced Austin to her daughter 'and would gladly have sent him away if her daughter would have promised her to do so but she would not'.

All the fraudsters took great care over their dress and were notable by their impeccable manners. It is curious how important a role various tailors and outfitters would inadvertently assume in this unfolding saga – not least with their latest arrival. 'By our direction [Hills] went to an obscure hotel in Manchester Square,' Austin Bidwell later wrote, 'and then purchased clothes more suitable for his new position than the fashionable tailor-cut suit he wore from New York.'

During his first week in London, the prosecution later established that Hills had passed variously as Brooks, Williams, Hills and Estes. The week before Christmas (19 December) he went to buy various items of expensive clothing from tailors on the Strand and Regent Street which included a hat and a tweed suit. He did not give a name and said he would collect these purchases in person when they were ready. The prosecution noted a peculiarity: 'His legs are much longer than those of ordinary individuals, and his clothes, therefore, are easily identified.'

The day after, Mac (still posing as Colonel Mapelson) and George Bidwell (or Horace Arthur, as he was calling himself) went to a familiar haunt, Newton & Company in Hanover Square. They were 'old customers and were well known and they introduced Mr Williams as a new customer'. Hills spent about £25 on clothes while the others tried on bespoke suits that they had already purchased.

While staying at the Langham Hotel – in whose register Hills' writing was recognised and matched to the alias of E.C. Estes – he visited the Nelson's Portland Hotel which was nearby. He gave the name E.N. Hills to the proprietor, Kate English, who was not surprised. Both Georges Bidwell and Macdonnell had visited her over previous months and left various notes for him. 'Are you the Mr Bidwells' friend?' she asked, shortly before the New Year. Hills replied that he was. 'I have several letters for you and have been expecting you for some time.' On this first visit, Miss English then gave him the various letters which George Bidwell had left for him. He opened and read them in her presence.

'Will you take in my letters for me?' Hills asked. 'I had at first proposed stopping at this hotel. I have changed my plans and I think I shall stay a little way out of town with a friend.' Miss English agreed, and recalled that he returned two weeks later.

By then, 'Mr and Mrs Bidwell' had moved to new lodgings. Since the disaster of Christmas Day, George and Nellie Vernon had had dinner with 'Mr Howe' on a couple of evenings. They made a nice, easy social grouping. On the afternoon of New Year's Day, the hail and driving rain had cleared to allow them all to go riding. On the following Saturday, 4 January, they went to the Crystal Palace together. The couple returned to their new apartments near to Regent's Park.

Claiming it was too expensive, George and Nellie had checked out of Ford's Hotel on 1 January. For the rest of his time in England, George lived with 'Mrs Bidwell' in rented accommodation in Upper Gloucester Place. 'We rather suspect that he considered he had been long enough in the place and was known,' the prosecution recorded. 'That the forged bills would be soon ready to issue and that he must destroy all trace of his whereabouts. He was therefore desirous of going to see some place where he would be more difficult to find.'

⸎

Perhaps as a result of their drunken behaviour, Austin Bidwell and George Macdonnell spent a few days in Brighton immediately after Christmas. They went down to the Bedford Hotel, where Mac checked in using his own name on 27 December. Austin Bidwell joined him three days later. They spent New Year's Eve together, drowning their sorrows and wondering what the New Year might bring.

On his return to London on New Year's Day, Austin went to his old room at the Golden Cross Hotel. This, the prosecution believed, was 'possibly that as soon as he began to discount Bills, enquiries might be made for him there'. At the best of times, Austin Bidwell was 'locomotive' (in the prosecution's estimation) and there was never any evidence that he ever slept or ate there until Saturday, 11 January 1873. The next day he checked out and headed to Paris.

That same evening, there was a tearful goodbye at Victoria Station. But the tears were not Jeannie Bidwell's. Like all the other forgers, Austin had wandering eyes. On this, for once, the prosecution was uncharacteristically diplomatic. 'No doubt, however, Austin Bidwell did not see as much of Miss Jeannie as he desired and as she would not dispense with marriage he had to form acquaintances elsewhere.'

⸎

The Turkish Divan was a bar and restaurant on Haymarket that saw many foreign, especially American, visitors. 'A great number of gentlemen go there to have cigars and coffee,' said one barmaid, who was later interviewed by the police. Frances Catherine Gray was a good-looking woman in her early twenties who was employed there from time to time. One night in December 1872, she had been introduced to a gentleman called 'Theodore Bingham' whom she later found out was actually called Austin Bidwell. George Macdonnell was also introduced as his doctor.

This 'rendezvous', as one of the prosecution termed it, was the cause of much speculation, not least about what kind of encounter it had been. Under a later cross-examination, Frances Gray provided an innocent snapshot in an almost other worldly way. 'I suppose there was smoking going on?'

'Oh yes.'

'And coffee?'

'Yes.'

'And Lemonade?'

'Yes.'

'Anything in the shape of drink?'

'Yes.'

But what counsel and the other lawyers did not ask the witness was what everybody else in court, or who read about the case, thought – was she a woman of loose morals? Because prostitution was exactly what the Haymarket was known for, an infamy that had spread in one contemporary estimation as 'a cancer in the great heart of London'. The street that links Piccadilly with Trafalgar Square, which housed many famous theatres, displayed a more curious form of drama each evening.

The Haymarket was a den of iniquity. To be fair, by the 1870s it had cleaned up its act from the heyday of its greater notoriety, but even so the reputation as 'the wicked street' remained. 'It was not just a simple promenade,' one recent historian writes, 'It was the piazza of an entire district turned over at night to sexual commerce.' And a remarkable sight too, for 'the troops of elegantly dressed courtesans,' another observed, 'rustling in silks and satins, waving in laces, promenading along these superb streets among throngs of fashionable people.' This involved what others had termed 'the lamentable Haymarket march past', the 'mutton walks' where prostitutes simply handed out their cards. Invariably, even respectable women found themselves accosted. If enticed into saloons, visitors found that the owners had ingeniously united 'the profits of a tavern to those of a brothel'. In some estimations, places like the Turkish Divan were little more than glorified 'knocking shops'.

As a result, there was certainly an abhorrent fascination about Frances Catherine Gray, who would play an unusual role in this saga. Described as a 'fair syren' in one newspaper report, the prosecution had already damned her with the faintest of praise in its assessment of her character. 'She was a lively, talkative, tolerably good-looking woman,' they would write. She only worked the evening shift, as the prosecutors noted, 'to assist and make herself agreeable to the customers frequenting the Divan'. Just how agreeable became another matter of prurient speculation.

The prosecution determined that Austin Bidwell often escorted her home to Pimlico, a choice of district which was also well known as a haunt of what were termed 'ladies of the night', amusing her with stories about himself and his travels and life abroad.

Day Five – Friday, 22 August 1873
Central Criminal Court, Old Bailey
3 p.m.

When she eventually came to give evidence on the stand, Frances Gray described herself as a single woman. There were a lot of nods and winks in the courtroom, not least when she was examined by Harry Poland. 'Used these three prisoners to come to the Turkish Divan in the evening?' he asked of the trio nearest her in the dock.

'Yes.'

'Were they friends?'

'I suppose so,' she said, a little uncertainly. 'They came in together.'

'Did Bingham tell you who Macdonnell was?'

'He said he was his doctor.'

'Do you know what Bingham was?' he asked. 'I suppose you know he was an American?'

'Yes.'

'And Hills – whose name you did not know – did they tell you at all what he was, either Bingham or Macdonnell?'

'Yes.'

'What did they say?'

'They said he was a genius.'

Mr Poland was now puzzled. 'Who said Hills was a genius?'

'Macdonnell.'

'Did he say in what way he was a genius?'

'He said he had come over to invent something.' And then the Central Criminal Court crowd erupted in laughter at this most surreal of statements which seemed to catch everybody off guard.

Austin Bidwell never gave up hopes of marrying Jeannie Devereux. As her mother would not let her anywhere near him, the lure of elopement grew stronger in his mind. In the first week of the New Year, he met a curate at a chapel off Regent Street and started to arrange the necessary legal proceedings. While visiting this place of worship, a ceremony was going on. Austin Bidwell then walked up to the altar, knelt down and, as he later told Willie Pinkerton, 'registered a solemn vow to High Heaven never to do wrong again as long as he lived'.

It was yet another forlorn hope. When the prosecutors came to look into the matter, they found that on Wednesday, 8 January he had obtained a marriage licence. It may well be that he intended to marry Jeannie Devereux that same day, for in a handwritten note, dated only '11 a.m. Wednesday', Austin wrote, 'My darling. I am so very, very sorry for you and am wretched to think that you should have suffered such pain today.'

He was supposed to have met her at 10 a.m. 'to the minute', but she did not show. 'Does your mother know of the church?' he asks, clearly worried. He had waited until 10.30 a.m., having driven around the corner and then back 'but knew it was no use doing more as we could not have got married after eleven'.

For the first time, he told Jeannie that he was compelled to go to Paris and that he would come for her again. 'The next time there will be no failure,' he promised her. 'I have the wedding ring in my pocket.' When Jeannie subsequently told her mother they were going to the French capital, she did her best to stop them. After Austin wrote to her to say Mac would pick her up, Mrs Devereux denounced them as 'thieves and swindlers', the first time anyone had accused them of such in the British Isles.

In reality, they had a rather more pressing need to cross the English Channel.

Tuesday, 14 January 1873
Rothschild Bank, Arondissement IX, Paris

It is not often that you get to meet a deity in person. The day after the rail accident that nearly brought him to his maker, Austin Bidwell was ushered into the presence of a god of the fiscal world, Baron Alphonse de Rothschild himself. After being greeted at the entrance, an undermanager expressed concern at the state of *le monsieur's* wellbeing. Milking it for all he could, Austin was then escorted into an inner sanctum where appeared a slight, sallow complected man in his early forties, who was held in sycophantic awe by his various attendants and retainers (one of whom recalled their visitor 'had pieces of plaster on his forehead and he looked very unwell altogether').

For someone who was so well moneyed, Monsieur le Baron struck an incongruously shabby figure in his suit of snuff-coloured garments. Atop his head was an old-fashioned stovepipe hat, which he removed as he spoke, clearly perturbed by the esteemed customer's suffering. 'Accidents are most unusual in France,' Rothschild said, offering a profuse apology. In Austin's recollection, the baron added that he would order his own doctor to treat him without any expense. Cleverly, Austin Bidwell made light of his obvious injuries, taking care to praise the railways and their management. He then gave the baron a substantial account of what happened. 'I stood quite close to them and heard what was said,' said one clerk, Ernest Lorelli. The baron replied by saying that he was very sorry, he very much sympathised with him. As he clearly wasn't angling for compensation, the prosecution surmised, the baron was more inclined to help.

'I would like to obtain a bill for £20,000,' Austin then said. More than he ever expected to get, it was a large sum of money to have locked up in any account. Despite his predisposition to kindness, Baron de Rothschild could not agree to this 'but at last he settled matters by giving him a draft on Messrs Rothschild & Sons for £4,500'. This was then prepared, during which time Austin handed over 99,000 francs in Bank of France notes. This was not quite enough to pay for the bill, whose total value came to 113,000 francs.

'At two o'clock I was at the hotel,' Austin says in his memoirs, 'and an attendant came with the bills and pointing to a signature on it, informed me that it was that of a Cabinet Minister, equivalent to our Secretary of the Treasury.' This was due to the 1 per cent revenue stamp required. According to Austin, Baron Rothschild had personally paid it himself at the Treasury. Whether this was one of Austin's embellishments, it hardly matters. 'I had been only eighteen hours in Paris,' he added, 'and by a happy fluke the business was done over which I had counted upon spending a good part of the month.'

Early the next morning, Austin Bidwell took the Dover steamer from Calais. He watched the nearly full moon cast its eerie light across the Channel. By the time he reached London after breakfast, he claims Mac was still in bed when he visited him at the Coburg Hotel. When his brother later showed up, both Georges 'deemed it incredible that I had succeeded within a day'.

Despite the distractions of his recent accident and forthcoming marriage, the greater fraud was progressing remarkably well. 'The plan was complete at last,' Austin Bidwell later wrote. 'Everything was ready to carry out our scheme in perfect safety to all, and I was now on my way to the bank for my last visit, with the Rothschild bill in my hand.'

Friday, 22 August 1873
Central Criminal Court, Old Bailey
3.10 p.m.

On the stand, Frances Gray looked decidedly uncomfortable. Under oath, Harry Poland asked her to confirm that she had become 'on friendly terms with Austin Bidwell'. She agreed and revealed that she had seen him off at Charing Cross Station 'some time in January, I should think'. She remembered him taking his ticket, then saying he was going away on business, 'not what particular business', and was away two or three days. They met up again at the Turkish Divan.

'Did you notice any change in his appearance?' Mr Poland prompted.

'His face was strapped up,' she explained, 'he had met with an accident.'

Mr Justice Archibald leaned forward. 'How do you mean strapped up?' he asked.

'He had a small piece of plaster upon the forehead.'

Mr Poland waited and then continued: 'I believe he told you that how it had occurred?'

'Yes,' she replied, 'that there had been an accident on the line.'

'What line?'

'The line to Paris,' she said uncertainly. 'I do not know.'

'Did he say what train it was?'

'The mail train.'

'I believe he said some persons were killed in the accident?'

'Yes, two persons I think.'

'Did he speak of his own escape?'

'Yes.'

'He only got injured?'

She replied yes. Mr Poland then wanted to know exactly when this conversation had taken place. 'At the end of January, I should think, as near as I can remember.'

Judge Archibald made some notes and addressed the prosecution, 'I suppose you have got further evidence of the accident?'

Mr Poland nodded before continuing. 'That was the date as near as you can tell?'

'Yes'

'And was that the last time you saw him?'

'Yes.'

'Had you any reason to believe from him that would be the last time? Did he say anything at all about his going away?'

'No.'

Saturday, 18 January 1873
St James Place, London

Trust Mac to find a doctor who was an expert on syphilis. To be fair, Walter John Coulson MRCS FRCS was a pre-eminent surgeon who practiced in one of the more exclusive enclaves of the capital, St James Place. But he was more than a fashionable doctor for the well-to-do. Dr Coulson had already written two standard references, *Stone in the Bladder* (1868) and two years later, *A Treatise on Syphilis*. For the last few weeks, he had been treating George Macdonnell, whose malarial symptoms had flared up again, with his own 'mercurial bath' treatment.

Even now, six months after his return from Rio, their severity occasionally laid Mac low, but that was nothing compared to the injuries his friend had more recently sustained. When Austin Bidwell was now introduced to his surgeon, Dr Coulson's eyes widened when he saw how badly injured he was. 'I intend to leave England immediately,' Austin said.

'If you do, you must travel at once,' Dr Coulson said, his Cornish accent obvious.

That was the way that George Macdonnell recalled it on the stand on the last day of the trial. According to Mac, Austin had taken up his advice straight away. Mac later claimed on the stand:

I thought it very likely that he might be induced to change his mind, and I had other cheques prepared, leaving a small balance on both accounts. These two cheques were cashed, and the proceeds left in my hands. The first forged bill was sent down to Birmingham on the 21st of January.

This money would then be invested in United States bonds which would be shortly obtained in Paris and later Frankfurt. On this, Mac was unequivocal:

> Up to this time a great deal of money had been thrown away in continually transferring and re-transferring the papers. The idea of losing that money and having no return for it at all did not please me very much; but as Austin Bidwell said he would leave, was determined to leave, and did leave, I could only let him go, and he went.

Before he did, though, a luminous presence returned to light up the wintry gloom. Jeannie Devereux came to visit Austin several times at the Edwards Hotel in Hanover Square (where Mac had also stayed) and his mood improved immeasurably. 'He made up his mind to marry her if she would have him,' the prosecution noted. When Jeannie all but fell into his arms on the spot, the final pieces of his life – and his escape – were in place.

'Everything now was ready for my departure from England,' Austin Bidwell says in his memoirs. 'For some weeks my partners had been busy preparing for the completion of the operation.' There was one last thing to obtain: the approval of his cohorts. Between all of the thieves of Threadneedle Street, Austin Bidwell later maintained to Willie Pinkerton there was always a code of honour. None could quit without the consent of the others. One day, that final week he was in London, Austin Bidwell got up from his sickbed and sought where the 'others' were staying (most likely the Coburg Hotel).

When he walked in, the two Georges could tell there was something up. 'Boys can you spare me?' Austin asked. 'I want to square it. I want to get married and if you will let me, I want to live honest.' They all congratulated him and cracked open the bottles of champagne. Austin Bidwell later claimed to Pink that he wanted to take his share of the capital – roughly $6,000 – as well as money he had saved in America. Austin assured them that the wedding would not take place for a few more weeks. In fact, he wanted to get married the very next day.

In his own memoirs, George Bidwell maintained that he did not want his brother to remain in England. Straight-faced, he claimed he refused to have anything to do with the forgery 'unless Austin was first beyond danger'. This clearly was nonsense. George Bidwell was certainly worried that his younger brother might be distracted by his new bride. 'Do not think of marrying her before you are settled in business,' George claims he said to his brother. 'Go home, and with the money you have, get into some legitimate occupation.' And then, he could marry in good conscience. 'But when did a person in love ever act from prudential considerations?' George asked, a hopeless, yet hypocritical, romantic to the last.

Tuesday, 21 January 1873
London

The penultimate Tuesday in January was, as the prosecution later noted, 'an episode in the history of the Forgery'. That same morning Austin Bidwell had essentially withdrawn all his money from both bank accounts, as Warren at the Bank of England and as Horton at the Continental Bank, leaving under £100 (£47 4s 6d at the former and at the Continental Bank £49 5s 10d), before he departed that evening for France.

'The inference clearly is that it was the intention of the forgers to draw out as much of their Capital as they could with safety and to send the greater part of it out of the country in a shape in which it could not easily be traced,' Freshfields observed. As they were about to send up the first batch of forged bills to the Bank of England, it seemed a sensible precaution, not least, as the prosecution noted, it was 'probable that Austin Bidwell left England intending not to come back if he could possibly help it'.

This had less to do with the fraud – rather an act of vengeance. On either the day before or that same Tuesday, he had made arrangements at St Martin's-in-the-Fields to get married. However, on one of those final two days in the city, there was a scene that he was likely never to forget. When he later told Willie Pinkerton about the circumstances, a rueful smile played across his face, 'Just as I was stepping into a cab with my fair bride, along came the cruel mamma'. The wailing banshee who was Mrs Devereux tore her daughter from his side, gave him a piece of her mind and took the weeping daughter home. 'She gave her a fearful pounding,' Austin added (though did not elaborate).

As Pink later recorded, 'all his hopes were blasted in a moment and he cut off to the Continent.' Though he liked to claim he had left earlier than this Tuesday, the prosecution noted that 'this – like all the rest of his stories – cannot be believed, but we do believe that he left on the evening of the 21st'.

George Macdonnell, in the meantime, decided to move thanks to a suggestion by Dr Coulson. The surgeon owned a private hotel at No. 17 St James Place, and at some point he suggested Mac should hire rooms there run by Agnes Green, daughter of the famous lawyer Paddy Green. He eventually moved there at the start of February and remained there until the forgeries were discovered.

Friday, 22 August 1873
Central Criminal Court, Old Bailey
3.20 p.m.

On the stand, Frances Gray shifted uncomfortably. All present were hanging on every word as she recalled the circumstances of what had happened once Austin Bidwell left for France.

'After Dorey left,' Mr Poland continued, 'did you receive any letters from anyone except from Hills or from Macdonnell?'

'No, never.'

'You say you are really sure that it was Hills that brought you the letter?'

'Yes.'

Mr Justice Archibald wanted to be certain. 'It was one of them?' he asked.

'Yes.'

Austin's counsel was not happy. 'That does not show that this letter was written by Austin Biron Bidwell because she never saw him write and cannot speak to his writing,' Mr McIntyre stated.

Mr Justice Archibald disagreed. 'The evidence is that she always called him 'Dorey' – that was the name he had and she also says that one of the prisoners – either Macdonnell or Hills – brought her this letter.'

'She said in answer to my friend, Macdonnell or Noyes always brought her letters,' Mr McIntyre corrected.

'And that no one else ever brought her letters from Dorey except them,' the judge interjected.

Mr McIntyre realised he would have to try a new approach. 'Will Your Lordship ask her whether she had seen any letters given to her from any other man except Macdonnell or Hills?'

'Signed Dorey you mean?' the judge replied, nodding towards the witness. 'She has said so. Was that what you want to say?'

'Yes.'

The letter itself was now read out in court and was hardly a billet-doux:

Friday PM

My dear Daisy

I will be unable to see you, I am sorry to say, until I change my quarters, which I hope will be on Monday, and I shall do so almost only because I can see you. My friend will tell you how I am I can only write with difficulty, so I will write no more, only to say that I am, dear Daisy, yours very truly, Dorey.

In his later writings, Austin Bidwell claims that he left London 'serene and confident of the future', two days before the first batch of forged bills had been sent in (though the prosecution determined it was the day before). Either way, he could not be connected with the execution of the crime.

The prosecution had already anticipated such a gambit. On the first day of the trial, Hardinge Giffard, had elegantly demolished it with what became known as 'the Kamchatka defence'. Even if he was out of the country, Giffard noted, Austin Bidwell was still responsible:

A man may be at Kamchatka or Rome and yet be just as much guilty as if he were in London if he was a party to the fraud, and I need not tell you what a very strange system of jurisprudence it would be if the laws were otherwise, if it were only necessary for a man to go across the water to another country and then to say he had not committed any offence in the country to which he sends the paper.

Giffard prepared the sucker punch which he hoped the jury would bear in mind when they came to consider the evidence:

There is a very old legal maxim, the importance of which occurs to me that a man who does it by another does it by himself. A man who utters a forged bill in London for the purpose of proxy it to be passed on as a genuine bill is simply the longer hand of the man residing in Rome or Kamchatka and both will be equally responsible but as I have said, the scheme was that Austin Bidwell should be protected and accordingly he appears to have left London.

Friday, 22 August 1873
Central Criminal Court, Old Bailey
3.30 p.m.

There was an expectant hush in the court as Mr Justice Archibald leaned over towards Frances Gray. He addressed her directly. 'I see that letter is addressed to you as "my dear Daisy".' She nodded.

'I suppose that was your familiar name?' Mr Poland asked, his insinuation clear.

'Yes,' Frances Gray said.

'Was he in the habit of calling you by that name?' the judge wanted to know.

'Yes.'

Mr Poland then asked about a £20 note sent by Macdonnell. 'Did he say who had sent it?'

'Yes.'

'Who?'

'Dorey.'

'Did he say where Dorey was going?'

'Yes, to the south of France.'

'Macdonnell said that, did he?'

'Yes.'

'Did he say for what purpose?'

'For the benefit of his health only.'

To be fair, there was a grain of truth in this claim. Austin Bidwell would eventually head to Frankfurt for his health, or so he claimed to his future fiancée, who thought it an excellent idea. Jeannie Devereux said as much in one of the many letters she sent him after his departure, 'Mama was at school there when a girl and says there are some very fine minerals in the vicinity of the city at a place called Schawalbach quite the colour of milk and warm, very efficacious for rheumatism.'

This correspondence, gladly handed over to the prosecution by the Devereux family, shows just how badly the wedding preparations played out. Their efforts at elopement were hampered at every turn. 'I am writing this under extreme difficulties Mama being just at my elbow but dear old soul she would never suspect me,' Jeannie wrote on one occasion (the note is undated). Her sister had begged her to write and would deliver it but, if she ever became aware of it, that would 'make Mama very cross'. It ended abruptly, 'Leave no more time to put down here as Mama is coming nearer. Ma looks can't write more. 12 o'clock tomorrow p.m. at your hotel.'

When Austin Bidwell subsequently left London, everything became even more complicated.

Friday, 22 August 1873
Central Criminal Court, Old Bailey
3.40 p.m.

Harry Poland wanted to know what happened once Austin Bidwell evaporated from her life. 'After that did you see Macdonnell and the other prisoner Hills?' he asked Frances Gray.

'Yes.'

'Used they to come to the Divan?'

'Yes, sometimes.'

'And did you ask [either] of them about Austin Bidwell?'

'Yes.'

'Which one did you speak to about that?'

'Macdonnell generally.'

'What did Macdonnell say about him?'

'He said he was very ill, suffering from the accident.'

'And did he tell you what he was going to do to him? You understood he was the doctor.'

'He said he was suffering from a shot wound.'

'That Austin Bidwell was suffering from a shot wound?'

'Yes.'

'Did he say what it was with reference to the accident as to that?'

'That he would have to have the ball extracted from his side I think he said.'

'I understand you to say that he said he was going to extract a ball from his side?'

'Yes.' After acknowledging that she had received 'two or three letters from Dorey', there was a discussion over who exactly had brought them. Looking at them on the stand, she was asked about one letter in particular.

'Who brought you the letter?' Mr Poland asked.

'I think it was Noyes.'

Hills' defence counsel stood up. 'Did you say that Noyes brought it?'

'I think so.'

'Then you are not sure.'

'No I am not sure.'

'It may have been somebody else.'

'I am almost certain, but I am not sure,' she said. 'I think it was Noyes.'

Mr McIntyre interjected. 'Did you even see Theodore Bingham write?'

'No,' she agreed, 'I never saw him write.'

'Did you see him at any time in reference to that letter?'

'No, I never saw him again after I received the letter.'

Austin Bidwell never gave Frances Catherine Gray another thought.

Thursday, 23 January 1873
Paris, France

Austin Bidwell had arrived in Paris on Thursday, 23 January and stayed for six days. In a letter dated Sunday, 26 January he informed Jeannie that he was not well enough to come home — yet. Mac would either show up in person on the Monday to tell her his latest plans or he would send a further letter. In this particular communication, Austin was revealing about his near contemporary, 'As you know he is a friend of mine, trustworthy and true and tried for many years and a Gentleman.' Anything that Mac suggested should be taken as though coming from Austin himself. 'He knows nothing as to my troubles with your mother,' her fiancé concluded. 'I have told him that we were probably married against the wish of your mother.' The spectre of Mrs Devereux remained omnipresent.

To avoid any unpleasant scenes, Jeannie should join him as soon as she possibly could. 'Of course, under ordinary circumstances this would not be the course I would pursue, but then needs must when the Devil drives,' he confessed. All would be fine he reassured her. Arrangements were on track. 'In conclusion, I must say that I dread these long delays,' he wrote, 'they are very discouraging.' Calling England a strange land 'so far away', he steeled himself, noting that 'soon if I am not wide awake the river will run by and leave me asleep on the banks'. Signing himself 'Your devoted lover Austin', in a postscript he added that he had also sent £100 to Mac to give to her but 'please do not open before him, he does not know the contents'.

When George Macdonnell went to deliver this money, he missed her. In Jeannie's reply to Austin's letter — 'so mysteriously delivered' dated Tuesday morning, most likely 28 January — he now informed her that Mac would see her in a couple of days. As for her mother, Austin lamented, 'I have absolutely no terms to make with her just now'.

In those final days of January, it felt like Austin Bidwell's world was falling apart. All he really wanted to see was Jeannie's signature on a marriage certificate. In the surviving correspondence sent from Paris, he was alternately excited and worried by the impending nuptials. All Jeannie had to do was write and make sure that the gorgon that was her mother would not be there when they met. But the time delays from his travels meant that it was difficult to maintain continuity.

And on that last Tuesday in January (though undated, it was the only date possible), Austin Bidwell was preparing to leave for Frankfurt but wanted to offer her guidance. Jeannie should not hesitate to telegraph. 'Do not forget how I desire to have you act under certain circumstances with your mother,' he warned. His intentions were now clear. 'It is possible that I may telegraph you from Germany to meet me in Paris. Have no fear of starting alone as I will meet you on your arrival.'

Austin suggested she take the 8.40 p.m. train from Charing Cross. Given that she might have to leave when her mother was not looking, he could not be certain he would be in France to meet her. She should go to a hotel or the one he was staying at in Paris – Grand Hotel St James, on the rue St Honoré – and wait. He would always reach her by telegraph. 'Above all remember that you will have plenty of money in your pocket,' he wrote, 'and that makes all the world your slaves and you can never be embarrassed.'

The wedding plans were now taking on a life of their own. When she attended to the details, she should go alone and not depend on friends ('ordinary mortals'). 'You are not purchasing your entire wardrobe,' Austin warned, somewhat schizophrenically adding that she might just need a dress to travel in and evening wear. She should, he said, only purchase the best. Jeannie also should buy a large ladies travelling trunk or a travelling basket, 'that is a very large wicker work basket about £4 cost covered with black canvas and with two straps', which would be useful for linen, dresses and light bulky articles. So as to confuse her mother, when Jeannie bought the dresses she should have the trunks taken to the same shops, too, to be packed. 'I am sure you can manage it.'

That same afternoon of the last Tuesday in January, George Macdonnell had joined Austin Bidwell in the French capital. They both checked in to the same hotel, the Hotel Richmond, where Austin had previously stayed with his brother in September 1872. That same day, he bought 'handkerchiefs at Longuervilles in Paris – orders them to be sent to Frankfurt'. He left for there on the Wednesday night, 29 January, after buying various bills of exchange which had the stamps that George Bidwell had used to forge acceptances on them.

'He paid these bills with French money,' Freshfields noted on the eve of the trial, 'but where he obtained this money from we have not yet ascertained.' These were a couple of cheques for £1,000, about which the prosecution came to believe 'that Austin Bidwell suggested the name of Clark to Macdonnell and the letter did the business, he being the better French scholar of the two'.

Thursday, 30 January 1873

On the last Thursday in January, George Macdonnell returned to London, where he assumed a new role: that of a go-between. Over the next ten days, Mach was constantly delivering letters to Jeannie and passing her information from telegrams that he either sent or received from his friend in Germany. No wonder the poor girl was soon bewildered. At 11.30 p.m. that same Thursday, Jeannie wrote to Mac from Edgware Road, thanking him for his letter and the 'strange mystery that ran through Austin's letter'. This seemed to be a statement that they would never meet again.

Certainly, she was keen to meet Mac the next day, Friday, 31 January. She would wait at 2 p.m. on 'the corner of Connaught Terrace, the first turning on the left hand from Marble Arch'. He did not need to reply, but strangely that same Friday, she sent him another note timed at 7 p.m. from Richmond Road, Bayswater. If needed, he could send a telegram, 'Harry, my little brother turns out particularly useful in going up there for me three times a day. I really shall not know what to do when he does return to school.'

Certainly, she seemed to think Austin's melancholy had more to do with recent events. 'I hope he does not suffer from that horrid accident,' she wrote. 'If he ever forgets me, kindly let me know that he is better.'

Thursday, 30 January 1873
Frankfurt

Austin Bidwell arrived in Frankfurt late on the Wednesday night when he checked into the Hotel du Nord and signed the register as F. Aldrich. On his arrival, he found a telegram had been sent from London by his brother using the alias of Harry Bedford, 'Buy immediately several small London sight at Frankfurt. Mac's address: Edwards Hotel, Maddox Street.'

This was an important link in the evidence chain. As the prosecution later noted, it was the 'answer to A. Bidwell's suggestion that he had no part in the forgeries after he left London'. The next day he moved to Wiesbaden and stayed at the Hotel Victoria as F. Bidwell. Over the next few days, he criss-crossed between the two, presumably to lessen the chances of his being caught should any of the forged bills not pass muster.

Early the next day, he returned to Frankfurt from where he sent another telegram to Mac. 'Make no more in this matter except to telegraph me Miss D address and tell her to write full particulars. Impossible to come to London.'

When he checked out of the Hotel du Nord a week later, he failed ('we say "forgotten"', the prosecution noted, 'because we think he was too wise to do so intentionally') to pay his hotel bill. As a result, Mr F. Aldrich made a lasting impression on the proprietor. As the prosecution noted, 'but for this little incident we think it very probable that Austin Bidwell would not have been remembered from the number of visitors at the Hotel in Frankfurt.'

Frankfurt, in that later winter of 1873, was ridiculously busy despite the ominous fear that the world's economies were overheating. Though never as important a financial centre as London (Great Britain remained the world's foremost trading nation), it had always been an important mercantile powerhouse since Charlemagne had established his fort there in the eighth century. The city had also been surprisingly liberal towards its Jewish money lenders whose influence was welcomed by all the ruling families of Europe. Foremost among them was another financial dynasty, one of whose forebears had been aptly termed *le Roi de Francfort* by admiring French suppliants. The Bethmanns might not be as important as the Rothschilds, but in Frankfurt they were equally grand and revered as patrician supporters of the arts.

For now, on this cold January morning, Austin Bidwell walked into what was known as Bethmann Frères, where he carried out a couple of transactions in false names. For the first time, he used forged bills of exchange which amounted to many thousands of dollars. His victims were upper-crust burghers, the heads of the private Bethmann Bank. In fact, he had already visited these same premises the previous October where he had been received by the anglophile Moritz (Baron Ludwig Simon Moritz Freiherr von Bethmann, to give him his full name) and now, three months later, in the guise of F. Aldrich, dealt with his younger brother Hugo.

'He came with some United States bonds which he asked us to sell for him,' von Bethmann said, on the fourth day of the trial. Mr Aldrich had presented nine bonds consisting of seven separate $1,000 bills and two of $500. 'A little more than £2,000,' as Hugo von Bethmann clarified.

Subsequently, a complaint came in 'about one bond that was a little torn,' as Baron Hugo put it. It was paid out even though it was returned to Bethmann Frères who did not pass it back to their customer as they normally should have done. 'How was the rest of it paid?' Giffard asked.

'It was paid in money of the Frankfurt Bank.'

'That would be paper money?'

'Paper money,' he agreed.

Given that this was the new, unified German currency, no wonder Mr Aldrich looked happy when he left. Indeed, he returned the next day, wanting a further $10,000 of the same kind of bonds to be sold. On the stand, Hugo von Bethmann explained that they were often selling American bonds at that time. Though he did not personally perform these transactions – they were done by underlings – Baron Hugo had re-examined his records the week before the trial. 'We had a great many bills in our possession that morning,' he also recalled, 'I did not read them all.'

'Was Bidwell there when you read it?' Mr McIntyre prompted.

'He was in the other room,' Hugo von Bethmann said. 'In the next room.'

The bills were endorsed by a W.J. Spaulding and a Charles Gordon Brown, aliases later traced back to the forgers. On this point, Baron Bethmann was re-examined by Hardinge Giffard. 'You have seen that endorsement now and the Bill itself and have you any doubt that was the Bill given to Austin Biron Bidwell.'

'No doubt.'

Saturday, 1 February 1873
Frankfurt

Austin Biron Bidwell had other things on his mind that same Saturday. At one o'clock that afternoon from the Hotel du Nord in Frankfurt, he wrote Jeannie Devereux what he termed a 'long and important letter'. He sent it via George Macdonnell in the hope he would deliver it in person. 'Please be careful that he learns no more than possible of our affairs,' Austin warned, 'though he is so good a friend.'

That same evening, Mac himself received a telegram from Austin. 'I regret to say as usual with English telegrams from the Continent,' Mac explained to Jeannie in a note, 'this one is somewhat obscure.' This was George Macdonnell at his disingenuous best. 'I understand from it that he went to Frankfurt a/m the day after I saw him in Paris,' Mac wrote to Jeannie, pretending he did not know. 'He says the doctors forbade him to travel and consequently he would be unable to come to London as he proposed.' As soon as he received anything, Mac would be certain to bring it over 'with my very sincere wish that the circumstances which seem to conspire against your happiness may be speedily removed'.

By the Monday, Jeannie was revealing more of her steely resolve. Thanking Mac for the above note, she complained how 'unkind' it was for Austin not to write to her directly. She had already replied to another correspondence. Though her original letters are lost, Austin referred to the fact she had accused him of 'such depth of villainy' in his later reply. As Jeannie now explained to Mac, 'I know I sent cross letters but I felt so dreadfully unhappy and angry I did not know what I was doing.'

She was full of remorse. 'I will write to Austin immediately,' she added, thanking Mac for all his troubles. 'Fancy you going out to post my telegram in all this snow,' she said, obviously unsure if they would ever get to meet up – or marry.

Just how industrious the forgers had been came with the testimony of other bankers in Frankfurt. Auguste Fleischman, a clerk for Messrs. Koch, Lautéren & Co., recalled via a translator that Austin Bidwell had visited that same Saturday, 1 February, to buy some bonds which were given to him in exchange for Frankfurt Bank notes. Herr Fleischmann made a note for the files recording the purchase. There were $15,000 US bonds which were bought in the name of Mary Ann Kellogg. Austin Bidwell, as ever, did not give his name.

'Was he a perfect stranger to you?' asked Mr McIntyre in cross-examination.

'Yes,' said the translator, 'he was quite unknown to him.'

'A perfect stranger', a phrase that had resonated throughout the trial.

Another foreign money lender called Bias Schwarzchild recognised both Bidwells, 'I knew George Bidwell as H.E. Gilbert,' he explained, and had seen him in the previous October 'where he gave an order to sell some American bonds for a Mrs W. Hall'.

When cross-examining, Mr McIntyre asked this witness a variation on his earlier theme. 'Whoever the man was that came – he was a stranger to you?'

'Yes.'

Joseph Bruckheim, another clerk who had worked in the Frankfurt Bank, recalled that on that first Saturday in February, Austin Bidwell had walked in, introduced himself as Henry C. Clark and wished to buy two bills. Mr Bruckheim asked for him to endorse one for £19 4s, in favour of a 'Miss Jane Pavy'.

The final foreign witness, Isidore Wolff, was a clerk at Messrs Morepurgo & Weisweiler, who had been taken to Newgate and had recognised Austin Bidwell. He had originally known him as A.H. Trafford. 'I only saw him once and I never saw him before,' he said.

Tuesday, 4 February 1873
Wiesbaden

By the Tuesday of the following week, all seemed to be resolved with the forthcoming nuptials of Austin Bidwell – badly.

The groom later told Willie Pinkerton that the reason he had gone off to the Continent was because all his hopes were 'blasted'. While staying in Wiesbaden, he had received a telegram from Jeannie which read simply 'Everything is lonely'.

When next he had heard from her, it prompted feelings of sadness and wonder. 'Did I not know that you are so good, so loving and amiable and so lovable, too,' for which he could only protest that his 'more than honourable, my loving intentions to you for I know that with you I need no advocate'. Worrying about 'how slight a thing may cause misunderstandings between those that love' Austin said that 'if we are separated for a little while I will not give you up'.

And then came the most intriguing part. 'I have not heard from you in reference to my proposition of Saturday. I am in great hopes that you and your mother will meet me in Paris as I propose in that letter.' It seems he had bitten the bullet and asked the elder Mrs Devereux's permission to marry her daughter. Claiming that he might have to leave Europe for purely business reasons, he had provided 'directions for our communicating, preparing for every contingencies'.

And then came words which would hardly have reassured her. 'At the worst, dear, our marriage may be postponed for a year. Direct to Paris as I told. I am dear Jeannie, with kindest love, Yours affectly, Austin.'

❧

By the Thursday of that last week in January, Austin Bidwell had returned to the French capital. To say he was on tenterhooks was an understatement. As he had put it in his final, surviving note to Jeannie Devereux, 'I can scarcely frame the language to express my thoughts as I would like to'.

It provides a unique insight into Austin Bidwell's emotions in the raw, not how he rationalised them many years later:

> If you knew the opposition I have already had the friends of years I would alienate the prospects of an easy life, I would have to forego the loss of both wealth and powerful friends if I make you my wife. You could call me a very brave man to even think seriously of it. But all this is but as dust in the balance if you love me everything I could throw to the wind.

If she no longer wished to marry him, 'I will take no offence'. Austin reassured her that there would be no trouble from him nor any 'scenes', he simply requested to see her face to face.

But now, as he checked into the Hotel Richmond, he had received no further communication from her. The wedding was now scheduled for the Saturday and he hadn't heard a further word from her since the previous weekend. He was beside himself with worry. Had he blown it?

'Austin Bidwell left Paris on the morning of the 7th,' Freshfields noted, the day after he had arrived in the capital for the purposes of matrimony. 'He stated he had been to Amiens to meet his bride.' But there was never any trace of this visit and in the end, everything went right up to the wire. The greater truth was that he was in a constant state of nervous excitement that week. Jeannie Devereux had not quite said yes, nor had she said no. Austin Bidwell was, the prosecution determined, 'sending telegrams to ascertain where his future wife and mother-in-law were'. And, it is clear, increasingly frantically.

On the Friday before the wedding, for example, he sent one to Mac in London in the early evening. 'After five. No news, very anxious'. The Devereux family turned up the next day. Mrs Devereux had somehow sufficiently become calm enough to accompany her daughter for what she would term 'a big match'. For someone who liked to wax lyrical on such matters, Austin Bidwell made very few comments about the ceremony. All that is mentioned in the official files is an extract from an American register, 'Mr Austin Biron Bidwell of Chicago was married this morning at the American Legation, Rue de Chaillot to Miss Jeannie G.M. Devereux of the same city – the religious ceremony was performed by the Rev. D. Hitchcock.'

Jeannie later wondered why it was stated she came from Chicago. Equally puzzling was the fact her mother fainted during the ceremony. It would seem that the presentation of a dowry had gone some way to assuage the elder Devereux's fears. Austin had also sent £1,000 to a banker in London to act as life insurance in case anything went wrong.

The previous week, despite the gnawing anxieties, Austin Bidwell – as he claimed in his memoirs – had hired a servant called Harry Nunn who would play an unusual role in the developing saga. Harry had met Austin for the first time in Paris the previous September 1872. While he waited to see if his bride would ever appear, Nunn provided him with a distraction in driving him all over the city. 'I now engaged the coachman I had met before as my valet,' Austin later wrote, 'and a very good all-around handyman he proved to be.'

Hiring a four-wheeled coach, they visited Fontainebleau and Versailles, where in Austin's memory, Nunn brought him a telegram. 'All well. Bought and shipped forty bales.' That meant the first £40,000 had gone through. Whether this was ever sent remains a moot point, but by leaving the country, Austin had certainly erected the first Chinese wall in protecting the greater scam. 'The plan was complete at last,' he later wrote. 'Everything was ready to carry out our scheme in perfect safety to all.'

9

Strange Messengers

The briefest and truest way of describing Lombard Street is to say that it is by far the greatest combination of economical power and economical delicacy that the world has ever seen. Of the greatness of the power there will be no doubt. Money is economical power. Everyone is aware that England is the greatest moneyed country in the world; everyone admits that it has much more immediately disposable and ready cash than any other country. But very few persons are aware how much greater the ready balance the floating loan-fund which can be lent to anyone or for any purposes in England than it is anywhere in the world.

Walter Bagehot, *Lombard Street*, written in 1873 as the events described here unfolded.

Saturday, 1 March 1873
Holding Cells, Mansion House, City of London
1.45 p.m.

Immediately after his arrest at the Continental Bank, Edwin Noyes Hills was escorted by the pair of policemen from the chaos to the calm of the Mansion House for his first remand hearing. As a matter of routine, he was searched and handed fatigues. In Hills' various pockets, Detective Sergeant John Spittle found a gold watch and chain, a diamond ring and various memoranda and letters. Many were from his employer, the mysterious Charles Johnson Horton, including the 'contract' he had signed to legitimise his work. There were also newspaper cuttings from where he had advertised his desire to work in partnership in a light business.

Sergeant Spittle started to fill out the charge sheet and wanted to know where the prisoner lived. 'I have no settled address,' Hills replied. 'I have been stopping at different places.'

'Will you say where you slept last night?'

There was an uneasy silence. 'No, after the manner I have been treated.' When pressed, all the American added was, 'I can only say in giving my former address I did so at Horton's request. I should go back to Durrant's Hotel, again.'

That establishment, the policeman knew, was in the West End. But he was tired of this silly game of pretence. 'Mr Noyes,' he said with exasperation, 'you gave at the police station your address as Durrant's Hotel, Manchester Square. That is false, as you have left there these three weeks.' The prisoner said nothing. It was going to be a long afternoon. Hills' silence somehow seemed rehearsed and calculated, something that was remarked upon throughout his time in England. 'In January the prisoner Noyes appears to have come on to the stage,' the prosecution noted, with an obvious nod to his theatricality, which had begun with a greater charade that had struck one bemused onlooker as 'a certain pantomime action'.

Seven Weeks Earlier – Friday, 10 January 1873
Durrant's Hotel, George Street, London
9.30 a.m.

It had been yet another cold, cheerless and endlessly rainy day in the capital. The hotel wasn't particularly busy, and the waiter noticed Mr Noyes sitting alone in the coffee room. He was quietly finishing up his breakfast and reading the paper. He'd been here nearly a couple of weeks now and, in recent days, had received a deluge of post. So when another American visitor – somewhat dashing and heavily bearded – came in and asked for Mr Noyes by name, James Richardson was not surprised.

The waiter pointed Mr Noyes out. The visitor did not introduce himself as they walked over, so Richardson did. 'There is a gentleman for you.' The two Americans exchanged greetings, and in that moment it struck the waiter as odd. When they shook hands, it seemed to him that they had met before.

Fairly quickly, the visitor left, and Mr Noyes then walked into the hall and put on his own hat and coat. By the front door, a hansom carriage pulled up with the other American already in it. 'Shall I go straight away with you?' Noyes asked him as he leaned in. The waiter was wondering what to make of this, when Mr Noyes turned and asked him a question. 'What is the nearest underground station? Is it Charing Cross?'

'No, Baker Street,' Richardson replied, pointing in its direction, 'which is only a few minutes' walk.' And with that the two Americans left in the carriage towards Regents' Park. Later, when James Richardson came to relate this story to Freshfields, the lawyers noted, 'It is thus perfectly clear that this scheme so far as that was concerned was premeditated'.

Edwin Noyes Hills returned to Durrant's that same Friday evening. The next morning there followed another surreal conversation with the waiter. 'I will need to get up much earlier in the morning, James,' Hills told him.

'Oh indeed,' Richardson replied.

'Yes, I think I have been fortunate in obtaining so soon what I wanted. Being a stranger in the country, I advertised for a situation.' Hills then referred to the number of letters he had received. Slowly, their sheer volume started to make sense ('I should think fifty or sixty in three successive days,' Richardson later remembered). The previous day, Hills said, he had paid his visitor £300 as security.

'You ought to be very careful in whose hands you place that amount of money,' Richardson warned. 'You are a stranger in this country.'

'Oh not with such gentlemen as these,' Hills replied brightly. 'Besides this, in the course of time as I come to be better known to them, I shall have to travel about for them. I guess I'm alright.'

Later Hills claimed that he had not answered any of the letters, thus explaining why the other American had called on him unexpectedly. He had wanted to discuss the offer of a job in person. They had spent the day together, Hills related. The stranger had introduced him to his bankers. Fairly quickly, they had come to terms. He never mentioned Mac's name, what his business was nor where his offices were.

The waiter was bemused. Hills continued to pretend that Mac was a complete stranger but so too, in a wider sense, was Edwin Noyes Hills; in the greater fraud since he went through the charade of entering into a more formal contract with his enigmatic employer. This had more to do with formal protection in case things went horribly wrong.

Hills' greater role was to keep his mouth shut. 'When arrested, he would not betray us, even though the prosecution offered to permit him to turn Queen's Evidence,' George Bidwell would marvel, 'the acceptance of which would have freed him as soon as the trial should be finished.'

This first public incarnation of Charles Johnson Horton was carried out by George Macdonnell. Curiously, the prosecution never did find out where he and Hills had spent the rest of that Friday together. It hardly mattered, for as Hardinge Giffard had put it, 'Everything was prepared for the performance which was afterwards to take place'.

By this point, the waiter, James Richardson, knew Edwin Noyes reasonably well. 'He came on the 27th December 1872, about half past ten o'clock at night,' he later testified. 'He had no luggage with him.' The next day, when it arrived – 'one was a black one, the other what I call an American box' – he moved bedroom and said he would stay for a month or two.

In the event, Hills remained for about two weeks. Though the waiter often spoke to him, that particular conversation with the arrival of his friend was the only one of any substance, which was why he recalled it so vividly. On this point, when he was later cross-examined on the stand, James Richardson was most insistent. 'I have reported all the conversation word for word,' he said. 'My memory is just the same as if it occurred yesterday.' Clearly, he wasn't born yesterday, either.

The whole business – which he had termed a pantomime – stemmed from an advertisement which had appeared in six successive supplements to the *Daily Telegraph* in the first week of January 1873. 'A gentleman of active business seeks a situation of trust or of partnership in a light business not requiring over £300,' it read. 'Address with particulars – Edwin Noyes, Durrant's Hotel, George St, Manchester Square.'

And here, in terms of pantomime, was the equivalent of a trap for a demon king.

Every caper needs a catspaw. Though he was never much to look at and struck several onlookers as something of a dimwit, it was a well-rehearsed act. Edwin Noyes Hills was, as Austin Bidwell wryly noted, 'no puritan'. The son of a farmer, 'Ed' was quiet, diffident but, most important of all, could play the role of the outside man to the hilt – that is, the bewildered dupe.

'He was a trifle older than myself,' Austin Bidwell later recalled, 'of a steady reserved nature, and a discreet and safe friend. This was the new member of our firm.' Though his shtick fooled nobody who knew them, Edwin Noyes Hills was able to play the patsy to perfection. To his dying days, he always maintained that the details of the plan were hardly known to him and he was only ever tangentially implicated in the scheme. This gathering absurdity was repeated by George Bidwell, who claimed that they never even told Noyes where they were living.

The 'chance meeting' with Mac at Durrant's was part of their opening overtures. Thereafter, he became an integral part of the forgery as a business partner to Charles Johnson Horton (subsequently played by Austin Bidwell). Noyes was their cut-out in case anything went wrong, protected by what one prosecutor called 'an expedient and an extremely cunning one'. The formal, legal contract was designed to make his employment with Horton look legitimate. It began:

> Made this 11th day of January, 1873 between Charles Johnson Horton, now of London Bridge Hotel in the County of Surrey, manufacturer of one part, and Edwin Noyes of Durrant's Hotel, Manchester Square, in the county of Middlesex, merchant's clerk of the other part. The 'said Edwin Noyes' agreed to serve 'the said Charles Johnson Horton' as clerk and manager in his business of a manufacturer at a yearly salary of £150.

The terms and conditions were that the said Edwin Noyes 'should and will faithfully, honestly and diligently serve the said Charles Johnson Horton as clerk and manager as aforesaid for the term of one year determinable as hereinafter contained'. As he told his waiter in his hotel, Noyes had paid £300 as security. There followed details of payment, schedule and return on the investment.

'Faithfully, honestly and diligently'. Words that were horribly ironic under the circumstances.

Intriguingly, there was a curiously familiar name at the end of the contract, 'Witness to the signature of Mr Horton and Mr Noyes, David Howell, 112 Cheapside, Solicitor – C.J. Horton – Edwin Noyes'. It was signed and sealed on 11 January, with the 'above mentioned sum' of £300 (which Austin tried to make out Noyes had 'swindled' from him when arrested in Cuba).

The role of Howell – who would later defend George Bidwell at the Old Bailey – was the cause of much speculation. George claims that he sent Noyes to Howell's Cheapside office to see if he would act as witness to the agreement. Later, when under remand, George himself met Howell and claimed he was 'quite reliable' in a letter to Nellie Vernon but, according to his brother, the lawyer was a 'thoroughgoing, unprincipled rascal'. After their subsequent trial, George, too, had changed his tune. Howell had, he claims, simply played into the hands of the prosecutor.

On their part, Freshfields were no less puzzled. 'We cannot help thinking that Mr Howell knows more of the prisoners than he had intimated at present or will state as he defends them all except Macdonnell,' they wrote on the eve of the trial's opening.

Friday, 17 January 1873
Lombard Street, City of London

A week later, on yet another bitterly cold January afternoon, Austin Bidwell walked painfully (because of his recent injuries in France) with Edwin Noyes Hills along one of those constricted, often anonymous streets within the City of London. Earlier this Friday he had been to see Colonel Francis on his last ever visit as Frederick Albert Warren. Now he would assume the identity of Charles Johnson Horton and together he and Mr Noyes would enter 'the golden heart which kept world trade in circulation'.

If Dick Whittington had really wanted to find gold in the streets, he should have headed straight to Lombard Street. It was named for Jewish traders expelled from medieval Italy who had subsequently lent gold to the kings of England for centuries. All around were the very establishments that were now underwriting the western world's fast growing economy.

Foremost among them were the bill brokers who were driving the first, putative global financial market. Hitherto, lack of communication and differing interest rates had made international credit difficult. 'But after 1870, the tempo of change quickened,' writes one historian. 'International financial intelligence was improving;

foreigners made increasing use of the London capital market and international influence grew swiftly.'

As Mr Horton and his clerk walked along, they could appreciate the febrile activity from the number of red-coated messengers and carriages which were disgorging top-hatted bankers. Given that so many walked 'a narrow ledge between prosperity and ruin, peace of mind and lunacy', as one recent chronicler has put it, the two Americans fitted right in.

The rise of the British economy had been accompanied by reckless gambles, with ever growing scams in bonding, insurance and limited companies. This very 'commercial profligacy of the age' would shortly inform one of the great moralists of the time to fulminate in his most trenchant work. As several people have noted, Anthony Trollope did not have very far to look when he started work on *The Way We Live Now* in 1873.[15]

Now, as Mr Horton and his clerk made their way towards the discount house where an account had already been opened, the greater fraud was about to widen and reach its most dangerous consummation.

Day Four – Thursday, 21 August 1873
Central Criminal Court, Old Bailey
2 p.m.

And to think he had no idea.

Looking across at them now in the dock, John Thomas Stanton still seemed shell-shocked from having witnessed the fraud fall apart before his very eyes on the first Saturday in March. As the manager of the Continental Bank, Stanton's testimony now 'occupied the court for the greater portion of the afternoon', as the *Standard* later reported.

The questioning was begun by Harry Poland. 'You know the Prisoner Hills by the name of Edwin Noyes do you?' he asked Mr Stanton. The manager confirmed that he first saw him at his bank at No. 79 Lombard Street. 'Who introduced him?' Poland prompted.

'Horton.'

'That was Austin Bidwell,' Poland said for the benefit of the jury. 'What did Horton say when he introduced him as his clerk.'

'He said he was to be treated as confidential clerk – that is, to say we were to treat him exactly as we should himself in his absence.'

'When he said this what did you say?'

'I asked if Noyes was to be allowed to sign cheques.'

'What did Horton say to that?'

'He gave a direct negative – "By no means" – or words to that effect.'

There was a curious silence in court. Here was another stroke of genius. Who would think that a forger would caution his accomplice *not* to carry out the forgery by cashing cheques? It would simply establish his credentials, especially after Mr Horton's departure just a few days later when the forgers started their third and final act of the scam.

When Edwin Noyes Hills was first arrested, the prosecution was still saying that his function was 'to remove suspicion to a great extent from F.A Warren', as nobody in London realised that Warren and Horton were actually the same person in Austin Bidwell. 'Warren therefore took rooms at the London Bridge Hotel and the Cannon Street Hotel (no. 6 at the former and no. 8 at the latter) in the name of Horton and installed the prisoner there.' It was left to Edwin Noyes Hills to deal with Mr Stanton alone.

On the stand, the manager was then asked about various sums which passed through Horton's account. 'The examination extended to very considerable length,' one newspaper reported the next day, 'but if the details were given they would, to a certain extent, be unintelligible.' And that was exactly what the forgers were aiming for. At the time, though, neither Noyes nor his master, Horton, ever drew attention to themselves.

'Did you know what countryman he was?' Harry Poland asked.

'We assumed that he was an American,' was all Stanton could say.

'Did he say at all what he was?' Poland pressed.

'We understood from him mostly that he was an American gentleman.' Which all made some perfect sort of sense for there was something impossibly glamorous and clever about their actions. The Bank of England was clearly outclassed by what the fraudsters would call 'smarts'. 'Alas! The only establishment that never allows an Englishman to overdraw his account was thoroughly done by these astute but vulgar Yankees,' exulted one newspaper.

It was a point echoed by Mr Stanton about Mr Horton. 'I do not know that he represented himself as being anything at all,' the bank manager would later claim, reiterating that he 'appeared to me to be an American gentleman.' Observing what Stanton termed his 'intimate connection with the Bank of England', no further questions were asked. 'We did not make any inquiry,' the cashier said under oath, 'because the evident connection of the account with respectable persons put it on one side.'

In all their subsequent dealings, Mr Stanton recognised either the writing of Horton or his clerk. There were also supposedly 'genuine' communications between businessman and clerk which were discovered about Hills' person after his arrest:

E. Noyes esq   28 January
Sir:

In order that it may be more convenient to business you will give up the room at
the London Bridge Hotel and go at once to the Terminus Hotel, Cannon Street
Station and pay one month's rent for a sitting room. Secure one not more than
one flight up if possible and also secure one that is comfortable and convenient.

Secure through the proprietors of the Cannon Street Hotel or some other
advantageous manner a trusty porter for messages. You can also send him with
deposits to the Bank and if at any time inconvenient to yourself to go.

Horton added that he would hire another clerk 'to save you from so much running
about', and should be prompt when instructed to meet.

Needless to say, staff recalled them in both hotels. Mr Noyes had used a private
sitting room at the City Terminus Hotel for the whole of February. A waiter recalled
visitors and various unknown messengers arriving. Mr Noyes himself only ever
made fleeting visits, and the proprietor of the London Bridge Terminus Hotel also
saw little by way of business activity. Albert Gearing positively identified Horton
as Austin Bidwell and recalled that the businessman said that he might require the
room 'for two or three days, or possibly weeks, until he got suitable accommodation
in the city'. He did not recall his clerk but once saw Mr Horton looking in the lobby
for letters.

The 'relationship' between Charles Johnson Horton and his clerk was equally
stormy – or rather Mr Noyes was a rather dim-witted, lazy fellow who could not get
out of bed in the morning. Horton wrote:

How is it that I was at the Hotel at 10 and you had not arrived and I heard that
you left there before three yesterday. I am especially desirous that you should
always be prompt on hand when I send you word beforehand. Please look out
that this doesn't happen again.

Doubtless they had a jolly giggle about that undated note.

As Austin Bidwell prepared to leave the country he was, as the prosecution marvelled, 'protected':

He was Frederick Albert Warren at the Golden Cross Hotel as at the Bank
of England. He was Charles Johnson Horton of the Terminus Hotel as at the
Continental Bank – at Jay Cooke & Co. he was not known except as a Casual
Customer. He had therefore only before any forged bills were uttered to leave
the country and he was, as he thought, safe.

But then the prosecution finished on an ominous note. 'He had, however, forgotten
his mother-in-law.'

Mrs Devereux may have provided a more pressing reason for fleeing the scene of the crime. 'On account of her insulting him so ruthlessly in Paris,' Willie Pinkerton later noted a conversation with Austin about his mother-in-law, 'he determined not to go to England again.'

To coincide with Austin's departure, they needed to draw out as much money as possible and 'send the greater part of it out of the country in a shape in which it could not easily be traced,' Freshfields observed. 'This was done in anticipation of the step they were going to take or probably taken on that day namely sending up the first batch of forged bills to the Bank of England.' They had insured themselves for either outcome. 'If this succeeded their capital was not wasted in England,' the prosecution brief noted. 'If it failed then capital was in the main safe.'

Figuratively, as well as literally, all throughout Mr Noyes' visits to the city, the Old Lady of Threadneedle Street loomed large, impassive and dark against the rainy skies of that cold and miserable winter. Its reputation was as solid as its original granite exterior. 'The stability of the Bank of England is equal to that of the British Government,' Adam Smith had famously written in 1776.

London's financial clout came about because of sterling's basis as a world currency. The gold standard system pioneered in London had been adopted worldwide. The Bank of England's bullion reserves underpinned much of the economic expansion of the west; 'the great steam engine of the state' in one earlier estimation, but also it was the lender of last resort for the various discount houses that had grown up in its shadow. 'These were the greatest days of the London bill brokers, the Lombard Street houses,' one official historian of the bank has written of these times. Ultimately, the buck – or rather, the vast amounts of sterling guaranteed by the bills of exchange – stopped at the entrance to the Old Lady of Threadneedle Street itself.

While they had transformed the money markets, these bills were not regulated. This very laissez-fair attitude meant they were open to abuses. Discount houses often raised cash by sometimes selling these bills at a reduced value too, essentially loaning the cash at interest for a fixed time (usually for up to three months). Specialised dealers trading in bills or acting as brokers operated with money borrowed on short-term loans from commercial banks. All were underwritten, in effect, by the Old Lady of Threadneedle Street.

Here was the great strength of the British economy and, ultimately, its great weakness due to unprecedented expansion. Railways, the telegraph and steamships had been the harbingers of globalisation. The years of the forgers' greater roguery – from 1866 to 1872 – had coincided with, in the phrase of the official historian of the bank, 'a gigantic hinge on which the history of the later nineteenth century turns'. He termed it 'furious' industrial activity around the world that had been underwritten by British investment. 'The normal pulse of international finance,' wrote Sir John

Clapham in his official history of the bank, 'is becoming such as once would have suggested high fever.'

And now it looked like the world's economies were catching cold, plummeting towards recession. Lending was at its maximum and some wondered whether Her Majesty's Government was over extended. The danger was simple: what if all the accumulated liabilities were greater than the reserves? With this in mind, that same year of 1873 somebody had pointed the finger towards the Bank of England for the very first time.

Walter Bagehot was a pre-eminent Victorian writer, a radically minded liberal and former editor of the *Economist*, whose multitude of misgivings were distilled into a magisterial tome simply entitled *Lombard Street*, which stripped much of the mystery away. 'There never was so much borrowed money collected in the world as is now collected in London,' Bagehot wrote. Lombard Street ran on credit which meant 'for a certain confidence is given, and a certain trust reposed. Is that trust justified?'

The bank, as ever, remained aloof. Its standard refrain was that the money market took care of itself. How many times had that been heard then, or since? The inherent danger behind it all was first diagnosed with crisp simplicity by Walter Bagehot. 'Money will not manage itself,' he wrote, 'and Lombard Street has a great deal of money to manage.' Most of that, he argued, had become, by default, the responsibility of the Old Lady of Threadneedle Street. 'This is by far the safest place for [other banks] to use,' he noted. 'The Bank of England thus has the responsibility of taking care of it.'[16]

And, as events in the early part of the year had shown, not particularly well.

Thursday, 21 August 1873
Central Criminal Court, Old Bailey
2.30 p.m.

As Mr Stanton now testified on the stand, there was never any hint of recklessness in Mr Horton's financial affairs. The manager carefully went through all the details of the money he had paid out. Mr Noyes never did anything to draw attention to himself. Mr Stanton claimed he recognised the handwriting on all of his cheques as those of Mr Horton himself. Yet on one transferred in the name of F.A. Warren, Mr McIntyre noted that one of the acceptances bore the name of Stanton's colleague, Mr Hartland

The judge wanted to know if his partner was in court. 'Is Mr Hartland here?' Judge Archibald asked.

Harry Poland looked across, 'He is in town, I believe.' There was then a detailed discussion about whether he should be called as he had made the entry. 'It is not necessary to call every clerk who made every entry here,' said an exasperated Harry Poland. All he wanted to do, he explained, was to show that Horton's 'was a sham account from beginning to end for the express purpose of getting the proceeds of the forged bills from the Bank of England into this account'.

The judge pondered this for a moment.

'This account of Horton's is fed by the account of Warren,' Harry Poland continued. 'That is our case.'

'Well it may prolong the matter very much,' the judge agreed, 'but if you were to give this evidence and it is objected to I think you must call the persons who made the entry I am afraid. So possibly if you call one, Mr McIntyre may not think it necessary to call the next.' And then Judge Archibald smiled. 'We have the whole of the long vacation before us.'

And so the court filled with sycophantic laughter.

There was not much laughter in banking circles that summer of 1873. The storm clouds that had been gathering in financial markets burst like a thunderclap. What was later known as 'the panic of 1873' had many origins. From today's perspective, however, the symptoms are depressingly familiar. Inflation, trade deficits and rampant speculation, particularly on the railways, were the cause. Increasing turbulence in the money markets, which George Bidwell had noticed the previous autumn when Germany abandoned its minting of silver thaler coins and went over to the mark, would have several knock-on effects.

On 9 May 1873, the Vienna stock market had crashed in a bursting bubble of insolvency and fraudulence. Around the world over the next few months there was a slump in trade, more bankruptcies and galloping unemployment, which culminated, days after the trial finished, by claiming the scalp of the 'modern Midas' of American finance.

Jay Cooke had been the P.T. Barnum of the merchant banking world, one of the original robber barons, whose influence stretched across the United States and beyond. In London, Frederick Warren and Edwin Noyes had been regular visitors to Cooke's offices, purchasing bonds or cashing cheques from their respective accounts. These purchases were simply a drop in the ocean. 'We put American bonds on the market to a large amount,' testified one of Cooke's clerks by the name of Alfred Joseph Baker. '$75,000,000 in the course of a year by our house alone.' Though he never did meet the mysterious Mr Horton, Baker recalled he had met his confidential clerk on several occasions. 'We are going to have an office in the Poultry,' Noyes later told him. Mr Baker also stated that 'there was nothing unusual to attract my attention in any way' with their dealings at Cooke's.

The same could not be said for his own boss, Jay Cooke. The fall of 'Midas' himself that summer was spectacular. When he began selling shares in the Northern Pacific Railroad as an exclusive agent, their uptake was a disaster. His various banks and all his associated houses in London too could not cover their liabilities. The money soon dried up. A few weeks after the trial of the forgers at the Old Bailey finished, so too was Jay Cooke.

On 18 September 1873, his Wall Street offices closed. Within days, other banks failed and the New York Stock Exchange was closed for ten days at the end of September. Factories laid off workers, wages were slashed and profits evaporated. The panic of 1873 became the first great recession to engulf the United States – and beyond. It is curious to speculate that the gang might not have been able to carry out their forgeries had they started six months later.

Jay Cooke would go to his grave never able to solve one lingering mystery. Eighteen months before his empire collapsed, someone had tried to swindle his New York bank out of $130,000 in United States bonds. An elegantly dressed lawyer called J.W. Kenney[17] walked into Cooke's Wall Street offices claiming to be the executor of a large estate in New Jersey. And now, on this cold winter's morning, the same confident, well-dressed person entered the gold weighing room in Threadneedle Street following in illustrious footsteps. His real name was George Macdonnell.[18]

'The art of forgery is becoming of the fine arts,' one British newspaper would later marvel, after the fraud unravelled. 'When a man can adroitly forge, it is as if he could coin money, or as if he were an alchemist, capable of transmuting lead to gold by a touch.'

Such criminal chemistry would now reach new heights with the transmutation of paper into gold – or rather, the presentation of forged bills of exchange which the thieves of Threadneedle Street would launder using this rarest, most elusive metal imaginable. If there was one remaining weakness with their scheme, it came from the fact that money – as in sequentially numbered notes, bills and bonds – could be traced. They needed another step to insulate themselves against discovery. They had to break the connection between the forgery and its actual products.

On several occasions, Edwin Noyes Hills changed the notes he had obtained from the Continental Bank into gold sovereigns at the Bank of England just across the road. But to ensure that nobody could trace them completely, they would need one final step: to launder the gold inside the Old Lady itself. There was clearly only one of them bold and brave enough to do so.

Tuesday, 28 January 1873
Gold Weighing Room, Bank of England, Threadneedle Street
10 a.m.

It was a salutary experience to enter the Bank of England for the very first time. As George Macdonnell walked through the archway that towered over its entrance on this gloomy, foggy morning, he appeared, as he always did, urbane, well dressed and confident. The reality was that even he felt the stomach-wrenching fear that everything might unravel.

Everything about the Old Lady of Threadneedle Street was designed to make the visitor feel overwhelmed. The building itself was a menacing, one storey edifice with no external windows that reminded many of a prison. Mac would no doubt have felt a growing sense of anxiety and paranoia as he came across a grand, gated entrance through which he now had to pass. 'The gate does not strike one as solemn and imposing as might be expected in a gate leading to the laboratory of a great wizard,' was how another visitor described it in almost quasi-mystical terms.

Once inside, the building was a revelation. 'The interior is far more lightsome and pleasant than one might suppose from the heavy outside,' another visitor noted. After crossing a small court yard, Mac would then have crossed the great hall of the bank, before coming across a veritable hive of activity in a large, noisy room with a parquet floor. This was the gold weighing room.

One side was filled with desks and counters. At its centre were a handful of small, brass machines driven by steam belts, sifting and regurgitating full weight and light sovereigns. If George Macdonnell was trying to be anonymous, he singularly failed. He made a meal of making sure the clerks got his name right. When one of them was about to write 'Macdonald', he corrected him. This – surely another form of pantomime – stuck in the memories of those who dealt with him.

For starters, the American simply informed a clerk, Henry Hughes, that he had some gold that he wanted to change for notes. 'I have £6,300,' Mac blithely said. Today, that would be equivalent to over £50,000. So far as such large sums of cash were concerned, the bank always referred upwards. And so the superintendent of the room, Mr Miller, was called in along with another principal, Mr Adams.

'Where does the gold come from?' Mr Miller asked Mac.

'Lisbon.'

Mr Adams was puzzled. 'It is not usual to have so many full weighted sovereigns,' he said. 'Probably you got them from Knowles, Foster & Co. of Lisbon?' This was a brokers in Portugal that exchanged a lot of money for the lucrative South American market, as Mac well knew. He had done exactly that on his return from Rio de Janeiro the summer before.

'I did not get them from Knowles, Foster & Co.' Mac replied. There was an uneasy silence. Had he been found out? The moment passed. Even though he said little, they continued to take him at face value. The officials never enquired too deeply. Hughes took the sovereigns into the weighing room and then, as he later testified, 'We weighed the lump and found it was £6,320'. In other words, there were twenty sovereigns too many. Mr Hughes then checked by weighing them all separately.

When he informed Mac, the fraudster seemed to expect it. 'Oh, I wondered where it was,' he replied with characteristic nonchalance. Once again, it stuck in their minds. And then when he came to write his name, Mac said, 'I have great difficulty in getting people to spell my name correctly.'

Nothing was said in Mr Hughes' presence about where the money came from. George Macdonnell left shortly afterwards, to return on a further three occasions.

'Robbing Peter to pay Paul' is a concept all fraudsters employ. But here the thieves of Threadneedle Street had then paid Patrick and Philip. As the amounts of money they laundered became ever larger, so grew the financial footprints they left behind. On that last Tuesday in January, for example, the amount of money Mac exchanged back into drafts would have been, in the opinion of one of the clerks, 'about three-quarters of a ton altogether'. They could hardly store such vast amounts of gold in their hotels.

So they developed a routine that was ingenious and beautifully simple to the point of genius. After paying in Warren cheques to the Horton account at the Continental Bank, Edwin Noyes Hills would buy gold at the Bank of England. This was handed over to him in sealed bags, each containing 1,000 new sovereigns. The seals were broken by the gang and the slips recording when they had been filled out removed.

Those pristine gold sovereigns were then swapped with coins already in circulation. These were also randomly chosen for 'it is impossible to trace the gold,' the prosecution noted, after Hills had first been arrested. Then George Macdonnell would take these bags of used gold coins back to the Old Lady of Threadneedle Street where a bank draft would be issued. As he had now discovered, nobody checked on their provenance. 'We never enter the numbers and dates,' said one of the clerks who dealt with him, 'we simply put down the amount and the name of the party presenting the note.'

Once he left Threadneedle Street, Mac could purchase US bonds which would then be spirited away. On this first occasion, Hills was handed $1,000 as a present, which he forwarded to his brother in New York City.

All the links of the chain that could connect them to the separate stages of the forgery were broken. By any reckoning, over the next few weeks they were supremely successful. 'The prisoner Noyes between the 21st January and the 28th February changed notes for gold at the Bank of England to a sum amounting to £23,650,' the prosecution noted in the immediate aftermath of the discovery. 'Macdonnell between the 28th January and the 25th February exchanged gold for notes to an amount of £16,950.'

As a result, Hills and the two Georges soon celebrated their good fortune over a bottle of Veuve Clicquot. 'It appeared as if the bank managers had heaped a mountain of gold out in the street,' George Bidwell later remarked of how easy it all was, 'and had put up a notice "Please do not touch this" and then had left it unguarded.'

The final, concurrent strand of the forgery could now also play out to its natural conclusion. 'Frederick Albert Warren' needed to be in two places at once – or rather, George Bidwell would now assume the role by repeatedly travelling to Birmingham in the next few weeks.

Why Birmingham? It was a question that many people wondered about. The answer was – for the sake of obscurity. Geographical separation alone added a convenient smokescreen to obscure their fraudulent business dealings. For this, George needed to use the post and did so for the first time, as Colonel Francis had learned to his cost, on 21 January. 'The letter is written in the handwriting of George Bidwell but it is signed by Austin Bidwell,' the prosecution noted of this first letter sent from Birmingham to the Western Branch.

Subsequently, George Bidwell needed to make several visits to the Midlands for the sake of continuity. In the same way that George Macdonnell drew attention to himself in the gold weighing room inside the Bank of England, so did George Bidwell on his various visits to the Queen's Hotel close by the railway station in Birmingham. 'He had an overcoat on and a light coloured scarf, almost a white scarf,' recalled waiter Josiah Winspear, 'a dark overcoat and a satchel over his shoulder.'

On the stand, David Howell QC had asked an obvious question. 'Did you notice anything remarkable about his face?'

'Yes, I noticed that he was a kind of foreign-looking gentleman.'

'Birmingham has the pleasure of seeing a great many gentlemen of this description has it not?' he prompted, clearly enjoying the sarcasm.

'Yes.'

On this and a later occasion, George Bidwell rented a private sitting room and took care to lock the door for good reason. Unseen, he now forged various letters to Colonel Francis in the name of Warren. This, of itself, was a minor forgery, for various blank bills had been signed by Austin Bidwell before he left for France. If the bills passed muster, the note would be taken for granted. All George had to do was make a passably good signature in a false name which would, as he speaks metaphorically in his memoirs, allow the forgers 'to enter the bombproof vaults of the greatest financial fortress of which history gives account'.

Thursday, 20 February 1873
Queen's Hotel, Birmingham
Afternoon

Despite his air of apparent nonchalance, when George Bidwell walked out of the Queen's Hotel on this cold and foggy afternoon he was worried. At about three o'clock, he drew the attention of a cab driver waiting outside the hotel. 'He gave me a piece of paper and told me to go to the Post Office and ask for the letters for that name on the paper,' Alfred Morley declared on oath at the Mansion House. The cabbie added that he did not recall the name on the letter, thereby making it difficult to establish the evidence trail:

He gave me a two shilling piece to buy a shilling stamp. I presented the piece of paper to the post office clerk and I bought the stamp. The clerk gave me one letter and I gave it with the stamp and shilling to the prisoner. He remained in my cab while I went to the Post Office.

After returning to the hotel, George Bidwell hailed another cabbie at 3.35 p.m. There followed a repeat of his earlier visit. 'He gave me a large letter and told me to go in and register it,' this driver, John Barker, also testified. 'It was stamped. I went in and registered it, and got the receipt for it, and gave it to the prisoner, who tore it up and threw it away in the road. The letter was to America; I did not notice the name.'

This time George Bidwell walked across the station to catch the London train at 4 p.m. and now had a perfect alibi, and he could claim that he had met a man on the train. 'Had I been arrested,' George Bidwell later recalled of this occasion:

I should have said that I met a gentleman on the train and fell into conversation with him and just before arriving at Birmingham he remarked that he must continue his journey to Liverpool, and would feel obliged to me if I would call for his letters and forward them.

When the Birmingham witnesses – the waiters and cab drivers – had originally appeared before Sir Sydney Waterlow on Friday, 18 April 1873, all had used the same phrase independently of each other. 'On or about 20 February'. This caused much excitement for the legal teams as it implied there had been some sort of collusion. George Bidwell now argued that, as he alone had been taken from his cell and paraded in front of them and others in a downstairs room, he was bound to be identified as the perpetrator. The Birmingham cabbies were all in cahoots, he had argued, presenting tarnished evidence.

The lord mayor was having none of it. 'The men you refer to have no interest in stating what was untrue,' Sir Sydney had said. 'You can interrogate them all, if you like, as to the surrounding circumstances under which they saw you, and their evidence would be recorded as part of the case.'

George Bidwell was equally insistent. 'It would be a fairer course, if, where the object was identification, to have him put with other men, and if possible, men like him. If a man wanted to recognise him, rightly or wrongly, of course, he would stick to what he said afterwards.'

The lord mayor was annoyed. 'Any man guilty of perjury would be liable to severe punishment.'

George Bidwell then argued that he had been put in an unfair position. Politely, Sir Sydney Waterlow asked him to cite any specific instances of malfeasance.

George Bidwell said the matter was as he stated it, then smiled. 'I do not want to get anyone into trouble.' It was, as several onlookers thought, already a little too late for that.

Establishing Edwin Noyes Hills' presence in Birmingham was equally important for the prosecution to complete the nexus of connections within this part of the fraud. Freshfields established that both he and George Bidwell made separately – or possibly together – a dozen or so journeys to Birmingham, often via Rugby from where they telegraphed to London.

Many of the Birmingham cab drivers also remembered seeing Hills on 20 February, as his behaviour was also quite peculiar. 'He was only four or five yards from me at the time,' John Barker had already testified. 'I believe he wore a blue pilot coat, and a black high-crowned hat.' On the third day of the later trial at the Old Bailey, George Bidwell's own counsel tried to get the cabbie to say he was mistaken. 'Was it not nearly five o'clock in the afternoon?' David Howell QC prompted him.

'No,' Barker replied firmly.

'What time was it?'

'It was about twenty minutes to four o'clock when he got into my cab and I was away about for ten minutes.'

'About twenty minutes to four in February?' Howell asked.

'Yes.'

'Were the lamps lighted?'

'No, sir. It was quite light at that time of the year.'

'Quite light was it.'

'Yes.'

'What, even in Birmingham?'

'Oh yes.'

Barker was then cross-examined by Hills' own defence lawyer, Mr Hollings. By the time he had returned George Bidwell the short distance back to the hotel, the cabbie had seen Hills standing at the entrance to the station waiting under the arch which lead to the booking office. George Bidwell joined him and they talked for about a minute. Hills walked directly away from him and went into the station, while Bidwell returned to the hotel which was under the same roof. 'That was the only opportunity that you had of seeing Noyes?' Mr Hollings asked.

'That was the only time that I saw him.' When quizzed further, Barker said that he had seen him for a minute and a half or two minutes. It was now established that it had started raining earlier in the afternoon.

'Surely you could not see anything?'

'No it was not raining,' Barker added, 'but it had been raining.' The main reason he remembered these events was because George Bidwell had not paid him his fare, a strange omission for someone trying to remain inconspicuous and defraud financial institutions across the world.

The clock was running. The gang had just eight weeks to extricate themselves before their forgery would be discovered when the various endorsed bills of exchange would come due. As a result, they became ever bolder with each new transaction, steadily increasing their haul as they laundered the money.

Between 25 January and 1 March, Noyes had been into the Continental Bank nearly every day – 'certainly two or three times a week' in Stanton's estimation. Porters from the Terminus Hotel and messengers brought messages for him which the manager thought a little out of the ordinary. In fact, Mr Horton's clerk was soon characterised as a strange messenger issuing forth a series of strange messages. On 13 February, Mr Stanton received a note from Noyes from room 6, Terminus Hotel, London Bridge, with a small amount of money contained within it.

'Do you remember when you received that letter,' Harry Poland asked, 'whether you sent the £65, whether you declined to do it?'

'I believe I declined to do it.' Mr Stanton recalled

'And did you afterwards see the person you know as Noyes at the bank?'

'Yes.'

'And did you speak to him about the letter about sending him the money by a strange messenger?'

'Yes,' Stanton replied, 'I said it would be necessary in future to give a fuller direction.'

'Did you say anything about the letter?'

'Yes, that it merely contained a direction to endorse an amount in an envelope.'

'That it was rather vague?'

'Yes.' There was another curious silence as the implications struck home. Had Mr Stanton enquired further then it was entirely possible the fraud could have been stopped in its tracks in the middle of the month.

'What did he say when you spoke to him?' Poland prompted.

'He said that he should desire me to obey the instructions of his letters and to trust the persons he sent: that the persons he sent could be trusted and it would be alright.' And, amazingly, John Stanton took him at his word and carried on regardless.

By the end of February, the forgers were nearly done and, as Freshfields noted in its pre-trial briefing, were 'quite aware that the first forged bill which fell due on 25 March would explode the whole scheme and it was necessary for them to be well out of the way before this catastrophe took place'.

Though the thieves of Threadneedle Street remained breezily confident – certainly from the tone of their recollections – what is interesting is how misplaced such self-belief actually was. There were so many near misses in the last few days of the forgery.

On Friday, 21 February, a cheque for £4,500 on a cheque of Warren's was banked by Hills at the Continental Bank. It was made payable to 'C.J. Heorton', as Mr Stanton recalled on the stand. 'It was presented at the Bank of England and they wrote upon it "Endorsement Irregular",' he explained.

The court was once more attentive. 'And that the cheque was returned to you?' Harry Poland clarified.

'It was.' When Noyes subsequently signed a debit slip, nothing was done about it – and he continued to present forged bills of exchange for discount as though nothing was wrong.

The next day, Saturday, 22 February, George Bidwell made his last ever visit to Paternoster Row to see Thomas Straker. The printer had seen him on average twice a week since Christmas and, as he had testified at the Mansion House, his visitor had never furnished an address nor indicated what his business was. As bidden, Mr Straker added different names to the master plates the customer had previously ordered and also printed the names of the banks on the body of some of the bills.

Earlier that month, he had engraved some scrolls on a separate piece of copper and transferred them to some bills which used the names of D.R. Howell and Juan Perez. The latter had caused an explosion. 'In printing Juan Perez at first, I spelt the name wrong, "Jaun" instead of "Juan",' Mr Straker later testified. 'The prisoner was very cross about it, and I of course said I would alter the name and print them over again.'

That Saturday, George Bidwell took away all the bill forms and plates apart from four scroll-blocks which he accidentally left behind. It was a significant blunder, which was later used by the police to trace him. In the meantime, George Bidwell wanted to obtain as much money as he could.

On Monday, 25 February, at one particular discount house, Clews, Habicht & Company on Old Broad Street, he posed as W.J. Spaulding. The chief cashier there recalled him being quite concerned whether the bills he presented had good acceptances. Alfred Lidington was more worried about the provenance of the parcel of bills themselves. 'I got them from private friends on the Continent for private business transactions,' Mr Spaulding claimed when challenged.

Mr Lidington said it was normal practice to leave bills for a few days before they were discounted. That way, they could make their own enquiries. George Bidwell did not miss a beat. The cashier then asked him to add his name and address in their signature book. He was puzzled when he wrote just 'W.J. Spaulding, Brighton'. 'Brighton is a large place, Mr Spaulding,' the cashier said. 'You must have some address there?'

'No,' he replied, 'Brighton is sufficient. It will find me in letters or telegrams.' Mr Lidington said that this was all too vague. So in the last week of February, Mr Spaulding had reluctantly come in to collect the money in person and, in the cashier's recollection, 'looked distinctly ill at ease'.

On the Tuesday, 25 February, George Macdonnell made his last visit to the Old Lady of Threadneedle Street to launder a final £1,000 of gold. All the weighing machines were in use when he got there. There was a delay of thirty minutes to three-quarters of an hour while he waited in the outer office. The clerks remembered the occasion very well. 'He rang the bell once or twice while he was waiting,' Henry Hughes recalled. When he went to see what the matter was, Mac was clearly thunderous.

'I am surprised I have been waiting so long,' the visitor said.

Patiently, Mr Hughes explained to the American what had happened. On the previous occasion – when Mac had brought in £9,000 – all the machines were free. Today, he would simply have to wait his turn. 'He seemed in a very excited and fidgety state,' Hughes added, 'and I gave him a newspaper to read.'

On the Friday evening, 28 February, if George Bidwell is to be believed, George Macdonnell was back to his usual insufferable self. Dusk was already gathering in their luxurious St James' rooms when Mac held up one of the last forged bills to the light. 'Boys,' he said to the others, 'these are perfect works of art.'

The next morning, the first Saturday in March, Hills made two separate visits to Lombard Street. The first was just after the Continental Bank had opened, when a cheque for £6,000 – a sizable sum – was paid out. Hills had wanted to be paid in French francs and thaler notes. Mr Stanton had come over in person to explain that there would be a slight delay. In that case, the American had said, he would come in on the Monday to collect the foreign cash.

In fact, he returned about an hour later when, in Hardinge Giffard's understated phrase, 'that for one of those accidents which must disarray the best devised schemes of fraud it was all but successful'.

All throughout the greater fraud, accidents, small and large, had accompanied them to their pinnacle of ambition. In Austin Bidwell's later estimation, this was something greater than just a mishap. 'No, it was nemesis,' he remarked, 'it was anything you want to call it, but it was not an accident.'

Thursday, 21 August 1873
Central Criminal Court, Old Bailey
4.45 p.m.

Towards the end of his testimony, John Thomas Stanton recalled his own gullibility when cross-examined by Mr Ribton who was acting for Hills. 'It is perfectly certain that until Mr May made his appearance you never suspected anything wrong about him?' he asked.

'Never.' The Continental Bank – like so many others – had no suspicion whatever. Despite some of the eccentricities associated with their customer, they did not suspect a thing, 'either from the large sums or the address given' of the hotel.

'You did not look upon it as eccentric?' Ribton asked.

'No.'

Hardinge Giffard took to the stand with one final line of enquiry. How, he wanted to know, did Mr Stanton realise that Mr Horton was a customer of the Bank of England?

'I did not know it,' Stanton observed. 'I merely observed a connection with a large customer of the bank.'

'You refer by that to the cheques by Warren which were being constantly paid into his account?'

'Yes.'

'You ascertained by inquiry I supposed that Warren's cheques were good.'

'We did not ascertain by enquiring but by the fact that large cheques were being continually paid. We only took care of ourselves.'

It was a stunning admission. The city only ever looked after itself, a charge as relevant today as it was in 1873 when Walter Bagehot noted that 'no one in London ever dreams of questioning the credit of the bank and the bank never dreams that its own credit is in danger'. As a result, he had been arguing for years that the Bank of England needed to change. He concluded, exactly as Austin Bidwell and the boys had, that the Old Lady of Threadneedle Street was run by well-minded amateurs. Significantly, however, nobody – least of all the governors or commentators like Bagehot – ever envisaged that criminals might take advantage of its very amateurishness.

By the time Mr Stanton had finished on the stand it was nearly 5 p.m. He looked like he had been through the wringer. Both witness and onlookers were exhausted. By then, nobody was in any doubt as to the cleverness and efficacy of the fraudsters. As with Colonel Francis at the Bank of England, Mr Stanton now admitted that he had never made enquiries at the Golden Cross Hotel about his customer. He had obtained a 'specimen' signature from Mr Noyes but could not be sure whether he saw the American clerk sign any of the slips which were now examined in court. 'We always find some slight difference in signatures,' the manager said at some point, 'but it appears to me practically to be the same.'

As a final line of questioning akin to clutching at straws Mr Ribton wanted to know if there was a particular reason why Stanton had asked whether his client could sign cheques for his 'master', Horton. 'I suppose you have known cases where confidential clerks have been known to sign cheques?' Ribton asked.

'Certainly.'

'It is not at all out of the ordinary course of business?'

'Not at all.'

'The ordinary course of business'. An omnipresent spectre that had hung over the city immediately after the discovery of the forgeries was that, given the worsening financial situation, they would nudge the Old Lady of Threadneedle Street and by extension, the British economy, into a nightmare of financial ruin. Currencies were vulnerable and would fluctuate wildly at the barest hint of trouble. 'If the Bank of England can be so easily misled there is no question that minor establishments may be victimised,' one newspaper would later remark. There could be a knock-on effect with a run on the pound – or worse.

Something similar had occurred just seven years earlier. Fresh in the memory was the biggest cause of failure ever seen in the city, when one particular institution had sustained 'losses so reckless and foolish that one would think a child had lent money in the City of London would have lent it better', in Walter Bagehot's assessment.

Overend Gurney had been the largest of the discount houses in and around Lombard Street. Its assets were ten times greater than any nearest rival, and it was 'the greatest instrument of credit in the kingdom', in one contemporary estimation. It was significant that many of the same lawyers assembled here in the summer of 1873 had also prosecuted Overend Gurney's directors for their irresponsibility. It was the Northern Rock of its day.

The directors had used short-term deposits to finance expansion in shipping and railroads, borrowing on bills of exchange 'equal in value to about half the national debt'. The City had been shocked, to say the least, when Overend Gurney went under in May 1866. As a direct result, Sterling's value had plummeted overnight. Financiers would often debate which was worse – that one of their own had failed or that the Bank of England had refused to bail them out.

Matters had come to a head with the events of 'Black Friday'. The Old Lady of Threadneedle Street had had to give emergency authority to issue notes in excess of the redemption funds it had to hand. To cover its debts, the bank had to hike interest rates to an unprecedented 10 per cent, thereby creating panic in the City. After under-writing many tens of millions to keep business flowing, the bank found that its reserve was reduced to just under £3 million by the close of business.

The Chancellor of the Exchequer recommended that the Bank Act be suspended. This was promptly agreed upon. The following morning the Bank of England was given authority to issue notes to whatever extent was necessary to quieten the fears of the market. Today, it would be called quantitative easing. Then, it was a close-run thing.

There was shock around the square mile. It was a Victorian version of overwhelming subprime debt that, in the worsening financial situation in 1873, could now be repeated in the wake of these forgeries. At that stage, nobody really knew how great the exposure of the Bank of England actually was. But when, in the immediate aftermath, the markets had opened on Monday, 3 March there was an eerie, curious calm.

It was clear that Frank May had stumbled across the fraud in the very nick of time. The *Daily Telegraph* had reported:

> The amount placed at hazard by these transactions is probably, to those who will be the ultimate losers, not very serious, but the feeling of insecurity created by the fact that notwithstanding every precaution, such frauds can be accomplished with impunity is, in such a mercantile community, a distinct evil.

The bank had missed a bullet. In one of the forger's estimations, it could so easily have been a howitzer shell.

Six weeks later in Cuba, Austin Bidwell boasted to Willie Pinkerton that if he had remained in England, the Old Lady of Threadneedle Street would never have known what had hit it. 'The bank would have lost three times as much money,' he boasted to Pink. 'I could have gone personally and presented bills for discount of £50,000 and had them cashed without question.'

Within a week, the thieves of Threadneedle Street would have made £3 million and left no trace. 'Had I been in London,' Austin claimed, 'the unfilled date which led to the discovery would never have taken place.'

Pink smiled. He'd heard all that before. 'If that is the case,' he said mildly, 'you are indeed unfortunate.'

Though both Bidwell brothers exhibited some contrition in court, George Bidwell later claimed that he felt no particular guilt, for they had left behind 'no ruined widows and orphans to linger out the remainder of their blighted lives in poverty'. Similarly, when he had discussed the frauds with Willie Pinkerton in Cuba, Austin Bidwell had alluded to the other excuse they invariably trotted out. 'There was no use playing against the Devil,' he said.

It was something with which his brother concurred. To understand what really happened once the fraud had been discovered, another variation on that same theme has a peculiar resonance. 'Tell the truth and shame the Devil, Nellie,' George Bidwell shouted to his mistress as he was lead from court at one of his first remand hearings, providing the link for the next, most extraordinary phase of their adventures – and certainly the most astounding day in court in the summer of 1873.

10

Devil to Pay

Q: With regard to the trunk, the large trunk I am speaking of, where was the last time you saw it?
A: Put into the train at Charing Cross Station.
Q: Had you packed it previously?
A: Yes, some time before.
Q: Was it full when you had finished packing it?
A: Yes, quite full.
Q: Did you look at it?
A: No.

Cross-examination of Nellie Vernon, trial transcript.

Yesterday a somewhat startling rumour was circulated in connection with the four men now under trial charged with the daring forgeries on the Bank of England. The rumour was to the effect than an attempt had been made to tamper with certain officials in Newgate.

Daily Telegraph, Saturday, 23 August 1873

Day Five – Friday, 22 August 1873
Central Criminal Court, Old Bailey
10.15 a.m.

It was another cool and cloudy August morning. There was definitely something different in the air. Yet it had nothing to do with the weather. It was obvious straightaway to the men and women who had dutifully filed in to crowd the public gallery. Heavily armed policemen now lined all the corridors, many congregating around the entrances to the courtroom. All nearby doors were locked. The warren-like walkways and passageways beneath the court were obviously guarded, too.

Something was most definitely afoot. There was a hush to every conversation, nervous glances exchanged between many officials. The barristers looked startled as they passed notes to each other. Even the judge, whose implacable, unsmiling face had remained serious throughout, seemed preoccupied when, shortly before the hour, he had walked in wearing his heavy, scarlet robes that seemed to weigh him down, slowing his progress.

When the prisoners had been led to the stand, they too became aware of it. They seemed to be hemmed in. The number of policemen had been doubled. All around were new faces. All the familiar guards were gone.

These were the most extraordinary circumstances on this, the fifth day of this most extraordinary trial,[19] confirmed when an otherwise carefree, yet beautiful, young woman now entered the Central Criminal Court escorted by unsmiling policemen. A frisson of excitement accompanied her to the stand.

Nellie Vernon looked younger than her 23 years. Her dark eyes were wide and gave her an air of sadness that seemed at odds with the carefree gaiety she normally presented. Uncharacteristically vulnerable, she was, as one newspaper described her, 'fashionably dressed'. Elegant and poised on the stand, Nellie felt no shame. In the hushed anticipation of the courtroom, the onlookers had already formed an opinion. Nobody had to spell it out because everyone knew what she was – a 'mistress'.

Hardinge Giffard QC was once again lead prosecutor for the morning. Effortlessly polite, with an air of mournful regret at having to prompt sometimes unworthy memories, he spoke to the witness directly, barely referring to his notes and occasionally politely acknowledging cues from the judge. 'In the course of last year did you live at 11 Duke's Road, Euston Square?' he began.

'Yes.'

'In the course of that time did you become acquainted with the prisoner George Bidwell?'

'Yes.' After confirming details of their European travels the autumn before, Nellie explained that she had returned to London due to illness. As the lawyers knew, she could be infuriatingly monosyllabic. But now, when she did speak, her voice was refined, measured and with the faintest hint of a foreign intonation. In the fetid atmosphere, sounds did not travel well.

'While you were absent from him and while you being in England and he being abroad, did you receive these letters from him?' The clerk moved forward and handed her a bundle – all sixteen of them – wrapped in ribbons and bound with an ornate wax seal.

'Yes,' Nellie said, after taking them.

Turning to face the judge, Giffard said, 'These, My Lord, are not important in themselves. Unimportant, except for examination at handwriting.' In fact, they were crucial to the prosecution's case. 'The letters of George Bidwell seem to afford conclusive evidence against himself,' the prosecution brief noted ahead of the trial, 'and unless he pleads guilty so as to prevent them from being used the evidence they contain is conclusive.'

Barely 12ft away, George Bidwell, as he usually did, looked at Nellie Vernon and smiled. There was a knowing twinkle, the telltale signs of the torrid passions which they had shared. Those letters were revealing about their relationship for, as he had written to her on remand, 'you know darling that with you I am safe from all tempters'. As always, there was his constant preoccupation with devilish temptation, and he had addressed her as 'My darling wicked eyed little *diabla*'.

Rather more simple terms of affection populated their correspondence: 'Nellie darling', 'Little Nellie', and 'My little sweetheart'. As well as all the foolish romantic fripperies that showed how unashamedly sentimental they could be in each other's company. 'There are many more things I shall reserve to whisper in your ear.' 'My pretty little baby does not know but can judge badly her "Old Turk" longs to obtain that sweetest kiss ever invented in "Old England".'

Among all this saccharine cooing, George Bidwell also wrote, 'you are now in my debt two thousand times [and] by this you know that I am a voracious creditor,' a telling metaphor under the circumstances.

Nellie Vernon felt no embarrassment as she handed the letters back. They were testimony to their love, many written in the peculiarly dreamy vein that George had made all his own. 'I have seen and see daily many beautiful women but not one can tempt me to be untrue to my sweet Ethel,' he wrote in one which bore a Dresden postmark. 'Beautiful cities filled with palaces containing works of art and appliances to luxury beyond belief,' he wrote in another.

As a counterpoint, there was a Victorian version of bling designed to appeal to his girlfriend when he visited the Royal Palace in Munich. 'Of course, you are interested in the bedroom,' he teased. 'The bed is canopied and with hanging curtains, also the bed has a cover or counterpane.' This evidently was where, 'the old Kings had their little fun with their girls: the walls and top are covered with looking glasses'. The latter seemed to have covered the whole of the room, so much so that:

> I sat thinking that if only I had my little Nellie, I would make the ghost of those old sybarites green with envy at sight of what might there take place. Lying there in whatever direction our eyes turned we should see reflected dozens of ourselves. Oh how jolly – go away peaches, I must not think of such things or I shall go distracted and now I have such good control over my passions.

That there was more to his travels was also apparent. 'I find that my mission is to be of a political nature and all my movements are to be very quiet,' he had written elliptically from Germany, concluding that particular letter with a serious admonition, 'You must destroy this at once.'

Friday, 22 August 1873
Central Criminal Court, Old Bailey
10.40 a.m.

Nellie Vernon composed herself as Mr Giffard prompted her about when she and George had moved to the Baker Street area at the start of the year. 'Do you remember while you were staying at Upper Gloucester Place seeing a black leather bag?'

'Yes.'

'I believe you kicked it accidentally or in some way or other?'

'Yes.'

'Did that cause you to open it and see what was inside?'

'Yes, it was full of money.' There was a flurry of excitement in the court.

'While you were also staying there do you remember buying a travelling bag at Baker & Crisp's?' This was a high-end haberdashery on Regent Street where Nellie often bought expensive trinkets for her boyfriend.

'Yes,' she said.

'Was that as a present for George Bidwell?'

'Yes.'

'About what time was that?'

'About the end of January.'

'Do you remember his taking that bag away with him?'

'Yes.'

'Did he come back with it, I believe?'

'No.'

'I think you were somewhat angry at his giving away a present that had been made for him by you?'

'Yes.'

219

'Did he tell you where he had been?'
'He said he had been to Calais.'
'Did he say with whom?'
'With Mr Macdonnell.'

Friday, 7 February 1873
Calais, France

It was late – close to midnight – and Austin Bidwell wondered if the two Georges, like his bride, would ever show. He arrived just ahead of the Dover steamer, and shortly thereafter so did they. At a nearby hotel, his brother handed him a heavy bag from which Austin counted out 'the very nice sum of $100,000 in gold, bonds and French money' (in reality, the prosecution believed it was roughly half that sum). There was also another golden ornament, a wedding present that the two Georges had bought two days earlier, a gold watch on which the inscription read 'presented to his friend, whom he hope soon to meet again,' engraved with Mac's initials. After half an hour's conversation on the dock, both then departed back to Britain.

Austin Bidwell promptly arrived back at the Gare du Nord early that same Saturday. Reunited with Jeannie Devereux on 8 February, his bride was beside herself. 'During our drive to the hotel, radiant with joy,' Austin recalled, 'she told me the separation had been a cruel one and she was so happy to know we should never be separated again.'

It was part of the groom's presiding genius to make his honeymoon his escape route. The first leg of their honeymoon was to cross France towards the Spanish border beyond Bayonne. The *Chemin de Fer* was hardly luxurious, nor particularly speedy, but it did not seem to matter. Mr and Mrs Austin Bidwell were delirious in each other's company, 'talking of the happy years that lay before us,' he later recalled.

Yet his duplicity had started to consume him. In all their time together, Austin Bidwell had pretended that he was a successful businessman. Should he not just come clean, he wondered? 'My secret cause of unrest had to be kept locked in my breast,' he later recalled, 'while my young wife, all unsuspecting, was merry and happy, chanting little snatches of song and telling me a hundred times she was the happiest of women.' Serene and oblivious, she slept as the night rushed by like 'a fairy dream'.

After crossing the Bidassoa 'we were on Spanish soil', in Austin's words, heading towards Madrid. Mrs Bidwell said, 'Now I will sleep', laying her golden head on his shoulder. Her husband wondered whether, as she dozed through the night, he shouldn't wake her to show her the magnificent scenery of the Pyrenees.

Fairly swiftly, the sun rose to announce a splendid Sunday morning. Suddenly, there was a twisted metallic discordance, followed by shots ringing out. The carriages came to a grinding halt and the mountains absorbed the echoes of the gunshots. Jeannie Bidwell woke with a start. Her husband, managing to reassure her, could not help wondering: was he about to end up the victim of yet another rail accident?

It was a random act of terror by the most enduring political separatists of the nineteenth century. The Carlists routinely shot at trains, so much so that the drivers often erected metal plates in their cabs as protection (which often failed). Moments later teenage brigands came aboard their carriage looking for spoils. One such fellow wanted Austin's chain and watch which he refused to hand over. The lad went away crestfallen.

After the passengers were ordered to alight, Austin pretended that he and Jeannie were an English duke and duchess. 'My wife thoroughly enjoyed the situation,' he wrote, 'and I should have done so too, had I not such strong reasons for quick passage through Spain.'

They were in the middle of nowhere high in the Pyrenees. Along with Harry Nunn, Austin Bidwell obtained an ox cart, removed all their luggage and then carried on their way. Though smiling to reassure his wife, he was deeply worried. 'My safe plan would have been to return to France, make my way to Brest and embark from there to New York,' he wrote. His appointment of a servant had been a triumph. Nunn, he says, 'proved to be thoroughly reliable, helpful and full of cheer'.

Marooned, the weather was atrocious. Snow was everywhere. When they arrived at a nearby inn, Austin was amazed to learn that storms like this could rage for a whole week – which they subsequently did. Another day, another blizzard, his sense of isolation becoming ever more acute. He was desperate to leave with a small bag containing the bonds and head back towards the French border. 'I would leave the greater part of the gold in charge of my wife,' he wrote. Harry Nunn was trustworthy enough to guard the rest of their spoils and look after Mrs Bidwell.

When he eventually told her of his plans to return alone to the United States, Jeannie pleaded to go with him. He relented. Mrs Bidwell was a model of common sense and enjoyed herself hugely after they found a donkey to take them. 'She came out warmly clad and mounted the mule,' Austin recalled, 'and I strapped some mugs and a bundle of lunch behind the saddle.' The villagers and other stranded passengers all came out to stare. Waved through by the military (including an English mercenary, who was in it, he shouted to them, for the excitement) they eventually made to the nearest railway town where Austin Bidwell marvelled at the 'sweet music' of a distant locomotive.

After another ride on a freezing train they made their way to Burgos, roughly 100 miles inland, from where they could connect to various trains heading towards Santander on the coast. The only news Austin could glean was that there had been a revolution in Madrid (King Amadeus had resigned and Castelar appointed as head of the Republic).

Among all the confusion, he had no idea when their train would leave, if ever. It was now 3 p.m. on the Friday. There would be just enough time to reach Madrid before boarding another train south-east towards Cadiz. He and Jeannie had a fine dinner in Avila, only to emerge to discover that martial law had been declared. The government had seized the roads in an effort to stop any insurrections.

The railways were next. That evening, there were no trains. According to his account, Austin then telegraphed both the new head of government, Castelar, and the Minister of War that he was an Englishman with his family who needed to reach Madrid in great urgency. After further desperate telegrams offering 5,000 francs if a special train could be laid on just for him, one did duly arrive at midday on the Saturday. The trio and all their luggage were loaded aboard. And then, nothing happened.

At this point, Austin Bidwell was virtually hyperventilating. Time — 'precious hours,' he termed them — was slipping away. 'I saw fate closing her hand on me,' he later wrote, wondering what he might be able to do to extricate himself from the mess.

Friday, 22 August 1873
Central Criminal Court, Old Bailey
10.50 a.m.

Hardinge Giffard slowly went through the minutiae of Nellie Vernon's time with George Bidwell. Routine enquiries had revealed that on Wednesday, 25 February, in the week prior to the fraud's discovery they had moved to the Albemarle Hotel ('for a few days' George had told her) obviously in case he needed to flee in a hurry as the bills started to come due. As this hotel was around the corner from St James Place, it also provided ideal access to their penman. 'Macdonnell came and helped them to pack,' the notes for Mr Giffard spelled out.

'Had you gone to take rooms, or had anyone taken them for you?' he now asked.

'Mr Macdonnell took them for us,' Nellie replied.

Mr Giffard referred to an earlier deposition. 'Has anything been said about the statement made by the prisoner at the Albemarle Hotel where you had come from?'

'Yes, it was said that we had come from Paris.'

'Did you say anything about that?'

'I said there was no need of a falsehood about it.'

'To whom did you say that?'

'To George Bidwell.'

'What did George Bidwell say to that?'

'As Mr Macdonnell had taken the rooms we had better keep the statement he had made.' At the time, she was furious and said it was stupid of him. Now, in court, something of her anger remained. All around her, there was an ominous quiet. Even the defence looked amazed. 'There was no need to tell a falsehood about that.' Why tell even a small lie if you were completely honest?

Under the circumstances, George's entreaty to his girlfriend was richly ironic. 'Shame the Devil and tell the truth, Nellie.'

Watching her on the stand, many of the court officials were only too aware that Nellie Vernon was not as innocent as she made out. In fact, she had presented the prosecution with several conundrums. There had been rumours of bribes, or at least money exchanged, for changing her story. While held in remand over the summer, George Bidwell had written Nellie a long, remarkable letter coaching her on what to say and what not to. 'Do not mention to any detectives that I have given you any information,' he wrote, 'only I tell you so in case the Messrs Freshfields do not seem inclined to speak for me.' This was a telling reference to their lessening his sentence if he fully co-operated.

She could, he was sure, tease out details and string them all along. 'The evidence against me is not the point,' he wrote, 'but of course, there is no saying what verdict a jury will bring in.' He had given as much information as he could to the Old Lady of Threadneedle Street. The more Nellie told them, the less helpful it would be. 'Do not let them think they are doing you any favour by getting me off with ten or twelve [years],' he wrote.

Ultimately, the prosecution feared just how much of a hold George Bidwell had over Nellie Vernon. In their correspondence he treated her with a Cinderella-like devotion, a princess whom he had elevated upon a pedestal, spoiling her with presents whose purchase he couched in terms of the oleaginous flattery which he had made his own. 'I send the bag – in the bag is a bundle – in the bundle is a slipper – in the slipper Geo hopes to see the "roly poly itsy footy" of his Little Nellie,' he wrote in one.

That was nothing compared to the fairy tales that he was still peddling about himself. 'I never had any low vicious nor vulgar habits, do not drink, gamble nor use tobacco,' he wrote. 'Steady in my habits, I have always been honest and faithful to my friends and have no qualifications that should win a fine position in life.' Also claiming that there was 'nothing mean nor treacherous in my disposition,' as ever, he blamed everyone but himself. 'I seem to have brought myself into a maze of difficulties out of which every track seems crooked,' George Bidwell had written.

And unbeknown to her, he was working on a way out. It stemmed from yet another fairy tale, when someone, who really should have known better, felt sorry for him and took one of his heartfelt pleas at face value. At his last remand before Sir Sydney Waterlow at the Mansion House six weeks earlier, George Bidwell had laid it on thick. He had looked genuinely contrite as he made what he termed his final request of the lord mayor. 'I have now been three months in Newgate,' he declared to His Lordship, 'undergoing the most rigorous solitary confinement.' Worse, he had been pilloried here in this very dock for that same amount of time. 'My position is greatly saddened by the fact that one who is so near and dear to me as my brother has been placed at my side on the same charge,' George continued, 'and under circumstances that were caused by me alone.'

This would be the first time he would make this ridiculous claim in public. And then, as he knew was sometimes allowed, he asked to share a cell with Austin Bidwell.

'I appeal to Your Lordship as a father, please allow us this last boon' he added, 'this last gleam of sunshine which we might ever be permitted to enjoy.' If convicted, he and his brother would be separated and never meet again. Austin Bidwell himself then stood up and, also with a completely straight face, added that it would allow them both 'an opportunity of preparing our defence and talking over family matters'.

Though Sir Sydney was at pains to point out that he could not decide what went on inside Newgate, the authorities there did, indeed, relent. They allowed the Bidwell brothers to share a cell. The family matters that resulted would lead to the most explosive denouement possible on the fifth and most extraordinary day of the later full trial at the Central Criminal Court.

Saturday, 16 February 1873
The Pyrenees

After various false starts, being shunted into side-lines and suffering breakdowns thanks to a wheezing engine, it was four o'clock in the afternoon by the time the train carrying the newlyweds eventually arrived in Madrid. It was too late to reach Cadiz that same evening. A sense of ominous dread fell over Austin Bidwell knowing that they had indubitably missed their boat. Then, if his memoirs are to be believed, his gaze alighted upon a timetable for transatlantic steamers. There was, he noticed, a French steamer sailing from St Nazaire for Vera Cruz, Mexico, which would briefly stop at Santander the following Saturday. They could make it if they returned from whence they came, retracing their steps northwards.

For now Madrid was perceptibly quiet thanks to the political situation, so Austin Bidwell made his way to the British embassy to read the English newspapers. There was no mention of any forgeries upon the Bank of England. '[All] was serene in London,' he later recalled, 'and that the Old Lady was without doubt giving out sovereigns by the tens of thousands for us.'

They left on the following Tuesday, arriving on the Wednesday night in Santander. The days dragged. It was a special kind of agony waiting for the weekend. The Bidwells spent an anxious Saturday sightseeing, but by the time they had returned to their hotel, the steamer had not arrived. 'Heartsick and anxious I went to bed half resolved to take my wife into my confidence,' Austin Bidwell claimed. 'It would have been a terrible shock to her but I began to fear that the truth would come to her ears some time.'

Early the next day, Harry Nunn woke them, grinning from ear to ear. When they looked out, there was 'a steamer of the largest size and magnificent in her beauty' across the bay. After a hurried breakfast, they embarked upon the *Martinique*, and later that Saturday afternoon, 23 February, set sail into what he seriously hoped would be a golden, happy future.

Austin Bidwell remained jauntily confident that the police would never find him, even though divine justice might. Watching the mountains and the continent of

Europe sink into the sea, he remembered some lines from his past, 'The days of my destiny is over, and the star of my fate hath declined'. But, as always, fate had other plans in store.

Friday, 22 August 1873
Central Criminal Court, Old Bailey
11 a.m.

It suited the forgers to portray their time in London as one of cosy domesticity, rising early and leading a blameless existence. On the stand, Nellie recalled that the two Georges often breakfasted together, excluding her, in Upper Gloucester Place.

'While you were living there do you remember Macdonnell showing you a bank note for a large amount?' Hardinge Giffard prompted.

'Yes.'

'What was it?'

'£500.'

A gasp of astonishment rippled through the courtroom. Even the judge looked amazed. It was a source of equal amazement that Nellie claimed she had no idea what the gang had really been up to. At one point George Bidwell had told her that he earned £20,000 a year. As a result money flowed freely, though there was one curious episode where she had lent money to 'Mr Hall' (Hills) via her boyfriend. As she came to recall this, her soft voice did not project and Mr Giffard had to lean forward. 'I am afraid what you said did not reach me,' he said patiently. At this, the judge interjected. Despite his seniority, there was clearly nothing wrong with his hearing.

'I gave him a box with some gold in it and told him to take what he wanted,' he repeated. There was another pause as Judge Archibald and the lawyers compared dates of when exactly Nellie and George Bidwell had stayed in central London. But now, as she came to relate this next sequence of events, Nellie Vernon's dark eyes clouded at the memory.

Nothing could ever come close to articulating what the experience of those first few days of March had really been like. In her heart of hearts, she had known something had been terribly wrong. That weekend had been a whirl of heady danger and excitement, but ultimately of lies and betrayal, passing like a vivid, abhorrent nightmare.

First Weekend of March 1873
Central London

That first Saturday in March, they had had lunch in the Albemarle dining room. Now she thought about it, George Bidwell had seemed jumpier, constantly looking over his shoulder. Suddenly, George Macdonnell rushed into their room around 2.30 p.m. that

afternoon and said something which she did not quite catch. Fairly quickly, the two Georges both went out together. Where they went, she never found out.

In his memoirs, George Bidwell relates a dramatic story of rushing to the Continental Bank from Garraway's Coffee House to find chaos, attempting to rescue their friend and hearing newsboys shouting about the fraud. The reality was more prosaic. The weather had been dreadful. They had stayed in all weekend. They would, he said, shortly be leaving for Paris. The next afternoon, George Bidwell had blithely informed Nellie to pack, and she was furious. He was in and out all day to see what she was up to. 'How are you getting on?' he kept asking, which made her even angrier, so she returned to her old lodgings to get help from her old landlady. When George sent for her at the Meunier's, she refused to come back.

Nellie Vernon had sufficiently calmed down enough to return to the Albemarle for dinner. George now told her that he had changed his mind. They would start for the south coast the next day, despite the fact rain was lashing the whole of the country. It was hardly going to be the jolliest of excursions.

'Did he explain at all how that came to pass?' Giffard prompted on the stand.

Nellie looked pained at the memory. 'He said he thought he should like to go to Hastings again before he left England.'

The next evening, the first Monday in March, they checked in at the Victoria Hotel, St Leonards. Later that same evening George Macdonnell followed them 'and George Bidwell ordered a room for him,' the prosecution determined. Further police enquiries revealed that the two Georges had spent much of the evening in Macdonnell's room. If Nellie thought this odd, she did not say when later questioned by police. Other guests later recalled overhearing a heated discussion. Some remembered there had been the smell of burning. Later, both Americans re-joined Nellie for dinner, both seeming extremely preoccupied. 'George Bidwell did not appear to have thoroughly made up his mind as to what he should do,' the prosecution later commented.

But, as they soon acknowledged, when he did make his mind up, he always did so in a hurry. It is a measure of George Bidwell's absolute faith in his invisibility – and, indeed, invincibility – that he continued to use his real name even after the fraud had been discovered. 'I did feel a certain exultation and full confidence in my ability to keep out of the way for all time,' he later wrote, as he and Nellie prepared to carry on sightseeing without an apparent care in the world.

Friday, 22 August 1873
Central Criminal Court, Old Bailey
11.40 a.m.

Nellie Vernon's memories were cloaked in claustrophobia. In the corner of the room at St Leonards were a couple of heavy, battered trunks, implacable and all the more menacing for being ignored by the two Georges. They provided a crucial evidentiary

link to which the prosecution now drew attention when Nellie admitted, 'We took all the luggage we had from London'.

On the Tuesday, 4 March, with one newspaper now reporting the fraud's arrangements as 'masterpieces of ingenuity and patience', it was time to leave. George Bidwell had told her that Mac was returning to the capital.

'Did he take anything with him?' Hardinge Giffard now asked.

'I believe he took a trunk of Mr George Bidwell's with him.'

At this point, Mac's defence attorney, Austin Metcalfe QC, interjected. He stood up to face the jury, almost shouting in anger. 'Don't believe anything,' he said. Metcalfe turned to address Nellie sharply. 'Did you see it?'

She shook her head. 'No, I did not see.'

Judge Archibald was clearly unhappy. 'Were you told anything about it?'

'Yes,' said Nellie. 'George Bidwell told me he had taken one.'

Mr Metcalfe, nodding towards the judge, was not happy, either. 'Surely that would not be in evidence against Macdonnell?' he asked. 'My friend is putting it in evidence against Macdonnell.'

Ignoring the sarcasm, the judge made a quick decision. 'It may be evidence against George Bidwell.'

Which swiftly provided Hardinge Giffard with a window of opportunity. 'It has an important bearing on evidence against George Bidwell.'

The judge agreed. Mr Giffard continued on his original approach. 'Was that a trunk that you packed?'

'Yes.'

'What sort of trunk was it?'

'A large black leather one.'

Mr Giffard paused, waiting to deliver his killer blow. 'I think it had better be produced at once.'

This self-same battered black leather trunk was now waiting in the anteroom behind the judge, guarded by policemen given the heightened state of security. The clerk to the court, Mr Avery, and his assistant now brought it in. Few people had actually seen inside it and now it had long since been emptied, but the contents were highly significant. Marked in evidence as 'certain property and documents', the trunk had contained letters and over $200,000 worth of bonds when apprehended in Manhattan.

There were also the items Freshfields had notarised as:

Two small engravers' boxes containing the wax impression of two seals. Steel discs of the Bidwell arms and monogram 'G.B.'; an engraved plate of 'Mr George Bidwell', with a card from the same plate; and a ticket of admission to the

Casino at Trouville, dated September 1872. There were also two watches and some coins in the trunk.

Friday, 22 August 1873
Central Criminal Court, Old Bailey
11.45 a.m.
....

While most of the court was staring at this luggage, Willie Pinkerton was paying more attention to the prisoners. There could no longer be any doubt. They were up to something. Pink had sensed it all along.

All week, the detective himself had been a welcome, occasional addition to the prosecution bench, squeezing in among the barristers. Nobody knew the intricacies of the case better, nor indeed, the self-same family matters to which Austin Bidwell had alluded at their final remand at the Mansion House. In fact, the greater Bidwell family had caused him the greatest puzzlement.

As a routine precaution, Pink had made it his business to intercept the correspondence between the siblings. Even at the height of their roguery, George and Austin regularly sent letters and money to their brothers and sisters back in the United States. Once they were on the run in the spring of 1873, their tone became darker. 'Don't let anybody bother you on pretence of being a friend of mine unless it be my brother or Mac or a bearer of a letter from one of them,' George had written to Joseph Bidwell in Michigan, the brother who had unduly influenced the Governor of Massachusetts to release him two years earlier. 'You may mail me money,' he had also written a telling note to this same 'Jo', 'as I will trust no one except my brothers. Do not on any account use the telegraph.'

In the spring, when Pink had talked to Austin Bidwell in Cuba, he was certain his brothers would come and help them.[20] 'Bidwell is determined to have John or Joe Bidwell come to England with about $50,000 to defend him and George,' Pink noted in a letter to his own brother, 'or to compromise his case for a light sentence and a plea of guilty if the Messrs Freshfields will accept it.' Though used to Austin's idle boasts, that was quite a sum. 'John has plenty of money belonging to me,' Austin had claimed. It was obvious where it had all come from.

The revelation that John W. Bidwell was also a justice of the peace and, in Austin's estimation, a fine upstanding citizen, had made Pink wonder most of all. If there was one thing William Pinkerton had learned it was surely the louder the protestations of honesty or innocence, the guiltier the party was likely to be so, as a matter of routine, he dispatched his operatives to rural Michigan to interview him at length.

Friday, 22 August 1873
Central Criminal Court, Old Bailey
11.55 a.m.

Most of the spoils from the fraud had, indeed, been hidden in their luggage, not that Nellie Vernon had appreciated it at the time. Hardinge Giffard was, as were most of the onlookers, staring intently at the trunk that stood in the middle of the court. Turning towards Nellie Vernon, he began his next line of questioning. 'So this is the box?' he asked.

'Yes.'

Giffard paused. 'I may as well ask you here at once was that the trunk with you in Trouville?'

'Yes.'

'You afterwards saw that box I believe after it had been brought from America – saw it opened?'

'I did.' That had formed the basis for her third and final deposition at the Mansion House eight weeks earlier.

'Did you see in it some of the shells that you had picked up in Trouville?'

Mr Metcalfe interjected, less certainly this time. 'I should like to see what the shells are that she has sworn to in this positive way?'

The judge was clearly irritated. 'You can ask about that when your turn comes,' he said.

Mr Metcalfe was livid. He turned to Nellie and angrily repeated his question. 'I'd said did you pick up these shells?'

Judge Archibald interrupted, looking equally annoyed. 'There was no objection to the question. When your turn comes you can cross-examine upon it.'

There was silence as Mr Metcalfe sat down. In his place, Mr Giffard stood up and turned towards the jury. 'It is very difficult to hear a witness in the middle of a running commentary.' Several onlookers smiled and soft laughter filled the courtroom. Giffard turned to face his witness who seemed unmoved by the legal niceties. The shells were never mentioned again, confirming that she had taken a ticket from the Trouville casino as she now attested. Watching her intently, George Bidwell had to smile. Now it was the time for the greatest gamble of all.

Friday, 22 August 1873
Central Criminal Court, Old Bailey
Noon

Willie Pinkerton had smelled a mouse where there was actually a rat. For someone who had been chased all over the world, George Bidwell's sangfroid in the face of adversity was remarkable. But now, uncharacteristically, the prisoner himself was growing increasingly agitated, his eyes flitting around the courtroom. He had noticed the greater police presence, but that was to be expected. They had made the authorities look foolish and they were simply taking precautions. But so had he, an insurance policy that required the presence of someone who seemed to be missing. He should have been here by now.

Watching him now, Willie Pinkerton could see George Bidwell's brow furrowed with anxiety. The detective could not help wondering why. The prisoner had already admitted he wanted to give it all up. 'In any event I am done travelling and shall settle down as soon as I see the end of these disasters,' he had written in one of his more recent letters to his estranged wife. 'I hope to be in shape to set us all up right.'

And, for George Bidwell himself, that meant there was only one nagging question remaining. Where on earth was he?

'Honest John', as Austin had termed his brother, was barely making ends meet. At the end of March, Pinkerton operatives had visited the Bidwell family farmstead at Black Lake, Michigan, where John W. Bidwell lived next door to their sister Harriet (whom they found 'to be one of those whining kind of women who appear melancholy or always under a cloud').

In nearby Muskegon, they learned that John Bidwell had received several bulky packages over the past few weeks. Honest John was apparently unsocial, uncommunicative and noncommittal when dealing with the staff at both the American Express and Post Offices. A lawyer in the town told them that he was always in debt. John Bidwell owed money to every store in Muskegon. He delayed his creditors by repeatedly claiming that he was expecting money from his brothers.

When challenged by the detectives, he said he did not want to 'criminate them', had not kept the letters but acknowledged that he had received a few thousand dollars at most. 'George Bidwell has never sent me any money,' he confessed. 'It all came from Austin.' John Bidwell also claimed that he had no idea about the provenance of this money, presuming that it was kosher until he read about his brothers' connection with the Bank of England forgeries in the newspapers. 'I am not his banker,' he added, of Austin, 'but he had sent me the money for the farm, to buy a boat and make the farm nice.'

His helpfulness was laced with determination not betray his siblings. 'I do not wish to lend my assistance in the capture of my brothers,' he said, refusing to give them any photographs of his brother. 'I have nothing more to conceal.' Taking no chances, the operatives thoroughly searched the property. They found nothing, certainly not the 'missing' money that Pink suspected had been sent to him in recent weeks.

When he later found out, Willie Pinkerton took it all with a pinch of salt. Among the more curious exchanges between the brothers was one where Austin had claimed he would be coming to the Pacific Hotel, Greenwich Street, with his bride in tow. He had wanted Honest John to meet them. 'Again, I say let nothing mortal prevent you coming as I direct (Joseph, too) for this is an absolute matter of life and death that I see you,' Austin had enigmatically written. 'Bring two or three thousand dollars with you, no matter in what shape.'

Pinkerton knew it was obviously some sort of bribe for the New York Police Department, where the fix had been in for years. Watching the Bidwells now in the Old Bailey, it gave him pause for thought. What would happen if they tried to buy protection here? Scotland Yard's finest were unimpeachable, Pink consoled himself, as he shook the notion from his mind. That was simply too ludicrous to contemplate.

The previous exchange, with the angry and at times inexplicable interjection by the defence lawyers, was the highlight of the day. In terms of theatre, the Old Bailey presented unparalleled spectacle. All the robes, theatricals and drama of the court had their own devotees, all now sitting back and enjoying the arguments.

These regulars at the court had, if not exactly become bound by friendship, at least shared kinship over the course of the week. All had more than a passing acquaintance with each other. Some even nodded at each other, sharing pleasantries. Many, understandably, were American. All had enjoyed the way in which Austin Metcalfe QC had overreached himself. Given the extra security, even the most dim-witted among them had known something had been up.

None of them realised that it was because of one of their number. For most of the week, there had been in attendance a well-dressed, bearded American who was quite clearly wealthy and pleasant. Today, though, he was absent. This was of little significance in itself: the court had been full of such types, there to gawp and watch, to wallow in the sense of occasion and enjoy history being made. But this fellow had been unusual in his modesty and self-effacement. If he spoke (in one account, with 'a strong nasal twang, and in a drawling, slow manner'), it was only in quiet acknowledgement. To all intents and purposes, he was exactly what his passport had claimed when he had passed through Liverpool docks six weeks before – a farmer, with a wife and family, who had never been in the British Isles before. But his name, had he given it, would have electrified the court – it was John Bidwell, 'Honest John'.

Nobody had noticed the family resemblance. Nobody had seen them exchange knowing glances. And certainly, as several others suggested, nobody ever suspected John Bidwell had, as detectives later believed, been carrying a gun in his pocket (and in a later account, so too had the policemen, lawyers and the judge, which hardly seems credible).

Nobody within the courtroom was aware that the police were now chasing John Bidwell down, having raided his lodgings the night before. That was why all the prison guards had been switched and the police presence had become so much heavier.

All morning, rumours started to grow that the prisoners were going to be sprung from the Old Bailey itself. 'The Bidwells and their associates are, in consequence, more closely watched than ever and at the Central Criminal Court yesterday, the redoubled precautions were obvious enough to the audience,' noted the *Daily Telegraph* the next day. 'The prudence of this case will hardly be questioned after what had now happened.' But what, exactly?

At this same moment in time, another trial was about to start at London Guildhall with an emergency sitting which would have a direct bearing on this one at the Old Bailey. Though dismissed as 'a tempest in a teapot' by George Bidwell, who vainly tried to claim his innocence in the affair, it was yet another manifestation of 'family matters'. It was so serious that it was held in camera (closed court), and some had wanted the same for these hearings at the Old Bailey, with not just the public galleries cleared but police officers stationed at every available exit point.

Friday, 22 August 1873
1 Mile Away – Guildhall, City of London
Noon

Unlike the crowded scenes at the Old Bailey, the police court sessions were shrouded in even greater mystery. There were no spectators or reporters and only the barest minimum of officials were allowed to participate. It was significant that the lead prosecutor, briefed in great hurry by the City solicitors earlier this morning, was Harry Poland QC, whose absence from the Old Bailey had been noted by a few more eagle-eyed observers.

This case was being held in camera for good reason. The accused, Owen Norton, aged 36 years, had been escorted in by fellow officers. He too was a prison guard, a sub-warder – or rather, had been until the evening before, when he had been searched by the City police and evidence had been found upon him. Now, as he walked in, he looked as though all signs of life had left him. Tall, with pinched eyes and dark, lank hair, Norton looked fairly down at heel.

Alderman Lusk, the only City Father available to take charge of the session, eyed him suspiciously. Though warders earned very little, this fellow seemed to have taken penury to heart. He looked like a tramp. Norton's discomfort was compounded by the fact he had spent the night before guarded by the men he normally drank with. They, too, looked disturbed as he now stood in the simple, wooden dock.

The clerk to the court read out the charges. Because they were so potentially explosive, details were sparse. The defendant was charged with attempting to convey three letters from one of the prisoners in his charge. 'It is contrary to the prison regulations to take any letters out unless they go through the hands of the governor and written on prison paper,' was the only explanation. The nature of this particular communication was only ever referred to obliquely.

Norton simply said 'Yes' to every question, pleaded guilty and within three minutes was being escorted back to his own holding cells. That was more than enough to hold him on remand in Newgate from which, ironically, the authorities had learned that the four American forgers would have been sprung that same Friday evening. There had been talk of making a run for it from the Old Bailey as they left for their own cells in Newgate at the close of the proceedings. A more realistic alternative was to make the attempt in the early evening once back at the prison. Both were, in essence, pipe-dreams. Desperate men will do desperate things.

Nobody was taking any chances. When the letter had been found about Norton's person the night before, the commissioner of the Metropolitan Police was so worried that he requested of Judge Archibald that the public be excluded from the Central Criminal Court. It was rejected. As a precaution, the Old Bailey and the prison at Newgate itself was flooded with extra police. There were more draconian lockdowns for prisoners, as well as greater numbers of patrols outside the prison walls itself, care-fully making their way along the warren of streets surrounding the jail.

As always, rumours soon spread, and the next day's *Times*, for example, reported that 'there was reason to believe attempts were being made to corrupt some of the warders of Newgate'. It had been Norton's misfortune to have been searched and held for remand along with the questioning of a pair of other prison warders who worked the same shifts. The newspapers learned they had 'received £100 each from friends of the prisoners'.

Very little was ever said publicly about the letter that Norton had been ferrying. Addressed to George Bidwell, it had been shown to various officials at the Guildhall and at Newgate who could hardly believe their eyes.

The whole extraordinary business had stemmed directly from the 'sob story' that the Bidwells had laid upon Sir Sydney Waterlow. Allowed to share a holding cell together, not only could the brothers hatch plans together, they had bribed Norton to bring in meals and exchange letters with Mac and Noyes Hills. The guards had been smuggling letters out to various 'associates', who were co-ordinating the plans to spring them. According to the letter, others were implicated, too.

The master key for all the cells was kept in the governor's office; he would have to give his official approval to let any prisoner out. As he had brought the police in to investigate when rumours circulated that something was afoot, his involvement seemed unlikely. What astounded the detectives who had found the letter was that the deputy governor was implicated.

At eight o'clock, one of the warders would say there was a change of clothes waiting for one of the prisoners. He would then be allowed the chance to change in the main prison office. As it faced down onto the street, they could open the window and the prisoner could jump down. Austin Bidwell and the others would quickly follow suit, either following through the window or else escaping when they were being escorted to another prison for safety. It all seemed hopelessly vague, yet the most interesting part of this unusual correspondence was the identity of the accomplice on the outside who would help spirit them away in a carriage to a waiting ship at Tilbury Docks – Honest John, or 'Brother Johnnie' as he had signed himself.

Friday, 22 August 1873
Central Criminal Court, Old Bailey
12.10 p.m.

Nellie Vernon was tiring, nearing the end of her testimony, wearily recalling the minutiae of her and George's travelling around the south coast on Wednesday, 5 March. They had visited Battle, St Leonards, and Ashford, and then in Dover she had pointedly had to wait outside in a carriage while George Bidwell stopped at a bank. Inside he exchanged a large sum of gold for a cheque for £300. The cashier at that branch of the London & County Bank, Richard Ely, remembered him. He signed 'James Esmart' instead of 'James E. Smart', the alias he had adopted for this transaction.

As he counted the money, Ely found there was an extra sovereign. 'Is it exactly £300 you want to pay in?' he asked.

'It might be one more or less,' the American added. George simply pocketed this sovereign. The rest would be used to hire David Howell QC to defend Edwin Noyes Hills, whose incarceration had been reported in the newspapers all week.

After then making their way to Canterbury that wet and windy Wednesday, George Bidwell suddenly announced that he had business to attend to in London. Not for the first time, Nellie Vernon was left in the lurch. 'Where Bidwell passed the night we do not know,' the prosecution brief for this part of the trial notes. 'Before leaving her he gave her a £20 note, but it is quite clear that she with great difficulty found her way back again on that evening to St Leonards.'

As she now explained on the stand, Nellie Vernon had been ordered by her boyfriend to retrieve two smaller bags from the station at St Leonards and come up to London the next morning. After examining her luggage claim ticket which had been entered into evidence, Mr Giffard prompted her.

'Now the next day, that would be Thursday, the 6th[21], did you come up to London?'
'Yes.'
'Had you sent a telegram to George Bidwell?'
'Yes.'
'And did he meet you on the platform at Charing Cross when you got to town?'
'Yes.'
'Did you notice any difference in his appearance when he met you?'

'His moustache was cut.' Later, Mr Giffard would make more about how much his appearance had changed as a result.

Now, Nellie could not help smiling. 'Yes,' she answered, 'a very great deal.'

'What became of you two then?'

'We got into a cab and drove a short distance towards Fenton's Hotel.' This was a luxurious establishment at No. 63 St James' Street, close by both where Mac had been living and the Albemarle where they had been staying until the start of the weekend.

Thursday, 6 March 1873
Charing Cross Station, Central London
Lunchtime

What neither Mr nor Mrs Bidwell knew at this stage was that the police had followed them from Charing Cross. Within hours of the fraud's discovery, both Scotland Yard and the City police had flooded the capital with their finest. Information had been pouring in to the latter's headquarters in Old Jewry and completely overwhelmed them. The City police was only a small force numbering fewer than 800 officers, and if there was one thing it would never do, that was to share information beyond the square mile. There was a great deal of antipathy between the City police and Scotland Yard, a cause of much speculation at the time. The police in London that spring of 1873 had already come in for a great deal of criticism for its handling of a number of prominent cases. These included a double murder in Hoxton the summer before and the release of an innocent German clergyman, falsely arrested for the murder of a woman in Coram Street on Christmas Day.

The apprehension of the thieves of Threadneedle Street was hardly any better. Leads were not shared, information was lost and witnesses were ignored, and despite the monitoring of all rail terminals in London, when Nellie and George Bidwell headed by cab to Fenton's Hotel, there was one salient detail which the police did not make public at the time – they did not know who he was.

To date, the only person the police could really connect to the forgery was Austin Bidwell in his guises of Frederick Albert Warren and Charles Johnson Horton. At this point in time, there was little concrete evidence to tie his elder brother to the crimes nor, as the prosecution noted, was there any 'evidence then in our power on which to arrest him'. At best, they could have held him 'under suspicion' – of what, though? The evidence against him was all too vague and circumstantial.

One officer, William Smith, of the City police, had been running around everywhere. Somewhat crestfallen, he later testified that on the Thursday, 6 March, he saw someone standing near the ticket office at Charing Cross Station. Waiting with witnesses who had dealt with Warren and Horton, they did not recognise him. Nor did he look like the description issued to all police of a heavily moustachioed dandy. A glamorous woman joined him, but they were not sure who she was, either, and so were, as the prosecution later commented mildly, 'baffled in their expectation of arresting' them both.

It got worse. Some distance away (it was only roughly ½ mile to Fenton's), George Bidwell slipped out of the cab, leaving Nellie to continue on to the hotel with their luggage alone. 'They did not see George Bidwell make his escape,' Freshfields added. When Nellie had arrived at Fenton's, she took some rooms in the name of Mr and Mrs Bidwell before leaving again in a hurry. 'I took Mr Bidwell's dressing bag and went to 11 Duke's Road,' was all she next said on the stand.

It is a measure of the police incompetence that they now missed her leaving Fenton's Hotel. They believed that a couple – whom they were certain were actually Austin and Jeannie Bidwell – had taken up residence for the evening. By this stage, Nellie Vernon was only too well aware that there was a large sum of sovereigns in their luggage. In a panic, she had gone off into the rainy evening in the hope of finding one of the few men in London who would be able to help her.

Friday, 22 August 1873
Newgate Prison, City of London
12.20 p.m.

As Owen Norton was returned to his own cell, the authorities at Newgate realised that they had been very lucky. It had not been clear exactly when the attempt would be made to spring the prisoners. At the prison, the guards came on at 6 p.m. and finished their shifts just after dawn in the summer months. But given the fact that Norton and the other two warders who had also been questioned would be on duty that same Friday evening for the first time in a fortnight, it seemed likely the springing was imminent.

Willie Pinkerton later determined that, in addition to John Bidwell, one of Mac's cousins, who lived in Brooklyn, called Pemberton (in some accounts, strangely, Pinkerton) and someone named 'Major' had been roped in to help. All three had come over to England especially for the trial. As Pink later told a San Francisco newspaper when he returned home a few weeks later, the warders 'were liberally bribed'. Norton and his colleagues would have received the bulk of the money once the forgers stepped outside the prison.

It seems they had already received a down payment. One warder, called Smith, had mentioned to a detective he knew that he was shortly moving to Tasmania. The other, Leach, had been carrying £50 in gold coins when he was interviewed. His claim that it came from his brother in Brighton did not fool anyone. All three warders had been seen drinking with the American friends of the prisoners and, as *The Times* later reported, 'from that time their movements were closely watched'.

Unlike the shambles in the spring when they repeatedly lost Nellie and George Bidwell, the warders were successfully shadowed now by the police. As they discussed the figure of £1,000 travelling on a bus, an undercover policeman was sitting behind them and listening in. The same shadowing led directly to John Bidwell who was also seen entering one of the warder's houses and was followed back to the suburbs.

Perhaps the most amazing detail came from the least boastful of the forgers. 'A plan was thought out of escape from the Old Bailey,' Edwin Noyes Hills recalled many years later. 'A hundred sovereigns, intended as a bribe, were upset from a bag in their haste and scattered all over the roadway.'

Friday, 22 August 22 1873
Central Criminal Court, Old Bailey
12.20 p.m.

It was in a state of suppressed hysteria that Nellie Vernon had made her way to No. 11 Duke's Road carrying George Bidwell's dressing bag which contained a small fortune in sovereigns. There, in a state of some consternation, she talked to her old landlord, Jules Meunier, when a cabman unexpectedly delivered a telegram from George Bidwell. 'In consequence of that,' Hardinge Giffard continued, 'did you go and meet George Bidwell anywhere?'

'Yes, at Marble Arch at 6 p.m.'

'Did you take the cab and the money and did you and Jules Meunier go together to the Marble Arch?'

'We went together part of the way.'

Judge Archibald seemed confused. He raised his hand after looking through his own notes. 'You say you took "a cab and the money",' he said directly to the witness. He turned to Mr Giffard. 'She said nothing about the money before.'

'I thought she did,' Giffard replied. 'She took the bag with the money in it.'

After clarifying that there were two bags, a dressing one and the other with the money in it, Nellie revealed that George Bidwell had told her in the telegram to change cabs. So she had left Jules Meunier en route and picked her boyfriend up at Marble Arch. The pair had then detoured along Bayswater Road, before doubling back towards Euston once more. Before arriving, George suddenly asked her, 'Will you go to the Victoria and Euston hotels and see if there are any telegrams for me?'

Reluctantly, she left George Bidwell in the cab to continue the short distance to Drummond's Hotel. Despite its name, Drummond's was actually a public house, known as something of a den of iniquity in police circles. 'That is close to Euston Square, I believe,' Mr Giffard said for the benefit of the jury.

'Yes.'

'Did you find him there?' he asked Nellie.

'Yes.'

'What passed between you then?'

The judge seemed puzzled, interrupting again. 'Did she get any telegrams?'

Mr Giffard addressed the witness directly. 'Did you get any telegrams?'

'I got one, but it was one that I had sent him myself.'

There was a ripple of laughter around the court. Mr Giffard ignored it. 'One that you had sent yourself from St Leonards?'

'Yes.'

Thursday, 6 March 1873
Central London

For someone on the run, George Bidwell had behaved with remarkable calm that gloomy, cloudy Thursday evening. At some point before Nellie had arrived from the south coast, he had visited Benjamin Nathan, the jeweller from whom he had bought the 'old family' bracelet the previous August. Today, Mr Nathan sold him four diamond lockets, two pearl pins, one turquoise and parrot pin ('in the shape of a parrot'), a small gold keyless watch and one fine gold Brazilian necklace. The total came to £114, and 'he seemed a little excited', in Mr Nathan's recollection.

What George Bidwell had actually been doing was to exchange all his money into diamonds, which would be so much harder to trace. As the prosecution later marvelled, all of the prisoners 'had their clothes specially adapted to the concealment of valuables by having short pockets made inside their waistcoats'.

That same Thursday evening, James Noyes ('I am no relation to the prisoner Hills,' he swore under oath) also received a note from a cabman to go to Drummond's Hotel. Surprised, he was reasonably well acquainted with both 'Mr and Mrs Bidwell' after having had several dealings with them. A few weeks earlier, George had ordered two bags from him which were later presented in court. On one of them, Mr Noyes had the initials 'H.E.V.' engraved. It was this particular bag which was now the subject of his telegram.

Mr Noyes did not want to dispatch it as it had not been paid for. When he arrived at Drummond's just after 8 p.m., Mr Bidwell paid him in person. Without his moustache, Mr Noyes did not recognise him at first. The fact he was wearing workmen's clothes and seemed so jumpy made him realise that something was definitely awry. George Bidwell's behaviour was so strange that James Noyes then immediately went to the police after he left the hotel. By now, though, the fugitive had other plans. As Nellie Vernon now found to her cost.

Thursday, 6 March 1873
Euston Station, Central London
8.50 p.m.

Where the devil was he? The station forecourt was chaotic and so were her emotions. Nellie Vernon looked through the crowds to see if she could make him out.

As the throng of passengers and porters moved through the steam and smoke, she could not make out anything at all. What had become clear from their rushed – and, at times, inexplicable – cab journeys was that her boyfriend was obviously in some sort of serious trouble.

Earlier she had asked him outright, 'Darling, what is the matter?' At first George had said nothing, then confessed, 'Some friend of mine had been doing something and he did not wish his name to be mentioned.' (When she later mentioned this on the stand, the judge looked amazed. 'His own name?' he asked.)

So now, still unsure of what has really happening, Nellie and Mr Meunier had come here to the station as her boyfriend had ordered her to do. George Bidwell had promised to wait for her, that he would never abandon her and that they both would, no matter what the trouble was, travel to America where they would live together happily ever after.

It was already dark when she and Mr Meunier passed under the three large archways at the main entrance of the original Euston Station. Lamps were being lit all over the concourse. They made their way towards the platform where everyone was crowding around the Irish mail train.

It was nearly time for departure. Her boyfriend was nowhere to be seen. And then, peering desperately in the distance, she saw something which made her heart skip a beat. Policemen, grim-faced and determined, marching towards them. 'Oh God', she thought, turning to her former landlord, who could tell that they were in deep, deep trouble.

It was only by accident that the police had picked up the trail of Nellie Vernon. At six o'clock this same Thursday evening, there had been a conference at the Bank of England Western Branch between various officials. For reasons that were never explained, it was suspected that Austin Bidwell and his wife were holed up at Fenton's. But then, suddenly and unexpectedly, Nellie Vernon had appeared once more, bidden by George Bidwell to retrieve any telegrams.

The City police again gave pursuit. PC John Spittle – who had arrested Edwin Noyes Hills in the foyer of the Continental Bank – observed her heading to her old lodgings. A few minutes later, she emerged with Jules Meunier, who was carrying a leather bag that obviously contained something heavy. 'Did you take them both into custody?' Harry Poland later asked him on the stand.

'I did upon the charge of the unlawful possession of the bag.' It contained what one newspaper later called a 'rascal's sword', though PC Spittle's words were less dramatic: '£2,717 10s in English gold'. That was enough to hold landlord and tenant for questioning, although it was very difficult to prove that these sovereigns were proceeds from the forgery.

'At any rate she does not claim the money,' Freshfields had written at the time, 'she says that it belongs to George Bidwell and that she wishes he had been apprehended.'

Accordingly, Nellie Vernon was promptly released after giving as much information as she knew, and, as she later testified, 'I have been living with some friends'.

Behind the scenes, the prosecution were not sure that she had told the police everything. The correspondence with her boyfriend was clearly evidence of that. The prosecution noted:

> The only difficulty is the mode in which the girl Ellen Vernon is to be treated, because it is quite clear that it will not do to let her go back to her former life [referring to her prostitution] until she has given her evidence and the bank must be very careful how they make any arrangement with her.[22]

Despite the fact that he had cleverly used Nellie Vernon to retrieve the money, George Bidwell's feelings for her were genuine. While subsequently on the run, he had corresponded with George Macdonnell via a lawyer's office in Manhattan and he was still touchingly concerned about her fate. Nine days after he had disappeared into the night, he wrote:

> It may be best to send someone over to get Nellie out of the way. Let someone go and tell her I have sent for her to come over to New York. She will come at once. My baggage seems to be all gone up. They can get track of her at 11 Duke's Road, Euston Road, St Pancras Church.

And three days later, aware from newspaper reports that she had been apprehended, George Bidwell realised he could make a more precipitate choice. He wrote to Mac:

> I shall try to get hold of Nellie, although I may incur some risk by doing so. Of course, I should not have got Nel and myself into this dam stew but for my anxiety to get over here to attend to matters and who would have dreamed they would take hold of her. It is all right as long as I keep inland but the moment I touch the border there is the devil to pay.

Friday, 22 August 1873
Central Criminal Court, Old Bailey
12.40 p.m.

With her arrest on Euston Station, Nellie Vernon's direct experience of the crimes and various misdemeanours of the thieves of Threadneedle Street had come to an inglorious end. With her questioning and cross-examination now complete, the court adjourned for lunch. The legal officers and the clerks dutifully filed out after

His Lordship, but for now, the prisoners were taken out to the holding cells. Each prisoner was given his own phalanx of police protection, forming a triangle around him. First, Austin Bidwell was escorted out and then, when he had passed through the doorway, his elder brother. Mac and Noyes Hills were lead out in this similar fashion. A few even noticed that all the doors surrounding the court, including those fanning out along the internal passageways, remained firmly shut.

The next day's *Times of London* also reported on the rumours of the attempted bribing of the warders:

> A good deal of mystery still prevails with regard to the transaction, and it was understood that a part of the plan proposed to be carried out was to attempt to rescue the prisoners from the dock while the trial was proceeding.

Its conclusion, however, could be better gauged from George Bidwell's reaction. As he was being led away from the Central Criminal Court, his defence lawyer, David Howell QC, handed him a note. His face fell immediately when he recognised the writing. It was all over. In its entirety, the note read:

> My dear bro.
> Just leaving for Paris, not daring to remain in London.
> John

Honest John had fled. The farmer and his two confederates had realised something was up and escaped as soon as they could. It was never clear what had alerted them and, equally importantly, whether they could have been charged with an offence. In some accounts, it is said that five years' imprisonment would have been their sentence.

Ultimately, if they had got away with it, the fraudsters would have had the last laugh at their helpers. The bribes for the warders would have been padded out to make it appear that they each contained £1,000 in fresh Bank of England notes. The packages would actually have contained, at most, about £100 each. It took the best part of two months to unravel all the threads of this particular riddle, which culminated with an independent inquiry at Newgate about the complicity of the warders.

For Willie Pinkerton, personally, it was an amazing discovery. Never in his wildest dreams had Pink ever suspected that John Bidwell had, for the best part of a week, been sitting literally just 15ft away from him, a sombre and outwardly respectable gent, watching events and imperceptibly weighing up all the options. 'It is understood that the Gaol Committee of the Court of Aldermen will hold a special meeting to investigate the affair,' the *Daily Telegraph* reported a week later, 'and it is very probable that some important alterations in the management of the gaol of

Newgate will result.' Foremost among them was never to let family members share cells, no matter how plausible their pleading.

During the prolonged agony of his incarceration, George had referred to himself as Nellie Vernon's 'poor found (foolish) lover' in one of his letters. Indeed, the subject of foolishness preoccupied them both, for he had also written, 'A wise fool like me suffers more than a foolish fool because the wise fool knows and appreciates his misery'.

Was Nellie Vernon a 'foolish fool', as George Bidwell had termed it, or a femme fatale? Just how innocent really was she? Or was her lack of knowledge a well-rehearsed act? As she made her way out of the Central Criminal Court, most people had already formed an opinion. The Devil had not only been paid, but in some sense had come collecting, for she would pay the ultimate price for their relationship.

The letters, now returned to the guarded evidence room, contained one last secret, a curious fact which nobody ever mentioned, least of all the forgers themselves. George Bidwell had written:

> From my poor heart overflows of devotion and love of God permits me to live to reward you to raise you to a place of honor by my side, for I can do wonders in these years of freedom with you to inspire me and our baby.

By the time of the trial, Nellie Vernon was carrying their child.

The irony was not lost on the father himself. These letters (and a lock of hair which he promised to send) might be the only mementoes of the father's existence. Nellie should, George implored, 'give them to our child for a keepsake of one it may never see'. There was never any doubt that their reunion could be a very long time in coming. 'Do not let anybody's opinion of the beauties of imprisonment convince you for one moment that we shall ever survive that enormous length of misery,' he wrote. This came the nearest to a summary of all their time together and all the vicissitudes Ethel Helen Vernon had had to endure.

11

Before Your Very Eyes

[The] police, after a fortnight's laborious search, seemed not much better off than they were at first. We come back, after all, to the old story, that a determined criminal who deliberately undertakes the risk can hold his own against the detective force.

Daily Telegraph, 15 March 1873

Saturday, 1 March 1873
Fitzroy Square, Central London
5.30 p.m.

Where the hell was he? He had said he would be home early, but it was already going dark and there was no sign of him. Her boyfriend had always insisted he would be home for dinner. If he was ever going to be late, he would always send a telegram.

Suddenly, there was a knock at the front door. To her surprise, it was his friend, the bearded one, 'Colonel Macdonnell'. Straightaway, she could tell something was wrong. 'I have some very bad news for you,' he said. Her boyfriend, he explained, would not be home for a week or two. 'I will come and let you know when he is coming home.'

If that was supposed to reassure her, it had completely the opposite effect. At this, Ellen was more perplexed than angry. 'It was very funny that he had not come back to bid me good bye,' she said.

The American at the entrance to their rooms smiled, 'He was called away, having to catch a train.' The colonel looked at the large trunks in the corner of the room. Her boyfriend, he now told her, had authorised him to take the boxes away. At this, she was even more bewildered. The weekend before, she had opened one and found it contained hundreds of dollars' worth of US bonds. When he had walked in on her, he had angrily ordered her from the room. Now, she stood her ground.

'You can take away one of these boxes,' she said, pointing to the larger one that had been packed in the previous week, 'but I cannot allow you to take that.' She pointed to the other one she had opened. In any case, her boyfriend had the key. Colonel Macdonnell seemed to accept this. As he lifted the first bag and prepared to leave, he was 'in a state of nervous excitement', as the prosecution later determined.

As always, he was in a great hurry, but when reached the front door, he stopped dead in his tracks. A stranger was walking up the steps from the direction of Charlotte Street. 'Who was that?' Colonel Macdonnell asked her landlord, who had materialised by his side. When Jesse White told him it was another potential lodger, Mac seemed relieved. As they went in again, Ellen came out and he spoke to her, pointing to the other trunk. 'I will come again and fetch that one or send for it Monday.'

Taking care to hand her a £20 note, he then drove away in a waiting cab. As promised, Colonel Macdonnell did return early the following week, removing the locked trunk in a four-wheeled cab before he too disappeared for good in front of her very eyes.

This was not Ellen Vernon, but rather, another Ellen whose surname of Franklin had also been appropriated by her boyfriend at her insistence (to make their living together seem more respectable). His real name, which she never knew, was Edwin Noyes Hills, who at the time of this strange encounter had been in the holding cells at the Mansion House for most of that Saturday afternoon.

In the last few days, though, Ellen Franklin had formed the idea that something was not quite right. 'Ned', as she called him, had seemed anxious. Their landlord, Mr White, had been with her when she had opened the trunk to find the bonds all rolled up together. Later, her boyfriend had wrapped the bonds in paper by use of two 'little seals', later produced in court, which had not been enough to fasten them. Mr White had provided some crystal cement, professing himself amazed at their thickness. 'There were more bonds of five hundred dollars each than those for a hundred dollars,' he marvelled, at the Mansion House, 'and there was a very thick roll of them.'

That was not the only oddity. On another occasion Ellen Franklin saw a printed cheque book which she had found in Hills' overcoat pocket. When he later found out, he was furious. 'You have no business to go to my pocket,' he shouted at her. Not only did she have no idea where they came from she had also noticed that there was a pocket book in the name of Noyes and a couple of letters addressed to 'Noyes' and 'Horton'. She had no idea who these characters were because as far as she was concerned, his name was Edward Hall of Newark, New Jersey.

He was clearly well-to-do even though he was something of a cheapskate. In fact, all the forgers were. Mr Franklin claimed he was earning £150 a year, with his board and lodgings amounting to just five guineas a week. Though he had showered her with many presents ('One was a sealskin jacket he had made me a present of,' Nellie recalled), the prosecution also marvelled 'that they were never (excepting so far as their own amusements were concerned) lavish of their money. They were prepared to spend anything on themselves but not to give money away.'

When she later thought about it, Ellen Franklin knew very little else about him. 'I do not know anything about his business,' she would shortly testify at the Mansion House. 'He never told me when he went out that he was going to business.' When asked about Horton, the person for whom he supposedly worked, Ellen Franklin was even more puzzled. 'I did not know the prisoner had any master,' she said on the stand. 'He never told me who his master was, or that he had one.'

It is fairly obvious that Edwin Noyes Hills had paid for her company the first night they met. He had originally picked Ellen Franklin up on the freezing, snowy evening of Saturday, 1 February. When she later testified at the Old Bailey, most onlookers jumped to the obvious conclusion. If Ellen Franklin was not possessed of loose morals, she had certainly prostituted herself in the company of Edwin Noyes Hills.

She was, however, hardly as brazen as the other Ellen who had testified immediately before her. This Ellen's naivety was equally astonishing. She genuinely thought they had a future together, and within days of meeting, they had taken lodgings together in the dining room floor of No. 7 Charlotte Street, Fitzroy Square. The landlords, 'most respectable people' in the prosecution's estimation, were the Whites, Sarah, a dressmaker, and her husband, Jesse, who worked as a commission agent. Mrs White later testified, like the waiter at Ford's Hotel, that Miss Franklin's gentleman friend was unusual for an American as he arrived without any luggage.

'Did he bring a large portmanteau with him?' she was asked.

'No I think he brought a pair of boots for Miss Franklin and a galvanic battery.' At this the court roared with laughter. Quite what had ailed her to receive electric shocks was never revealed. There had also been unintentional laughter in court when Ellen Franklin had been asked exactly what his business was in England. 'He told me he was inventing a way for milking cows,' she had said.[23]

By now, unfortunately, Ellen Franklin realised that the ultimate laugh had been on her. The only real milking had been that of her better nature, though to be fair, Hills had been reliable, attentive to her needs and 'was perfectly regular in his habits'. Nellie got used to him going out to the city, or out into the country.[24] 'He used to get up early in the morning, breakfast early, go out to business and come into dinner at about six.' Apart from that first day of March, he always came back the same day, rarely missing dinner and seldom went out at night. As the prosecution marvelled, 'were it not for the other particulars of the case, it might be said that he was having a respectable life in these lodgings'.

In retrospect, February 1873 – a cold, windy and overcast month – should have been the last of the lotus days, but as the prosecution noted, 'there is no doubt from the account given by the women that about the 25th of February the prisoners all became nervous and excitable and ill at ease'. For someone who always claimed he never knew what was happening, Noyes Hills was the most agitated of all. 'Towards the last of the month,' Ellen Franklin later recalled, 'he was very uneasy.'

She remained blissfully unaware of why. During their month together, George Macdonnell had been a regular visitor. He came perhaps half a dozen times and was always referred to as 'colonel', even though they were familiar, and called her boyfriend 'Ed'. But there was a great deal more mystery about another close friend of his. Ellen Franklin knew him only as 'Mr Bradley' of Belgravia, although he never gave too much away. Whenever Hills mentioned 'George', he always meant Mr Bradley, with whom he had some sort of business arrangement.

There was an even greater mystery about Mr Bradley's other half. One day Ned and Nellie Franklin happened to be standing outside Baker & Crisp's on Regent Street, the high-end haberdashery where the other Nellie had, as noted earlier, bought a travelling bag for her boyfriend after they had moved to Upper Gloucester Place. Hills had pointed out Mrs Bradley inside where she was buying a black silk dress. Pointedly, he did not introduce her but, as the prosecution determined, Nellie Franklin 'turned round and went into the shop to look at her'. When Edwin Hills later told 'Mr Bradley' about this, he laughed at his mistress's incorrigibility. When he teased her about spending his money, however, Nellie Vernon became very angry. 'You keep spies to watch me,' she exclaimed. She was even angrier when George Bidwell would not tell who had seen her inside the store.

In his later telling of what happened after everything fell apart that first Saturday of March, George Bidwell remained convinced that 'if all my precautions had been lined up, no harm beyond temporary inconvenience would come to Noyes'.

Ellen Franklin's ignorance and innocence was one thing, but her landlord was more perspicacious. Jesse White was struck by the rapid exit and general shiftiness of her visitor that Saturday evening. 'The circumstances, however, were so peculiar,' the prosecution noted, that Mr White 'particularly examined' George Macdonnell as he left. The landlord had the presence of mind to record the number of the cab and immediately informed the police, whose officers showed up a few hours later. There was little that Ellen Franklin could tell them. As far as she knew, 'Mr Franklin' had simply vanished off the face of the earth. 'He did not return on the first of March,' she said, a fortnight later at her first deposition, 'and I did not see him until he was in custody.'

If Ellen Franklin had been baffled about some of her boyfriend's behaviour, the antics of 'Colonel' Macdonnell, as he styled himself, had created greater puzzlement for the manager of the private hotel in St James Place where he had spent most of February. The American had strange habits and even stranger visitors.

The colonel had only been there a day or two before he insisted to Franz Herold that the servants should always knock loudly and only enter when he said come in. A few days later, the colonel said he was frozen. 'I would like to have the fire as large as they could be made,' Mac declared, pointing towards the grate. He explained that he came 'from a very hot country' in South America. 'The only thing he said about the fire was that it was not large enough,' Herold recalled. 'He would like to have a larger fire.' They were regularly kept up even when it was not particularly cold.

Then there was the day he brought in a box, more than a foot long, which he wanted to send to India. It was some 'sort of little machine' about which Mr Herold had no idea what it really was. On his own initiative, the manager had a box maker make one up that fitted perfectly when it was wrapped inside a cloak that Mac also gave him. But when Mr Herold fastened it up for him, the colonel just smiled. 'I don't think I'll send it today,' he said dismissively. 'It does not matter.' Once again, it stuck him as very peculiar behaviour.

By this point, George Bidwell was regularly visiting, usually around eight o'clock in the morning, occasionally bringing Nellie Vernon with him. The blinds were always drawn, no matter if day or night, and the colonel seemed to spend an inordinate amount of time in a large morning coat, writing. When Herold went in to deliver things, he noticed the two Georges were usually together in the bedroom or the sitting room and always looked busy. Doing what, the manager was never quite sure.

Because of the darkness, they burned so much gas that the light's glass cracked and the ceiling was blackened. There were always lots of papers lying around and, as always with Americans, a great deal of luggage. Fairly quickly, Mr Herold was convinced that they were 'makers of money', which prompted an interesting exchange on the sixth day of the trial. Mr Watkin Williams was trying to ascertain the general appearance of their rooms.

'I used to notice generally papers on the table where he used to write,' the manager said.

'Did you notice what kind of papers they were? What did they look like?'

'Like bills of exchange.' There was a murmur around the court.

Mr Watkin Williams smiled. 'Many?' he simply prompted.

'Yes,' the waiter agreed, 'many.' As Mr Herold later confirmed, the whole of their behaviour was very extraordinary.

As a rebuttal, all the defence really could do was to try to besmirch his good name. When Austin Metcalfe QC came to cross-examine him, he tried to portray him as the worst kind of nosy parker. 'I mean you seem always to have been in the room,' Metcalfe said with deceptive charm, 'always in the bedroom?'

The waiter was outraged. 'I beg your pardon?'

'You seem always to have been in the room and in his bedroom.'

Mr Herold recovered momentarily. 'Yes, when I had occasion to.'

At this point, the judge decided to intervene. 'Did you ever go in without being rang for?' Justice Archibald asked.

'Yes,' Franz Herold said, looking respectfully at His Lordship.

Mr Metcalfe continued his undermining of the witness. 'He admitted you into the bedroom while he was writing and all these papers about him?'

'Yes.'

'That was in the day time as well as the evening, apparently?' he asked. Several onlookers were amused at the inference.

'Yes.'

'You must have been continually there.' It was another electric moment in court.

'I could not say that,' Herold said sticking to his guns. 'I could not say I was always there.'

Monday, 3 March 1873
17 St James Place, Piccadilly
1 p.m.

Colonel Macdonnell was always in a hurry. Franz Herold had watched him rush in earlier that morning around 11 a.m. looking more than a little flustered. 'I think I am going to leave today,' he told the manager. The colonel had then been in and out of his rooms for the rest of the time. It seemed he was preoccupied with packing and looking at the weather outside. Conditions were appalling, a constant sheet of heavy rain. So much so that, once more, he changed his mind. The weather was simply too bad for travelling. 'Yes, I will stay,' he later said in Franz Herold's hearing, 'I won't go.'

Both the manager and proprietor, Agnes Green, were used to his comings and goings. It was just after one o'clock when Mac was still dithering that, all of a sudden 'and without warning', the prosecution noted, two cabs came down the street together and pulled up outside. The colonel had not asked the hotel staff to call them nor did he seek their assistance now. Mac went out into the rain with his luggage and told the drivers where to go out of earshot. Weighing it all over in his mind, the manager was certain the American was up to something.

'Very likely a friend of mine will call,' Mac had told Herold at some point earlier that morning. If he did, the manager should give him the *Continental Guide to the City of London* and a dispatch box which were left in his rooms. The colonel had also informed Mr Herold that he was likely going to Paris and that his bed should be kept. He left no forwarding address. Oddly, he had said that he would be back by the evening. 'You are a very quick traveller,' the manager had observed, certain that there was much more to this than met the eye.

There was, in truth, a certain method in his apparent March hare madness. George Macdonnell needed to remain in residence in St James for as long as possible. Reports of Americans suddenly leaving swanky apartments and hotels would be of interest to the police. If they were not careful, they would be followed and traced, so as George Bidwell would later remark, 'all we had to do was to lie quietly in London'.

As the prosecution noted, there was still much to be done 'because all the stock in trade – that is to say all the wooden dies and stamps, the spare bill papers, ink and all the paraphernalia of forging had to be got rid of'.

That Same Monday
6 p.m.

It was already going dark by the time Agnes Green, as was her habit, finally got to read the newspaper. Normally she did that over lunch, but it was early evening by the time she had picked up that morning's *Daily Telegraph*.

There, on the front page, was a headline that caught her eye – 'Extensive Forgeries In The City'. She was intrigued as she came across one particular paragraph, 'The fraud was said to be the work of a ring of smart Yankee swindlers,' followed by warnings about some bonds and then a description of the mysterious Warren or Horton, 'a man of about forty, about 5" 10', dark and sallow who speaks with a strong American accent'. There was, the paper added, no reason to suspect that he had been in the city to conduct the fraud on the Saturday.

She looked across at Mr Herold. A few days earlier, her manager had said in passing that their visitor's whole conduct had been 'very extraordinary'. And now, she was inclined to agree that Colonel Macdonnell might well have been involved in this astounding deception. The description did not sound like him, and there was one obvious way of confirming if their suspicions were true. When they entered the colonel's bedroom, Agnes Green found several newspapers, some foreign, but most importantly, some blotting papers strewn haphazardly on the bed. Nearby, on the floor was 'a sheet of note paper covered with strange impressions of the names of different banks'.

The blotter and these pieces of paper were a direct link to Mac's involvement in the crime. 'The nearest proofs to the actual signing are four pieces of blotting paper,' the prosecution would later establish. The first two read as follows:

No. . . . .
Accepted payable at
No. . . . .
Accepted payable at

Accepted payable at the
No. . . . London . . 1872
No. . . . London . . 1872
Accepted payable at the

Accepted for us for the
Accepted for us for the
London & Westminster

Bank & Loan Co.
Manager

Sub Country man
Secret
Sub manager

Care of
The Bank of Belgium and Holland Limited
No. . . . . London . . . 1872
Accepted payable at the
London & Westminster
Bank & Loan Co.
Care of
The Bank of Belgium and Holland Limited.

It had only been a fortuitous accident that all these papers were still lying around. Mr Herold would normally have tidied up the mess they left behind. Today, he simply had not had time to burn them after collecting their detritus together on the bed. The forgers had been careless, an act of omission that was, as George Bidwell later termed it, 'a fatal concession'.

As a result, Agnes Green sent for the City police straight away. Within a couple of hours the harassed Sergeant William Smith arrived. In addition to the blotters, when they came to examine the *City Directory* they found several underlinings and removals that were significant. Part of one page had been cut out. A list of engravers – Straker, Cheshire and Challoner – had also been removed.

And something else, too, which later caused amazement in court. 'If Your Lordship looks at page one of the *Directory*, you will find "Bank of England", Harry Poland said to Judge Archibald when he came to examine a copy. In the original, the names of all the officers, 'including governor, deputy governor and directors', were listed 'and you will find some initials in pencil against those names'.

Agnes Green's calling of the police was just one strand in the ensuing chase of the thieves of Threadneedle Street. Many claimed responsibility for their apprehension, not least with the offer of a substantial reward of up to £1,500 for information.

In one version of what happened next, it came down to Austin Bidwell's movements in Europe being picked up by routine police work. In another, it was because he had been overhead saying that if he ever had enough money he would venture to the tropics. It was also later claimed that one or more of their girlfriends had squealed.

In fact, the greatest breakthrough came from a vengeful source who had been the very first person to denounce them as scoundrels, thieves and liars. The lapidary words of the prosecution brief spell out how 'in the meantime, another adversary whom the forgers had least of all suspected had sprung up,' Freshfields recorded for the files. 'That is to say the mother-in-law of Austin Bidwell.'

Somewhere in the mêlée of his rushing around, Mac had bumped into Austin Bidwell's nemesis. It was, by any stretch of the imagination, an extraordinary coincidence. To say the least, Mrs Devereux was anxious to find out more about where her daughter and that ne'er-do-well of a husband had disappeared to. 'She would not believe that Austin Bidwell had taken her daughter straight from Paris to Madrid,' the prosecution noted. 'She believed that they were still in town and to be found.'

When advertisements subsequently appeared in the press which described Warren, George Bidwell and Macdonnell by name, everything came together in her mind. The fact that the main suspect was believed to 'be accompanied by a young woman eighteen to twenty years of age, looks younger with golden hair', was more than enough to prompt her into action. Mrs Devereux went to a solicitors who swiftly took her to Freshfields, where she told them everything about her 'missing' daughter and son-in-law.

'She was accordingly prepared to give any amount of information,' the prosecutors noted. 'She gave tolerably accurate information of all the prisoners and thus assisted materially.' The mistakes, the police could make for themselves.

Though nothing was ever said about it in the Central Criminal Court, there was a widespread feeling that the City police had made a mess of the investigation. 'Inspector Bailey, the head of the police at the Old Jewry was evidently overworked and overpowered with the magnitude and complexity of the case,' the prosecution noted. 'He did not see the bearing of this piece of blotting paper.'

Amazing as it may seem to posterity, after his return from St James, Sergeant Smith kept the blotter in his desk. For three weeks. Only when Freshfields' own investigators went to No. 17 St James Place at the end of March did they learn about its existence. They had the desk broken open and, as they noted for the files, 'the pieces of blotting paper showed indubitably that George Bidwell and Macdonnell had used that paper in the process of their forgeries'. Had they known sooner, the two Georges might have been apprehended during the first week of March 'and probably the plunder searched before it went to New York'.

Yet, herein was a paradox which was not lost on Freshfields. 'It is however to be observed that allowing them to be at large secured a much larger amount of evidence than could possibly have been obtained had they been taken into custody immediately on the forgery being discovered.'

Wednesday, 5 March 1873
Cheapside, City of London
11 a.m.

A ripple of raucous laughter echoed around the store. Everyone was amused, including the bearded American, about whose fellow citizens they were laughing. George Macdonnell grinned along with them, probably more amused by their obvious awe at their achievement. Around the city, what were known as 'the great forgeries' were the subject of fevered speculation. 'It's a very clever thing,' was all George Macdonnell said.

It was a measure of Mac's sangfroid that he blithely walked into the City this rainy, overcast Wednesday into what was known as Sir John Bennett's Store. He ordered another chronometer (similar to Austin's wedding gift) – very apt, given that his very own race against the clock was starting.

That same morning, he went to an outfitters and then a shipping agent to buy tickets for the *Cuban*, which would sail across the Atlantic at the weekend. Though George Bidwell was insistent that they had as many liquid assets to hand, Mac wanted to make sure he had as little as possible. The simple reason was that notes could easily be traced.

Around lunchtime he walked in to the Atlantic Express Company on Moorgate with a suitcase that Nellie Vernon had packed and he had retrieved from St Leonards Railway Station the day before. He told the manager, Alfred Rémond, that he wanted to ship it to New York. Mac wrote two notes, a consignment bill that was kept and a customs declaration which went with the package to Manhattan, and signed both in the name of 'Charles Lossing of Tunbridge Wells'. The trunk was addressed to Major George Matthews of New York and the customs form noted that it contained 'wearing apparel actually in use'.

This was, in fact, the same trunk which had subsequently been examined in court during Nellie Vernon's testimony. The jury and the rest of the onlookers had little appreciation of how it had been the subject of an intense police investigation on *both* sides of the Atlantic.

On this Thursday in March, however, George Macdonnell simply told the manager it contained 'personal effects' and should be kept in bond in New York until called for by this fictitious army officer. Mac signed the documents and confidently walked out again. The other trunk that George Macdonnell had hurriedly retrieved from Ellen Franklin's was later found at Charing Cross cloakroom and seems to have been left there on the Saturday the fraud was discovered.

With the chase now gathered, a familiar name reappears in the narrative. 'Warren and Macdonnell appear to have been intimate with some girls of the name of Gray,' Freshfields noted at the start of March. 'Waitresses at a coffee shop in the Haymarket, but this is not, at present of any great importance.'

How wrong they were. When Frances Catherine Gray later testified about her relationship with Austin Bidwell it caused great shock in the Central Criminal Court. Now, immediately after Ellen Franklin's revelations, came even greater outrage. Harry Poland, almost quivering with distaste, prompted Frances Gray about what happened after Austin Bidwell had departed from the scene. 'Afterwards,' he said carefully, 'after Dorey left, did you become Macdonnell's friend?'

'Yes.' Not only had she slept with one of the gang, but Frances Gray then began a relationship with another (and was rumoured to be connected with yet another international criminal whose surname she happened to share).[25]

On Tuesday, 4 March, Mac had returned from the south coast to the sweet embrace of his latest mistress. 'He did not return to his lodgings,' Freshfields recorded, 'but he went to 126 Stanley Street where the girl, Miss Gray – who generally passed by the name of Daisy – lived'.

To be fair, she knew little of his business. One day in February they had gone into the city in a brougham. He had retrieved some coloured papers in an envelope from a building she did not recognise. 'Bonds, I think they were American bonds,' she said on the stand. 'I had never seen any before.' The week before the forgery was discovered, Mac had promised to take her to New York at the start of March, before telling her they would be delayed for another week. On the Saturday that Hills was arrested, he had told her that he was going to Paris for a few days. 'He said he should be back on Thursday,' she recalled, 'but he came back on Tuesday.'

Her lodgings were close enough to Victoria for him to walk from there. At some point, he had gone out to dinner. On his return, he told her that he had overheard some German diners talking 'about a forgery case'.

'It was just what an American would do,' Mac had said, translating their words for his mistress's benefit. 'They will be down on all Americans now.'

Wednesday, 5 March 1873
Stanley Street, Pimlico
Afternoon

The next afternoon, Frances Gray received an unexpected gentleman caller. 'Is Mr Macdonnell in?' he asked. Though obviously American, she had no idea who he was. 'He hasn't kept an appointment with me,' he confessed, clearly agitated. This, it transpired, was at the Grosvenor Hotel, also within walking distance.

'I am expecting him again,' Frances Gray replied. 'He has just gone out.'

Later, she believed her visitor was George Bidwell. When she thought about it afterwards, her own boyfriend had been behaving oddly. That morning, Mac had left early ('Between 7 and 8 o'clock I think,' Frances Gray recalled on the stand), at which point she was still under the assumption that they would be leaving the country that same night from Liverpool.

She was wondering quite what to make of George Bidwell's visit, when she received a telegram from George Macdonnell which informed her that they could not leave until the nine o'clock train this same evening. Pondering what he was playing at, Miss Gray later met him at Gatti's Restaurant, near the London Arcade, to take tea. 'Go to Liverpool and meet me there,' Mac said, appearing preoccupied. He handed her a ticket and she was immediately suspicious.

'Why have you not taken one for yourself?' Frances Gray asked.

'I have,' he replied. 'I have taken it at another office.' He implied he was going to go and get it after they had dined. She and an unnamed friend returned to Pimlico to retrieve all their luggage. When questioned on the stand, there was no doubt as to why. 'For the purpose of going to Liverpool and on to America?' Mr Watkin Williams prompted.

'Yes,' Frances Gray replied, the memory clouding her face. It had been a barefaced lie. By this point, George Macdonnell was certain of one thing that he should have done days before – jettison his woman, for as the prosecution noted, 'Macdonnell had made no arrangements for taking Miss Gray with him to America.'

Towards the end of this first week in March, the peculiar strain of patriotic inevitability that the 'Yankee rascals' would be caught had evaporated. The Bank of England had cautioned the public about negotiating certain specified five-twenty and ten-forty United States bonds, in total amounting to $220,000, which were believed to have been obtained with the proceeds of the forgeries. Even with the inducement of a substantial reward, nobody had come forward.

Because the fraudsters were American, the police suspected the mysterious Warren would seek 'the most expeditious mode of getting back to his own country', as the *Standard* in London put it. That meant they were dispatched to 'various parts of England, Ireland and Scotland where there was reason to believe the fugitive or fugitives might be overtaken'. Seaports such as Glasgow, Southampton and Liverpool were obvious boltholes. As a precaution, one policeman was sent to Queenstown in Ireland, 'whence he returned late last night without obtaining a single clue as to the whereabouts of the suspected forgers'. Without realising it, he had missed one of the forgers, who may well have passed before his very eyes.

Friday, 7 March 1873
Liverpool
Afternoon

Where the hell was he? Now, as Frances Gray and her friend waited in the foyer of the North Western Station Hotel, slowly everything started to make sense. While they had been out on Wednesday taking tea, she had learned that a policeman had called at her lodgings.

George Macdonnell was in serious trouble. He was not going to show. Nor had he ever intended to take her away with him. To Paris, Manhattan or anywhere else in the world.[26] His concern for her had all been some sort of act. All he'd said to her as she stood outside the restaurant in the rain on Wednesday afternoon was that she should take the earliest train from Euston. When later recalling the details on the stand, Frances Gray was certain that it was the mail train. 'I think it was the nine o'clock,' she recalled, 'between eight or nine it started, I do not remember exactly the time.' So, after retrieving their luggage, she and her friend went by cab to Euston Square Station.

As instructed, they had checked into the Liverpool hotel in the early hours of Thursday. 'In the meantime,' Harry Poland later prompted her on the stand, 'Macdonnell had not come there to meet you as he said he would?'

'No.'

'When you found that by the Friday he did not come to you did you and your friend afterwards return to London?'

'Yes.'

'When did you return to London?'

'We arrived in London on Saturday morning at seven o'clock.' She only had her own luggage when she was arrested at Euston Square, where the police took charge of it.

'They examined your luggage?' Poland asked.

'Yes.'

The judge wanted to clarify this. 'Was that on your return?'

'Yes.'

Mr Poland let the moment pass. 'I think the next time you saw Macdonnell was in New York?'

'Yes.'

Under very different circumstances that none of them could ever imagine.

255

⚮

The irony was that George Macdonnell may very well have arrived in Liverpool some time that Friday. In one account, he arrived at Lime Street Station, saw the waiting police and then jumped back on another train that was just about to depart. In another, he slipped off the train at Chester while en route. Either way, he doubled back to Southampton and then crossed the English Channel.

As for the other George, he had made it across the Irish Sea. George Bidwell had managed to elude the police on Euston Station on the Thursday evening. After sending a porter to buy a ticket, George Bidwell waited until the last minute to board the nine o'clock mail train unnoticed. In his own compartment, he finally could relax. After midnight, he took the overnight steamer to Dublin from Holyhead. Driving rain welcomed him on Irish soil at seven o'clock the next morning, after which he then made his way to Cork, where his own troubles were just beginning.

Friday, 7 March 1873
Cork, Ireland
4 p.m.

He spotted them straightaway. George Bidwell had been around enough policemen to know that these two were paying him way too much attention. As he walked from the rail station he was exhausted but was all too aware that 'as I passed into the street, two detectives were watching the passengers, turned and followed me'.

A few yards later one of them caught up with him. 'Have you ever been here before?' one of them asked.

'Yes,' George lied haughtily and then carried on. He made sure that he did not look back and, if his memoirs are to be believed, then walked on for about a quarter of a mile through what seemed to be a business district. To see if he was being followed, he went into a pharmacy to buy some liquorice. As nonchalantly as he could, he looked out. The detectives had seen him but passed on by.

At this point, George claims he had another stroke of luck. He happened upon an enclosure which turned out to be the wharf from which steamers departed to America. Better known today as Cobh,[27] it had been renamed two decades earlier after a visit by Queen Victoria. When George arrived, the Queenstown wharf was crowded with a throng of passengers all waiting to take their place aboard the next available steamer.

Somewhere in the chaos, George Bidwell glanced back and saw the two detectives staring towards him. At this point, he then threw down all his papers before making his way out of the mêlée. He headed back into the town, walked on up a hill and passed by the impressive residences owned by the obviously well-to-do. He hailed a cab which took him back to Queenstown Station where he waited for a train.

It would, he knew, take just a few minutes to head back to Cork from whence he had arrived earlier.

A train soon pulled in. As he entered a carriage, there was a surprise. The two detectives were waiting for him.

∽

Never panic. There is always a better way out. If he drew more attention to himself, George Bidwell would create more problems. Looking out of the window, he sat in silent contemplation, certain, as he later wrote, that nothing 'had been discovered to show my connection with the fraud'. He knew he could still bluff his way out. He'd had enough practice.

When the train returned to Cork, George purposefully walked out onto the concourse of the station and made his way across to the post office. In his memoirs, he claimed that he was expecting a dispatch from Mac, but in reality, he actually sent a package to New York to a G.C. Brownell at Brevoort House, 5th Avenue, New York, which bore 'the Cork post-mark of March, 1873,' as the prosecution later determined. It contained some $17,500 of bonds and was sealed with the same seal as another letter that he later dispatched to New York.

As he came out of the post office, George Bidwell noticed that the two detectives were on the other side of the concourse. Wondering where they had come from, he made his way out into a busy thoroughfare. Once again, they were following him. He accelerated, stopping occasionally, turning three or four times, and eventually, eluded them. Fairly swiftly, he found a temperance hotel where he booked a room for the night in the name of George Burton. In the lounge, he came across a commercial traveller who gave him a rail map of the country, 'which, in my subsequent flight through the country, proved of incalculable service to me'.

Saturday, 8 March 1873
Cork, Ireland

Exhausted, George Bidwell had spent most of the following morning in bed. When he awoke, he knew the simplest way to disappear was to alter his appearance.

As it was a showery day, he went out to buy a Scotch cap (a bonnet) as well as a large bag and what he called a cheap 'Frieze Ulster', the kind of long, loose overcoat worn by any self-respecting Irishman. In other words, he could pretend to be either Irish or Scottish should he need to. Very quickly, he then hired a covered cab to take him back to the temperance hotel.

According to Freshfields, he then made further contact with the North Atlantic Express Company that Saturday by sending the cabbie to the nearest post office. In one account, the cab driver was arrested there; in his own recollection, George

257

watched two detectives follow behind the cab as he returned. He had fortuitously given an address on the other side of the road and left unnoticed. Taking care to now wear his Scotch cap, George took another cab to a canal boat wharf, crossed a bridge and then took yet another cab north.

Two miles outside of Fermoy, they stopped at a tavern, where he got the cabman drunk so he would not be able to return home in daylight. As darkness fell, George Bidwell then made his way to the railway station where he noticed someone watching all travellers who were buying tickets. So instead of heading back towards Dublin, he took the first available train in the opposite direction.

Later that night, he awoke in Lismore Station all alone with the porters putting out the lights. He then made his way to the Lismore Hotel where he was 'utterly dumbfounded, bewildered, paralysed', in his later recollection, wondering how much longer he could elude the forces of law and order.

In London that same Saturday, Edwin Noyes Hills made his second remand at the Mansion House – where Dr Kenealy had insulted the lord mayor – and that evening, the police had issued a description of 'Warren', 'Macdonnell' and George Bidwell, alias Burton, the name he had used most recently in Cork. George was described as aged 40–42, height 5ft 8in; with black hair, sallow, cleanly shaven and described as 'rather strong built man with short neck; supposed to wear brown mixture suit, probably an overcoat and carried a black bag'.

But it was all too little, too late. 'The police ought at once to have telegraphed after him, but they did nothing and George Bidwell escaped to Cork,' the prosecution lamented in their files. Not that the Irish police were any better, despite their geographical proximity. 'We had a good laugh at those blunderheads, the Cork officers letting you slip through their fingers,' George recalls one of the detectives from the City police later telling him.

At best, they were only a few hours behind him but, as Freshfields noted, 'the police followed him next day but he had got a good start'. Early on the Sunday morning, George Bidwell slipped out of the Lismore Hotel, bill unpaid, as dawn was breaking. When they later found out, the Irish police did not know which way he might be headed. Despite a general alert being issued over a radius of 50 miles, once again the suspect disappeared – before their very eyes.

Sunday, 9 March 1873
Cahir, Ireland
Late evening

The knock at the door was urgent. When the householder went to investigate he found a shivering workman, hiding from the rain. When he spoke he was apologetic, but his voice, which had an American accent, was tinged with desperation. 'I am a Fenian leader and the police are after me!' he said. 'I have been dodging them for two days.' At least the latter claim was true.

After escaping from Lismore to Clonmel by cab earlier that Sunday, George Bidwell had then taken another to Cahir where the householder now took him at face value. George Bidwell claimed he was carrying important papers he did not want to fall into the wrong hands. Given shelter, he waited until a mail cab went by which he hailed. He then returned back to Clonmel, where he stopped at a tavern at which the only food available was eggs ('I hesitate to divulge how many [I] disposed of that evening,' George says).

It was pitch black when he went to the rail station to take the 11 p.m. train to Dublin. In a waiting room, a man asked him if he was an American. George Bidwell immediately took him to be a plain clothes policeman. In fact, he seemed more interested in claiming the £500 reward. George said he understood his zeal and hoped he would be successful.

When he arrived at the Maryborough Junction just before one o'clock in the morning, he took a cab to the Cathedral Hotel in Dublin. He was shown up to his room at two o'clock in the morning. Five hours later, George Bidwell was awake and out of the door. Despite the rain, he visited a street market where he bought some rather more spiffy clothes and a valise. Then he went to a better locality where he procured a silk hat 'draped with mourning crape'. He put the Glengarry, as he also termed his traditional Scottish cap, in his pocket. The older clothes and the Ulster cap were placed in the case, and then, as he says in his memoirs, he resolved not to speak another word of English 'and became a Frenchman'.

George Bidwell's elusiveness was amazing. That same Monday, newspapers were reporting 'up to a later hour last night, no further arrest had been made in connexion with the recently discovered forgeries upon the Bank of England'. Though there was a sense that the net was closing in – 'photography and extradition treaties render ultimate escape much more difficult than formerly,' *The Echo* in London had presciently noted – the only problem was that George Bidwell was not the only forger at loose in Ireland.

On that same Monday evening, a well-known counterfeiter by the name of Wolf (in some accounts, Wolfe) had been arrested on the outskirts of Dublin with £500 about his person. 'Inquiries today proved him to have no connection with the frauds on the Bank of England,' the *Standard* in London reported the next day. That Tuesday, 11 March, a gentleman by the name of Flanagan, with two shabbily dressed associates, entered the Provincial Bank of Cork before leaving for America. When arrested, it turned out he was just a rag merchant from Shrewsbury, who also had £500 in his pocket.

The Irish police were faring no better than their British counterparts. They had no idea where to look or, at times, who they might be looking for. But the next day, when George Bidwell left the Cathedral Hotel, he realised he had made a final, fatal mistake. In his rush to leave and assume yet another identity, he had left behind a silk scarf in his room – the monogrammed one that Nellie had bought him as a present the previous Christmas.

Tuesday, 10 March 1873
Dublin Railway Station, Ireland

Later that same day, an impeccably dressed Frenchman was seen buying a ticket to Drogheda. It was a disguised George Bidwell, who had 'not dared to purchase one through to Belfast' even as the train was already pulling in. As he walked out onto the platform, two figures alighted, staring at him. When these two plain clothes cops enquired of the station master who this dandy was, they were told he was French. He could hardly speak a word of English. Once more, George Bidwell managed to escape before their very eyes.

If this does sound like one of his taller tales, there is at least a contemporaneous record to support it. The following Thursday, 13 March, he wrote to George Macdonnell care of the general post office in Manhattan and described what happened after landing in Ireland:[28]

> Your friend has had a series of the most extraordinary adventures since you saw him, a hell's chase, and no mistake. His nerve has stood him through two taps on shoulder, and four encounters. He has been a Fenian, a Priest, a Professor, a Russian, who could speak only '*veree leetle engles, mais un peu de Français et Allemand*', a deaf and dumb man with a slate and pencil – all in the space of a week.

The police clearly never expected the fugitive to head in the opposite direction. Maintaining his disguise, George Bidwell doubled back and headed north towards Belfast, where, in a second class carriage, he was amazed to hear a drunken farmer reading to a friend from a newspaper about the great bank forgery. 'Those Yankees did a mighty thing when they attacked that powerful institution,' the drunken one said. Realising that he fitted the description, George asked the farmer to buy him his ticket as his English was not good enough. The good farmers obliged.

After arriving in Belfast at nine o'clock that night, he took a cab and arrived at the docks in darkness. He took to the Glasgow steamer unobserved and, passing the saloon, noticed the purser. *'Parlez vous français?'* George asked him. A head shake. *'Une billet à Glasgow?'* This was then handed over, his berth noted as he paid the money. Entering the washroom opposite a few moments later, he heard footsteps and then an Irish voice speaking with some alacrity. 'Purser, a cab just brought a man from the Dublin train. Where is he?'

'Oh, you mean the Frenchman? He's in the washroom.'

When the two detectives entered, they encountered a dandified fellow in a silk hat, who was standing preening himself before the mirror, removing some lint or dust from his coat. They left. 'That proved to be the last ordeal through which I passed in the hunt through Ireland,' George Bidwell later recalled. He returned to his berth, promptly fell fast asleep and woke as the steamer sailed down the Clyde at about three in the morning on Tuesday, 11 March 1873.

According to his memoirs, George wondered if he shouldn't just head back to London and travel to Marseille and thence to Rio. (Just under a year before, they had made the reverse journey from Brazil to France). 'But, feeling that my escape from Ireland had cut all traces of me,' he says he was emboldened, and once again, disappeared off the face of the earth.

That same second week of March, everything went quiet so far as the whereabouts of George Bidwell was concerned. There was, however, news from the Old Lady of Threadneedle Street itself. It held its half-yearly meeting for shareholders in the parlour of the bank. Though it was Friday 13th, it was hardly an unlucky occasion.

The governor of the bank, George Lyall, announced that the forthcoming dividend would be £4 15s per cent, a total payment that would amount to just over £3 million (£3,006,191 17s 2d), with just £77,000, 'the full amount of the loss sustained or accruing in consequence of the recent forgeries'.

There were, according to press reports of the event, resounding cries of 'Hear! Hear!' A seconder said that he agreed with pleasure, despite the write off. The shareholders' dividend would be smaller, Sir George acknowledged, due to 'the circumstances of the past half year have been peculiar', a tacit reference to the worsening worldwide financial situation.

Old habits die hard. George Bidwell had a need to stay in touch with the wider world. He spent much of his time writing to friends and relatives. And, indeed, a note that he had sent to George Macdonnell on his first day in Scotland would lead to his undoing. 'After the lapse of about a fortnight, we received a telegram from America,' is how

Freshfields recorded it, 'stating that a letter dated 11th March bearing an Edinburgh postmark and a seal marked GB had arrived addressed to Macdonnell.'

As a matter of course, Freshfields appointed an old Edinburgh firm of lawyers to enquire further. Local police and a private detective were hired and spent a week looking in both Glasgow and Edinburgh 'but without any definite results', as one newspaper reported.

In the fortnight it took for the post to cross the Atlantic, he could be anywhere by now. As if emphasising the point, two days later George Bidwell had written once more to Mac. 'Your Irish friends were too warm for me, but I avoided their attentions by coming over here, and shall remain quietly here until I hear from you.' He then pointed out that he had much less money than he wanted. 'You better send me £100 in English or Francs bank notes, not by registered letter,' he wrote. He asked his friend to divide it into three sums – to be sent separately to here, Copenhagen and Barcelona. 'Do not telegraph,' he asked. 'It may be some time before I reach home.'

Day Six – Saturday, 23 August 1873
Central Criminal Court, Old Bailey

It was unusual for the chief clerk of one court to testify at another, but these were the most unusual of circumstances. So when Mr Oke, the chief clerk at the Mansion House, now swore under oath about the depositions of a witness who had earlier appeared there, several people wondered why.

James McKelvie was a private detective who lived in Edinburgh. After testifying twice before at the Mansion House, he had passed away just six weeks earlier on 15 July 1873. So, as was required by law, the clerk at Mansion House read out Mr McKelvie's death certificate, which recorded he was 36 years of age and had succumbed to 'typhus fever'.

Judge Archibald, who was a stickler for propriety, wanted complete assurance that Mr McKelvie was exactly who he said he was. 'I have someone here who knows the handwriting,' explained Hardinge Giffard. 'I rather think the identity of name is sufficient evidence.' And so another Edinburgh detective, David Ferguson, now took to the stand.

'Did you know the late James McKelvie who was a private detective?' Mr Giffard asked.

'I did.'

The clerk handed over his death certificate. 'Just see if that was his signature,' Giffard continued as Ferguson looked at it. 'You have seen him write I believe and know his writing?'

'Yes,' the policeman replied. 'I have no doubt that this is his signature.'

'And he is dead we hear.' A curious uncertainty lingered. Was Giffard being sarcastic?

'Yes.' As with all policemen, Ferguson then went through the monotonous minutiae of how Mr McKelvie had been hired by Gibson, Craig & Co. of Edinburgh, 'writers to the signet'. As a result of that commission, he had been watching a house, No. 22 Cumberland Street, Edinburgh, on Wednesday, 2 April 1873 'from about twenty-five minutes past ten o'clock in the morning'.

What happened next[29] had been astonishing even by the standards of this trial, and one newspaper termed it 'a most exciting chase'.

Wednesday, 2 April 1873
Cumberland Street, Stockbridge, Edinburgh
Afternoon

If only he had remained indoors. Or been more wary and less regular in his habits. Certainly, the private detective hired by the Bank of England presumed that such a clever and experienced criminal as George Bidwell would not be stupid enough to draw attention to himself by doing the same things over and over again. That included mailing letters and buying all the newspapers.

Yet George Bidwell's vanity knew no bounds. The solipsistic certainties of how the story about the forgeries was playing out in the press consumed him. Virtually every day since he had arrived in Edinburgh, George Bidwell had called on a bookseller in Dundas Street – a glorified newsagent – to purchase copies of all the London newspapers.

'He gave the booksellers to understand that he was a foreigner,' the prosecution later noted, 'that his name was M. Courant and had just recently come from the West Highlands of Scotland.' Mr Anderson, the owner of the bookshop, was increasingly puzzled. Why would a Frenchman live in the highlands? And come to the city to improve his health when the weather continued to be unremittingly awful? And what would anyone want with all those newspapers?

One day, Mr Anderson mentioned it to another customer who just happened to work for Gibson, Craig & Co., appointed on behalf of the Bank of England. It came at exactly the right time. The detective's enquiries had proved fruitless, but now he had an address to investigate thanks to the newsagent's ledger.

So on this cloudy, cold Thursday morning, James McKelvie made his way over to Cumberland Street in the company of a plain clothes detective (identified only as M'nab in subsequent reports). After gaining entrance to No. 22 he asked the landlady about her visitor. Ann Laverock told them that Monsieur Courant had arrived later that same Tuesday after landing on the Clyde. Carrying with him a portmanteau, the Frenchman had promptly rented the sitting room which faced the street. He asked if there were any French or German lodgers in residence. It seemed an odd question, not least when he later claimed he had French parents. He just wanted quiet, Mrs Laverock explained to the detectives.

Armed with this information, the two detectives waited outside in a partially obscured stairwell that led down to the basement. When, at 12.49 p.m., someone emerged, Mr McKelvie looked up to see Mrs Laverock standing by an upstairs window. She nodded, he's the fellow.

∽

M. Courant paused, looked up and down the street. He'd come out to see what the weather was like and then went inside again. To the detectives, the lodger already looked suspicious. Twenty minutes later, he re-emerged and walked up to the nearby pillar box, posted a letter and then went to another newsagents from where he emerged holding a bundle of newspapers. 'From his appearance, I suspected he was George Bidwell,' Mr McKelvie had testified before his untimely death. 'I watched him and saw where he went.'

After leaving Dundas Street, their suspect looked around and suddenly shot around a corner. By the time the detectives followed, George Bidwell had already set off at a run 20yds ahead. Giving chase, McKelvie was amazed to see him emerge from a blacksmith's, in the opposite direction. The two detectives then turned and closely observed their suspected fugitive dodging in and out of side streets ahead of them.

In other words, he was more than aware that he was being followed. McKelvie pretended to take no notice of him as he passed by. The stranger then walked on for a little while and then suddenly started to run again, amazingly, for the best part of an hour and a half.

It is harder to say who was the more tenacious, the hunter or the hunted. Certainly, the Edinburgh constable quickly fell by the wayside. But McKelvie kept up the pursuit, and more than his stamina, it was George Bidwell's agility at scaling garden walls that kept him from being apprehended. Though the private detective repeatedly came within striking distance of his quarry, he continually managed to evade him.

The fugitive became ever more desperate and, as the *Daily Telegraph* reported the next day, the detective 'followed him through a number of private gardens'. After jumping wall after wall, McKelvie then pursued him as he went 'through a private house'. In one account he leaped through an open window; in another, he smashed through the window or glass door.

Whichever it was, George Bidwell badly injured his leg on the glass, yet he kept on running. With the detective at his heels, George desperately entered the back door of another house, ran along the passage and exited at the front. There, McKelvie testified, he had jumped 'over the Church railings, jumped over several stone walls, one after the other'.

By now, he had emerged from a graveyard into Scotland Street, nearly 2 miles away from where the chase began. 'I got round to the street by another way,' the detective added, 'and was in the street as soon as he.' The chase continued until he came to a standstill in Duncan Street. Both were now exhausted. Turning towards the detective,

264

George made several thrusts at him with a stick which he had in his hand. McKelvie responded in kind, warding off the blows with a small baton that he always took care to carry. 'I held it out as if it were a pistol,' he later testified.

Momentarily, the stranger paused. 'Stand and be a gentleman,' McKelvie declared, 'to be a brother and not a coward.' This was a reference to his being a Mason, the cause of much comment at the time. 'I got hold of his hand and held him,' McKelvie added. By now, the detective had gained the attention of a coal porter who was standing about 50yds away. McKelvie called out to him to come and assist. He arrived to hear the prisoner shout that, irony of ironies, he was not an Irish troublemaker. 'I know that,' McKelvie replied. 'I am not looking for any Fenians.'

By now it was clear that his prisoner had seriously hurt his leg. It was gashed and bleeding from the jump through the glass window. On nearby Pitt Street, McKelvie and the coal porter found a cab. The detective took his prisoner to the solicitor's office on Thistle Street. 'You are George Bidwell,' he said when they got there. 'You are wanted for the forgery on the Bank of England.' At this point, George spoke in 'some foreign language and I don't know what he said'. At various points, he pretended to speak English with a French accent. By the time he was taken into a private room for questioning, McKelvie asked him to give an account of himself.

The exchange became even more surreal. 'Why did you run over those private grounds and stone walls?' he asked. The prisoner would not give him an answer. On the stand, Detective Ferguson just about kept a straight face as he read from McKelvie's original statement. 'A few minutes afterwards he said he was subject to giddiness in the head,' Ferguson said, 'and took to those fits of running off.' The courtroom erupted in resounding bellows of helpless laughter.

By four o'clock that Wednesday afternoon it was all over. James McKelvie had bound up George Bidwell's still bleeding leg and handed him over to the Edinburgh police. 'I had nothing more to do with him,' the late Mr McKelvie had testified.

George Bidwell was locked up in a cell at the police station on the High Street. Around the same time, other officers had removed his luggage from Mrs Laverock's premises. Inside the portmanteau he had bought while on the run in Ireland were several valuable diamonds, a large amount of jewellery and, most interesting of all, several letters addressed to George Bidwell, as well as his cufflinks, which showed the initials 'G.B.'

Later that afternoon, Police Constable John Spittle of the City of London Police arrived with the long-suffering Sergeant William Smith, who now had no doubt who he really was. Entering the cell, they identified themselves as police officers. Spittle told the prisoner that he held a warrant for his apprehension by the Lord Mayor of London.

Whenever he replied, the prisoner continued to use a silly accent. 'He spoke like a continental person,' Spittle later recalled, 'a person accustomed to speak French or

Italian as it might be, but knew very little English.' His first question for the policeman was downright bizarre. 'Political, anything political?' George asked. 'Are you sure there is nothing political about it?' (This was probably another futile attempt at pretending to be a Fenian.)

'No,' Spittle replied, 'I am sure the Lord Mayor of London granted this warrant, upon sworn depositions.' Spittle informed him that he would have to come with them to London. But first there was the matter of his apprehension under Scottish law, and so he was quickly arraigned before Bailie Wilson at the police court later that afternoon. He was identified by both James Noyes (no relation), who had last seen him at Drummond's Hotel with the engraved luggage and Alfred Lidington, who a week earlier had known him as W.J. Spaulding of Brighton.

Later that evening, he was escorted by Smith and Spittle in a cab to Waverley Station. As they headed for the 11 p.m. overnight train, according to press reports, a large crowd watched the sickly looking prisoner hobble painfully towards their own first class carriage. Still resplendent in what was described as his 'Ulster' overcoat and block 'billycock' hat, George Bidwell enjoyed the attention. Tellingly, he seemed to possess a great deal of luggage, but most of it, according to later press reports, contained clothes.

The journey back to London took the better part of a day. The detectives had plenty of time to chat to their prisoner, who had now stopped pretending to be French. The warrant that had been served on him also mentioned the other prisoners by name – Edwin Noyes, Macdonnell and, in Sergeant Spittle's recollection, 'Warren'.

'I suppose the Mr Noyes in custody is a person I knew by the name of Hills,' George said in his normal accent. 'He was introduced to me in that name.'

'Are you a naturalised American?' Spittle asked.

'Excuse me,' he replied, 'I would rather not answer questions.'

Their train arrived at Euston Station at around 9.30 p.m. on Wednesday, 3 April. Along with police escorts, a cab took the prisoner to Bow Lane Station. A full inspector quizzed him and an assistant commissioner witnessed the proceedings. When Inspector Bowman asked him to confirm his name, George was hardly forthcoming. 'I would rather not give my name now,' he said. 'I wish to see my solicitor.' He also said he could not remember the exact address where he had stayed in Cumberland Street, Edinburgh. He was kept overnight in the Bow Lane cells.

They were taking no chances and the prisoner was guarded by a duty policeman. However, neither was George Bidwell for, as noted before, he refused to give a name when he appeared the next morning for his first remand before Sir Sydney Waterlow. Despite his play-acting over the next few weeks, in reality he was overcome by depression. 'I had determined when first arrested to end it in my life in order to save the family name,' he wrote to his brother Joseph in South Bend in May. 'Of course it is a wretched affair and it will be a sacrifice for you to come but I leave it to your blood to decide what you will do.'

On this first Thursday in April, as George Bidwell was taken to his cell in Newgate, word had spread that his brother and bride had also been apprehended – in Cuba, of all places.

12

Cat and Mouse

It is unsatisfactory to reflect that all the efforts made here by our most experienced lawyers and detectives, backed by the willing concurrence of every Government affected, and aided by the sympathy of all to whom the immunity of daring criminals is a source of dread and danger, have been to the present baulked by accident or superior dexterity, and that the men now in custody, if guilty at all, are but inferior instruments in the great Bank of England forgery scheme.

Daily Telegraph editorial, 14 April 1873

Saturday, 15 March 1873
Havana, Cuba
Sunset

Finally, it was good to make landfall.[30] Yet as Austin Bidwell, his bride and manservant quickly disembarked, danger lurked all around them, hidden within every shadow. Crowds were milling around on the dock, and somewhere in the gathering darkness was a swarthy man of medium build, with long black hair, moustache and whiskers much like his own. His small brown eyes missed nothing, especially not such a striking couple who were rushing from the *Martinique* with all that luggage.

His name was Lucas, and though he was often mistaken for a Spaniard, he was actually an Austrian in his forties. He spoke several languages and worked as an interpreter at the Telegrafo Hotel, one of the more salubrious in the Cuban capital. In this guise, he kept a watchful eye for potential customers.

More often, he was ever alert for the main chance, or in this case, the highest bidder, as Lucas took care to examine the passenger list. The conspicuous couple fitted a description that had been widely distributed. The gentleman was 'thirty to thirty-five but sometimes looks older, very thin and bony' and was indeed 'accompanied by a young woman eighteen to twenty years of age, looks younger with golden hair'.

Fate smiled upon him. The new arrivals were oblivious. In Austin Bidwell's later telling, their disembarking had been a last minute decision. During their eighteen day voyage, the newlyweds had enjoyed themselves tremendously aboard the *Martinique*. Their fellow passengers viewed them as a young, glamorous couple celebrating their good fortune with endless formal dinners. 'We always finished a bottle of claret and two of champagne,' Austin later wrote.

Eventually, the West Indies beckoned like a siren of old. After coaling in St Thomas, he and Jeannie caused quite a stir when they stepped ashore, all in white 'from canvas shoes to white umbrella'. His wife was deliriously happy and found time to write to her mother. After staying in a hotel overnight, they left for Havana the next morning. The *Martinique* would continue on to Vera Cruz, Mexico, from where Austin Bidwell had originally wanted to disappear.

After spending most of this Saturday shadowing the beguiling coast of Cuba, the *Martinique* berthed in time for the sunset gun. With just thirty seconds to spare, in Austin Bidwell's account, they rushed ashore and made their way to the Telegrafo Hotel, where he was convinced they would be safe. 'Not a soul in Europe knew I was in Cuba,' he later wrote, 'and so long as my name did not transpire, I was as safe in Cuba as if in the desert.'

Third Week of March 1873
Cuba

After the freezing cold of an English winter – not least with their more recent experiences in the Pyrenees – the newlyweds were enchanted by Havana. They hired a suite of rooms in the hotel with servants who, as Austin relates, 'took all worry and household cares from my wife's shoulder'. With a lovely sloped garden that looked over the Gulf of Mexico, it felt as though they were living in a tropical plantation.

There, in the sunshine and carefree atmosphere, the Bidwells enjoyed a second honeymoon. It was, Austin recalled, more like an American club. There was a party atmosphere as they mixed among the 'nice but gossipy society' in various bars and restaurants. Austin Bidwell freely spread his money, which helped cultivate favours, not least from General Torbert, the US consul as well as the local Colonel of Police. Such bribery, Austin later claimed, would ensure 'no speedy action would be taken and ample time given me to escape' in the event of discovery.

In his memoirs, Austin implies they spent the best part of a month at the hotel. In reality, it was less than a week. During that time, Jeannie, admired by fellow socialites, spent her time attending picnics and dances. Privately, she took a very different view of the fast handsome men. '[The] ladies here, I hear, have no morals', was how she later described them to her mother. Many of the Americans, including Lucas, who had family in Brooklyn, were there for the sunshine and the warmth.

The newlyweds spent their time resting in the tropical breezes, lazily swinging in hammocks. Austin Bidwell took great delight in watching his wife unwind. 'It was well she had a few happy days,' he later wrote, 'enough misery lay not too far ahead.'

Three Weeks Earlier – Monday, 3 March 1873 Manhattan

He did not even bother making his way to the office. After having left Europe a fortnight before, Willie Pinkerton, tired and more than a little annoyed that his prophecy to the Old Lady of Threadneedle Street had come true, took a cab straight down to Broadway near 28th Street. There he would pick up the latest whispers, knowing full well that, as the telegraphed reports coming from London showed, the perpetrators were American.

At the top of his list of suspects was George Wilkes, whom he soon learned had gone to ground. The 'King of the Forgers', as he was generally known, had suspected he was being watched by Pink's operatives. Though some said he had already left the city, he hadn't. Wilkes was later traced to an address on 20th Street but did not, from the available evidence, seem to be involved. Pinkerton took that with a pinch of salt, not least with various vehement denials that came from several of Wilkes' associates.

In London, Pink himself had come across Joseph Chapman, 'formerly a member of Wilkes' Gang of Forgers', he now minuted to the bank's American attorneys, Blatchford, Seward, Griswold & Da Costa. Pink had seen him in the company of Austin Bidwell in the tailors on the Strand.

He had also encountered another ne'er-do-well called Samuel Perry, both in London and now in his first week back here in Manhattan. Known as 'Bottle Sam' thanks to his fondness for the booze, Perry would shortly be selected by Walter Sheridan to dispose of the spoils from some of the elaborate frauds he was planning. Perry had been boasting that there was 'big money' in something that was being planned in Europe. All Bottle Sam would say was, 'They will never get the men who did this as they are smart men.' Whether that was a reference to Walter Sheridan, Pink was not sure.

Wilkes, Sheridan and others were all connected as well as, in the later phrase of a NYPD chief, 'numerous other American burglars, sneak thieves and forgers then residing in London'. Ironically, Perry was dropped by Sheridan because of his drinking, even though the same police chief marvelled that, 'in his time, he has been associated more or less with the ablest thieves in the country'.

At this stage, only the names of Warren and Horton had been publicly announced. In Austin Bidwell's later telling, Willie Pinkerton had quickly concluded that the mysterious Frederick Albert Warren would either be a resident of Manhattan or Chicago, 'because I was young and evidently had a good knowledge of finance and financial matters'. But waiting for solid information that would pan out as useful leads was a special kind of agony for the greatest detective in America.

Third week of March 1873
Havana, Cuba

In Havana, the news about the forgeries detonated throughout the expat community. When Jeannie Bidwell read about them, it produced a surprising reaction. 'Who had the audacity to rob the Bank of England?' she exclaimed to her husband one morning. 'He ought to have a whipping!' Austin Bidwell wisely said nothing.

Though he had tried to keep his bride from reading the newspapers, she had soon heard about the forgery from the gossipy Americans in Havana. As they had recently spent time in Europe, Austin Bidwell was constantly asked about who might be behind it all. 'Some clever young scamp, with plenty of money of his own,' he would remark, 'who did it for the excitement of the thing and from a wish to take a rise out of John Bull.' Which, for once, probably wasn't too far from the truth.

In his memoirs, Austin Bidwell claims he took the news hard. Rather than panic, he took a long walk along one of the endless, white sand beaches and pondered his fate. How had Hills been found out, he wondered? At worst 'arrest for him only meant for him a brief incarceration', and thankfully his own name remained unknown. For now, at least, there was still a great deal of leeway. He and Jeannie could still proceed to Mexico, lie low and then travel incognito. He was safe in the knowledge that there was nothing concrete to connect him to either the mysterious Warren or Horton.

But Cuba was full of Americans who gossiped. Would he come under suspicion by them? During this first week in the tropics, Austin says that he became acquainted with a rich young plantation owner who had his own estate on the Isle of Pines – 'One of the loveliest tropical isles imaginable' – and soon joined him and some other fast friends in shark fishing, hunting turtle eggs and, ironically, participating in slave hunts as the island was full of runaways.

By the time he got back to the capital, it was clear from the New York newspapers that his earlier optimism had been misplaced. Austin Bidwell knew he would have to assume an alias and, inevitably, let his wife in on his great secret. Given her earlier outrage, he wondered exactly how, but was 'tolerably certain she would forgive me upon my promise never to do wrong again'.

As it was, a steamer to Mexico was due to leave on the following Sunday, 23 March. So, according to his memoirs, a dinner party for all his friends was planned for the Friday night. As they prepared for it, his wife was still 'unconscious of the frightful calamity impending, entered upon the last half day of happiness she was to know for many long years'.

Friday, 7 March 1873
Manhattan

Never panic. It was as true for the detectives as the forgers themselves, especially when distracted by all the various false leads that came thick and fast, such as the one about a Mrs Warren who supposedly lived in the Bowery.[31] But when news came on this Friday morning, by telegram overnight from Queenstown, that one of the suspected forgers would dock at ten o'clock, Willie Pinkerton knew what he had to do. He dispatched two further operatives to see if, as the telegram suggested, George Macdonnell would disembark from the *Calabria*.

Someone who was younger than Mac's telegraphed appearance, with 'dark side whiskers and moustache, yellow skin, dark spots on his face, large nose', in their later report, made his way to the 5th Avenue Hotel where he registered as 'George Alvoici, San Francisco, Cal.' As it was one of the known haunts of the forgers, he was kept under discreet surveillance until another telegram arrived from London stating that Austin Bidwell had been in Paris on 1 March (which was most likely incorrect). 'G.B. and Mac were here two days ago trying to escape,' it added, 'may now be on a steamer. Extradition papers follow by first mail.'

This Friday was crucial in terms of the unfolding investigation. 'Arrest Warren, Macdonnell and Bidwell – charge forgery, newspapers of Monday last gave particulars,' Freshfields now telegraphed their American associates. 'Macdonnell and Bidwell were here two days ago.' The net was tightening.

Mrs Devereux's statement that Mac had told her that her daughter and son-in-law were headed to Madrid from Paris had been enough. A quick check of passenger lists had revealed that Mr and Mrs Bidwell were en route to the Caribbean aboard the French steamer *Martinique*. The problem was that they could well disembark anywhere en route, though the later receipt of Jeannie's letter from St Thomas narrowed their landfall most likely to Cuba or Mexico.

An 'all parties alert' was sent to various British consulates in and around the West Indies. When Lucas, the translator, reported their arrival in Havana, everything came together. The local British consul telegraphed the City police in London to dispatch two of their finest, who were headed first for Manhattan.

Willie Pinkerton, too, had sent enquiries to all US consuls in and around the West Indies. A couple of dozen possible Warrens were narrowed down to just one, Austin later noted, aided by an American surgeon in Cuba who had come across him and also reported his suspicions to the authorities.

George Macdonnell's own voyage had begun on Saturday, 8 March when the Bremen-based *Thuringia* had left for New York. Another tip had come from an all too predictable source. Frances Gray, as a later New York police chief noted, 'became enraged at the disappointment, and suspecting the route her lover had taken to get away, betrayed him to the police'.

After being arrested at Euston Station on Saturday morning, her testimony led to the release that afternoon of the names and descriptions of Warren and the two Georges. Fairly quickly, it was established that George Macdonnell had arrived in Paris two days earlier on 6 March. 'He did not stay there, however,' Freshfields recorded, 'but went next day, Friday, to Havre.'

It was a simple matter to consult the passenger lists. Someone calling himself Frederick Macdonnell would dock in New York on the penultimate Thursday in March. That was now just over a week away. Throughout the voyage, the fugitive himself was his usual insufferable self. Mac behaved as though he did not have a care in the world. Enjoying himself in his luxurious stateroom, he became friendly with a Frenchman whom some of the ship's officials were certain was a smuggler, and fairly soon became 'intimate' with a young lady. Whether Mac proposed to her is not known, but he did hand her the diamond ring which the original police all-points bulletin had suggested belonged to the other George.

Anticipating his arrival, many American officials were somewhat apprehensive, for George Macdonnell's elusiveness was legendary. So it would prove now, because he had already taken extraordinary measures for his own protection even before he had left French territory.

Thursday, 20 March 1873
Manhattan
5 a.m.

Dawn was breaking as the large, steaming police boat headed out to meet the *Thuringia*, a growing, ever looming presence in the half-light as it was making its way towards the Battery. The authorities had been waiting for two days now, and what followed was not just a race against time, rather a classic game of cat and mouse. Except in this case, the authorities felt it was they who were being watched, misled and, indeed, hunted. The circumstances of George Macdonnell's apprehension were so convoluted that at times it was difficult to know who the prey was and who was stalking whom.

In one version of the story, Mac's apprehension started with a race between the police boat *Seneca* – on which a pair of New York's finest were located – and a tug with a pair of deputy sheriffs and Pink's men aboard. In reality, there was only one boat and there were no Pinkerton operatives aboard. Two deputy sheriffs from the US Marshals' Office, along with a customs official and a police pilot, were with the arresting officers on the *Seneca* as it pulled up alongside the *Thuringia*.

They all had one aim: to get hold of George Macdonnell. But as became abundantly clear within minutes, their ultimate intentions were very, very different.

The Bank of England was hardly going to take any attack lying down. As soon as the Old Lady of Threadneedle Street became aware of the real identities of the forgers, they instructed Blatchford, Seward, Griswold & Da Costa to issue a lawsuit in the New York Supreme Court regarding their assets – namely, to seize all the property of George Macdonnell and Austin Bidwell, 'fugitives from justice'. The claim was for £100,000, procured, they explained, by means of forged paper in March 1873.

The US Marshals' Office in Lower Manhattan would now be responsible for getting hold of any property in Mac's possession. Deputy Sherriff Judson Jarvis had received the writ of attachment the Friday before the *Thuringia* arrived on 13 March.

Yet already, there was ill feeling as to who would actually serve it. A few days earlier, a policeman had appeared in his office to politely request that the sheriff stay on land when they intercepted the boat. 'I would prefer to go with you,' Jarvis said. The policeman had reluctantly agreed. There was at least some logic in his reasoning. Rather than openly attempt to arrest George Macdonnell, they needed to do it as quietly and discreetly as possible. The last thing any of them wanted was for someone as resourceful as Mac to be tipped off so he could hide either himself or, more to the point, his valuables. It hardly helped that the *Seneca* was a large boat over 100ft long and well known for the belching smoke that always seemed to signal its arrival.

Behind the scenes, there followed a good old-fashioned bailiwick dispute. After a series of arguments that had become ever more byzantine, complex and vitriolic, it was half-heartedly agreed that a customs official should join two of New York's finest as well as a pair of deputy sheriffs (Mr Jarvis and a colleague by the name of Curry). They would all pose as health inspectors for the simple reason that it was normal for a 'health boat' to dock first, and so they could pretend they were carrying out a common or garden quarantine inspection.

Manhattan Harbour
5.30 a.m.

What happened next could be characterised by chaos, calumny and counter-accusation.[32] As the *Seneca* heaved to, for some reason the genuine medical officer, Dr Mosher, let everyone on board the *Thuringia* apart from Mr Jarvis. It seemed to the others, despite the earliness of the hour, that the doctor was already drunk. While the deputy sheriff argued to be let aboard, his colleague Curry, sensing that something was amiss, ordered the *Seneca's* pilot to drop him on the other side of the looming liner.

By now, the two detectives had long since scrabbled aboard with the customs officer, J.H. Storey. By the time both US Marshals eventually arrived in George Macdonnell's stateroom, the suspect had already been apprehended. With the customs man in tow, he had noticed one of the cops stop to speak to someone who was standing in front of a state room. 'He gently pushed him backwards and they went into the room,' Storey recalled.

This, it transpired, was George Macdonnell. It was this same Mr Storey to whom the honour of inspecting his belongings had fallen. When Mac's luggage was searched, all that was found was a package of kid gloves, two small gold watches and, in his pocket book, six diamonds, later described as 'African coast diamonds of little value'. But there were no bonds. Anywhere.

Understandably annoyed, when the sheriffs eventually got there they searched him for a second time. George Macdonnell openly laughed in their faces. 'I'm clean,' Mac said. 'You can't prove anything on me. You cannot take me back to England on any such charge.' As a precaution, other guests with whom Mac had been friendly were also searched. He had not handed any of his belongings to anyone else. A short time later, Mr Storey made another discovery. The captain of the *Thuringia*, Meyers, quietly informed him about Mac giving the valuable diamond ring to a young lady. 'I saw this lady,' J.H. Storey later said under oath, 'who told me that she had returned the ring to the giver. I afterward saw the ring on Macdonnell's finger.'

And that, as the customs officer reflected sadly on the stand a few months later, was the last time he ever saw it, about fifteen minutes before George Macdonnell was taken away to Ludlow Street Jail. There he was to be held indefinitely until the due process of law could extradite him back towards the British Isles.

One detail not reported at the time was when all the officials were back on the *Seneca*, the lead detective had seemed in great spirits. Captain Jimmy Irving showed the others a pistol which he had confiscated from Mac. 'This is all I want,' he said with a lupine grin. 'For once I've had my own way. The job has been done just as I wanted it done.'

So far as the waiting world was ever aware, the breathless pursuit and successful arrest of George Macdonnell – also known as 'Swift' or 'Sweet' in some accounts – added 'another instance to the notable list of captures by aid of the electric telegraph'.

In Manhattan, as in London and Cuba, there was exultation at a job well done. Certainly, news of Mac's capture by the brave and resourceful Captain Jimmy Irving and Detective Philip Farley of the New York Police Department was soon wired all over the world. Their vigilance in maintaining a steely gaze upon all the ships that had been arriving in New York Harbour seemed part of their dedication and industry.

More intriguing details, however, were kept secret. In Judson Jarvis's mind, something did not ring true. The day after Mac's apprehension, the deputy sheriff turned up at the police central precinct, where he served Phil Farley with an order to deliver all money or property of the prisoner to him. The detective claimed he had none. A short while later, one of the named partners of Blatchford, Seward, Griswold & Da Costa had a quiet word with the other detective. 'Irving,' Clarence Seward privately said, 'if you and Farley give up the property, I will take no further action in the matter and the public will know nothing about it.'

Some of the mystery about the proceeds of the forgery was resolved the next day when Jarvis headed to the downtown post office. A package had been addressed to George Macdonnell, care of the brokerage firm of Duncan Sherman. It had arrived a few days earlier and was found to contain bank notes, drafts and other 'sundry bills of exchange'.

There was also a heavier package addressed to 'A. Biron Bidwell c/o Safe Deposit Company'. It had arrived on 18 March and had been marked 'not known to care'. In other words, it had not been claimed and was lying in wait. Rather than open it, the officials left that for the courtroom. From the size and volume of the contents, it was obvious that it contained a great number of bonds.

The authorities, while waiting with interest to see what else might turn up in the post, had clearly caught the scent of a rat.

The events surrounding George Macdonnell's capture subsequently took on a whole new complexion. Why, for example, had the police not been charged with sequestrating all his property? Partly, this explained why Blatchford's had subsequently issued suit against the two detectives personally.

There was something more going on. Nothing was ever quite what it seemed in this story. Who was chasing whom? Who exactly was the cat and who was the mouse?

The events that immediately followed in both Manhattan and Cuba were a case in point. In the narrative which follows, there was no straightforward sequence of events. Telegrams crossed in the ether; police reports were mislaid; information and misinformation mingled; letters were known to have been posted and were sometimes 'accidentally' destroyed, but invariably on purpose. Worse, when the story came to be reported, there was much dissembling, exaggerating and, in the case of some, pure fantasy, particularly concerning the exact details of how Austin Bidwell was apprehended in Havana.

Friday, 21 March 1873
Havana, Cuba

In Austin Bidwell's later telling, the dinner party which he and Jeannie had been planning was a hit. A dozen guests, mainly plantation owners and their wives, were treated to the finest food and wines, with warm air wafting in from open windows which looked out onto the ocean. Shortly after eight o'clock, there was a knock at the door. Through the windows, they could see a number of officials making their way across the verandah.

A 'resolute-faced' American appeared in the hallway and introduced himself as William Pinkerton. 'Mr Bidwell, I am sorry to disturb your dinner party or to annoy you in any way,' Pink supposedly said. 'But I am forced to tell you I have a warrant in my pocket for your arrest upon a charge of forgery upon the Bank of England.'

Austin Bidwell, at his most nonchalant, asked Pink if he would like a glass of wine.

'Yes,' he replied, 'but I never drink anything but Clicquot.'

The host walked over to a desk and quickly removed a revolver from a drawer. Without warning, Austin Bidwell turned to shoot Captain John Curtin, the head of the Pinkertons' San Francisco office, at point blank range before attempting to jump through a window. He was stopped by another officer who appeared from behind the curtains and then wrestled him to the ground.

The only problem with this remarkable story is simple. It did not and, more to the point, *could not* have happened. Pink did not arrive for nearly another fortnight, the day after John Curtin on 1 April. Nor did Austin shoot anyone (certainly not Curtin, whom he got to know and like well in later years). Yet if Austin Bidwell exaggerated, so did Willie Pinkerton, who did not exactly help the historical record in later years. 'Yes, I arrested and landed Bidwell, the great forger and bank robber behind the bars,' he boasted to one reporter. 'Being well acquainted with [him], I started off myself to intercept him and made a bee line for Florida.' As an example of how time conflates memories, when Pink had arrived in Havana, 'we passed the very ship that had Bidwell on board while rounding him into port'. This, too, made for a more dramatic telling of an already spectacular story.

The most accurate, and oddly the most innocent version of what really happened, as she, in fact, described herself, came from the pen of Mrs Jeannie Bidwell. In a letter that Pink later intercepted and had copied, she told the full story to her mother. 'One evening we were romping, Austin and I, and a knock came very loudly,' she wrote. 'Evidently they had knocked twice and I opened the door and in walked the police.' Her husband's arrest was a decidedly more low-key affair than he allowed. As he was taken away, Austin turned to his wife and exclaimed, 'Don't say a word about who you are, what you are, where you are from, or anything about us.' It would prove to be a forlorn hope.

Jeannie Bidwell was wracked by tears of bewilderment. 'I tried to soothe my wife's fears,' Austin later recalled, 'but it was attempting the impossible.'

In a later letter to her mother, she was also livid at the way the authorities had treated her husband. 'I was so frightened,' she explained, clearly believing it to be some sort of cruel mistake. Repeatedly protesting her husband's innocence, she soon made herself very ill.

In his memoirs, Austin Bidwell described how carriages took them all into the Cuban capital. In fact, the suspect was only separated from his wife and they spent the Friday night apart in the same hotel, the Telegrafo. Early the next day, the local police chief, Colonel Morano de Vascos came in, indignant and ordered that his friend be released. He later told Willie Pinkerton that he would be responsible for the prisoner.

'So about twelve o'clock the next day I was transferred to the police barracks,' Austin remembered, 'and put into the lieutenant of police's room and a guard of soldiers placed over me.' This is borne out by contemporaneous press reports about him and his manservant. 'Warren and Noyes or Nunn are confined at the military barracks and deprived of all means of intercourse,' the *Daily Telegraph* reported. 'The wife is under surveillance at the hotel.'

For all the implied hardships, it was hardly a severe regime as he was already a close friend of the colonel. 'My wife spent many hours with me daily,' Austin remembered. 'All meals were brought from the hotel.' The prisoner was never searched properly ('only his pockets turned out', according to Pinkerton a few days later), was not shackled and could wander around the barracks at will. About his person, he had managed to hide some bonds, jewellery and cash.

In fact, the Cuban police did not seem unduly interested in him at all. Austin Bidwell was openly disdainful about his own treatment. 'I never saw such a set of fools in my life,' he later told Pink. 'We were never really searched and destroyed articles of value under their noses.'

A day or two after the arrest, Jeannie had handed over $5,000 in US bonds, which was, so far as she knew, all the newlyweds' money. At this stage, Austin claims he was not that bothered. 'So at last justice had laid hold of me,' he later wrote, 'but I thought it a very shaky hold – so much so that I could break away from her.'

Whenever he read the papers, Austin was gently encouraged. 'His arrest is not justified by any treaty of extradition between Spain, England or the United States,' was how one report had it. That wasn't the half of it, because by this point, in the final week of March 1873, lawyers in three different countries and working in many different jurisdictions were trying to determine the fate of all of the thieves of Threadneedle Street. The relevant statutes were arbitrary, tortuous and without precedent, which meant a carve-up for the lawyers, not least in Manhattan with the first of many extradition proceedings against George Macdonnell.

Mac's first appearance in an American courtroom, for at least a couple of years, was also enlivened by the unexpected appearance of a 'fashionably dressed' girlfriend whom he thought – and probably fervently hoped – he would never see again, the archetypal woman scorned, whom he had left waiting in the lurch in Liverpool three weeks earlier

Wednesday, 26 March 1873
Financial District, Manhattan

On this sunny morning, George Macdonnell was taken from Ludlow Street Jail to face Commissioner John R. Gutman, Jr at his Nassau Street offices, which formed part of the Southern District Court of New York. After his arrest the week before, Gutman had agreed to the prisoner's continued remand.

Mac's extradition hearing was opened by the first witness, Sergeant Harry Webb of the City police in London, who dramatically announced the details of a telegram he had just received: 'Full depositions, certified by consul, sent by special messengers.'

In vain did Mac's counsel call for the case to be dismissed due to lack of evidence. Mr Marbury of Blatchford's argued for the prosecution that the British authorities needed time to prepare their depositions. 'It is not the duty of a US Marshal to facilitate, by the admission of technicalities,' he suggested grandly, 'the escape of a prisoner accused of a great crime.' The judge had little option but to continue holding the prisoner on remand. Mac's full examination was put back for another two weeks.

The highlight – though, hardly for the prisoner himself – was the appearance of Frances Catherine Gray. Somewhat reluctantly, it transpired, she had accompanied Harry Webb across the Atlantic and now on the stand was hardly forthcoming. 'I suppose I was required as a witness,' she said, when prompted.

After detectives had searched her property in Pimlico, she had not been detained. Somewhat blithely she was told that criminal proceedings might be held against her if she did not help the police. She was later only given three hours to get ready to leave for Manhattan. 'I was told my position was rather awkward,' Frances Gray said. That was classic British understatement.

'She was asked whether she ever saw Noyes with Macdonnell,' *The New York Sun* later reported. 'After much legal quibbling, she answered that she went to the Old Bailey with a police officer to identify Noyes, who was then under arrest as an accomplice of the Bank of England forgers.' On this day in Manhattan, she also swore blind she did not even know his name. Under cross-examination, it became clear her main preoccupation was the compensation she would receive for having given her help. Frances Gray did admit, however, that she had talked very little with Harry Webb. 'During the voyage he said I was wanted to identify Macdonnell,' she said. 'I did not tell him what I was going to say.'

In Cuba, the legal complexities now reached combustion point with what Austin Bidwell later termed 'the firing of many legal fireworks'.

Alfred Thomas Archimedes Torbert was a genuine Civil War hero, a cavalry officer who was serving as the US Consul General on the island, the kind of diplomat whose will was iron and whose instructions were absolute. The general was soon meeting

Austin Bidwell several times a day and, as the prisoner recalled, 'assured me he would see that I should be treated with every consideration until such time that as the unfortunate mistake was corrected'.

It was hardest on the bewildered Jeannie Bidwell. After what she termed 'a lot of fuss', she was allowed to visit her husband. 'He said how innocent he was,' she later explained to her mother, 'and convinced me so thoroughly that I made a great many enemies.'

In the lieutenant's room, Austin was frequented by any number of visitors from both the US and British consulates, who were arguing over exactly what the fate of their prisoner should be. Just about the worst indignity was that Austin Bidwell was suffering from fleas.

As an American, the Spanish had no automatic right to detain him. It hardly helped that, at first, the local authorities seemed to think he was a British citizen. A first class diplomatic row was brewing in the background, not least because relations between the United States and Spanish governments were already badly strained.[33] Smiling with great satisfaction, Austin Bidwell was clearly happy that the matter of his incarceration was becoming a cause célèbre all over the world.

Tuesday, 1 April 1873
Havana, Cuba

Perhaps it was appropriate that Willie Pinkerton finally arrived in Havana on April Fool's Day. He did not actually leave Florida until two days *after* Austin's arrest, so he clearly could not have arrested the prisoner as soon as he had slipped off his own ship in Havana. The Pinkerton records reveal that he had left Manhattan for Cedar Keys on Sunday, 23 March, when news reached his offices that Austin Bidwell had been arrested in Cuba (the same day that the Bidwells should have headed to Vera Cruz). Bad weather delayed Pink's own departure from the Florida Keys until the end of the following week.

As soon as he arrived in Havana he realised he had walked into an intractable nightmare. 'The great difficulty here is not being able to speak the language,' he soon lamented. With temperatures in the shade of 85–95° Fahrenheit in the middle of the day, a short while later, Pink feared he had caught sunstroke, entering a nearby store 'til I cooled my head'.

On this Tuesday, his first stop was the British consulate, where he presented a photo of Austin Bidwell. Mr Dunlop – 'a kind hearted and really excellent man', in Pink's estimation, who was the acting vice consul – confirmed that he was in Cuban custody. However, Pink was told that the most senior American consular officials were now interfering in the due process 'claiming that Bidwell was a wealthy and respectable citizen of the United States'. 'Here we go again,' Pink thought.

Worse, they had helped Austin Bidwell obtain a lawyer called José Conti – 'sharp, shrewd and unprincipled' in Pink's later estimation – whom he soon concluded was 'unscrupulous to a fault'. Senor Conti would play an intriguing role in this saga along with the US consul, who had been informed by Washington to defend Bidwell at all costs.

At his own meeting with General Torbert later that day, the detective and the diplomat soon developed a hearty dislike for each other. 'He is a noted professional thief,' Pink said of Austin Bidwell, 'has been all of his life as has his brother.' The US consul said very little, but he was rather more forthcoming later that day to reporters. 'A Reuter's telegram from Havana says that the American consul here demands from the Cuban authorities the release of the prisoner Bidwell, alias Warren, on the ground that he is an American citizen,' *The Echo* reported the next day in England.

General Torbert seemed to be taking it as a personal insult that Her Majesty's Government wanted to extradite Austin Bidwell. The US consul, Pink determined, was manipulating things behind his back. So too was the translator, Lucas, whom the detective came to realise was passing on information to the highest bidder. Fairly quickly, Pink employed the head waiter at the Telegrafo Hotel as his own interpreter. Significantly, he requested of his brother Robert in Manhattan to send any correspondence for his attention in future via the British, not the American embassy. The Cuban officials, in Willie Pinkerton's estimation, were simply plain incompetent.

Though the press reported that nothing 'criminating' had been found 'except a note book with some leaves torn out' in Austin Bidwell's possession, he had, however, been allowed to keep hold of the gold watch, the wedding present given him by, as one official termed it, 'his esteemed friend George Macdonnell' and £50.

Pink was beside himself with rage. Worse, was there more? He quickly picked up the rumour that Austin Bidwell was oiling things with money that he had hidden about his person. It was high time to meet the miscreant for himself.

That same Tuesday afternoon, when they arrived at the barracks, Willie Pinkerton and his Californian colleague, John Curtin, were told that the prisoner was 'too ill' to see them. They returned to the Telegrafo Hotel and chatted at length with Harry Nunn, who was helpful.

By now, General Tolbert had informed Austin Bidwell that Willie Pinkerton had arrived. He was, in Pink's later telling of the story, excited by the news. 'I do not know him,' Austin Bidwell had lied, 'and have never seen him.' At this stage, the prisoner was certain that he would never be sent back to England as the charges against him would not hold. He was an American and he had left England before the forgery began (the 'Kamchatka defence' that Hardinge Giffard would later demolish at the Old Bailey).

He also took care to tell his wife that Pinkerton would only deceive her and she must not communicate with him. The detective, he made clear, was their enemy. Jeannie should remain in her room and refer him only to the slippery Senor Conti and avoid him at all costs. But such pleas had fallen on deaf ears, for Jeannie Bidwell's self-proclaimed innocence was soon shattered. Like all naive and simple-minded people, when the truth hit her about what her husband had really been up to, it was akin to a vase being smashed by an express train.

Tuesday, 1 April 1873
Telegrafo Hotel, Havana, Cuba
2 p.m.

He could not believe how young she was. On meeting Jeannie Bidwell, Willie Pinkerton concluded that she was a simple girl who was out of her depth. She was naive, she was lost and she was very, very upset. He had presumed that she would have been vociferous in protesting her husband's innocence, much like Martha Bidwell had done with her misbegotten brother-in-law. Ironically, Austin had made it clear that he also wanted Jeannie to stay in Chicago with one of his sisters and start up some sort of business together. That was clearly no longer on the cards.

To Pink's amazement, as they took tea in the hotel parlour on this sweltering afternoon, Jeannie Bidwell told him that she would have nothing further to do with her husband, that she had nothing to say to him and would not go near him at all. 'She told her story in a simple, heartless manner,' Pink later noted, 'and I am convinced she told the truth. She is certainly not skilled in the ways of the world and is nothing more than a very foolish young girl.'

Austin Bidwell's version was that his wife 'now basely deserted me'. When his memoirs were published two decades later, he added very little else about their time together. All he ever said was that he could never 'have foreseen that this woman, on whom I had settled a fortune, would have married another soon after my sentence, I should not have felt so sorrowful on her account'.

When it happened, it happened quickly. Within a matter of days of his imprisonment, Jeannie had read a newspaper account of what her husband had really been up to. More than the forgeries, the revelation of what Jeannie later called 'all these other women' got to her. 'I could not bear to see him stand before my sight,' she fulminated in a letter to her mother. 'We had two dreadful rows (excuse the vulgar word, ma dear) – Enclosing some of his insulting letters.'

She had torn a lot of them up, but now informed Mrs Devereux that she was going to come home as soon as possible. 'Oh ma dear, I am so miserable I hope I won't live long – I am not worth even life now. Oh I so wish I had taken your advice. Signed your loving child.'

In the days that followed, the correspondence between husband and wife became ever more vitriolic, particularly after she learned that Austin Bidwell already had a wife and children. In vain, did Austin point out this was his brother George. 'You must, dear, come down and see me for this is a cruel mistake,' Austin implored of her the following week. 'Those children of mine and the wife that that detective spoke to you of are my brother's property', which was a curious phrase to use. Explaining that George's children were now teenagers then 'you must yourself allow dear that if I was a father at twelve years of age, I began very young'.

The letters continued with a curious mixture of bluster and tender concern:

I swear to you by the virtue, the name and the grave of my sainted mother that you are the first and only wife I ever had and that no woman living or dead ever called me husband. You will certainly break my heart for I never dreamed to have so very cruel a blow from you. Do for heaven's sake come down to see me so I can make arrangements to send you to my home where peace and love await you.

Austin desperately wanted his bride to stay within the Bidwell family and be taken care of by them. Jeannie Bidwell wanted to have nothing to do with any of them. 'She declares she never wants to see her husband again for the way he represented himself,' Willie Pinkerton noted after this first meeting with her.

In the days that followed, Pink befriended her and this was not purely for altruistic reasons. As he observed to his brother, he wanted to control her and the flow of information from the prisoner. As he was reading all their correspondence, he was pleased to note that, in one of her letters, Jeannie told her mother that the detective 'is so kind'.

'He is certainly a bad, wicked man,' Pink told her in no uncertain terms. And on another occasion he told her that she should never have married him. 'You were no match,' he sadly concluded.

Jeannie was also taken care of by the British consul and some English people who happened to live on the island. A nurse in the hotel called Denise was also reporting Jeannie's thoughts and actions to Willie Pinkerton. When Austin Bidwell found out, it was the cause of even greater vituperation. When the oleaginous Lucas had run the San Carlos Hotel in 1872, he wrote that this nurse had been thrown out for being a strumpet, or as Austin indignantly spelled it out, 'in other words a whore'.

Perhaps the most remarkable of Austin Bidwell's various missives concerned his requests to his brothers in Michigan that they journey to New York to meet Jeannie, whom he had described before their falling out as a faithful, affectionate wife. 'She is young (only nineteen) talented and beautiful and thinks all the world of me,' the proud husband had written, 'loving her tenderly as I do, you can fancy how painfully I feel for her.' Specifically, he asked that they all stay at the Pacific Hotel, Greenwich Street, because 'a friend of mine' would escort her and meet them there.

At first, Willie Pinkerton presumed that this was either another of his siblings or else an associate from the extended criminal underworld. When a few days later Jeannie Bidwell revealed his identity, Pink was stunned – it was Detective Irving.[34]

If it had not been clear that something was definitely awry with George Macdonnell's arrest in Manhattan a fortnight earlier, it certainly was now. This revelation went straight to the heart of police corruption. Despite his tendency to exaggerate, Austin Bidwell was uncharacteristically honest about Captain Jimmy Irving in his memoirs. Irving was a complete creation of Tammany Hall and the Tweed Ring and it came as no surprise to Pink to learn that Austin Bidwell was in his pocket. After having joined the 20th Precinct as a patrolman in 1857, Irving soon fought and overcame the 10th Avenue Gang, rising ten years later to the detective force at police headquarters.

His fierceness was already notable. Time and time again, Irving had been observed drunk on duty, beating suspects, and on at least one occasion he had shot someone who simply annoyed him. Yet he was the original Teflon man – nothing could ever stick to him. 'Irving rose in general favour and reputation after these events,' *The New York Times* eulogised on the later occasion of his death. 'His successes also multiplied.' And in words that are richly ironic, the paper concluded, 'The arrest of Macdonnell, the Bank of England forger, was one of them.'

According to Austin Bidwell, he had first encountered Jimmy Irving in the mid-1860s among the gambling dens and faro banks of Manhattan 'dining and wining and being dined and wined'. His description of the detective was of a man of medium height, heavyset with a blonde moustache and pleasant eyes. The latter did not fool him. With his 'weak mouth and chin, and a flush face, telling a tale of dissipation' he looked like a scoundrel and, in Austin's estimation, was 'not possessed of any quality which would paint him out as a fit man for the place'.

So far as Austin Bidwell was concerned, Jimmy Irving was certainly the most corrupt of the city's detectives. His power and influence was without parallel. Ironically eulogised in his later *New York Times* obituary as 'one of the most daring and successful detectives ever employed on the police force', Irving ran his squads as an extension of the power elite.

In young Austin Bidwell he had found the perfect money launderer. 'I was the go-between of the most dangerous syndicate that ever existed,' Austin Bidwell later claimed, 'a gang which was composed of bank burglars and public officials of New York City.' Here was one of the mysterious supporters of Austin's earliest criminal enterprises.

Ultimately, though, he who paid the piper had little option but to dance to his tune. On a bright spring afternoon in 1870, Austin joined the detective on a horse ride through Westchester County. Later, over dinner, the detective made an offer he could hardly refuse. 'Go to Europe and negotiate some stolen bonds we have, will you?' For this, he would be paid $10,000.

At first, Austin Bidwell claims he declined. In his later telling of the story, he says that his rent arrears and tradesmen's bills were overdue. In other words, he had little choice. With police protection, it certainly helped propel Austin, Mac and George Engels on their first ever foreign foray.

Now, three years later, as Willie Pinkerton was finding out in Cuba, Irving would act as a go-between if Jeannie Bidwell ever made it to the United States. As Willie Pinkerton noted at the time, the detective was 'a particular friend of [Bidwell's]' and, significantly, Austin had warned his bride 'to be aware of all other men that might claim to be friends of his'.

Third week of March 1873
Manhattan

By now, as Willie Pinkerton pondered such matters, he could tell there was much more to this association than met the eye. In fact, he already had a pretty shrewd idea of what was going on. Two weeks earlier, Pink had pointedly been excluded from joining the arresting party of George Macdonnell. In part that could be explained by the bad blood which had long existed between the Pinkertons and the NYPD, but there was something else behind it, stemming from the reward of £500 for the capture of the man himself.

Ironically, it had all begun on Friday, 13 March. According to an affidavit later brought by Blatchford, Seward, Griswold & Da Costa, they had wanted Pink's detectives deputised as US Marshals. The lawyers acting for the Bank of England wanted Willie Pinkerton to serve the arrest warrant himself. When Detectives Farley and Irving heard about this, they were incandescent. The NYPD detectives refused and Irving and Farley turned up at the law offices on Nassau Street brandishing an all-points dispatch from across the Atlantic. It read:

> Arrest Geo. Macdonnell, charged with felony, on board *Thuringia*, from Havre to New York, Sgt Webb will follow with extradition papers. Macdonnell armed.
> Inspector Bailey,
> City of London Police.

Their services, the lawyers imperiously declared, would not be needed. The cops were understandably livid. 'We'll see about that,' one of them said. There then followed a series of mean-spirited arguments. 'We cannot recognise them as police officers,' Irving himself had said to one lawyer about the Pinkertons. 'They have no power to arrest and cannot even serve a Justice's warrant.'

When another attorney continued to make his case, Irving asked, 'Do you doubt our ability to make the arrest?' The Blatchford's lawyer backtracked. He wanted Pink personally to join them, so that the lawyers could be sure that their interests – and by extension, those of the Bank of England – would be best served. The two detectives then, 'in the nature of a threat' as it was reported, went to see the British Consul General in Manhattan, Mr Archibald. Here they were somewhat more emollient, reiterating that they wanted to arrest the suspected forger.

They were also quite open about claiming the reward from the Old Lady of Threadneedle Street. 'We had been so long on the force and made so many arrests, many times without any hope of reward,' Phil Farley later testified, 'and now was there was a little chance to make some money, we thought we should have the chance.'

In Willie Pinkerton's estimation, what was most revealing was something Phil Farley had said in his hearing. 'He said he knew Macdonnell,' Pink later testified, 'he kept calling him Livingston, I kept calling him Macdonnell.' Farley had arrested him in March 1871 under that name. But what Pink later determined – and never revealed at the time – was the fact that a telegram was found to have been sent from Le Havre to Jimmy Irving:

Meet *Thuringia* not Cuba about Eighteenth.

Livingston[35]

Easter Week: 6–11 April 1873
Havana, Cuba

Publicly, Austin Bidwell kept a brave face over what Willie Pinkerton called 'the daily sad interviews with his wife'. During the subsequent court case at the Old Bailey, he took care to keep Jeannie's name out of it. In a later petition issued on his behalf, it was stated, 'He would not permit the fact of his marriage and absence from England to be made known to the jury declaring that whatever the consequences to himself, he would not have his bride's name dragged into the publicity.'

Such chivalry was hardly apparent at the time. Hell had no fury like an international fraudster wronged. Vitriol alternating with self-pity poured from his pen. Austin was heartbroken, 'and now until the last moment of my life you will be what you have always been, my first, last and only love', he wrote as though writing to her for the very last time.

Jeannie Devereux told Pink she was very hurt that Austin was not just satisfied with the injury he had caused. If she did not come to see him, her husband had threatened that she would be turfed out of the hotel with her baggage. 'I will never go near him again,' was all she could say.

Pink took that with a pinch of salt. He feared poor Jeannie was weak-minded and would, if she ever came into direct contact with Austin Bidwell again, do what he wanted, for, as he later noted, her husband 'is said to have great control over her for fear he may be able to influence her to do wrong.'

For now, the war of words continued and intensified, as did the games of cat and mouse. Austin's friends on the island were, the detective feared, clearly up to something. They were sending too many telegrams and 'almost everyone here thinks money is being used liberally'. As a precaution, John Curtin appointed a couple of Spanish-speaking shadows to monitor the shadow, the consul and the dodgy lawyer.

'The shadows report that Conti and General Torbert have been very busy and have come together a number of times during the day,' Pink later reported to his brother.

Privately dismissing Lucas as an idiot, the prisoner's lawyer clearly was not. A few days later, Senor Conti had managed to evade his shadows. 'I fear he has gone to the States on some business for Bidwell', Pink wrote to his brother in New York City on the Wednesday of Easter Week, having not been seen since Saturday. There was clearly something going on but, as Pink bemoaned, they could 'do very little but watch persons about the hotel'.

Torbert and friends would stop at nothing to get him free or at least released into American custody. Whatever was going on, the general was, in Pink's estimation, severely derelicting his duty. Pink had also picked up the fact that the consul was being very well paid for his efforts on Austin's behalf. 'I cannot help believing it is,' he noted.

General Torbert and some reporters, it seemed, were using 'every honourable and dishonourable' means to muddy the case. The most obvious was in spreading disinformation and playing the sides off against each other. But help was on its way. London City Police detectives were now on their way via Manhattan with the equivalent of international arrest warrants. Despite his bluster, Austin realised the British cops 'would never have made the mistake of coming to Cuba without full papers'. In other words, that he could be extradited.

Ultimately his fate all depended on the actions of the Spanish Government in Madrid, whose failures Austin had experienced first-hand on his honeymoon. The *Daily Telegraph* editorialised:

> What seemed beyond doubt is that neither the Spanish nor the American Government wanted to screen a man charged with so serious a crime, and if both were willing that he should be given up to justice, the right of the power of any authorities to interfere was not very obvious.

As Easter week progressed, things went from bad to worse for Willie Pinkerton. Looking back, Pink knew something was up when he noticed that Austin Bidwell was still wearing the watch which Mac had given to him, as well as his wedding ring and chain. Estimating they were worth $1,500 in gold, he knew they were perfect bargaining chips. Unless they were confiscated, Pink knew only too well what might result. It wasn't as if he was being particularly well guarded by the local police. 'They were,' he exploded, 'the most worthless lot of dogs ever I saw.'

Pink had also come to the conclusion that the British embassy officials were clearly scared of General Torbert. The US consul had threatened the Spanish Captain General not to make any move on Austin Bidwell. When Pink found out, he exploded in the hearing of the Brits. 'He is being treated more like an American gentleman than a damned thief!'

Worse, he now learned that the prisoner was ordering in 'large quantities of wine and the very finest cigars'. Through Lucas, he was distributing them freely to the police. Pink protested to anybody who would listen, but to little avail. On Good Friday, he intercepted a note passed by Lucas for the attention of Jeannie Bidwell, where her husband was quite clearly in agony.[36] Austin Bidwell wrote:

Hereafter you can believe what you like once for all I swear by the virtue of the grave of my mother that I never had a mistress or that any woman ever travelled with me but you. I say that I am tired of all this, it is agony to have your hand ever ready to strike the first blow.

Chiding her that she was being very silly to even look at the newspapers, he instructed her not to make such a 'parade of your self-respect'. She should keep silent and not tell anyone, 'servants and everyone you are on speaking terms with', of her troubles. 'Don't you be so mad as to talk of the good home and friends you left for me or I shall be tempted to tell (though I would not) of your weak (I could use a stronger word) mother, that had repeatedly beaten you,' he ranted.

What worried Pink most of all was that on Maundy Thursday, Austin Bidwell had received 'an unusually large number of visitors'. At one point, up to twenty of Havana's worst ne'er-do-wells had been in his room. When Pink found out that Lucas had spent four and a half hours with him from six o'clock on another evening, he hit the roof. He protested to the authorities that the interpreter should not be allowed to do so unless someone 'reliable' was also in the room with him.

Though Torbert had not seen him so much, letters were still being passed along. Pink insisted that his colleague John Curtin sit with the prisoner at all times. He was politely refused. In the meantime, Austin Bidwell continued to send alternatively begging and threatening letters to his wife who, in his estimation, had showed him nothing but 'cruelty to a heart that was tenderness and love for you'. Her affection was great 'more particularly as soon as I will require all the care and attention that attention can bestow'.

But it was to no avail. 'It seems that now I am utterly deserted by everyone and it is doubtful if I will have the opportunity to send this, still I write it in the hopes that I can,' he wrote on Maundy Thursday. That same day, Austin sent Jeannie an ultimatum. 'In conclusion, if I don't see you before six o'clock tonight never show your face to me. I am done with you and thank heaven that the laws of my country will soon lose the legal tie that binds us. Your husband, Austin.'

Easter 1873

In London that weekend, a sense of smugness had returned in public perceptions of the case. The forces of law and order were doing their job. 'One by one the alleged chief actors in the late forgeries are falling into the grip of the law,' the *Daily Telegraph* had already exulted:

When a comparatively trifling blunder broke up the grand conspiracy, they fled to the four winds, but the secret was so hot that pursuit reduced the fugitives to extremities. Electricity anticipated them across the ocean, and keen vigilance tracked them in London.

On both sides of the Atlantic, speculation remained rife. In the United States, it was reported that Austin Bidwell's extradition would be blocked, while the opposite appeared in the British newspapers. The greater truth was that very few people knew what was really going on – least of all, the participants.

On Good Friday, it was reported that Mac's latest application for habeas corpus had been thrown out. 'Macdonnell was remanded until Wednesday next', a Reuter's dispatch confirmed that it would be a simple matter to have him extradited. The *Daily Telegraph* in London predicted that Mac 'will probably be placed in the dock before the lord mayor' in little more than two weeks. In other words, it would all soon be over.

But then, that weekend came an even more astounding piece of news. It was a snap, issued by Reuters, dated Easter Sunday, 13 April 1873:

Advices from Havannah state that Bidwell has escaped from prison and is supposed to be hiding in the city.

13

Means of Escape

I did what I thought was for the best. You may forgive me but I will never forgive myself and now as my last wish it is my last request and I ask you by your former love by all you hold sacred to accept a home from me for the sake of the child that will soon call you mother if not for my son.

Austin Bidwell's final plea to his estranged wife, Maundy Thursday, April 1873.

Maundy Thursday, 10 April 1873
Havana, Cuba
Midnight

Ten seconds. That's all it took, and as Austin Bidwell later claimed, it was all the time he needed to make an impulsive leap from an opened window into a crowded street below. This dramatic decision to make a daring escape from the police barracks was a story he would repeatedly tell and embellish at the time, and over the years.

Desperate men will do desperate things. And so he had. Thanks to Jeannie Bidwell's coldness towards him and his sensing that things were not going his way, the prisoner felt he had little to lose. 'Soon after 8 p.m., General Torbert came in to smoke a cigar and have a chat,' he recalled. 'He remained until nearly ten and then departed.' Some time before midnight, Austin Bidwell claims he made an impulsive run for it even though he was being escorted by soldiers with fixed bayonets. 'My room was in the second storey of the barracks,' he later explained, 'but I was allowed to go freely through all the rooms on that floor.' A guard had hollered, but nobody on the street below took the blindest bit of notice. So far as he was concerned, Austin noted with relief, the Spaniard 'was not a suspicious animal'.

Badly bruised, Austin was escorted by his waiting manservant, who handed him a disguise – bushy whiskers and a cloak – and they soon disappeared into the shadows. Though Austin claimed this was the ever loyal Harry Nunn, Pink later interviewed his manservant at the hotel. It was obvious Nunn had not been involved at all. It was yet another of the prisoner's stories. The culprits were much closer to home and much more surprising.

His escape, though, came as no surprise to Willie Pinkerton, aware that the prisoner had been 'getting desperate'. Earlier that same evening, Pink had remarked to Mr Crawford at the British embassy that 'Bidwell means business'. Within minutes of the escape, Willie Pinkerton was informed. He rushed to police headquarters where his rage was unconfined when he learned about the circumstances from the Superintendent of Police himself. Austin Bidwell, he said, had jumped from a high window on a balcony and 'made good his escape' through his own office.

Pink remained unconvinced when they showed him the extent of the drop. 'I am satisfied that he did not jump out of the window as described by the police,' Pink wrote to his brother a couple of days later. What he called the 'jarring' would have been too much. Had he jumped from that height, which Pinkerton estimated at 22–24ft, all his bones would have been broken. '[Besides] that, he is not yet recovered from a fractured leg and has many sores from three broken ribs received in a railroad accident between Calais and Paris last winter,' Pink noted. 'Now a man in this condition would never have taken the leap he is said to have made.'

It was going to be a long night. Willie Pinkerton soon learned of the rumour among most of the English speaking expats 'that Torbert and Price, *New York Herald* correspondent, are all concerned in the escape' and knew where Austin Bidwell was hiding. The Spanish 'shadows' hired by John Curtin had seen them regularly conferring. Word on the street was that Austin Bidwell would pay Torbert $2,000 for services rendered.

A heated exchange followed with the Superintendent of Police – a dead man 'and perfectly stupid' in Pink's estimation – who was insistent the Cuban authorities were doing their job. All means of escape were being watched. No boats or vessels would be allowed to pass without a search. Later, Pinkerton learned that the officer who should have been on duty outside Austin Bidwell's room had not been. Worse, Pink now observed for himself various Cuban cops discussing the escape in Spanish and it was clear 'they appeared to regard it as a matter of very little consequence'.

An obvious way of putting a firecracker under their investigations was to offer a substantial bounty. 'I will pay a reward for the return of Bidwell dead or alive of $500,' Pink simply said in the hearing of the several bored officers. Exhausted, the American returned to the Telegrafo Hotel to close his eyes for a few hours, determined as always, to find the prisoner – and quickly.

Austin Bidwell's own relating of his escape was, like all his writings, a tale of derring-do that often veers into the bizarre. It is a breathtaking narrative of diving into jungles, nonchalantly pausing to light cigars (he had about his person a hundred of them, he claims), swimming through shark-infested waters while being shot at by guards and, while stopping for provisions, being ultimately betrayed by a howling conclave of peasants. It certainly read like a penny dreadful melodrama designed for the more febrile of Victorian audiences. Most can be dismissed as fabrication.

In his memoirs, Austin Bidwell claims he was hardly bothered by the heat as he headed towards the interior: 'I had a chronometer, several valuable diamonds, a revolver and a gun,' he recalled. Wearing a panama hat and a sturdy pair of English walking boots, he took care to only travel when it was dark – 'Neither night travelling nor the situation had any terrors for me' – with just a couple of bottles of water.

Helped by his sympathetic friends, he had been provided with maps of the island. But so, too, had Willie Pinkerton, who also soon concluded the route the fugitive would take would be east along the coast, or else south down towards Spanish Honduras. Obvious places where he might show up were telegraphed in notes that Pinkerton took care to send himself. 'We are as busy as two men could be,' he reported to New York. The most immediate task was for him and John Curtin to search the harbour and its ships. By now, they knew the trail of the prisoner would have long since gone cold.

Good Friday, 11 April 1873
Havana, Cuba

At 3.30 a.m., the two detectives rose and headed over to the depot where trains left for Matanzas as well as the interior of the country. Their hearts sank straight away. The police on duty there had not even been told that a prisoner was on the loose. A night-watchman told them that at 1.30 a.m. somebody claiming to be an engineer had appeared and said he wanted to board any available train. As he fitted Austin's description – tellingly, including a panama hat and in shirt sleeves – they searched a train that was about to leave. It proved fruitless. Pinkerton left Curtin to keep tabs on all the other departures.

By 4.45 a.m., Pink had arrived at the harbour master's office in the port, where a policeman had only just arrived with a note from the Captain General describing the escaped fugitive. The harbour master himself did not actually arrive until about 6 a.m. They compiled the names of all ships and fishing smacks which were about to sail. The Telegrafo boat, they agreed, could leave but would be thoroughly searched. Pink said he would return in due course.

By 8 a.m., he was meeting Mr Crawford from the British embassy. 'He's obviously got himself into a scrape,' the diplomat remarked of the Cuban chief of police. Fearing difficulties with Torbert, the Cuban cops had obviously been complicit in the prisoner's escape so as to keep in with the US consul. 'He'll be rid of a very large elephant,' the Englishman added.

When they both met the Captain General himself, it became clear that he had not received instructions from Madrid over what to do. On one point he was insistent: the prisoner would not be handed over to the British.

Despite his tiredness and the growing heat, Willie Pinkerton was a characteristic whirlwind of activity. Later that morning, he sent a flurry of telegrams to the United States, particularly Florida where the fugitive would most likely surface. He ordered photographs of Austin Bidwell to be printed up and distributed around Havana.

Back at the Telegrafo Hotel, he saw Austin's wife, whose eyes widened at the news. 'Mrs B is very much alarmed lest he should come and murder her,' he later wrote, 'but I don't think there is any danger.'

The rest of this boiling Good Friday was a bust. 'I nearly died with the heat, over exertion,' Pink later lamented. It was yet another stroke of genius for Austin Bidwell to have made his escape over Easter. Havana was a deserted ghost town and, as Willie Pinkerton later put it, everything was as still as the grave. No shops were open and there was a deathly quiet. Pink, in his later reports, said that he had been 'unable to get a cab or any conveyance for love or money'.

Suspecting that the fugitive might try to lie low in Cuba with some of his sympathetic friends, Pink put watchers outside all his normal haunts and their houses. Dutifully watching one of them himself, Pink ended the day at 11.30 p.m. Exhausted, he returned to the Telegrafo and went straight to bed. Pink later concluded, in a letter to his brother:

> I can only say this Good Friday has been a bad Friday for me, I cannot express to you how I feel about this escape but I have been in anticipation that he would make an attempt of this kind. All that human man can do I will to get Bidwell re-arrested.

Easter Saturday, 12 April 1873
Havana, Cuba

At 4 a.m., Pink arose and watched a heavy rainstorm pass over. By the time he returned to the harbour, the promise of money had changed things considerably. All ships were being searched and examined, especially American ones. Down at the dockside, the police were on full alert.

After sharing breakfast with Curtin, Pink obtained a note from the French consulate addressed to the captain of a French steamer, giving them his authority to board the ship before it left the next day for Vera Cruz. This, it became clear, was the self-same ship that Austin Bidwell had originally wanted to take. When they arrived, the detectives were pleased to find three Spanish policemen already on board 'having been there since last night'.

The local police had already searched other ships bound for New York and Baltimore. Not that Pink thought this would do much to effect Austin Bidwell's apprehension. Aboard the SS *Liberty*, which was headed for Maryland, the captain was insistent that he would not pick up a man in the harbour. But there was 'no feeling' what he might do for money if someone pulled up in a small boat. This prompted Pink to send telegrams to as many ports as possible in the United States when he got back to the Telegrafo, cursing the incorrigibility of his fellow citizens.

That same Easter Saturday morning in lower Manhattan, George Macdonnell's attorneys began their fight against his extradition orders issued by the British authorities. Over the next few weeks Mac would become a regular visitor to the chambers of Judge Woodruff of the US Circuit Court on Nassau Street. His lawyers repeatedly argued – as they did today for the first time – that Her Majesty's Government had no jurisdiction over an American citizen.

After three hours of argument, Judge Woodruff came to what was described as 'an elaborate decision' in one account. His trial should take place before the commissioner. After that first hearing, if found guilty, the prisoner would then be released to the British. That afternoon, Mac was remanded to the US Marshals and this first writ of habeas corpus which had demanded this hearing was now dismissed. The prisoner was ordered to appear again before Commissioner Gutman in ten days and was returned that evening to Ludlow Street Jail.

Overnight, the news crossed the Atlantic by cable, where the *Daily Telegraph*, among others, noted that, along with Austin Bidwell's escape, the legal contortions 'leads us to fear that long delays may yet intervene between pursuit and justice'.

Easter Saturday, 12 April 1873
Telegrafo Hotel, Havana, Cuba
11 p.m.

Willie Pinkerton returned to his room exhausted and was, he later claimed, sick and 'could have cried'. But a few moments later, salvation – apt, for it was about to become Easter Sunday – came quickly. Despite feeling 'very blue', as he confessed to his brother, a messenger suddenly appeared in the dining room. The Cubans had apprehended a suspect 50 miles away at Bora Rocks where a coastal captain had alerted the police. 'Curtin and I jumped into a cab with an interpreter,' Pink recalled, 'and drove at once to the Punto, the most secure gaol on the island.'

In the early hours of Easter Sunday, they eventually gained access to the most isolated cell after some considerable difficulty. There was an armed guard outside. On the floor, camped at the back, was a huddled figure. When Pink called him to come into the light, he obeyed. 'Yes, Pinkerton, it is me,' came a familiar voice. A hirsute figure emerged in ragged and stained clothes. Austin Bidwell felt as dreadful as he looked. Despite his later claims, he had not eaten anything for thirty-six hours and had walked continually through night and day, so much so that his shoes were worn to the soles.

Needless to say, his later version of his capture was melodramatic. It had, he later recounted, taken place on a desolate beach after what he termed 'a terrific hullabaloo' as troops gathered around him. The press also reported at the time that 'he was seriously bruised in the hands and legs while escaping from prison'. In reality, the fugitive had been stopped and searched on the street by a local police captain and another person (whom Pink never identified at the time). Fairly quickly, they realised that he was an American who carried no passport. When they examined a notebook in his pocket, the name 'A. Biron Bidwell' appeared at the top.

'He made a desperate resistance,' Willie Pinkerton reported to his brother, 'and tried to get the sabre of the captain away and seized it by the blade but the captain drew it through Bidwell's hands, cutting him severally.' According to Pink, Austin had pretty well pounded up both of them 'when he was disabled from a blow of the sabre'. Despite his later claims of a posse of soldiers and fifty pairs of hands grabbing at him, Austin Bidwell did truthfully reveal one telling detail. Sabre in hand, the captain 'flew at me like a mad bull'.

This time, the authorities were taking no chances. 'I was taken by a guard of soldiers,' Austin says, 'not to the police barracks, but to the common prison, where an entire corridor was cleared of its inmates to make room for me and my guards.' Everything else on him – the gifts from Mac, diamond studs, sleeve buttons and scarf pins – were removed. There was also the gold watch which George Macdonnell had given him as a wedding present. It showed all the signs of its inscription having been vigorously rubbed with sand to remove it, presumably on a beach while he was on the run.

In his memoirs, Austin Bidwell says his first visitor was William Pinkerton. 'I am delighted to see you,' Pink said, adding that he hoped his prisoner would not escape again. As Pink and Curtin left, the prisoner begged of him to come and see him again with an almost Lewis Carrollian twist. 'There are many things I want to talk with you about,' Austin implored.

Over the next few days they did get to talk, despite the fact the American detectives encountered difficulties in getting in to see the prisoner. Later that same Easter Sunday, 13 April, Pink and Curtin found the prisoner cleaned up and back to his usual boastful self. 'I will fight it out here all summer,' he said defiantly. 'I'll be alright until next winter.' For reasons he did not elaborate, they would never be able to get him out before that.

'I pity you sincerely,' Pink told him outright on a later occasion. 'I am not going to let you escape while you are here, I will do all in my power to make you comfortable and contented.' On this particular visit, they brought him pen and papers so he could write to his cronies in the United States (which the canny Pinkerton could intercept and read).

Austin Bidwell thanked him profusely. 'I will never forget it and you will never regret it,' he said with emotion in his voice. A few days later he reiterated the same to his long-suffering sister-in-law, '[Pink] has been so very kind and considerate'. Ironically, he had used virtually the same words as his estranged wife about the detective. Austin professed himself still 'very anxious' about Jeannie. The correspondence continued. Pink told him he had not given her the last couple of letters before his escape. 'They were written in the heat of passion,' Austin later confessed, 'when I was almost driven crazy', and was glad that they had not been delivered.

So, too, would Jeannie have been. For all his later claims of chivalry, the prisoner's anger towards his wife was horrible to behold. 'You have been a false wife to a husband that at least was all tenderness to you,' he wrote. 'It is not too late to repair the wrong you have done me, but if this remains unanswered I curse you with forgiveness.' She had, he claimed, been taking too much notice of others. Repeating that the nurse Denise was a whore 'who was siding with her', he would 'make no insinuations for I know you to be pure but remember the world will judge you by the company you keep'. Later, he scribbled that she should not keep the company of a prostitute, 'or you will soon be one yourself'.

His sense of abandonment was complete. 'You have for a few days past so tortured me that my heart is turning cold and dead to you.' And though she had written that she hated him, he would, however, consider her a model for baseness. 'Why,' he mocked, 'murder could be respectable by the side of your action.' And in another missive he warmed to his theme. 'The money you have is from the proceeds of three different murders I committed so being stained with crime you will not keep it,' he mocked, when he had heard she no longer wanted to associate with him because of his past.

Easter Monday, 14 April 1873
Cuba

It was amazing how quickly the mood of officialdom had changed. Austin Bidwell had committed the ultimate sin, that of embarrassing the authorities. The Havana police, it was clear, had turned against a prisoner who had made them all look foolish. As Willie Pinkerton now concluded with the greatest of satisfaction, 'depend on it, no favour will be shown him now'.

Even more significant, the prisoner could sense it, too. 'So now he has nothing and the severity shown him is stronger than the laxity was before the escape,' Pink noted on this same day. The former darling of the city was now a pariah. The authorities wanted him gone, a bitter irony which amused the cause of all the anxiety. 'The laugh would have been against you if I had succeeded,' Austin told Pink of his escape. 'Only hunger drove me to take the course I did.'

By the time he returned to Havana, Willie Pinkerton made sure wine and cigars were sent to the pair of arresting officers. He also made a stop at the Telegrafo Hotel where he told Jeannie that her husband was recaptured. 'I am very glad, indeed,' she said. 'I am well pleased.' So, too, was Willie Pinkerton. 'Tired as I was, I could not sleep that night,' he wrote to his brother, 'for I was too happy knowing he was secure.' After not having what he termed 'an hour's refreshing sleep during his absence', he fell into a deep sleep for hours.

Easter Monday, 14 April 1873
Havana Harbour, Cuba
Early Morning

The first that Sergeants Michael Haydon and William Green of the City of London Police were aware that something was seriously amiss was when they returned to their cabin. All throughout their voyage, they'd had the curious sense they were being watched. Certainly, their Manhattan hotel room had been tossed. As a result, Haydon had lost £40, a memorandum book, some letters, unimportant papers, a silver snuff box, shirt studs and pins. Sergeant Green's valise was broken into and a memo book, personal letters, three pictures of Mac and cigars were also taken.

The night before, Easter Sunday, as their steamer arrived in Havana they were certain their cabin had been entered again. Early the next morning, the *Morro Castle* was immediately quarantined. By the time Willie Pinkerton heaved to aboard a gondola with John Curtin, the quarantine officer would not let them aboard. Wondering if history was going to repeat itself, Pink had waved and recognised Haydon. The City police's finest had made sure they had left their extradition and legal papers away from their room for safekeeping. Whoever had tried to burgle them had not found what they were looking for.

When Pink looked over the passenger list, he saw a familiar name, Oscar Wilson, who 'had the cut of a New York swell thief', as Pink called him. Haydon agreed, they had him up for it, too. About 35 years of age, with a medium build and dark complexion, Wilson was what Pink would call a 'silk hat' (although the one he wore was black). As a precaution, the purser had already looked through Wilson's valise and found clippers, skeleton keys for doors and trunks, a small jemmy and the usual tools that would make a 'complete outfit for a first-class hotel thief'.

But there was no money or papers. Pink wondered why the Brits had not just put the frighteners on him. 'It was too late now, however, as he had been alarmed and could see he was suspected,' he wrote to his brother two days later. Apart from the Spanish gold and a few greenbacks, they had nothing to hold him.

Reluctantly, Oscar Wilson was let go and made his way to the San Carlos Hotel, where he was put under observation.

Later that day, Wilson's tools were found in Sergeant Green's bed and under his work stand. Among all the keys was one for the room Green had stayed in after landing in Manhattan. Pink and Haydon now had Wilson arrested. The thief was taken to the same jail as Austin Bidwell and then thrown in the dungeon. He would be held until the Britons departed, because Pink had learned from Austin Bidwell that someone had been sent by corrupt New York cops to put a 'beat' on them. In another version of the story, events had taken a completely different turn in Manhattan.

Michael Haydon, the *New York Dispatch* later reported, had become 'smitten with the charms of a fine-looking woman whom he met one evening on one of our thoroughfares'. Foolish enough to accompany her home, it transpired that she was a 'panel thief' who had removed the sergeant's pocket book, a gold snuff box 'and worst of all, the extradition papers for Austin Bidwell'.

A while later, these papers were thrown through the window at City Hall and forwarded to Cuba – or so the newspaper reported. 'It is understood that Sergeant Haydon believes this was a rough joke put on him by the detectives at police headquarters,' the *Dispatch* reported.

Certainly, this was a variation on the story that Austin Bidwell now told Willie Pinkerton. He said that he had heard from his friends in New York that Oscar Wilson's robbery 'was a damned good joke'. That seemed to be confirmed when, a week later, the New York papers arrived with 'indignant', as they saw it, coverage. William Green said there was obvious collusion between the police and the thieves. While in New York, they had only seen Philip Farley one night and when they left, he had waved them off. According to Michael Haydon, Farley had also been spotted in the company of Wilson before the boat sailed for Havana.

When the Brits later discussed the matter with Willie Pinkerton, they suspected they knew why. It was significant, the British police thought, that they were probably robbed that first night in New York. It could only have happened while they were talking to the cops. Oscar Wilson – whom they suspected of handing things to a confederate – had been able to 'clean them out effectively and succeeded in doing so in all but getting possession of the right papers'.

The Week after Easter
Cuba

Austin Bidwell was clearly feeling desperate once more. Willie Pinkerton was sure that he would, if given half the chance, try to escape again. Pink ensured that the prisoner was held 'severe and sure' in his cell. At this point, he was also unsure exactly how Oscar Wilson would be dealt with. On one of his visits to the prison, Pink saw him in the distance and the 'swell thief' walked away.

Pink wanted the authorities to search Austin's cell twice a day, morning and night, and allow him and Curtin to spend most of the day in his company. Both suggestions were rejected. 'I am in constant dread lest Bidwell escape again,' Pink wrote, 'for he cannot do it without collusion.'

On one of his visits, Pink was distressed to see a stone in the cell wall had been moved. That would, he was sure, have allowed someone to 'operate on the cement' so that the prisoner could easily escape into the yard and over the wall. In other words, Oscar Wilson might not be the only envoy from New York.

Pinkerton and Curtin were also keeping an eye out for suspicious characters who had been arriving from the United States. Every day, they noticed men 'loafing around' in the city, including a Reverend Strong, who had also been seen in the vicinity of the consulate and the prison. 'They apparently have no business and it is now too hot to come here for pleasure,' Pink noted. He was having them shadowed, allowing him to boast to his brother that he was 'watching everyone here' in the hope of foiling yet another desperate attempt at escaping.

Tuesday, 22 April 1873
Nassau Street, Manhattan

If at first you don't succeed, try another courtroom. George Macdonnell's extradition hearings began again when the prisoner, looking elegant and as though he did not seem unduly worried, was brought once more before Commissioner Gutman.

Imprisonment, it was clear, had hardly impinged on his lifestyle. 'He showed a handsome gold watch and peculiar seal,' *The New York Sun* reported. 'These were taken from him at the time of his arrest but were returned.' Later, Mac had the watch assessed at Tiffany's and rejected the $450 they offered. He subsequently handed it to his cousin in Brooklyn (whom it was later believed sold the watch to fund his trip to London in the aborted attempt to spring the prisoners from Newgate). While in Ludlow Street Jail, Mac somehow managed to amass a wardrobe of 'eighteen suits, including a full dress suit, a velvet suit and several walking suits and a splendid dressing gown'.

Today's hearing lasted five hours. After dismissing the original warrant, another was now formally served. A great, prolonged argument took place – one newspaper termed it 'a considerable dispute' – but, eventually, it was agreed that in the interests of justice, many of the original witness statements and depositions brought from the Mansion House should be submitted.

It took most of the afternoon to read them out, which the prisoner seemed to enjoy hugely. 'That he will be sent to England ultimately there is no doubt,' *The Times* in London later reported in the wake of this hearing, 'but no one can say when.' Looking exhausted, the commissioner took all the material, including a photo of Mac with a light wrap over his arm, and locked it in his safe at the end of the day.

They were not the only possessions now in the arms of the law. The day before, the Bank of England's solicitors had retrieved the same trunk that George Macdonnell had sent from Moorgate on 5 March. Various lawyers and policemen from the City of London Police and Pinkertons had witnessed its opening in the Broadway offices of the North Atlantic Express Company. The contents – as would be noted during Nellie Vernon's examination at the Old Bailey – amounted to $220,950. Also within the trunk were cards and a card plate with the name of George Bidwell and various other memoranda involved in the commission of the crime.

The odd thing was that a woman had earlier called to collect the trunk. Whoever she was, the woman had shown the supervisor a note from Major George Matthews (in whose name it had been addressed) that she could collect the trunk from storage. In some accounts, it is stated she was Mrs Matthews. Either way, she had disappeared, never to be seen again. The mystery was compounded by the fact that in Ludlow Street Jail around this time, George Macdonnell showed a picture of a woman with a baby whom he implied was one of his girlfriends. It was one mystery about Mac that was never solved.

When Austin Bidwell subsequently heard about the seizure of what was generally later termed his brother's trunk, he was very downhearted. 'It destroyed all of George's chances,' he told Willie Pinkerton, 'except what Masonry would do for him, George being a high Mason.' And according to several witnesses who happened to overhear him when he read a newspaper account, his reaction was even more extreme. 'That finishes him,' he said of George, 'I am certainly done for.'

But he reserved most of his anger for someone whose terrible loathing was heartily reciprocated. 'I wonder if that **** in London had a hand in it,' he said, leaving no doubt how he felt about Nellie Vernon.

Third Week of April
Cuba

In all the subsequent meetings between Austin Bidwell and Willie Pinkerton, there was one recurring theme. The question of his sentence. The prisoner was clearly preoccupied with how long he might remain behind bars. Often, he just voiced his fears aloud. If he returned as much of the money as he possibly could, surely the Bank of England would treat him more favourably? At this point, Austin was not exactly sure how much had been retrieved in New York. He claimed that he could easily get hold of $5,000 from his own share of the forgeries. At this, Pink was amazed. Surely, he thought, Austin's share would be somewhere around $23–35,000?

In the meantime, lawyers and diplomats argued over his own extradition. 'Will I be taken to England?' Austin Bidwell asked one day.

'Yes,' Pink said emphatically, 'unless you escape again.'

'It's useless to talk to that. No one would escape from where I am.'

Pink was certain, given the opportunity, that he would. When Austin asked what his punishment in England would be, Pink told him straight. 'Very severe,' the detective said, 'unless you make arrangements with the Queen's Counsel, Freshfields, then by restitution of money stolen and pleading guilty, you might escape with a light sentence.' Austin asked what Pinkerton meant by that. 'About five years.'

His other major concern was for his wife's welfare. Austin Bidwell repeatedly told Pink that he wanted his wife to move to Chicago and live with Martha Bidwell, his sister-in-law and George's long-suffering wife. Austin said he would give her $5,000 in gold and then if she still wanted to she could return to England.

The problem would be Mrs Devereux – 'a violent tempered woman' – and he was worried Jeannie would not be treated fairly. On one of his visits, Austin begged Willie Pinkerton to help her come to this conclusion.

'I have no influence with her,' Pink said somewhat nonplussed.

'If you tell her,' Austin insisted, 'she will believe you.'

By now, Jeannie Bidwell was determined to divorce her husband. She wanted to leave on the first available steamer. 'I can't forgive him since I knew of his guilt,' she lamented to her mother. 'Oh, I can't forgive him for deceiving me, an innocent girl and a fool as I was.' His behaviour since his arrest, the insults and the re-escaping showed the extent of her naivety. 'Oh how he deceived me,' she added, 'and here I am in a helpless state.'

She was visited and helped by the wife of General Stuart, who the Devereux family had known in India. 'This is a capital place for single girls and married ones, too,' she added. At this point, she reported to her mother, she was being wooed by a rich Cuban widow who 'is madly in love with me. He talks rubbish and you should see his letters.' He was rich, with plantations, slaves 'and keeps two nurses, one a very nice English girl,' and 'a little baby', a subject close to home.

Jeannie Devereux was pregnant, a fact confirmed, in one account, by the same doctor who had alerted the Pinkertons to Austin's presence in Cuba. From the surviving correspondence it is not clear when Jeannie Bidwell discovered she was in 'the family way', as she now termed it to Willie Pinkerton. Not that it modified Austin's subsequent behaviour when he knew. Her husband was much more concerned that his wife thought he had been playing the field. Again, he had reiterated that he had not already fathered any children in Chicago:

> You make me out quite a Don Juan hereafter, do as you please. Believe what you like only don't trouble me with repeating any newspaper falsehoods, I have offered you a home and a fortune do as you like about accepting where I give you until a month after your child is born to decide.

Last week of April 1873
Cuba

Waiting, endless waiting, in the sunshine. That was Willie Pinkerton's abiding memory of the final days of his stay in the supposed tropical idyll whose charms had long since depleted. The weather was even hotter and several people he knew ended up contracting yellow fever. Their number included the unfortunate Harry Nunn, who was now quietly recovering at the hotel.

Finally, on 23 April, the Spanish Captain General ordered Austin Bidwell up for extradition, which, as Pink reported to his brother the next day, 'was very welcome news to all of us'. Austin Bidwell became even more desperate to communicate with his estranged wife. Two days later, he even offered the detective $1,000 if he could arrange a meeting or just pass on a note. (Pinkerton already knew from the shady translator, Lucas, that Austin Bidwell had previously asked him to change a $1,000 bond.) 'I want to make this agreement in case I cannot effect a short sentence in England,' he said. Mordantly amused, Pink reminded him that, in the past, Austin had already confessed to paying people off with counterfeit money.

'Oh no,' he protested, 'this deal would be on the square.'

During another conversation, the prisoner admitted something that had been obvious all along. He finally confessed that he had bought himself out of the Havana police headquarters, but he would not say with whom he had done the deal. 'You would have laughed to see the pantomime he and some of them went through in making the bargain,' Austin said. When pressed, all he would add is that 'Money done it'. 'I would never betray a man who has ever done me a service,' he declared.

In those last few days of April, the only light relief for all of them came in the hollow laughs department. When Willie Pinkerton told him that Lucas had not only insulted his wife, he had put in a claim for the reward offered in their capture, Austin Bidwell went ballistic. 'Lucas is a damned scoundrel,' he shouted.

Oscar Wilson was now also severely sick at the hospital. It would, Austin chuckled, be the last laugh to his friends and the cops in Manhattan if the 'swell thief' were 'to pass in his cheques'. By now, it was glaringly obvious to Willie Pinkerton just how much protection all the forgers had been afforded by the New York Police Department. Austin Bidwell had already boasted that other criminals were annoyed about the 'pull' they had at police headquarters and that George Macdonnell had many friends in high places – and lower ones, among the seething underbelly of the Manhattan underworld.

Desperate men will do desperate things. Willie Pinkerton was certain that if Austin Bidwell could attempt to escape in Cuba where he did not know the lie of the land, there was a far greater chance that George Macdonnell would do the same in Manhattan. One afternoon, the detective had a long chat with the prisoner about the New York detectives.

'I am extremely sorry if Detective Farley or Irving should get into difficulty over this affair,' Austin said matter-of-factly. The two cops, he was quite insistent, had arrested Mac 'to prevent him falling into someone else's hands'. He also revealed that after lying low he too would, as Pinkerton recorded for the files, have slipped 'as quietly to New York, settle some accounts with his friends' and then give what he termed 'a percentage with Detectives who knew his business'. Ominously, Austin Bidwell ended with a dire warning about the consequences of his friend's extradition. 'They had better look out or they would be mixed up in a bigger sensation than the Bank of England forgeries,' Austin bragged.

These were not idle boasts. It was abundantly clear to an increasingly worried Willie Pinkerton that Austin Bidwell should not be allowed to set foot anywhere in the United States. Fairly quickly, Pink decided to play the criminals at their own game. He would simply 'play' Austin Bidwell with trash. In these last few days of April, he confided in the prisoner that his steamer would head home via New York City. They would all have the chance to disembark and stay there for three days.

'He jumped with joy at this and asked in what manner he could get the word to his friends', Pink had the satisfaction of noting. The wily detective said he would forward any letters that he wanted. With what sounds like a conspiratorial wink, Austin asked that any information they contained should be kept in strictest confidence. 'If you do this,' Austin gleefully replied, 'one day you will be handsomely paid.'

A few days later, Pinkerton was amazed when he read Austin's letter to Jimmy Irving, from an apparently unfamiliar correspondent. 'Hearing that you are the head official of the police of New York,' Austin ingenuously began, 'though a stranger, I have taken the liberty to write to you as you may know I have been arrested here.' He then explained that he would be leaving on 7 May, arriving on the 15 May and would be in New York for two days. 'Should you hear of anyone that knows me,' he added, 'will you be as good to inform them of the fact. I should be happy to have any one come out and see me onboard of ship.'

That same first day of May, Austin Bidwell also wrote to another old friend, George Engels. 'Have had no word from you or anyone else,' Austin said, after repeating the same proposed itinerary he had sent to Irving. 'The government have finally given me up.'

Reading all this correspondence in his hotel room, Pink was struck by the intimacy existing between the cops and 'this gang of thieves', as he called them. 'What a pack of fools he must suppose we are to take him to New York and allow thieves and his police friends to assist him ad lib,' Pinkerton wrote to his brother.

A few days later, however, Austin Bidwell suddenly enquired about his earlier letters to Jimmy Irving especially the one of introduction to his wife. 'It should be destroyed for Irving's sake,' Austin sincerely now claimed.

'It's not in my power,' Pink replied. 'The British consul has it in his possession.' A look of consternation crossed the prisoner's face. 'That is most unfortunate.'

Thursday, 1 May 1873
Punto Prison, Havana, Cuba
Afternoon

She was reluctant, as he knew she would be, yet when Jeannie Bidwell walked into his cell, it seemed to light up. Austin Bidwell certainly did. His wife was still as demure and radiant as ever but her eyes signalled only sufferance. Jeannie did not really want to be there. Austin Bidwell knew this would his last chance to persuade her to stay. When William Pinkerton happily escorted her in, it was obvious to him how things were going to play out. Austin Bidwell was effusive and warm. Jeannie was not so much cold, Pink thought, as indifferent. Their departure for Britain was only days away but her ship had clearly sailed.

So far as Austin was concerned, they were still man and wife and should share a state room on the journey home. There was little chance of that ever happening and so, as he had known in his heart all along, Austin Bidwell came clean. First, he told her about his role in the recent forgeries on the Bank of England. 'In the United States,' he boasted more for Willie Pinkerton's benefit, 'it would have been compromised for half the amount.'

Jeannie was stonily unimpressed. Shamefaced, he sketched out his earlier life, which, as he had maintained throughout, had been nothing less than a struggle. Listening to this litany of misfortune, Pink could not help marvelling at how most of it was untrue. 'Please go to my folks in the United States,' Austin implored her when he had finished, 'and accept a home amongst them.' If she had to go home to England, fine, but please consider staying in Chicago where his sister-in-law would have a great deal of sympathy with Jeannie's current situation.

'I will return to America after seeing mamma,' was all that she would allow.

Relieved, Austin then turned to Pinkerton. He had, he claimed, seen Oscar Wilson the day before. 'I know all about that,' Pink lied, surprised but managing to maintain his best poker face. It transpired that Austin had bribed a guard to let him upstairs and he had spoken to Wilson for five minutes. As none of their guards could speak English, they did not seem to care. Wilson had given him $5, which Austin asked Pink to keep for him. He then claimed he did not know the swell thief beforehand but laughed out loud on learning that he wanted to sue the Spanish Government for damages. Quite what Jeannie Bidwell thought of all this was not recorded.

After discussing Hills ('You know how to take a sinner,' Austin concluded gnomically, 'but beware of hypocritical thieves who serve the Lord.'), the prisoner told his wife what Pink later called 'a romantic story' about George Macdonnell's younger brother.

Michael Macdonnell had been arrested along with Hills in the late 1860s, that much Pink knew to be true. What he did not know was that, according to Austin, aged only 19 years of age Mike Macdonnell had run away with and subsequently married the daughter of the former Canadian Prime Minister, John Strong of Quebec. Soon afterwards, Mike Macdonnell was arrested and was still in jail. Even though she was quite young, his wife continued to live with Mac's family in Canada despite all that had gone on. 'She still sticks to him,' Austin said, leaving no doubt that Jeannie should do the same. And with that, in Pink's contemporaneous account, both he and Jeannie left.

On their way back to Havana, Jeannie told him that she still wanted to divorce her husband, but, unsurprisingly, sought his reassurance that he would 'make some permission for their child'. And that was how the matter was left, hanging uncertainly in the air.

Later that same day, Austin pleaded with his wife by letter:

Leave all this misery behind you, and go to my brother (you will need no other introductions to them) there you will find love and a happy home. Try and forgive me. Think how wretched you will be in London.

It is my last, my dying request. That all things good may watch over you is the ayer and the farewell of your loving & devoted husband, Austin.

Friday, 9 May 1873
Havana Harbour, Cuba

With a sense of growing inevitability, Austin Bidwell faced up to his fate. A rowing boat drew up along the landing stage and the prisoner, who seemed resigned to his future, with his wife pointedly standing away from him, walked along with the British vice consul to Cuba and the two Scotland Yard sergeants to board it.

They were quickly transferred to the gunboat *Fly*, which would take them to St Thomas, where they would transfer to the Royal Mail Steamer *Moselle*, which then headed back to the British Isles. They would pass nowhere near Manhattan. If Austin Bidwell's later memoirs are to be believed though, he was still contemplating desperate measures. 'I had secretly resolved never to be taken back,' the prisoner later claimed, 'but intended the first night out of Havana to jump overboard, possibly with a cork jacket.'

At the time, it was variously reported that Jeannie Bidwell would turn state evidence and, indeed, ask for a divorce. 'Her six weeks of married life not savouring of anything which would induce her to continue it', was how one newspaper put it. According to Austin's memoirs, her presence aboard the ship was there to stop him from even considering suicide or anything intemperate 'so that my wife might be spared long years of agony and me the misery and degradation of prison life'.

Third week of May 1873
Manhattan

It was a fate that George Macdonnell would avoid at all costs. In New York, Mac's legal contortions continued, and in the amazed appreciation of one newspaper, 'succeeded in protracting the proceedings for an extraordinary time'.

Some thought all the legal shenanigans were characteristically elaborate and elegant; others, as time had gone on, detected an air of desperation. Certainly, the endless hearings had taken their toll on the prisoner, now reported as 'careworn' and betraying 'considerable nervousness', the week before.

As the arguments rolled on in the US District Court in Manhattan it did seem, however, that the end was in sight. On Wednesday, 21 May, concluding arguments over the prisoner's extradition were held. Rumours were floating around that a record $300,000 had been spent in legal fees alone to ensure that the due process of extradition was successful.

Such expenditure was needed. In this one week alone, George Macdonnell, or rather his legal representatives, managed to get writs issued and orders countermanded on an almost daily basis. Not only was there now a serious conflict between two governments, there were involved bailiwick disputes between the various s and federal authorities, the police and private investigators. Even on the day th was being ferried to the steamer that would extradite him from American t a final set of papers were being handed to the Supreme Court to halt his ex on. No doubt George Macdonnell enjoyed it all. He had created chaos.

On Thursday, 22 May 1873, his extradition was finally approved by the US District Court of Manhattan after what one local newspaper marvelled had been 'an eight weeks' wearying discussion of legal technicalities'. As Commissioner Gutman read out his ruling, George Macdonnell sat, by one account, coolly stroking his whiskers, apparently without a care in the world.

One reason was predictable. That same evening yet another appeal would be lodged with the Supreme Court in Washington to countermand the decision. But now, as George Macdonnell was once more returned to the custody of the US Marshals, the prisoner smugly boasted to the one to whom he was chained as they were headed up town: 'Jack,' George Macdonnell said to US Marshal Robinson, 'if they convict me, I will make it hot for them'.

But, to his amazement, the authorities had got the better of him. When Mac arrived at his cell in Ludlow Street, it was full. Extra security had been laid on. There was a pervasive sense of menace. 'Macdonnell was vigilantly guarded that night,' one newspaper later recalled. 'In addition to the regular keepers on duty in the jail he was surrounded by ten deputy marshals and keepers.' As if that wasn't enough, five of Pinkerton's finest were on the lookout outside. Willie Pinkerton himself had sounded the warning. After his final discussions with Austin Bidwell, he was certain that an attempt to spring this other prisoner was imminent. 'If Macdonnell is given up, look out for attempted rescue and a desperate one,' Pink had warned the authorities in New York. 'Recollect how deep the police are in this thing and you can expect no real assistance from them.'

As a result, the extra security was not, as several onlookers noted at the time, overkill. It had been obvious for some time that George Macdonnell's 'crooked friends and various influential authorities', as the first chronicler of the case aptly called them, would try to extricate him from jail by any means available.

Austin Bidwell's boasts a few weeks earlier in Cuba were not hollow threats. Neither were the prisoner's own words to US Marshal Jack Robinson. Every effort, Austin had told Willie Pinkerton, would be made to save George Macdonnell while he was in Manhattan. If the US Marshals were interested, enough 'green' would be available to make it worth their while to spring Mac.

What worried Pink more, though, was what might happen if the guards *did not* comply. 'If they don't,' Austin had warned him, 'they are liable to be knocked on the head and may be killed if they resisted.' This would happen, he said, either when Mac was taken back and forth to his jail cell or, as a last resort, when he was on his way to the ship that would take him back to Britain.

As was already abundantly clear, the fix was in with the police. But who might actually do the job? Austin Bidwell name-checked two of the more notorious criminals of the day – Johnny Dobbs, a bank robber and known associate of George Wilkes, and Davy Cummings, who had started out as a waiter in Chicago and robbed all the boats he had ever worked on, before progressing to safe breaking. Neither were what Pinkerton called 'silk hats' or 'gentlemen burglars'. Both, he implied, could be prevailed upon to help Mac and neither would show a second's hesitation in having to use the rough stuff. According to Austin Bidwell, men like this would organise a 'target company' so as to separate Mac from his jailers. The cops would look the other way. Either the driver of the cab or a US Marshal aboard it would be paid to go a certain route down to Nassau Street, either on his way to an extradition hearing or during his transfer to the docks, and would, Austin Bidwell assured Willie Pinkerton, 'rescue him even if they had to kill every man with him'.

They had done such things before. 'This was how Davy Cummings was sprung from Massachusetts officers,' Austin noted of one of his escapades. Even allowing for the prisoner's capacity for hollow threats, Willie Pinkerton had to take the matter seriously. 'Bear in mind these men have lots of money besides that stolen from the Bank of England,' Pink now presciently informed his brother, 'and their case is a desperate one and only desperate measures can "bear it" and I feel desperate measures will be resorted to.'

Tuesday, 27 May 1873
Plymouth, England

A rather more English greeting awaited the prisoner. Everywhere he looked, there were people. Austin Bidwell was amazed at the attention he had garnered. As he emerged smiling and blinking in the sunshine he was cheered both literally and figuratively by a heaving mass of onlookers who were clearly eager to see who this remarkable fellow was. 'So great was the crowd,' reported *The Times*, 'that it was with some difficulty that Bidwell and his escort managed to reach a cab.' In some estimates – not least his own – there were 20,000 people at the docks gathered to glimpse him.

The prisoner was taken across the harbour to the Duke of Cornwall Hotel where he was allowed to change and have dinner before leaving with his detective handlers on the mail train at 7.45 p.m. Early the next morning, as the train came into London, he was swiftly taken towards the looming, terrifying presence of Newgate, his home for the next few months.

The next morning, with three officers in tow, Austin Biron Bidwell made his first appearance on his own in front of Sir Sydney Waterlow. Described as 'a gentleman late of Havana', the hearing was perfunctory and he said very little. The proceedings concluded when he asked Sir Sydney if he would 'kindly give an order for the transfer to his wife of the clothing which had been taken from me'. He was remanded to appear that Friday with his brother and Edwin Noyes Hills. The feeling in court was that, for all his contortions on the other side of the Atlantic, it was only a matter of time before George Macdonnell would be joining them. And when he did, the case could then be concluded as swiftly as possible.

Tuesday, 3 June 1873
Manhattan, Chambers Street

Desperate men will do desperate things. And so came the final, desperate attempts at delaying the inevitable as George Macdonnell's attorneys issued even greater numbers of writs in state and federal courts. Far from slowing the due process of law as they had intended, the two now tended to work against each other.

'The extradition case of the forger Macdonnell is a singular illustration of the absurdities of the laws in like cases,' the *New York Tribune* thundered. Though it was obvious Mac was guilty, 'some of the best lawyers of both England and this country are splitting legal hairs over his identification with a vehemence quite amusing'.

Nobody was laughing during these final hearings, which, despite a last minute appeal, were successful. Judge Woodruff finally agreed to the extradition of the prisoner. After being allowed to say goodbye to his counsel, George Macdonnell was carefully shackled to a deputy marshal.

When they emerged from the court just after noon, there were crowds here, too. Word had spread. Yet not everyone was an innocent bystander. Surrounding the prisoner as he emerged were US Marshals, sheriffs and policemen, some of whom, it was said, were looking extremely sheepish. As they came outside, they mounted the nearest carriage. Two other marshals jumped up (one in the box with the driver) and another cab followed as they headed off. The gathered crowds had, as *The New York Herald* later put it, 'very little time to feast their eyes on the champion expert'.

The authorities had turned the tables. Instead of heading uptown, the carriages rode away at a fast clip down towards the Battery. Mac, amused by it all, jokingly said to one of the deputy marshals that he would not mind having another look at the new court house, as it might be his last ever time in New York. The prisoner smoked a Havana and merrily chatted away.

The cab made its way down Broadway in what seemed like record time. At Battery Park, he was escorted onto a tugboat which then steamed to a military boat. Their final destination was a military installation on Governor's Island, a remote crag of rock off Manhattan, where he was kept in his own casemate and served meals from the military mess. 'The authority for his confinement is said to come from Washington,' reported *The New York Herald*, from where also it transpired this same day a final writ for habeas corpus was served to the Supreme Court by George Macdonnell's lawyers. In some accounts, even the president himself had been consulted.

Wednesday, 4 June 1873
Fort Columbus, Governor's Island, off the Coast of Manhattan

Nobody was willing to tempt fate. 'Desperate chances will be taken to effect Mac's release,' Austin Bidwell had boasted to Willie Pinkerton, 'even murder.'

It was something the prisoner himself seemed to be aware of, too. After his first night of confinement in a military prison, George Macdonnell appeared restless. Reading all the newspapers and smoking several cigars, he was not allowed anywhere on his own. His cell was strictly guarded, US Marshal Robinson was never far away and when he was allowed out to take in some air, he was heavily guarded.

And on his last night in the United States, there was a very peculiar occurrence which, in its most credible version, was later related by Allan Pinkerton in his ghosted memoirs, *Thirty Years a Detective*. 'That night was one of the most beautiful of the season the moon shone brilliantly,' the elder Pinkerton recalled, 'lighting up the harbor for miles, and enabling one to view the broad expanse of glistening water that surrounded them.' At around nine o'clock that evening, a small boat containing two men was observed approaching the fort. It was apparently drifting towards Governor's Island and came to rest just below the walls of the fort. There, it could not be seen, but when the prison guards went to investigate, they heard its occupants whispering just under the walls. 'Macdonnell stepped outside to the closet several times in company with the officers,' Allan Pinkerton wrote, 'and each time he gazed anxiously in the direction of the boat.'

Nothing happened, because the guards kept him in their sights at all times. A few days later, one of Mac's cronies – probably a policeman, though he was never identified as such.– asked one of the marshals if he had noticed anything unusual about the fort that particular night. The reason, it transpired, was that the boat had been sent to rescue him and the occupants had been paid $50 each for the task. If the prisoner jumped into the water and swam towards them, they were expressly told not to fire at him. But in Pinkerton's explanation, US Marshal Robinson, who was directly responsible for him, might aim more accurately. In the event, Macdonnell took fright and decided not to jump. And when he awoke the next morning, it would be the last time he did so in the United States for a very long time.

Thursday, 5 June 1873
Fort Columbus, Governor's Island

And so came the inevitable, organised and executed with appropriately military precision. It was a sweltering summer's morning and, despite the heat and the fear there might be last minute delays prompted by the lawyers, everything went without a hitch – or a heist. Just after 9 a.m., all the various US Marshals and British policemen left for the Battery barge dock together, from where they then travelled out to Fort Columbus. By the time they reached the prisoner's casemate, he had only just finished breakfast.

Deputy Marshal Jack Robinson was with him. The plates were still on the table. George Macdonnell was, true to form, enjoying himself hugely, looking natty in what one newspaper later termed 'a new dark suit of the prevailing fashion'. Escorted along a corridor in the fort, he gave a cheery 'good morning' to his guards. He smoked a cigar as he left, joking with the deputies, 'but his occasional furtive glances and trembling lips betokened an innate fear regarding his future fate', according to another contemporary newspaper report.

As a final precaution, they had not told the prisoner how he was going to head back to Britain. Various authorities whispered the name of another ship to lay a false trail. They also ensured that Mac would not land in Manhattan. He would head straight to the actual steamer that would take him across the Atlantic.

Accompanied by Sergeants Hancock and Webb, the whole party left the island on a heavily guarded tug just after 10.30 a.m. It made its way to Pier 46 but arrived way before the *Minnesota*, the steamer that would take the policemen and their prisoner to the British Isles. So the tug sailed around the harbour until the steamship eventually arrived. By half past one, Mac had been successfully transferred to the *Minnesota* without incident and was finally on his way to Liverpool, thus ending what one newspaper termed 'the successful capture of his whole gang of unparalleled delinquents'.

Saturday, 14 June 1873
Newgate Prison, London

It is not clear whether Jeannie Bidwell travelled with her husband back to London on the mail train from Plymouth, nor if she ever saw him again. She certainly heard from him by post a fortnight later when he wrote his final letter to his estranged wife. He began by noting that her solicitor had informed him that she really did not want anything further to do with him. 'I will not believe that of your own will, you, my dear little wife, keep away from me,' he wrote. 'I know that you would not and that you would forgive me if you knew how I suffer.' And then after talking of such anguish, he asked a plaintive query: 'Do you realise the fact that in three weeks – more if I am convicted – we will be almost as much separated as tho' one of us were in our own graves?' Signing it 'your affectionate husband', he never received a reply.

In the same folder in the Bank of England archives, is another letter written to Jeannie that same day by his brother. It was penned in a similar vein, a sob story which doubt-less enraged her as George Bidwell described the suffering of his brother. 'A stranger in a strange land' is how he described Austin, 'penniless, deserted by the wife he loves whose actions are those of her friends and to crush him whose adherence to him will equally aid to free.' And as always, George Bidwell tried to maintain that he was the bad influence:

> Believe me, he has been misled, but has a good kind heart. He loves you most sincerely and upon your decision now depends his future and your happiness for I would pledge all I hold dear that he will prove to you a kind, faithful and loving husband and a good citizen.

But by far the most remarkable of the surviving correspondence from this day is the note that Austin Bidwell sent to his mother-in-law. Addressed abruptly to 'Madam', it is a tour de force which begins by noting that she had shown him no mercy and he would do the same in return. Referring to a particular night when she was drunk and abusive, he continued, 'You see, Madam, that I shall break you on the wheel you meant for me'. He was heartbroken, he claimed. Jeannie had been kept away from him because of her mother's express instruction. Austin threatened to reveal her true nature and expose her:

> All I have to do is to prove a motive for my leaving England when I did. I will prove the cause of marrying my wife when I did was because of her cruel mother, her wretched home and the trials and temptations you caused her to be exposed to.

The wronged husband would have no qualms about exposing this 'in half the papers of England'. His price for silence was simple. That he should be allowed to see Jeannie and to have her address.

'All very simple and what Christian soul would not refuse a husband,' he continued. Calling it a base thing to keep her away from him, he would turn the tables. 'By the heavens above I will make you repent of it,' he wrote. 'I have blame or reproach for her. Do you know that you are making her doubly perjure herself?' He gave her a deadline of the following Wednesday to reply. 'The consequences be on your own head,' Austin wrote. 'Don't think I will fail to do as I say. Your own disgrace or not lays in your own hands.'

Needless to say, nothing ever came of these veiled threats. Austin Bidwell never saw Jeannie Devereux or her mother again, even after one final ignomiv, which came a few weeks after her estranged husband's trial at the Old Bailey with yet another court case.

Monday, 29 September 1873
Three and a Half Months Later
Central London

All was quiet – or as quiet as it ever could be off Oxford Circus – when late on this clement evening agonising screams pierced the night. If anyone noticed, nothing was said. Inside a virtually unfurnished apartment, a terrifying episode of almost gothic horror had played out. A young mother helplessly writhed in agony as she went into labour two months early.

A little girl briefly came into the world, but shortly before midnight she passed away. The impoverished family were beside themselves. The mother of the child had nearly died herself and was now gently sobbing and wracked by guilt and the onset of a fever. It was the culmination of a truly *annus horribilis* which was clearly going to get worse yet. Everything had fallen apart. They'd had to move to the lodgings as they were destitute. Shortly, the mother of the child would soon be sent to a workhouse in nearby St Giles.

So her family did the only thing they could only do under the circumstances, and that was the problem. The dead baby had been wrapped in a nightshirt and laid in a wooden soap box 'with a towel, newspaper and some bran', in one account. She was dispatched by parcel, along with an anonymous note, to an undertakers in Lambeth chosen at random from a directory. As there was no death certificate, the undertaker was legally bound to report the circumstances.

They were suspicious to say the least, even in age where infant mortality was an all too regular occurrence. An unidentified tip-off and simple detective work found the child's mother and, two weeks later, on 15 October she was arrested even though she was still seriously unwell. That same Wednesday, she was taken to Bow Street Magistrates' Court where she was charged in her full name – Jane Georgina Mary Bidwell.

Her defence counsel was someone who knew her and had taken pity on her – Harry Poland QC. Seven weeks earlier, the greater trial of 'the forger Bidwell' had come to an end with Mr Poland in attendance. Now it would be poor Jeannie's turn to face the law, but it was obvious in this smaller court that there was a great deal of sympathy. 'No evidence has been produced against Mrs Bidwell sufficient to enable a jury to convict,' Mr Poland said, by way of explanation of the unreported death of the baby. Mrs Bidwell was so young, ill and had already suffered so much at the hands of her estranged husband, he argued.

Clearly her elders should have known better. They too were being charged. Jeannie's own mother, described in the press as 'a well-dressed woman of respectable appearance' and a servant, Catherine Bassett, were also placed in the dock to stand trial. A short while later, Miss Bassett was identified by an agent of the Parcels Delivery Company to whom she had paid sixpence to send the box to the undertakers.

All three were bailed immediately, but a week later the case was dismissed. Wiser and cooler heads had prevailed. The stated reasons were that there was insufficient evidence but, for once, the legal system was compassionate and realised that, for all the negligence that may have been charged against her, the poor girl had suffered more than enough.

14

The Melancholy of All Things Done

> All four men deserve the credit of having maintained in an unusual degree the honour which is rather proverbial than customary among thieves. They have been staunch to each other and have fought the law with extraordinary audacity and resource.
>
> Report on the pre-trial, *The Times*, 27 August 1873
>
> It is an almost intellectual treat to follow in detail the concoction and execution of this amazing plot. There is no hurry, bustle or flurry. All things are done decently and in order.
>
> Report on the summary of the trial at the Old Bailey, *Daily Telegraph*,
> 27 August 1873

Final Day (Eight) – Tuesday, 26 August 1873
Central Criminal Court, Old Bailey
7 p.m.

Nobody ever thought the trial would last this long, and nobody thought they would be finished by the end of this final day. Several thought the accused might change their pleas to reduce their sentence, or that they would exonerate some of their colleagues; that the Bidwells would save Hills, who they would claim was subordinate, or even each other.

Nobody ever anticipated George Macdonnell addressing the court with his heartfelt plea that Austin Bidwell was ever only peripherally involved in the forgery, suggesting the probability that he was entirely innocent. The astonished judge had then pointed out to him that such a confession 'cuts away the ground of any defence from under your own feet'. No one thought that Austin Bidwell would apologise to Colonel Francis, or that the judge's own 'short summary' of the case would take over an hour to complete. Wryly noting that the steps the defendants had taken were not those usually to be traced in honest transactions, he urged the jury to use the very rectitude of Victorian sensibilities in considering the evidence. 'Nothing demands more the exercise of intelligent and manly common sense,' Justice Archibald had said.

And now, with darkness descending, nobody was in the slightest doubt as to how it all might end, 'commensurate with the enormity of a crime which has no parallel in criminal history', as one newspaper later aptly summarised it all.

The Old Bailey had once more filled to capacity after an extraordinarily long day. At times, the proceedings had dragged, hardly helped by the atmosphere becoming increasingly oppressive. Occasional bursts of bright sunlight had followed the noise of heavy rain surrounding the court. Throughout the day, thunder rumbled in the distance following on from some of the most violent and persistent electrical storms in recent history.

Some detected an equal measure of thunder in the features of His Lordship Sir Thomas Dickson Archibald as he waited for the jury to return and hear their verdict. All the lobbies and antechambers surrounding the Central Criminal Court were hushed with anticipation. Outside, there was another large crowd, in places three or four deep, all eagerly waiting to see what would happen.

Policemen still shepherded the prisoners in case an attempt was made to spring them. Several officials later claimed that they thought such a scenario might happen in these closing minutes of the trial. The atmosphere remained electric. 'The judge, having summed up,' the *Daily Telegraph* reported the next day, 'there was an interval of a quarter of an hour or twenty minutes, during which the jury box was empty.' In fact, the jurors were absent for just nineteen minutes. There was a call for silence as they returned to their seats. The prisoners were brought in by a phalanx of unsmiling policemen, who stood behind them.

The judge looked across at the foreman. 'Are you all agreed?' he asked George Spooner.

'We are.'

'How say you – do you find Austin Biron Bidwell guilty or not guilty?'

'Guilty,' Spooner said.

This was then repeated for the others in turn. When he was done, Mr Spooner sat down and the prisoners were allowed to make their final pleas before His Lordship passed judgement. Austin Bidwell used the opportunity to apologise to Colonel Francis. And then, as only he would ever do, tried it on for the very last time.

'My Lord,' he began, 'Would it be of any use for me to make an application for the postponement of the sentence for a few days?'

'None whatever,' came the haughty reply.

'Then My Lord I have nothing to say for myself.'

Then George Macdonnell – whom the judge clearly disliked – made another plea on behalf of Edwin Noyes Hills. Finally, George Bidwell repeated a version of the sob story he had tried before Sir Sydney Waterlow. He turned sad eyes towards his brother:

> There is one here some twelve years younger than myself who would never have been here but for me and I ask Your Lordship to have mercy upon him. He is young and is just married. Let him have a chance in the world to retrieve the past. He promised when he left England and took my hand – he told me of his own accord solemnly that he never should have anything to do with anything wrong, and I do ask Your Lordship that you will have mercy upon him.

And then it was the turn of Edwin Noyes Hills himself. By nature, he was the quietest and least likely to emote in public. He had clearly learned from his brother, the Reverend Hills:

> I had thought that I would not ask for mercy but it is human, it is natural, and it is God-like to ask for mercy, and it is God-like to extend mercy. Every man, every woman, all human beings pray for mercy and the very prayer of our maker teaches us that those who have it in their power to render mercy should do so. I hope Your Lordship will see that these are some mitigating circumstances whereby you can exercise mercy with justice.

Central Criminal Court, Old Bailey
8 p.m.

There was clearly going to be little chance of that. By now the atmosphere was very tense as the prisoners stood up together.

His Lordship looked at them directly, pensive yet determined in the darkened court room. He looked at each of them in turn:

> Austin Biron Bidwell, George Macdonnell, George Bidwell and Edwin Noyes Hills. You have severally been convicted of this offence with which you are charged and although the indictment only charges you with the forging of the one bill of exchange referred to in it, it has been necessary in the evidence offered on the part of the prosecution to bring before the court and the jury evidence which shows that you are each implicated in a scheme of fraud which perhaps for the audacity of its conception, and the magnitude of the fraud contemplated as

well as the misdirected skill and ingenuity with which it was attempted to carry it into effect is without parallel.

The words were absorbed by an eerie silence. His tone was matter-of-fact, yet precisely intoned:

I can see no palliation or mitigating circumstances in your offence. You were not pressed by want. On the contrary, you appear to have been embarked in this nefarious scheme with a very considerable amount of money, how you became possessed of which does not appear. You are not persons who are ignorant, not knowing and unable to contemplate the full effect of the crime that you were committing. You are persons of education so far as I can give that name to mere intellectual training without any apparent development of the true moral sense.

You appear to have been possessed – some of you – with the knowledge of different European languages and all intimately acquainted with the details of commercial and banking business. The success of your scheme was only rendered possible by the fact that in these days with the eminent commercial operations that are going on, it is necessary to extend to those who present themselves with apparent means and apparent respectability, and apparent business engagements the utmost confidence, and besides the loss that your crime has inflicted upon those whom you have defrauded, it is not the least pernicious consequence of it that you have given a severe blow to that confidence which must be maintained and protected and those who like you who seek to abuse it for criminal purposes – who are not restrained by any restraints of conscience or honesty must expect to be met by the law with a terrible retribution, and it must be well known that those who commit crimes which only persons of education can commit will be sure to meet with a very heavy punishment.

It was obvious what was coming:

I cannot see any reason to make a distinction between you in the sentence I am about to pass upon you, and with regard to that sentence, if I could conceive any case of forgery worse than this I might have endeavoured to take into consideration whether some punishment less than the maximum might have been sufficient for your case, but as I cannot conceive any worse case than this I feel no hesitation at all as to the sentences which it is my duty to pass you.

He paused, and then gravely reached his conclusion:

The sentence of the court upon each one of you is penal servitude for life and in addition to that sentence I order that each of you shall pay one fourth of the costs and expenses of the prosecution.

A strange, stunned hush descended over the Central Criminal Court. The accused appeared to shrink as the words hit them. 'I never will forget the moment when the old judge solemnly condemned me to what was death,' Austin Bidwell recalled twenty years later. What another newspaper later termed 'a low, indescribable murmur of amazement' ('pervading awe', in another newspaper account), ran through the courtroom. The prisoners had regained at least some of their composure as they were led from the court, the last time they would see each other for the best part of two decades.

'We turned from the judge and went down the entrance to the underground passage leading to Newgate,' Austin recalled. 'There we halted to say farewell.' They shook hands and promised, so that they would each know what the other was thinking they would read the same chapter of the Bible a day. The prisoners vowed to each other that they would never give in. 'The "primrose way" had come to an end,' Austin Bidwell later wrote, 'but we were comrades and friends still.'

There was a great deal of head shaking about the verdict. Nobody had been killed. No one had lost their houses or livelihoods. Losses would be recouped since the banking system was insured. The Bank of England had retrieved most of the money. 'Is not this one of the biggest things in the way of forgery ever attempted on this or the other side of the Atlantic?' the *Daily Telegraph* asked. 'Has not the Bank of England been victimised and would not the dear Old Lady of Threadneedle Street spend a million to punish the bold offenders?'

In the event, the dear Old Lady said very little publicly about the trial, apart from a few matter-of-fact statements from its officers at the Bank of England's subsequent half-yearly meeting on Thursday, 12 March 1874. It was just over a year since the frauds had been discovered, and its first announcement was that there had been a small reduction in the dividend. 'At that time last year we wrote off £77,000, which was the total loss,' said its new governor, Mr Benjamin Buck Greene. Since that time the bank had recovered property which had realised £73,420 13s 3d, leaving a total loss of £3,579 6s. He then explained that 'a large sum' had been expended to trace and retrieve the money that the thieves of Threadneedle Street had successfully swindled.

Though he did not explicitly mention it, the governor was referring in part to a final court case in Manhattan the previous October. It had been served by their American attorneys against Captain Jimmy Irving and Detective Phil Farley in the police commissioner's court. A great deal of dirty linen had been aired with the 'trial of the detectives', the aim of which was to trace the final $50,000 that seemed to be missing. The pre-trial submissions were enlivened by the participation of someone, it was rumoured, who had been put up to it by Michael Haydon, the City policeman who had been humiliated thanks to the efforts of the NYPD.

On 26 August, the night before the book was thrown at him, George Macdonnell had sworn on the record in Newgate that when arrested in March he had been in league with Irving and Farley. When apprehended, he claimed he had handed them some bonds that he had in his possession in the belief that they would be used to pay for his defence. 'Although I sent repeatedly to both Irving and Farley to ask for my property,' Mac had written, 'I received only $600 in bonds from them.'

But this, and all the other claims of malfeasance, were hard to prove in the trial that followed in New York. A letter that had been sent to Farley's residence by 'Harry' — an alias of Mac's — had not been signed for. There was no way of knowing whether the detective had ever received it. All the various officials who had boarded the *Thuringia* the previous spring contradicted each other and made things worse. Jimmy Irving, defended by a former mayor of New York, was at his belligerent best, denying every charge that was laid at his feet.

Accusation and counter-accusation might well have continued but soon, as rumours abounded that it would, the trial collapsed at the start of November 1873.[37] For reasons that, once again, were never fully explained, the Bank of England withdrew its lawsuit.

Though the detectives were acquitted, their reputations never recovered. A short while later, Captain Irving was transferred to command the Harbor Police where, embittered and drunk one evening, he crashed the *Seneca* and was ignominiously booted out of the force.[38]

For once, neither George nor Austin Bidwell needed to exaggerate. Both their subsequent prison sentences were draconian. That first night of imprisonment, all four members of the gang were kept in separate cells in Newgate, then dispatched to other prisons around the country. That first night, in the pitch dark of solitary confinement, it hit Austin Bidwell with a resounding thud. He had no idea when he would see his friends or family ever again.

After another week in Pentonville, Austin Bidwell was taken to Chatham prison, where he was greeted by an unsmiling warder. 'You were sent here to work and you will have to do it or I will make you suffer for it,' he said, by way of welcome. It was a variation on a theme they all would hear. Suffering would be the keynote to all their subsequent incarcerations.

Imprisonment took its greatest toll on the older Bidwell brother in Dartmoor. 'Before I had been six months in prison, heavy band-irons were riveted around my ankles,' George later wrote on the first page of his memoirs. 'These were connected by a chain and I was condemned to wear them day and night, in bed and out, for six months.' As a result, his legs atrophied. 'Throughout these various periods of solitary confinement, I never saw the blue sky, the sun or the twinkling stars,' he also added.

What was later described as 'probably the most remarkable case of malingering on record' resulted, in the recollection of Dr R.R. Quinton, governor and medical officer at Holloway Prison. 'Bidwell was in good health on conviction,' he wrote, 'but never did any active work in prison.' He feigned the loss of power in his legs, he 'lay in bed from day to day', while throughout his incarceration, he defied 'all efforts of persuasion and resisting all unpleasant coercive measures devised to make him work'.

After nearly a decade's imprisonment, Dr Quinton noted that George Bidwell's lack of motor ability had made him almost a cripple. His muscles were wasted, his hips and knees bent double 'so that he lay doubled up in a bundle'. Nobody ever determined what his illness was, and all the medical authorities could really say was that it was the result of George's firm decision 'never to do a day's work for the British Government – a threat which I believe he ultimately carried out'.

In a fit of despondency, he attempted to commit suicide by cutting his throat. He lost consciousness through loss of blood, but he recovered and was moved to Woking Jail. There, George Bidwell then taught himself foreign languages and wrote endless reams of poetry, including this one:

Tis fourteen years since on me freedom smiled,
While banished far from country, wife and child:
Misfortune's arrows sharp have pierced my heart,
My spirit, too, with most envenomed dart.
In solitude wild fancies thronging,
The heart for home is ever longing.
Then heed the captive's cry and set me free,
Almighty God of Grace if God there be.

The prisoner made at least one further escape attempt and then tried to commit suicide with a blunt knife. 'Has been poisoned and ill-treated both here and at Dartmoor and has suffered a long term of imprisonment,' the authorities at Woking Jail noted in August 1880.

His brother found his imprisonment hard to take at first. Austin Bidwell, too, had been incarcerated in his own little stone box 'eight feet six inches in length, seven feet in height and five feet in width', where he was just fed on bread and gruel. During these first couple of weeks in Chatham, he was convinced that he was going mad. He thought he could walk through walls. He could hear voices. But after a church service – the only time the prisoners were allowed out of their cells – he grabbed a Bible that was left in his cell and found that an entreaty to Job gave him strength. 'He hit on the idea of preaching sermons to himself,' it was later reported, 'and on each Sunday, he rattled off addresses at a rapid rate until he was forced to leave his cell to exercise.'

Eventually, he was allowed out to work and could see the sky. Fairly quickly, he made sure he would not be consumed by self-pity. 'I determined then and there to live in the future,' Austin wrote, 'and never to dwell on the horrible present or past.' A few weeks later, another prisoner gave him a pet rat, which became 'the solace of an otherwise miserable existence', buoyed only by hope and the promise of what might be.

'A man dreams of two things in prison,' he later said, 'liberty and good eating.' Austin put most faith in the former, 'but heaven knows the eating was bad'. The staple diet was tons and tons of potato. He even saved the wedges, 'and when they got hard, I ate them for dessert.' Prisoners were effectively starved, for they were only allowed 5oz black bread, 5oz meat 'and five days a week, a pint of soup is allowed for dinner'.

His greater memory, though, was of immersion in the mire. 'Mud, mud everywhere, with groups of weary men with shovels, or shovel and barrow, working on it,' he later wrote. Employed in a nearby brick factory, he found that the regime was unceasing and unwavering. 'For seven years, I worked in the slimy mud in the ship basins, hauled cement for several years and did masonry work and bricklaying the rest of the time.' Eventually he assumed the role of foreman of the bricklayers but received no special dispensations.

The regime took its toll on others. Austin Bidwell witnessed twenty-five men deliberately cripple themselves by throwing their arms and legs under loaded trains; he claims he saw seventy-four men commit suicide. Observing their agonies was, he said, worse than a thousand deaths. 'I never gave up hope, however,' he later claimed, 'as I knew my family and friends were working hard for my release.'

Not that he was ever allowed much contact with them. Visits and letters from the outside were strictly rationed. 'A visit of half an hour in three months is permitted,' he later wrote, 'but this is a favour that is only granted upon the same condition as the privilege of letter writing.'

Ironic then, that behind the scenes, a letter writing campaign had been begun on his behalf by one of his most devoted family members, who within a fortnight of his incarceration wrote, 'how disappointed we are that you didn't come home, or do you think we didn't care?' Their sister Harriet was indefatigable. She, at least, did care and spent the next two decades working on her brothers' behalf repeatedly petitioning for their release.

'My sister came over from America,' Austin Bidwell noted, 'and for ten years lived near the prison working for me.' While that does seem like an exaggeration, it was true. 'I have sold my home in America to enable me to come each year to England,' she wrote in one letter to Princess Victoria of Teck, 'hoping that I may be instrumental in the release of my brother.' She repeatedly pointed out that Austin Bidwell had 'repented of the intention and endeavouring to break away from the gang'.

It seemed to a fellow resident of the Windy City that she was in his office every week trying to find out what was happening. Or at least that was how Willie Pinkerton chose to recall it. 'Ten years had slowly dragged by,' Austin later wrote, '1883 came, and my devoted family felt that I, and my comrades too, had paid as was right, our due to justice, and we ought to be liberated.'

Wednesday, 3 August 1887
New York City

They were waiting for him, as he knew they would be. No sooner had the *Wisconsin* docked, than Sergeants McGuire and Doyle came aboard and arrested George Bidwell as he prepared to come ashore. They were not taking any chances, even though he could hardly walk. The British had relented; the Americans would not. Several onlookers wondered if wasn't just overkill.

The supposed master criminal was no longer the carefree young man who had left these same shores fifteen years earlier. He was now, in his own estimation, 'a grey haired cripple', and to the expectant throng of reporters he presented a curious spectacle. Now in his mid-fifties, he looked much older. 'But there's little chance of his ever becoming dangerous again,' noted one reporter. 'While chatting with the officers, at times, he was incoherent and senile, but he had intervals of lucidity.'

Whatever his real mental state, George Bidwell seemed to take it all in his stride, happily smiling in the sunshine on the docks, delighted that he was, once more, the centre of attention. Even though the two sergeants had no warrant for his arrest, he was shortly taken to police headquarters on Mott Street. Sunburned and irrepressible, he had to be helped to the carriage. The stories about his damaged legs were clearly not his own exaggerations.

His arrest ushered in something new, which he found baffling. George Bidwell was formally photographed for the first time by the American authorities. Some thought he seemed to enjoy this introduction to a very modern chapter of celebrity and notoriety with his first ever appearance in the 'Rogues' Gallery'. 'My photograph had never before appeared as a star in that ill-omened galaxy,' he later wrote.

At the time, though, there was a general feeling of outrage at the NYPD's high-handedness. 'He was charged with no offense,' *The New York Herald* thundered the next day, 'and as far as appears, suspected of none.' And, when appearing before the duty judge, he was as baffled as the prisoner and the reporters. There were no grounds nor reason to deprive him of his freedom. 'For those reasons, I order that Bidwell be forthwith discharged from custody and be allowed a fair opportunity to take a fresh start in life,' the judge ordered.

Helped outside, George Bidwell once again could play to the crowd. 'I have come here to put myself in the hands of my wife and redeem the past,' he said. Despite the front page news of his earlier dalliances with Nellie Vernon (and their illegitimate child), he soon retired to the family home, 'a neat and verandahed country residence' in Hartford, Connecticut, an otherwise 'obscure village', in one newspaper record.

The year after his release, George Bidwell published a colourful, yet ultimately misleading account of his life in crime, *Forging His Chains*.[39] He was proud of the fact that it had taken him six months to write. 'I have nothing to conceal,' he said on the eve of publication, 'and I offer my life record as a warning to others against crime.'

All throughout, he continued to claim that his younger brother was hardly involved in the great forgeries at all. Though vivid, it was hardly an accurate account of his life to date. As Austin was still in jail, George Bidwell obviously had good reason to down-play his younger brother's involvement. The prisoner himself joined in with his own missives from Chatham Jail. 'Counting from my birth to this hour, I have passed more than one-third of an ordinary lifetime in a Chatham prison cell,' he petitioned at the end of the decade.

The indefatigable Harriet entered into correspondence with members of the royal family, Lord Randolph Churchill and Joseph Chamberlain MP. But most revealing was George Bidwell's own encounter with another member of the British Establishment whom he happened to bump into on the streets of Manhattan. Sir Sydney Waterlow was little changed since he had last seen him in the dock at the Mansion House. They greeted each other if not like long lost friends, then certainly with warmth, despite the circumstances of their original meeting. 'Your brother ought to have been freed years ago,' the former Lord Mayor of London insisted. It was a measure of Sir Sydney's equanimity that he felt the forgers had done their time.

Sir Sydney lived and prospered, remarrying and eventually dying in 1906 when his obituaries noted his charity and devotion to duty. The Waterlow company prospered, not least with the printing of most currencies around the Continent, and that included some 580,000 Portuguese bank notes in 1932 thanks to a conman who fleeced Sir William Waterlow, one of Sydney's sons. Its perpetrator, Alvos dos Reis, better known as 'the Man who Stole Portugal', achieved notoriety, not least when one news-paper reminded its readers that its precedents included 'one of the most skilful and daring forgeries ever perpetrated was the great Bank of England forgery'.

As one newspaper reported in the 1880s, it was thanks mainly to Harriet's pluck that efforts to release Austin Bidwell continued on their native side of the Atlantic. 'Hattie' was indefatigable in petitioning the Marquis of Hartington, several members of Congress and Mr Phelps, the US ambassador. 'A life sentence on a young man of twenty-five years of age for an offense against property seems to me very harsh and inconsistent with the better feeling prevailing in our time,' she began. Another later petition was signed by several prominent authors, including Harriet Beecher Stowe and Mark Twain.

It was Twain who had famously declared that reports of his own death had been greatly exaggerated. Bizarrely, that was a claim that George Macdonnell could eventually make. In the summer of 1886, it was widely reported that Mac had died. Newspapers were full of appreciation for his exploits, nodding, perhaps uncon-sciously, towards the words of Hardinge Giffard, in noting 'for the audacity of its conception, the magnitude of the fraud perpetrated, and the misdirectional skill and ingenuity with which it was attempted, to be carried out, this great crime stands without a parallel in criminal history'.

But it was all a surreal mistake. George Macdonnell was still very much alive, though soon his actual mental state became the cause of much speculation. So too did Austin Bidwell's.

By the turn of the new decade, it seemed that sickness, insanity or suicide were the only possible ways out for Austin Bidwell. 'My fate seemed inevitable,' he later wrote, 'but never for a moment did I cease to believe that future's frowns would one day disappear and that I should yet again feel the warmth and sunshine of her smile.'

Harriet's letter writing campaign continued, and in 1890 she travelled with her brother to London. She repeatedly made the point that, though five murderers had been released in that time and Austin had even saved a fellow prisoner from drowning, the authorities would not allow his release. But in the autumn of 1891, the Home Secretary unexpectedly remitted eighteen months from the prisoner's sentence.

On a cold, frosty evening the following February, nearly twenty years since he had left for Paris after the near fatal derailment, Austin Bidwell had settled down for the night in his dark, freezing cell. All at once, there came a rush of feet and a warder gave him the good news. 'You're free!' he said.

It was, Austin later thought, some sort of hallucination. Thinking he was dreaming, the prisoner was led to freedom, and in the freezing sky he made out the shining iridescence of the Milky Way. 'At the sight of that miracle of glory,' he claimed, 'my heart beat fast.' Austin Bidwell still could not quite comprehend what was happening. 'My release came as a dream,' Austin later remarked, 'and I did not realise that I was a free man for several days.'

Escorted by warders, his greater champion was reunited with him in Liverpool. Accompanied by his 'faithful sister' Harriet on the *Cunarder*, they left for home that February of 1892, never to return.

The rigours of his incarceration had taken their toll. Austin Bidwell was ridiculously thin, weighing less than 130lb. He looked even more gaunt, the full extent of his hollowed-out cheeks hidden by whiskers. His hair was still coal black, but his face was now florid. When he spoke, it was with a distinct English accent. And how that voice had changed. The confidence of youth was replaced by a hoarse raspiness, almost like a ventriloquist without a dummy. When he talked, he did so without moving his lips, a habit, he later explained, that avoided untoward interest from prison guards.

Gradually, his confidence and his voice returned. Eighteen months later, on his return to New Orleans for the first time in twenty years, he was asked by a reporter from the *Daily Picayune* what the moral of his life story was. 'It is this,' he enunciated slowly and clearly:

Wrong doing never pays. If men are indomitable and refuse to be conquered, they can rise from any position, no matter how far down in the mud they may be. In other words, when a man goes to the Devil he must not remain there, but struggle to come back.

'I had gone into prison a vigorous young man,' Austin Bidwell later said. 'I came out worn down; youth was gone, middle age fading and old age seemed settling down on me.' Though he was actually only in his mid-forties, he felt much, much older and, like his brother, he began his own memoirs, which were later published with the same breezy disregard for facts and chronology.

In the interim, Austin and George Bidwell campaigned for the release of their fellow conspirators. In this, they enlisted the help of the Duke of Norfolk, who intervened with the Home Secretary. 'We four have stuck together through twenty years of misery and our friendship has never sustained a flaw,' Austin later said. 'We propose to stand together for the rest of our lives and if hard work and knowledge of affairs will bring success we hope to attain it.'

Their release was not long in coming. Both George Macdonnell and Edwin Noyes Hills met for the first time in two decades on Euston Station before they too headed home. The press reports from the time were unequivocal. Mac had been the genius behind it all, and Hills was now described as 'a snowy-haired, hopeless though perfectly harmless idiot'.

There was a great deal of press interest when, in the company of Mac's sister, Mary, they came to depart from the main terminus for the north-west and Liverpool. They chatted to reporters as best they could. Curiously, standing close by them and singularly failing to be incognito, were two men who looked like farmers. They were warders whose task was to make sure they did leave and never return.

Most relieved was Mary Macdonnell, who had been a toddler when her brother was incarcerated. It had been hard on their family, too, she said. In 1886, their mother had been allowed to see her son for all of two hours in Dartmoor and died shortly thereafter of a broken heart. Her dying wish was to have her daughter carry on the quest and gain a pardon for her brother. 'She has worked ever since as only a woman can work for the object on which her heart was set,' one newspaper reported.

Suddenly, without warning the week before, Mac had been hauled in before the governor. Despite the rigours of incarceration, he quickly returned to his usual overbearing self when told he was about to be freed. Far from being relieved, he was concerned. 'What clothes are we to travel in?' he asked. The governor could hardly believe his ears. When he told George Macdonnell that he would have to leave in the clothes he was wearing – his prison fatigues – the prisoner was defiant. 'Then I decline to go.' The governor said that the provision of a 'liberty suit' (clothes for release) was not in his remit. Characteristically, Mac persisted and, as ever, he took it right up to the wire. Ten minutes before he was taken to Pentonville Prison, he was given a fresh set of clothes.

Shortly thereafter, he met his sister, who had taken the first steamer over. Though showing all the signs of imprisonment ('No one looking on his face could feel anything but pity for the man's wasted years,' one reporter noted), Mac still was chivalrous and helped his sister onto the train. Just before it left, he was asked about his time in jail. 'It is bad,' George Macdonnell replied. 'It is calculated to make men either madmen or brutes. Thank Heaven I have done with it forever.'

March 1892, 5th Avenue Hotel, New York

It was fitting that the thieves of Threadneedle Street were all reunited at the same hotel where, two decades earlier, they had left with such hopes for the future. Now, it was a disorientating experience for all of them, as all around them the city they had once known so well had changed, in many ways beyond all recognition.

So, too, had one of their number, obvious in his eyes and from his deteriorated condition. 'Poor Mac', people would soon say. Although newspapers had reported that George Macdonnell was in good health and Hills 'a jabbering idiot', George Bidwell was soon lamenting that 'the reverse was nearer the truth'.

While the others faced life with what Austin Bidwell characteristically termed 'courage and fortitude unbroken', Mac just would not listen. That night of their reunion, when the drink and food flowed, he didn't make much sense. Despite the other George telling him to take rest for a few months, he promptly got himself arrested under a false name in a foreign country. In September 1892, George Macdonnell told his friends he was returning to France where he was determined to find some of his money from their forgeries two decades before. It had been prompted by his seeing the name of one bank missing from a list of places where they had deposited cash all over Europe. In vain, the Bidwells and Hills told him there was no missing money. 'Nothing would satisfy him but he must go himself,' George Bidwell told reporters.

And when he promptly headed back to France, nobody heard anything from him or about him. His long-suffering sister, Mary, was worried and went in pursuit a few months later only to find her brother imprisoned. He had written a check to cover his hotel bill and for money to return home, but it bounced and he was arrested. It was Willie Pinkerton's brother who filled in the details. 'It is felt that Macdonnell was arrested under an assumed name,' Robert Pinkerton told *The New York Times*. 'Even now, the French police do not know who their prisoner is.'

But it was clear that all was not well with their friend, who was escorted home with his sister. On this, both Robert Pinkerton and George Bidwell were in agreement; they thought Mac had gone mad. George went so far as to say that George Macdonnell should be placed in an asylum. The last word, if there ever could be, came from Austin Bidwell. 'We did not save a dollar of the millions secured from the Bank of England,' he flatly declared, and was living proof that crime did not pay.

George Bidwell had done his best to reap the commercial possibilities from repentance. As Harriet noted in the late 1880s, 'since that time he has spent his earnings and talents in lecturing and writing with the hope that he may warn others from falling into evil ways'.[40]

On one such an occasion a newspaper reported that he had an honest face. 'His hair is iron grey and bushy,' the paper added, 'and he has a heavy iron-grey moustache'. His photograph adorned some of the handbills he distributed to promote a publishing company and the magazine he had created called *The Crusader*, where he warned his readers of the dangers of crime. 'Twenty years' experience among the criminal elements causes me to say,' he fulminated, 'Tremble for the future of this country into which is being poured the desperadoes of all nations.'

In the first issue, for example, there were articles on 'Advice for Young Businessmen to Heed', 'Honest vs. Dishonest Money' and pointedly, 'Salaries of Detectives Cause of their Dishonesty'. George travelled widely throughout the United States to promote his magazine, with the long-suffering Mrs Bidwell in attendance. 'In behalf of that noble wife,' he had announced in his inaugural lecture in 1891, 'I thank you for your generous approval.'

Austin joined him on his release and together they publicly discussed their time in jail to small, but generally appreciative, crowds.[41]

Redemption invariably brings with it blessed relief and, in trying to rebuild their lives, the Bidwell brothers invoked it often. George Bidwell later wrote:

> Success won in honest fight is sweet, but I know from my own experience that the success of crime brings no sweetness, no blessing with it, but leaves the mind a prey to a thousand haunting fears that made a shipwreck of peace.

Certainly, all the thieves of Threadneedle Street were afflicted by what the poets once called the 'melancholy of all things done'. The Bidwells seemed haunted by their deeds, stalked by uncertainty as most of their subsequent business ventures failed, including their publishing firm and *The Crusader*.

Redemption ultimately came to have a greater meaning for someone who had died and then lived again — a claim of messianic fervour that only one of the four forgers could ever make, for he too had found little solace nor peace of mind.

The redeemed seek absolution in death and so when, in the late summer of 1903, several citizens of California received letters from Pastor J.B. Taylor of the Church of the Redeemed, Emeryville, a small city on the San Francisco Bay, they took notice. It came with a plea for forgiveness and redemption:

The indorsed pawn ticket is sent to you by way of restitution. The sender is at the point of death as the result of an accident. He wishes me to say that he once stole some money from you which he is unable to return, but that difference between the value of the locket and the amount it is pledged for is considerably more than the sum stolen. He hopes that you will be able in this way to reimburse yourself.

Some recipients were so moved that they did exactly that. After all, it was one of the tenets of Christian charity to do so. But not everyone was so generous, for as a later press report simply recorded, 'There is no Pastor J.B. Taylor at Emeryville and no Church of the Redeemed', and the person behind it, when arrested by police, was described as 'an old man of about eighty years old and is thought to be slightly abnormal in his mind'. And when charged, they used his full name, as with all notable criminals – George Taylor Macdonnell.

Sunday, 4 October 1903
San Francisco

Poor Mac. He never really ever gave up. A shattered life, a shattered mind and an addiction to crime that he could never overcome. Though only in his late fifties, he looked so much older. A shadow of himself, pained and painful looking. Here was a man who had once coolly laundered gold inside the Bank of England. Now he was attempting nickel-and-dime stuff. In recent months, it transpired, he had advertised for Grand Army veterans to work as an elevator attendant. 'The applicant was requested in the advertisement to inclose a two-cent postage stamp with his application,' one newspaper recorded. 'That was all the profit that Macdonnell got out of his speculation.'

Now he was being charged for defrauding the gullible at $12.50 a pop. In this latest scam, he had posed as H. Epstein, a pawnbroker on Kearny Street, and also as the Reverend Taylor. 'They were directed to return the pawn ticket and the money to "Epstein" whom Macdonnell,' the *San Francisco Call* reported, 'and received the valuable locket and the big diamond.' He had bought a golden locket with Epstein's on Kearny Street. If they returned the pawn ticket and money, they would get the locket and the diamond.

When arrested, he tried to run and was caught in a matter of seconds on the corner of Kearny and Sutton Streets. He was sent to the County Jail on the same day. For the law official who nabbed him, it was not his first encounter with the slightly shambolic figure who still thought he was capable of magic. George W. Hazen of the secret service had first come across Mac two years previously. The old rogue had been living at his sister Mary's house, but when she had become aware of what he was up to, she had thrown him out onto the street.

So Mac and a couple of like-minded ne'er-do-wells had rented a basement where they experimented for a number of months with steel dies and silver. Agent Hazen later found them in possession of 'nubs, dies and other appliances for making counterfeit money'. It had been Mac's idea to flood China and Hawaii with counterfeit dollars made from Mexican coins. As always, they had outsourced the engraving to someone who spilled the beans to the secret service.

Unknown to them at the time, Hazen had been watching their every move. Their arrests in late June 1901 were prompted by Mac's imminent attempt to flee the country (to Vancouver, it was variously reported). When on 14 June that year, the case came to trial in the US District Court, all three were acquitted because the dies found in their possession were blank. So, too, was George Macdonnell's expression as he shuffled away, yet still afflicted by what one newspaper termed 'the pleasure of being wicked'.

History seemed to be repeating itself. The Monday he was arrested in October 1903, it looked like George Macdonnell had packed his bags in case he needed to leave in a hurry. Agent Hazen searched Mac's luggage and found letters, enclosing dollar bills, from parents of soldiers who were on duty in the Philippines. Mac had, it transpired, sent them a group photo of their son and was charged with using the mails to defraud.

When the Church of the Redeemed case eventually came to the trial the following February, Mac's lawyers tried an ingenious defence. The gullible people who had responded to the letter had received value for money. It was not exactly a scam, Mac's counsel argued. 'The strangest part of the story is that Mac has furnished to his attorney a receipt or bill of sale from a firm of wholesale jewellers,' one newspaper reported. Two jewellers testified that the lockets used to entice them were worth 'ten to sixteen dollars' and his 'offer' of $12.50 was a fair price.

The judge directed the jury to acquit him if the lockets were 'of far less value'. Half an hour later, he was found guilty and, once again, because of his age, frailty and the fact he struck several people as not quite being all there ('bad for the love of crime', in one headline) he was given a suspended sentence.

Willie Pinkerton, who was asked to provide a character reference, wondered what to make of it all. A few years later, he was generous enough to say that Mac was simply twice convicted for petty frauds and left it at that.

March 1899
Butte, Montana

The Bidwells never made it into the new century. By 1899, George was in his sixties and Austin was in his late forties. Despite the hardships they had had to endure in prison, both were still good-looking, attractive men whose spirit had clearly been dimmed. They no longer attracted women with the promise of danger and easy money. They were eking as best a living as they could, fetching up in the frontier mining town of Butte in February 1899. They took lodgings together in the Mantle Block, hardly the most salubrious of locations but representing a long held dream.

When he was under arrest in Cuba in the spring of 1873, Austin Bidwell told Willie Pinkerton that his ultimate dream was to end up in either Montana or Kansas where he would live a virtuous and honest life, leaving crime behind and living happily ever after with his wife in tow. Two decades later, the brothers claimed to reporters that they wanted to start in the mining business. They had, they said, backing from several sources.

The reality was they were near penury, sharing a room and having to skip meals. An accumulation of genteel poverty and lack of nourishment, hardly helped by their time in English jails, meant that both were wrecks of their former selves. Few citizens of the booming mining town had any idea who the two tramp-like figures were who spent most of their time skulking along Main Street.

In the preternatural cold of the Rocky Mountain spring, Austin Bidwell was suddenly taken sick and died on 7 March 1899. The autopsy records he succumbed to 'natural causes', while newspaper reports said 'grippe'. A few days later, a grieving George delivered a lecture on his brother's life to enable him to meet the burial costs. Few came to listen. They were old news. 'After the lapse of a quarter of a century,' Reuters reported from New York, 'the details have grown faint, and are forgotten by most persons.' As George only sold fifty tickets, he became extremely despondent. Appeals to other citizens in the town failed to raise the cash needed. Accordingly, Austin Bidwell was dispatched to a pauper's grave.

While out begging for money George Bidwell slipped and fell, injuring his legs that had already been weakened from his incarceration. He was confined to bed in the same room at the Mantle House that he had shared with his brother. On 25 March, a cleaning lady found him dead in the same bed in which his younger brother had died. Once more, the autopsy showed that he had died from natural causes. George Bidwell could clearly no longer face living without his brother, and his inability to pay for a decent burial was the final straw. 'He died in want,' *The New York Times* dutifully reported the next day, 'and the body of his brother is yet unburied, although it has been three weeks dead.'

Neither brother left wills, for the good reason they had little money to leave behind. Nor were there any deathbed confessions nor letters of redemption left with solicitors to be read out as warnings to others. Austin Bidwell, though no less melancholic at times, had once asked, 'Is there any crime under heaven where property is involved that such an eternity of suffering ought not to expiate?' This serves as some sort of summary of a life that, as he himself had painfully acknowledged on that fatal, final day at the Old Bailey, had been wasted with so many opportunities lost.

Saturday, 22 August 1908
London
....

The last ever public sighting of one of the gang took place when a brisk, alert old man – 'with a heavy grey moustache', in one account – was back in the town where last he had been tried thirty-five years earlier. Now Edwin Noyes Hills was back in London with other reformed criminals lecturing about the dangers of gambling.

Though that same newspaper account eulogised 'a crime story which the world has not forgotten', the man himself was still claiming that he was only dimly aware of what happened. For now, he was travelling around England on an anti-gambling tour, led by John P. Quinn, 'the prince of card sharers', who formed the International Anti-Gambling Association of New York.

They had found willing and appreciative audiences in their native United States. All could have made millions from carrying on frauds, but instead, wanted to rail against its evils. For the rest of his life, Hills wanted to rescue people from the folly of gambling 'which was my ruin', and after a successful tour, came to England. When asked about his former colleagues, sadness clouded his eyes.

The Bidwells were long dead. As for George Macdonnell, 'he was killed'. How or where is difficult to establish but it is likely that he was one of the many hundreds who perished in the great San Francisco earthquake. Hills claimed he was writing his own version of the story and, with contacts made from acting as some sort of publishing agent, it would appear in print shortly. At the end of the evening, he left the stage, never to be seen publicly or heard from again, leaving no trace at all of that intriguing manuscript.

All the others in this story – like Hills – went on to greater glory or faded from view.

Willie Pinkerton assumed the role of the grand old man of crime prevention. Often wintering in California, he passed away at the Biltmore Hotel in Los Angeles in December of 1912, aged 78. He was buried in Chicago and many criminals whom he had helped over the years attended.

It was apt that the summer before, Pink had given a valedictory address to the International Association of Police Chiefs in Toronto.[42] Using it as an opportunity to relate his long litany of greatest 'hits', almost inevitably he referred at one point to the Bidwells. 'They both died in Butte Montana a few years ago and so far as I ever heard,' he said sadly, 'never went back to a life of crime.' The theme of his speech was simple. Crime was not genetic. Poverty and environment were the cause of criminality. Black sheep were in every family and the Bidwells were a prime example of that. 'I have always contended that there is no criminal class,' Pink expounded. 'I mean, hereditary criminals.' He cited various examples of miscreants who 'guarded the secret of their lives from their children'. 'I know there are scientists who claim that crime descends from father to son,' he told his appreciative audience, 'but I have known children whose father and mother were criminals and who developed into good citizens of useful lives.'

It was obvious that Pink had clearly never heard of Austin's brother, Benson, and his son, Charley, inventors, so they claimed, of a motor that would never run out. Benson Bidwell, who had buried his brothers nine years earlier, also claimed he had invented the trolley car and electric fan. In the fall of 1908, his invention of a perpetual motion machine had all the hallmarks of being a great breakthrough. But, as ever, it was a great con. A series of adverts solicited investors and something like $225,000 was raised. When shown at a subsequent trial, electrical engineers revealed that the motor was impractical.

Carbonic acid gas was poured in to make the outside appear covered in frost. During one exhibition, it became so hot that smoke started to blow out. So Charley Bidwell sat next to the machine and lit up and puffed on a cigar to hide the fumes. Both were arrested in October 1908 for fraud, and Benson, aged 73, was sentenced to a jail term of not less than one nor ten years.

So much remains and yet so little. 'When an honest man makes a mistake he has not only sympathy, but can always pick himself up again,' Austin Bidwell had once written. 'When a rogue makes a mistake it may easily be and almost always is fatal.'

And yet, even after his passing, the truth was at best elusive. Nobody at the time ever felt they got to the bottom of the story. Were the thieves of Threadneedle Street acting alone? Who else was involved? What about the other forgers like George Wilkes, Walter Sheridan and George Engels, who supposedly ran scared because of all the 'fallen women' they associated with?[43]

So many mysteries remain, but none quite as curious as an event that occurred just a few weeks after the Bidwell brothers' own demise.

Sunday, 11 June 1899
Bellevue Hospital, New York City

'You have a very short time to live' — and in the eerie quiet of the hospital, it was true. On this cool evening, there played out a final act, not of redemption but of compassion, when an old man slowly and painfully shuffled into the Bellevue Hospital. He had been found ill and emaciated at the junction between 16th and 5th Avenues. 'I am friendless and homeless,' he told doctors. 'I cannot obtain food.'

His name, he said, was Edward Errell and he was 61 years of age. For the last few weeks he had been living as a hobo in alleyways and in parks, begging where he could and foraging. Treating him for malnutrition, the doctor on duty, Dr H.M. Taylor, asked, 'If you have any friends, give me their names. You have a very short time to live.'

It was clear this wretched fellow was fading fast. 'Tell me something of yourself,' the doctor prompted him.

The old man let out a weary sigh. 'Must I give you something of my record?' he asked, his exhaustion eclipsing his defiance.

'You had better,' Dr Taylor said. 'You are close to death.'

For what seemed an eternity, as his breathing became shallower and shallower, the old man was quiet as he pondered this last act. Slowly, he gathered the strength to speak and what he said was astonishing. 'I am an engraver,' he said at last. 'Would to God that I had never founded an engraver's tool.' He paused, looking for forgiveness and absolution. 'I was last employed by Austin Bidwell, the Bank of England forger. My record is known well enough. Now I am homeless and unknown.' He paused, gasping for air.

According to the doctor, he would say no more. His breathing was fading now and the effort proved too much. He was consumed by silence and the memories. Ten minutes later, he passed away. His body was taken to the morgue.

So who was Edward Errell? Was he really involved in the Bank of England forgeries?

A search of contemporary records reveals nobody of that name in any of the lengthy reminiscences or official records. If his age on death was correct, that would have made him in his late forties when the bank frauds were being executed. He would have been much older than the thieves of Threadneedle Street. Possibly he might have worked with Austin Bidwell more recently, in the last decade or more. But it was clear that Austin had never returned to a life of crime.

And, in the final analysis, who knows? If their criminal history started with one ambiguity, it surely ends on this one. That would be the Bidwells' greater legacy – that in all their blind ambition, they were consumed not just by the fates and furies, but mysteries of their own making. Perhaps that is how they would like to be remembered best, that for all their human foibles and vulnerabilities, they and the mysteries they engendered remain unanswered.

Notes

1   Three weeks later, Sir Sydney exacted his revenge with a splendidly feline putdown. During the remand hearing of Saturday, 29 March 1873, the lawyers discussed the passbook used on one of Warren's bank accounts. 'I must confess that personally I do not like the idea of my passbook being possibly handed to a stranger,' the lord mayor said, 'even to a very respectable-looking person like Dr. Kenealy.' The Irish lawyer's often breathtaking lack of respect for judges would shortly come to a head with the Tichborne case that involved a convoluted claim on a title. A cause célèbre in fashionable circles, Dr Kenealy shortly took over the representation of Arthur Orton, the claimant. After various outrageous antics as the case played out, within a couple of years, Dr Kenealy was expelled from the Bar. Oddly, during his own later imprisonment, George Macdonnell claimed to have gotten to know Arthur Orton very well.

2   When the forgers first arrived in England in April 1872, George Macdonnell told Austin Bidwell that he wanted to be reconciled with his father. Mac said he was 'determined to send him $10,000 and so make good the money his father had given him to establish himself in New York'. This repayment would have come from the large sums they would remove from the Bank of England.

3   It is difficult to point to an exact time when Pinkerton and Shore encountered Austin Bidwell on the Strand. Austin's reaction is taken from Pink's note on p. 40 of F5/3 (referring to the documents in the Bank of England Archive), written on 16 April 1873. In his *Daily Inter Ocean* interview from September 1891, Pink suggests he had arrived in London in October 1872. This is supported by his sworn affidavit in TNA HO 144 20568 dated 26 August 1873. The Bidwell brothers, however, were only in London together at the start of September 1872. For most of October, they were travelling around the continent. This event most likely took place in November when they had returned (see p. 157). In some other accounts, it is said that Pink saw both Bidwells and Mac but this clearly was a misremembering compounded by his last ever interviews in April 1912 (see p. 331 and note 42).

4   By comparison, the collapse of Overend Gurney – the nearest equivalent in terms of byzantine legal proceedings – had generated 164 folio pages of printed depositions. The phone hacking trial in 2014 at the Old Bailey took three years of police work, 42,000 pages of evidence, seven months of hearings, the work of up to eighteen barristers at any one time and a dozen or more defendants facing their accusers (see Nick Davies summary, the *Guardian*, 25 June 2014).

5   The timing of their arrival from Brazil is hard to ascertain but pp. 26–7 of the Prosecution Brief (F5/8) suggests Mac had returned at the end of July/early August 1872. He was reported in Eastbourne on 3 August 1873. On page 105 of his memoirs, Austin Bidwell says they had a happy return with Mac in Paris but this cannot be so. The Freshfields timeline document F5/10 notes that the brothers were in London – staying at the Langham Hotel – by 20 August.

6   George Macdonnell's letter to 'Friend Phil' was dated on 26 August 1872 and may be found on p. 25 of the Prosecution Brief, F5/8. Nobody is certain who the intended recipient was. The best guess was either the detective Philip Farley (see Chapter 13) or else a forger in Manhattan known as Phillip Hargreaves. It was signed 'Harry', a name that Mac often called himself. The writing seemed to match George Macdonnell's. The related mystery of their 'German friend' was compounded by a handwritten note in the margin of this letter. 'Don't tell anyone but Engels that you have heard from me – James Doolittle.' The police never got to the bottom of that particular reference and the meaning remains obscure.

7   George Engels had also been referred to as 'George Eagle' in contemporary accounts, sometimes as 'Ingall' or 'Ingalls' and even 'Dutch George' 'He talks too much' may be found on p. 42 of F5/3 of Willie Pinkerton's letter of 20 April 1873 from Cuba. Sheridan and the 'disreputable' comments are found in both *The New York Times* of 31 March 1876 and *The New York Sun* account from September 1873. Further details concerning Engels may be found on p. 195 of Byrnes and also in *The New York Times* of 2 January 1881, which reported his arrest in Italy.

8   To understand the 'nominal value' of a bond consider what happens if you buy petrol at a garage. You will pay the market price per litre, which will vary depending on supply and demand The unit of measurement – one litre – is fixed. So it is with bonds, essentially IOUs issued by companies and governments. Each bond had a fixed nominal value, often £100 for a sterling bond. This is set when the bond was issued and remained the same until it was redeemed (bought back and cancelled by the issuer). On a fixed-income bond, the nominal value is used to work out the annual coupon. If the rate is, say, 5%, then the coupon payment each year will be £5. At the end of its life, the amount the issuer will pay to redeem it would have been set by the bond market. This would usually be less than the stated value.

9   As with the opening of the Millennium Dome in Greenwich in more recent times, bad organisation, unreadiness, confusion and exorbitant ticket prices (coinciding with a stock market crash) had caused a groundswell of grumbling about the great exhibition in Vienna. Even worse, there had been cholera attacks ('which cleared Vienna of strangers' in one account) and, in the summer of 1873, a fire.

10 In late Victorian times, somebody was killed on the rails virtually every week. Profit rather than safety was invariably the reason. Improvements such as block signals and brakes – of the kind Mr Warren discussed with Colonel Francis – were reluctantly added refinements. There is a telling anecdote from the Lord Mayor of London. As a Member of Parliament, Sir Sydney Waterlow had voted for the consolidation of railways in the 'Garden of England'. When asked by his biographer why the House had sanctioned the creation of a monopoly in Kent, Sir Sydney airily replied, 'Well, there were seventy-six railway directors in the House of Commons.'

11 As Austin Bidwell later noted (see p. 82), the bank spent slightly more than it had lost to retrieve the money. An exhaustive ledger, more than 700 pages in length, shows that the bank had paid £107,011 8s 10d to Freshfields in total (see p. 704 of F5/34).

12 During his preamble, Mr McIntyre had established that the colonel had been a bank manager for thirteen years, having been a sub-agent at Leeds and then agent at Hull. Peregrine Francis began his duties at the western branch on 3 March 1872 and had, he explained, inherited a well-ordered branch. He did not need to go over the banking account of existing customers with his predecessor as he 'had the same sub-manager who could give me all the information'. That was Mr Fenwick who had opened the account for Mr Warren (see p. 92).

13 There was another Liverpudlian connection that showed how slippery George Macdonnell could be. After he was jailed for the Tiffany's robbery at the end of 1867 (see p. 88), Mac spent three years and two months in prison. He was, by all accounts, a model prisoner who was allowed to work as a waiter in the prison coffee shop. According to Allan Pinkerton's account, some time after his release, Mac was travelling to Louisville, Kentucky, on a train with, he claimed, a ticket to Liverpool in his pocket. He struck up a conversation with a cattle drover who was liberally swigging from a bottle of brandy. He soon fell asleep under the influence. 'I had twenty-six hundred dollars when you took a seat beside me, and now I haven't a cent!' he exclaimed after he woke up. Mac feigned surprise. 'Do you think I would take your money?' he declared. George Macdonnell insisted on being arrested and searched to prove his innocence. 'Get my baggage and let the officers make a search that will satisfy them,' Mac added, 'and you.' While the cattleman had been sleeping, George Macdonell had removed all his money. At the next stop, Mac alighted to buy some newspapers and envelopes, folding the greenbacks within the newsprint. He then addressed the envelopes to various fictitious people in Manhattan and posted this haul at the next station where he alighted again. Typically, Mac eventually insisted on paying the cattleman's full fare and they departed the best of friends.

14 The details concerning Austin Bidwell's protracted wedding preparations may be found in F5/ 8 and on p. 17 of F5/10. The 'conversation with the boys' and the comment about 'cruel mamma' is related in Pink's letter from Cuba of 20 April 1873 on p. 43 F5/3. All the various shenanigans that preceded the ceremony are covered on pp. 89–125 of F5/8. As is clear from the text, some of the original correspondence is missing. In his memoirs, Austin claims that in the week before he had joined Jeannie and her family at the Hotel St James, rue Saint

Honoré where they all went sightseeing. As the Prosecution Brief makes clear, the Devereux family did not arrive until the wedding day. All subsequent details about Harry Nunn are taken from Pinkerton's 11 April 1873 letter from Cuba (F5/3, pp. 24–5).

15 *The Way We Live Now* 'grew out of the compost of a lifetime's observation, anger, amusement and writing experience,' in the words of one of Trollope's biographers. His book took shape in May 1873 at the same time the Mansion House hearings were playing out. The book concerns a financier called Melmotte who is believed to be the richest man in the world. He is vile, shameless and violent, an unappealing amalgam of all the various robber barons of the time. 'What are we coming to when such as he is an honoured guest at our tables?' asks one character. But nobody else sees through him and they fall over themselves to invest in his South Central Pacific and Mexican railway, a murky fraud based on limitless credit and commercial overkill. It was similar to the one Mac and the Bidwells said they were helping to build in Brazil the summer before (see p 109). In this regard, George Macdonnell preposterously claimed on the last day of the Old Bailey trial that Edwin Noyes Hills had thought he was going to be involved in a stock-mining business 'rather placing on the stock exchange of London depreciated silver mining stock of the United States'. When summoned to London, he had, Mac claimed, 'no idea of any forgery'.

16 As a result of the Franco-Prussian war, cash payments at the Bank of France had been temporarily suspended. In Walter Bagehot's estimation, the Old Lady of Threadneedle Street was left as 'the only great repository in Europe where gold could at once be obtained'. In other words, it was vulnerable. Not only could it attract 'hot money' the lack of reserves might break the bank if they were allowed to flow away Oddly, Bagehot assumed this would not result from direct criminal action but rather lack of oversight.

17 In Allan Pinkerton's ghosted version of the Kenney story, the lawyer said he wanted to invest the money in bonds to be sent to his office in the Union Trust Company's building. There they would be paid for by a certified cheque drawn on the National Park Bank. While in negotiation, the police got wind that something was afoot. Kenney then disappeared off the face of the earth It seemed George Macdonnell had planned to present two certified cheques. One, for a small amount, was genuine. the other was a forgery. When Cooke's messenger would have arrived at his office, they would have gone to the National Park Bank together. The genuine cheque would have been certified in front of the messenger; they would have returned to Mr Kenney's office and, en route, swapped the cheques. Even if the authorities did catch up with him, there was nothing they could do. Kenney had not actually carried out the act so could not be prosecuted.

18 The footsteps included those of an unassuming Bostonian called Alfred Charles Hobbs a couple of decades earlier. Termed a 'mid-century Melvillean trickster', Hobbs had been expressly invited by the Bank of England's managers to show that their security was not unassailable. Hobbs was a celebrated lock maker who had amazed Victorian England by cracking open supposedly impregnable safes. In September 1851, Hobbs became the sensation of the National Exhibition and, in one later account, introduced himself to officials at the Old Lady of Threadneedle Street. When he did enter the bank, Hobbs realised he had

met his match. He did not get anywhere near the vaults. Led through darkened alleys and narrow passages, armed guards were everywhere. 'It would be sheer folly for anyone trying to fleece the Bank of England,' Hobbs later declared.

19 A further aspect to this extraordinary Fifth Day of the trial was its sheer length, seven hours, the longest yet. As the jury were returned to the City Terminus Hotel in one account, they 'were taken for an airing in a coach'. The story of the guns in court seems to be a later embellishment, recorded in various American newspapers. In Ann Huxley's account, everyone in the court – the judge, too – carried a gun. Nellie Vernon's various letters which were produced in court may be found in F5/10 of the Bank archive. In an earlier hearing at the Mansion House, she had testified that she had recognised all sixteen of them. 'They are those I received from George Bidwell,' she had said under oath. 'I wrote him letters and received letters from him in answer.' Charles Chabôt would shortly pronounce that they were 'in the same handwriting as the letters produced, spoken to by Miss Vernon'.

20 The various Bidwell sisters and spouses were also used to hide money. Willie Pinkerton learned that Austin's sister-in-law, Martha A. Brewer, had received bonds from her estranged husband by post. 'You must hide it away well protected from damp and mice until you can get it into John's hands without mailing it to his Post Office', George had written when holed up in Edinburgh. He went on to explain, 'he has better places for hiding than you'. When the Pinkerton operatives encountered Hattie at Black Lake around the same time, she cheerfully told them that she could not 'imagine her brothers mixed up in anything as they were too well brought up etc.' Her brothers only ever did anything for John. Hattie then went into a rant about only getting a few lines from Austin or George – never any money. When she had calmed down, Harriet acknowledged a letter, stating that she could not recall the date but remembered it was from France. This, she claimed, 'was the only letter she had received from him'.

21 In the official court transcript, the date is given as 6 March, one of the few mistakes made by the stenographers Barnett & Buckler in many hundreds of pages.

22 In the original affidavit prepared against Noyes, Nellie Vernon and Meunier in March 1873 (F5/1), Freshfields stated that it would be hard to prosecute her. They would have liked to keep her in prison ('It would be infinitely preferable', they noted), but there was no legal basis to do so.

23 Edwin Noyes Hills had taken care to bring with him sketches of the milking device that Ellen Franklin never actually saw. She took this, and his other claim that he had been in the British Isles for three weeks, at face value. Pointedly, he never took Ellen to Ford's Hotel where he had been staying immediately beforehand. Curiously, there was another American counterfeiter of the same name who was suspected of being in England at the time. It did seem strange that one fraudster used the name of this other Edward Hall – who was well known to the police – to hide his own real identity.

24 Edwin Noyes Hills made several trips to Rugby – with and without George Bidwell (see p. 209) – and also to Birmingham and Stafford. Nellie testified that one evening she said to him,

'You have telegraphed from Rugby.' He replied, enigmatically, 'I know I did.' This prompted an extraordinary exchange on the stand on the fifth day of the Old Bailey trial. Mr Watkin Williams pressed her on exactly which date Hills had gone there. Ellen Franklin remembered receiving one particular telegram from Rugby that might well have turned up one Saturday 'Can't you identify it?' he asked. 'No,' she replied, holding them in her hand. 'Look at those three!' Watkin Williams exploded. 'I did not look at the telegram,' she explained. 'I only just read them when they came.'

25 Several officials wondered about the truthfulness of Frances Catherine Gray, who was widely believed to have been involved with this eponymous American fraudster. William E. Gray had started his career as a stockbroker before pursuing, as one newspaper later remarked, 'the sharp practices which subsequently made him a fugitive from justice'. That involved cashing bonds in Manhattan that he did not own: a crime for which he was jailed. Gray eventually ended up in London where he pretended to be the nephew of a great philanthropist. He lived in high comfort, 'leading a chequered and not unromantic life on the other side of the water', as another American newspaper noted. A few weeks after Frances Gray identified George Macdonnell in person, a newspaper reported that she had indeed 'left this country with, or followed, William E Gray, whose exploits so startled Wall Street some two years ago'. There was a school of thought that Frances was William Gray's mistress, either in his employ or involved in his nefarious schemes. However, nothing was found to connect her to him – or, indeed, his crimes.

26 The prosecution was convinced that both Hills and Macdonnell had originally thought it safer to take both Ellen Franklin and Frances Gray with them, so as to remove the two most obvious witnesses who could identify them. 'What they would have done with them if they once got them to America is a totally different question', Freshfields recorded for the files, 'but we cannot help thinking that part of the scheme was not only to go themselves but to remove those with whom they had been living'.

27 On p.157 of his memoirs, George Bidwell claims that on this day he nearly took another vessel: 'That was the last passage ever made by the magnificent steamer Atlantic', he later wrote. In fact, he could not have done. The Atlantic did not leave for another two weeks and sank off the coast of Halifax on 31 March 1873. It was, in several estimations, the biggest maritime disaster until the *Titanic* in 1912 and the *New York Herald* declared it 'another epoch in the history of the world's calamities'.

28 In this same letter, George Bidwell says they had 'foolishly' left London Their escape and the repeated remands of the Edwin Noyes Hills trials had been front-page news for several days. He enclosed several clippings about the most recent examination at the Mansion House, clearly delighted at the attention they were getting.

29 Details on the Edinburgh sequence are taken from newspapers published the next day, especially the 3 April issues of the *Daily Telegraph* and the *Edinburgh Daily Telegraph*. In his original testimony at the Mansion House, Detective McKelvie was not sure if anybody else overheard his surreal exchange with the prisoner. He also stated for the record that the coal

porter who came to help him would not have seen the thrusting of the stick, but he might have been aware of some of what transpired.

30 All previous accounts of Austin Bidwell's time in Cuba (including his own) contain inconsistencies and errors. According to the tabulated diary in F5/10, Austin had married Jeannie on Saturday, 8 February 1873, in Paris. In his memoirs, he says it was a Friday. The newlyweds departed for Bayonne that same weekend; it would have taken them a couple of days to reach the Spanish border. They were stuck in Spain for roughly three weeks. Contemporary press reports fix the timing of the train delays and the appointment of Castelar. The trip to Cuba aboard the Martinique took eighteen days, Austin says, and discusses the details from pp.172 to 175 of his autobiography. According to p.180 of F5/3, the Bidwells embarked in Havana on Monday, 17 March though the New York Herald of 21 March reported it as Saturday, 15 March. The couple were in Cuba for less than a week, as he was arrested on 21 March. Willie Pinkerton did not arrive until 1 April (F5/3, passim), the date on which the New York papers noting Austin's original arrest arrived in London. In his memoirs, Austin Bidwell says that the news of the forgery had not reached the island when he arrived in Cuba. This is not borne out by the record that clearly shows word had been spreading since the start of March, with the physical arrival of the New York newspapers. According to his memoirs, Austin says he first became aware of the story while eating breakfast on 14 February 1873. On that date, he and Jeannie were still stuck in the Pyrenees and the fraud was ongoing and as yet undetected.

31 On Tuesday, 4 March 1873, an overnight telegram from Freshfields in London pointed suspicions towards the Bowery. 'Who is a Mrs Warren supposed to live on 88th Street and Henry and Pike Streets?' it asked. 'Is her husband with her? Is he likely to be Warren the forger? Did a man passing by name of Macdonnell arrive by ship Calabria, leaving England on 22nd?' As a result, Willie Pinkerton put a watch on the steamer of that name upon its subsequent arrival. A couple of Pinkerton operatives also enquired if anybody – male or female – by the name of Warren lived at that New York City intersection. They diligently interviewed 'every person that any information could easily be got from', such as postmen, grocers and saloon keepers, but there was no trace of anyone called Warren in the neighbourhood.

32 The smelling of the rat once George Macdonnell arrived in Manhattan at the end of March later culminated with the 'Trial of the Detectives' in November 1873, which is covered on p.319. Many of the details reported about the boarding of the Thuringia came from various depositions and testimonies in that later trial, which may be found in F5/31 in the Bank of England archive. Document F5/17 contains the Bank of England's letters on the matter, while newspaper clips in F5/31 include: the New York Tribune, 31 October 1873 and 8 November 1873; the New York Sun on 24 October 1873; and the New York World, 11 November 1873, all of which were used in this chapter.

33 In his memoirs, Austin says those strains had been prompted by an 'international incident'. The Virgilis was a Spanish gunboat that captured a gang of American filibusters. Thirty of them had been accidentally killed. The only problem is that this event occurred in October 1873, six months after he was arrested and five after he left Havana.

34 Details about Jimmy Irving are taken from his New York Times obituary (20 February 1895), Austin Bidwell's interview with the St Louis Globe Democrat (2 November 1896) and the first few chapters of his autobiography That obituary erroneously records that one of Irving's greatest successes was arresting Mac as part of the Bank of England job in 1869.

35 In the Bank of England archive, Austin Bidwell's letters from this time are annotated 1, 2 and 3 in the prosecution exhibitions. These were all written and sent at the end of Easter Week. It is not clear which of all of his later letters (marked 4 onwards) were seen by Jeannie or forwarded by Pink after Austin asked the detective to destroy them. See Pinkerton's 16 April letter F5/3 and also other correspondence in F5/6.

36 In the 'friend Phil' letter that Mac had sent the previous August (p.114 and Note 6), the sum of $400 was mentioned. That was why Willie Pinkerton suspected it had been addressed to Detective Farley and was clearly some sort of protection money. An even bigger mystery surrounds what happened next. In the account given by George Dilnot, an emissary from the criminal underworld confronted Jimmy Irving directly. They wanted their cut. The detective said he did not know what the fellow was talking about and carried on about his business

37 The trial of Irving and Farley was not the final legal word. In September 1873, George Macdonnell petitioned the Manhattan District Attorney for the return of his diamonds. The Bank of England had kept them, as they were the proceeds of crime. While imprisoned in England, Mac had assigned them to his latest American attorneys in lieu of his fee. The later legal complications went all the way up to the United States Secretary of the Treasury who, as everybody expected, sided with the Old Lady of Threadneedle Street. George Macdonnell never saw the diamonds again.

38 Jimmy Irving bitterly resented his transfer to the Harbor Police. The Seneca became party central, which was why he was so drunk when he crashed it. A year later, Irving then started his own private detective agency but died in February 1885. When Austin Bidwell's memoirs appeared a decade later, Irving could no longer sue for libel, hence his identifying the detective by name. Equally significantly, Austin never mentioned Philip Farley by name, who was still alive (and later wrote his own memoirs).

39 According to Austin Bidwell, his elder brother had put pen to paper somewhat against his better judgement. Forging My Own Chains was, in one account, highly successful and allowed him to spend '$10,000 and five years trying to enact his brother's release', according to one later newspaper report.

40 There followed an unexpected and delicious twist of Schadenfreude at the end of November 1893 with a financial scandal involving the man who had unearthed their scam twenty years before. Frank May was forced to resign from the Bank of England as he had been inducing his colleagues to lend money on questionable securities. When these debts were called in, a loss of £50,000 was reported. The money had been used by his son, a stockbroker, to shore up insolvent trusts – perhaps May had taken a cue from the Bidwells

and kept it in the family? Though the Bank of England denied any wrong doing, May was pensioned off. A cartoon shortly appeared in Punch showing an old lady wearing a petticoat, crossing the street, whose shoes and lower layers were covered in mud. The Old Lady of Threadneedle Street had, it was clear, been sullied. Perhaps the shame was too much for Frank May, who died suddenly four years later.

41 During their lectures, the Bidwell brothers would show a cat-o'-nine-tails, as well as the ball and chain in which George had been placed in solitary confinement. It had, both of them explained, caused the most horrible injuries imaginable. 'His hands are large', another newspaper reporter noted of the elder brother, 'and the fingers are bent out of shape'. One thing had not changed: George Bidwell still loved an audience and invariably ended his presentation with pictures of his wife, Martha, who kept their home and stood by him, as well as his youngest grandchild, 'a pretty little thing', one newspaper report had it, 'who loved her grandpa'.

42 In this, his last major public speech, Willie Pinkerton once more gave vent to the unfound rumour that he had personally foiled the plot of the great forgeries on the Old Lady of Threadneedle Street. 'By a happy chance, I happened to be in England on business for our agency and met these men on the streets and told the English police all about them,' he said. Once again, he falsely claimed that he had arrested Austin Bidwell with the Cuban police, 'on his arrival on a steamship'.

43 One further mystery occurred over a year after their trial at the Old Bailey. In a US court it was suggested that the Bidwells had been involved in the Spence Pettis case, where a criminal had forged railroad checks in Massachusetts. Though Austin had confessed as much to Pink in Cuba, at the time that Pettis was arrested Austin was already in jail and one witness did not recognise Austin Bidwell in a photograph.

Acknowledgements

I owe a deep and sincere series of thanks to many people on both sides of the Atlantic for their help, advice and wise counsel. Given that much of the transatlantic story started and ended in Liverpool, so, too did my research. I would like to record my gratitude to several Merseyside institutions: the staff of Liverpool University library were unfailingly helpful as were their colleagues at the Maritime Archives & Library and the magnificently refurbished Liverpool Central Library. At the Merseyside Maritime Museum, Ian Murphy, deputy director, provided many insights.

Most of the detailed research was conducted deep within the Bank of England itself at its remarkably well-organised archive. I am particularly grateful for all the archivists' help, good humour and the fact that nothing was ever too much trouble during my repeated visits: former Head of the Archive, Sarah Millard, Archive Manager, Michael Anson, and Ben White, Lorna Williams, Clea Hodgson and Margherita Orlando.

For assistance on American aspects of the story, I would like to thank Kenneth R. Cobb, the former director of the Municipal Archives of the City of New York, Michael Chuchro of ChicagoCop.com, Lt Steve Kramer of the Greater Cincinnati Police Museum and Kevin Fredette at Western Virginia University. Others were prompt in answering queries and providing information: professors Dorothy Walkowitz and Carl-Ludwig Holtfrerich, Ellen Terrell at the Library of Congress, Lyn Crawford at the Royal Bank of Scotland archive, John Davies at the Mansion House, Charles Henty, Under-Sheriff and Secondary of London, at the Central Criminal Court, Smita Shah at the Bar Council, Emma Harris at the Law Society and Oksana Newman and all her staff at Cheshire East Libraries.

When I formally started work on this project in early 2011, a whole new world order was emerging in publishing. For their advice in navigating the various shoals and sandbanks in which even an experienced author might become accidentally stranded, I would like to thank Carrie Kania, Al Zuckerman, Angharad Kowal, Andrew Lownie, Will

Francis, Bob Dofrio and, alas, the late Nick Webb, whose peerless help over the years is now sorely missed. In his stead, though, comes the best agent I have ever worked with, Humfrey Hunter, and the best commissioning editor, Mark Beynon. I would like to thank them both for their tolerance, encouragement and, at times, forbearance as I wrestled with this complicated story. Their insights and humour were a boon and a blessing. I consider myself very fortunate to have worked with them on this project. At The History Press, many thanks to Juanita Hall, Jemma Cox and Sarah Wright who saw this book to press.

Various friends and family members read drafts and suggested improvements. I owe a particular debt of gratitude to my parents-in-law, Allan and Linda Jones (who have never had the dubious privilege of an author in the house before), and my mother Joyce (who has). That they are all still talking to me is testament to their better natures rather than mine.

All images in the plate section are from Austin and George's autobiographies unless otherwise credited.

Reading nineteenth-century references to extreme rascality struck a chord thanks to my wife's splendidly naughty cat, Tilly, who let me work unaided – well, most of the time. And finally to Sarah herself, my constant joy and soul mate. Without her love and support this book could never have been written let alone completed. I much appreciate her inspiration, not least for motivating me towards the computer on cold winter mornings and, come to think of it, warm summer ones, too. That my original work on the research started about the time we met and the fact this book has gone to press on the third anniversary of our wedding day is one of those – with apologies to Hardinge Giffard QC – accidents of history, rather more wonderful than those that befell the four forgers who inhabited our workroom for perhaps rather too long than was necessary.

Nicholas Booth
2015

Permissions

Grateful acknowledgement is made to the UK National Archive for its Crown copyright material, which is reproduced by permission of the Controller of HMSO. Similarly, all material from the Bank of England is reproduced by kind permission of the Bank of England Archive.

Photographs in the plate section are taken from the Bidwell biographies (no longer in copyright), the Library of Congress, the National Archive and, for most of the portraits, The Bank of England. They are reproduced here by courtesy of the Bank of England Archive and The National Archive.

Bibliography & Sources

The main sources of information for this book came from the archives of the Bank of England (BoE) and The National Archives, UK (TNA). The former material is collected together under the heading of 'The Freshfield Papers: Records of The Warren Forgeries'. There are thirty-five separate files referred to by number below. This cornucopia contains many original documents and copies that were all drawn up in 1873 by hand. It includes the full transcript of the trial of the four forgers at the Old Bailey as well as the various Mansion House hearings that preceded it. The bank archive has all the detailed investigations carried out by William Pinkerton (including his own contemporaneous notes and observations) and his operatives for Freshfields, the Bank of England's London solicitors, as well as those done across the Atlantic for Blatchford, Seward, Griswold and Da Costa in Manhattan.

Crucially, the Bank of England material includes the complete brief for the prosecution (document F5/8, which numbers 187 pages) and its associated timeline (more formally a 'tabulated diary') in document F5/10. Both provided the narrative spine for this book. They clear up many of the inconsistencies and errors in a lot of the coverage of the case. Much of the action was not linear and there was a complicated, interwoven tapestry of events and actions. Aliases and deliberate obfuscation were the norm. So far as possible, the author has made all names consistent, though there were many variations (even within the same documents).

In particular, the Freshfields timeline recreated precisely what the forgers were up to from when they arrived in England in April 1872 to their apprehension a year later. Alas, there is no such illumination concerning any chronology before that: the timing and exact sequence of events before 1872 often remain clouded in mystery. Many records have been lost or destroyed, such as the Pinkertons (as noted in the text as a result of the Chicago Fire in October 1871). Many other official US and county records around the time of the Civil War are also patchy. The originals of the Freshfields documents were destroyed during the Blitz (1940–41) when its offices in London were bombed. Other supporting material may also be found in the Pinkerton archive now housed at the Library of Congress in Washington DC as well as the '1873 forgeries' files at the western branch of the bank now managed by the Royal Bank of Scotland.

At The National Archives in Kew, the official British Government and police files on both Austin and George Bidwell may be found (ref. TNA HO 144 20568, particularly files B and C), which also contain a wealth of treasury solictors' correspondence. Significantly for this narrative, there is a sworn statement drawn up for Freshfields by Willie Pinkerton, dated 26 August 1873, which is a unique and accurate record of the Bidwells' history up to that time.

At the outset in writing this book, I decided to start from scratch in transcribing the full Old Bailey trial (F5/11, Bank of England archive), which was compiled by Barnett & Buckler, who were official shorthand writers of Chancery Lane. Although an edited version of their work appears on the Old Bailey website, this online version does not carry the full exchanges between the participants. As a result, there is none of the drama or the interactions between the various witnesses and lawyers in front of Justice Archibald. The Old Bailey website also does not contain the first day's three-hour opening by Hardinge Giffard, which outlines the scope of the fraud (and includes 'the Kamchatka defence' as on p. 182 of this book). All timings of the proceedings are estimated from my own reading of the transcript. Dialogue has been taken from the record and any errors of fact or transcription are my own – some editing was necessary for clarity and interpretation.

Some of the more useful material in the Bank of England's archive includes the Brief for Prosecution in F5/1 in the case of Regina v. Noyes, Vernon & Meunier. This shows exactly what the authorities had thought about 'Warren' in the days immediately after the fraud was discovered. All major correspondence surrounding the case may be found in file F5/3 and includes all letters and telegrams from Willie Pinkerton to his father, brother and colleagues (many from Cuba): correspondence from the forgers to George Engels and to/from Edwin Noyes Hills. File F5/3 also contains the often hair-raising correspondence between Austin Bidwell and Jeannie Devereux when their marriage foundered, as well as all her letters and telegrams to her mother. The F5/3 series carries interesting information about Yankee Bligh, his investigation in 1871 and the correspondence with Scotland Yard and William Pinkerton. The F5/3 files also include the reports from Pinkerton operatives who were sent to Michigan to trace the greater Bidwell family.

The official printed depositions from all twenty-three hearings at the Mansion House may be found in F5/5. Exhaustive and complete proofs for the prosecution – used by the individual attorneys on the stand – may be found in F5/9. The complete indictment handed down is in F5/8. All the various letters from the forgers entered into evidence at the Old Bailey are in F5/10. This includes all correspondence between George and Nellie, arranged chronologically from pp. 1–15; all letters from Austin to Jeannie during their courtship and to others during his later incarceration, pp. 15–41; all Edwin Noyes Hills letters to his family, pp. 42–8, and various other miscellaneous materials, pp. 48–52. Other miscellaneous documents, including the Lyon Signalement Importante, may be found in F5/4.

Further telegrams from Austin Bidwell are contained in F5/6, while greater background details on Noyes Hills from his time in prison and his brother's testimony may be found in F5/30. The complete accounts ledger for the bank's activities is contained in F5/34, while supporting information for George Macdonnell's various extradition hearings in the United States are collected within F5/7.

As noted throughout the text, I have been careful in my use of both Bidwell brothers' versions of their life stories. Though they contain a wealth of colourful information, much of it is suspect. Many episodes can be shown either not to have happened or details have been conflated, exaggerated, or simply made up. George Bidwell's autobiography, Forging His Own Chains, appeared first in 1888 in which he claimed he would 'correct all mistakes or false reports' that had hitherto appeared in press coverage. While his writings did have the advantage that they were written nearer to the events they describe, George was trying to cover Austin's tracks (see p. 322). Similarly, stories that Austin Bidwell relates in Bidwell's Travels: From Wall Street to Newgate is often fanciful. Consider his curious claim that he had an uncanny ability in remembering what he terms 'trifling details' at the most dramatic moments. 'I can never forget a flower worn by a lady guest at my table,' he writes on p. 170 of that book, 'when, in the midst of enjoyment and surrounded by friends, the hand of the law in the form of a burly detective was laid on me in Cuba.' He adds that he also recalled the 'peculiar color [sic] of the wood of a cigar box standing on the sideboard'. The only problem with this supposedly vivid recollection is that it did not happen: see p. 277 of this book and also the (F5/6) Pinkerton letters from Cuba.

Equally notable is Austin Bidwell's amazingly bad sense of chronology. To take one example, he recalls having dinner with Mac and his brother at the Grosvenor Hotel in London in the summer of 1872; in reality, they did not move there until the end of that year. He talks of leaving London that November when that did not happen until two months later. Both the Freshfields Briefing document (F5/8) and tabulated diary (F5/10) clear up most of these mysteries, though the errors still remain in published accounts to date.

The Bank of England's archive contains extensive contemporaneous press clippings that also include those of newspapers no longer published (Daily Chronicle, Daily News, Echo and Pall Mall Gazette). These are bound in separate volumes from British (mainly F5/22) and American newspapers (mainly F5/23), which proved – as with a number of nineteenth-century newspaper archives – invaluable. The American press reports are much less reverential about the Old Bailey trial; references to laughter, for example, are missing from the more sober British ones. All references to the mood in court and, indeed, the weather (at key points in the story, too) come from contemporary reporting.

One of the better contemporary newspaper reviews was a large feature in the New York Sun of 15 September 1873, which was also reproduced in many other American news-papers in the weeks that followed. Two interviews with Austin Bidwell – from the Daily Picayune of 22 February 1893 and Macon Telegraph of 27 November 1896 – contain hith-erto unknown insights into his life. Further details about George Bidwell's history come from Chicago Tribune of 20 May 1873 (when he was being held at Newgate) and the Pall Mall Gazette, 14 May 1888 (when promoting his autobiography).

As this book has shown for the first time, the Bidwell brothers started out in fraud far sooner than previously known while George Macdonnell continued right up until the end of his life. Newspaper reports from April 1864 tell the story of W. Austin Bidwell's arrest and shooting, especially relevant issues of the *Cincinnati Enquirer* and *Cincinnati Times* (see also *Quincy Daily Whig*, 24 March 1864 and the *New York Sun*, 31 March 1864). The tangled details of Mac's last criminal escapades in California come from various contemporary newspapers, especially the *San Francisco Call* of 6, 7, 14 and 17 October 1903 and the *LA Herald*, 26 April 1901. Details of the passing of the Bidwell brothers in Butte, Montana are taken from 9 March 1899, *Bligh Daily Tribune*, the story of Charley and Benson Bidwell are covered in *The New York Times* of 15 March 1908, 25 October 1908 and 25 April 1909, as well as Benson's own highly fanciful biography (which is even more preposterous than those of his brothers').

Austin Bidwell's reminiscences about his upbringing are taken verbatim from William Pinkerton's letters from Cuba in April and May 1873 (F5/3). Further details about the better-known figures were taken from the Oxford Dictionary of National Biography, *Who Was Who* and *The American National Biography*. The biography of Sir Sydney Waterlow provided a useful insight into his life. Allan Pinkerton's *Thirty Years A Detective* was written by a ghostwriter and contains many episodes – especially about George Macdonnell – relevant to this story. In particular, Willie Pinkerton's reminiscences in the *San Francisco Daily Evening Post* of 30 September 1873, *The Daily Inter Ocean News* of 17 September 1891 and the *Rocky Mountain News*, 4 September 1887, were revealing. Two standard references to the Pinkertons' own history are Frank Morn's *The Eye That Never Sleeps: A History of the Pinkerton National Detective Agency* and James D. Horan, *Pinkertons: The Detective Dynasty That Made History*.

Select Bibliography

Bagehot, Walter, Lombard Street: *A Description of the Money Market* (King, 1873)
Bidwell, Austin, *Bidwell's Travels: From Wall Street to Newgate* (Crusader, 1897)
Bidwell, George, *Forging His Own Chains* (Crusader, 1888)
Bidwell, Benson, *Inventor of the Trolley Car, Electric Fan and Cold Motor* (The Hennebery Press, 1907)
Bidwell, Edwin H., *Genealogy of the First Seven Generations of the Bidwell Family in America* (Munsell's, 1884)
Byrnes, Thomas, *Professional Criminals of America* (Cassell, 1886)
Chabôt, Charles, *The Handwriting of Junius Professionally Investigated* (John Murray, London, 1871)
Clapham, Sir John, *The Bank of England, Vol. 2 1797–1914* (Cambridge University Press, 1944)
Crapsey, Edward, *The Nether Side of New York: Or the Vice, Crime and Poverty of the Great Metropolis* (Sheldon & Co, 1872)
Davis, Richard, *The English Rothschilds* (Collins, London 1983)
Deane, Marjorie & Robert Price, *The Central Banks* (Penguin Viking, 1995)
Dilnot, George, *The Bank of England Forgeries* (Scribner's, 1927)
Eldridge & Watson, *Our Rival The Rascal: A Faithful Portrayal of the Conflict Between the Criminals of this Age and the Defenders of Society, the Police* (Pemberton, Boston 1897)

Fraser, Steve, *Wall Street: A Cultural History* (Faber, 2005)

Geisst, Charles R., *Wall Street, A History* (Oxford University Pres, 1997)

Giuseppi, John, *The Bank of England: A History From Its Formation in 1697* (Evans, 1966)

Holtfrench, Carl-Ludwig, *Frankfurt As A Financial Centre* (Beck, 1999)

Horan, J.D., *Pinkertons: the Detective Dynasty That Made History* (Bonanza Books, 1967)

Huxley, Ann, *Four Against The Bank* (John Long, 1969)

Kynaston, David, *City of London, Vol. 1 A World of Its Own* (Pimlico, 1995)

Levi, Michael, *The Phantom Capitalists: The Organisation and Control of Long-Firm Fraud* (Heinemann, 1981)

Lombardo, Robert, *Organised Crime in Chicago: Beyond The Mafia* (University of Illinois Press, 2012)

McCabe, James Dabney, *New York by Sunlight and Gaslight: A Work Descriptive of the Great American Metropolis* (Douglass, 1882)

Mihan, Stephan, *A Nation of Counterfeiters, Capitalists and Conmen and the Making of the United States* (Harvard University Press, 2007)

Morn, Frank, *The Eye That Never Sleeps* (University of Indiana Press, 1982)

Picard, Liza, *Victorian London, The Life Of A City, 1840–1870* (Weidenfield, 2006)

Pinkerton, Allan, *Thirty Years A Detective* (Dillingham, 1900)

Poland, Sir Harry Bodkin, *Seventy-Two Years At The Bar* (Macmillan, 1924)

Read, Donald, *England 1868–1914, The Age of Urban Democracy* (Longman, 1979)

Santé, Luc, *Low Life: Lures and Snares of Old New York* (Granta, 1998)

Scammell, W.M., *The London Discount Market* (St Martin's, 1968)

Smalley, George Washburn, *The Life of Sir Sydney H. Waterlow* (E. Arnold, 1909)

Shannon, Richard, *The Crisis of Imperialism, 1865–1915* (Paladin, 1986)

Shpayer-Makov Haia, *The Ascent of the Detective: Police Sleuths in Victorian and Edwardian England* (Oxford University Press, 2011)

Trollope, Anthony, *The Way We Live Now* (Wordsworth, 1875)

B B. Turner, *Chronicles of the Bank of England* (Sonnenschein, 1897)

Walkowitz, Judith R., *Prostitution and Victorian Society* (Cambridge University Press, 1982)

White, Jerry, *London In the Nineteenth Century. 'A Human Awful Wonder of God'* (Cape, 2006)

Academic Papers

Papke, David Ray, 'Legitimate Illegitimacy: The Memoirs of Nineteenth Century Professional Criminals', *Legal Studies Forum, Vol. 9, No. 2* (1985)

Dolan, Paul 'The Rise of Crime In The Period 1830–1860', *Journal of Criminal Law & Criminology, Vol. 30, No. 6* (Mar-April), 1940

Haller, Mark. H, 'Historical Roots of Police Behavior, Chicago 1890-1925', *Law & Society Review, Vol. 10, No. 20* (Winter 1976)

Mallalieu, William C., 'Exploits of Yankee Bligh', *Filson Club History Quarterly, Vol. 43* (1969, Kentucky)

Index

Albemarle Hotel 222, 225, 226

Aldrich, F (See Austin Bidwell)

Alexandra Hotel 157, 160

Amsterdam 97, 148, 151, 156, 157

Anthony, Mr C.W. (*See* George Bidwell)

Archibald, Judge Sir Thomas Dickson 84, 87, 89, 90, 106, 133, 136, 138, 144, 154, 178–9, 182–3, 202–3, 225–7, 229, 233, 237, 248, 250, 262, 285, 315

Bagehot, Walter 93, 202, 213, 214

Baker, Louis (See Austin Bidwell)

Barings 134, 156, 157

The Battery Park, New York 273, 309, 310

Bayswater Road 187, 237, 104

Bidwell, A. Biron 276, 295

Bidwell, Austin Biron 15–6, 22–34, 46–9, 53–5, 64–71, 74–5, 77–80, 86, 88–92, 96–8, 101–4, 115, 122–3, 128–130, 144–5, 164, 168, 171–2, 174–6, 178–82, 185–92, 215, 218, 220–22, 224–5, 268–272, 276–7, 280–1, 283–92, 215, 218, 220–2, 224–5, 268–72, 276–7, 280–1, 283–289, 290–2, 295–6, 298–305, 308, 311–2, 315–26, 329, 330

Bidwell, Benson 23, 332

Bidwell, Biron 28, 29, 108, 276, 295

Bidwell & Co. 18, 29, 68

Bidwell, George 16, 26–8, 29, 31, 32, 40, 42–5, 50–1, 61, 63, 68, 71, 80–1, 95–8, 115–20, 148–53, 155–6, 161–2, 170–3, 180, 206–10, 211–2, 215, 218–9, 222–4, 226–38, 240, 242, 254, 256–65, 268, 311, 316, 319–20, 322–3, 326–7, 329–30

Bidwell, F. (See Austin Bidwell)

Bidwell, Jeannie (See Jeannie Devereux)

Bidwell, John aka 'Honest John' 25, 230, 231,234, 236, 237, 241

Bidwell, Joseph, 27, 32, 69, 228, 231, 266

Bidwell, Martha Ann (née Brewer) 68–71,230, 282, 301

Bidwell, Harriet 'Hattie' 23, 321, 323, 324, 327

Bidwell, W. Austin 18, 20, 21, 44, 60, 68

Bidwell, W.W. 64

Bidwell, Winnie 68

Bill of Exchange 8–11, 15, 41, 64, 66, 77, 83–4, 96, 125–7

Bingham Theodore (See Austin Bidwell) 15, 174–6, 185

Blatchford, Seward, Griswold & Da Costa 270, 274, 276, 279, 285

Bligh, Captain Delos 'Yankee' Thurman 57–60, 62, 64–5, 67, 69, 70–5

Blydensteins 133–4, 158–9

Bowles & Co. 63, 114, 165,

Bradshaw, Captain Austin (See George Bidwell)

Brewer, Martha A. (See Martha Bidwell)

Broadway, New York 51, 68, 72, 270, 300, 309

Brown, Charles Gordon (See Austin Bidwell)

Burton, George (See George Bidwell)

Byrnes, Tommy Inspector 53, 117–8

Calais 97, 103, 129, 155, 178, 220, 291

Cannon Street 161, 199–200

Challoner, George Boule 153–4, 167, 250

Charing Cross Station 178, 186, 194, 216, 234–5

Chatham Prison 319–20, 323

Cheshire, William 151–3, 250

Chicago, Illinois 15–6, 28–32, 45, 49–51, 55, 60, 63, 68–71, 73, 192, 271, 282, 301, 304, 307, 331

Cincinnati, Ohio 10, 13, 33, 93, 139, 165, 172, 181, 193, 198, 200, 204, 206, 210–13, 226, 239

City Police, London 15, 142, 232, 235, 239, 250–1, 258, 272, 279, 287, 297, 318

Civil War, American 28, 31, 33, 45, 47–8, 50–1, 58, 62, 65, 279

Clark, Henry C (See Austin Bidwell) 15, 187, 190

Coburg Hotel, London 130, 178, 180

Continental Bank 10, 13, 33, 93, 139, 165, 172, 181, 193, 198, 200, 204, 206, 210–13, 226, 239

Conklin, H.B. (See Edwin Noyes Hills)

Cooke, Jay 124, 200, 203–4

Cork 67, 256–60

Cotton 62–3, 69, 79

Coulson, Walter John 130, 179, 181

Courant, Monsieur (See George Bidwell)

Crapsey, Edward 35, 46, 48, 54–5

Curry, Deputy Sherriff 274, 294

Curtin, John (Pinkerton's detective) 277, 281, 286, 288, 291, 295, 297, 299,

Dalton, James 147–8, 153

Dartmoor Prison 319–20, 325

Devereux, Jeannie 22–34, 46–9, 53–5, 64–71, 74–5, 77–80, 86, 88–92, 96–8, 101–115, 122–3, 128–30, 144–5, 164, 168, 171–2, 174–6, 178–82, 185, 192, 215, 218, 220–22, 224–5, 268–72, 276–7, 280–1, 283–92, 295–6, 298–305, 308, 311–2, 315–26, 329–330

Devereux, Mrs 103, 105, 115, 172, 177, 181, 184, 185, 191, 192, 201, 251, 272, 282, 301

Devereux, Harry 104, 187

Devereux, Jenny 103, 184

Drummond's Hotel, Euston 237, 238, 266

Dublin 61, 65, 67, 256, 258–261

Duke's Road, Euston 217, 236, 237, 240

Durrant's Hotel, George Street, London 194, 195, 196, 294

Ebro, the 113–114

Edinburgh 21, 40, 81, 262–6

Edwards Hotel, Hanover Square 180, 187

Engels, George 54, 55, 60, 62, 64, 67, 70, 76, 80, 86, 92, 96–100, 104,

110–1, 113, 117–8, 121, 157

Euston 99, 117, 238–240, 255, 256, 266, 273, 325

Farley, Philip Inspector 275, 276, 285, 286, 298, 303, 318, 319, 333

Fenwick, Robert 91–94, 120, 123, 124, 128, 136

Ferguson, David (Edinburgh detective) 262, 263, 265

5th Avenue Hotel, New York City 272, 326

Fitzroy Square 243, 245

Ford's Hotel, Manchester Square 159, 160, 164, 170, 245

Francis, Colonel Peregrine Madgwick 122–9, 131–145, 197, 207, 213, 315

Franco-Prussian War 65, 66, 97, 154

Frankfurt 15, 16, 66, 73, 97, 148, 154, 155, 156, 158, 170, 180, 183, 186–190

Franklin, Ellen 244–247, 253

Fraud, Long Firm 19, 28, 29, 44, 62

Freshfields 21, 33, 75, 82, 93, 150, 154, 194, 223, 251, 262, 272

Gates, Edward Wilson 163, 168

Giffard QC, Hardinge, 83–4, 89, 92, 153, 157, 159, 163–4, 183, 188–9, 195, 212–3, 217–9, 222, 225–7, 229, 234–5, 237–8, 262, 281, 323

Gilbert, H E. (See George Bidwell)

Gilmour (See George Bidwell)

Golden Cross Hotel, London 137, 174, 200, 213

Gray, Frances Catherine 174–176, 178, 181, 183–4, 253–5, 273, 279

Green, Agnes 181, 248–51

Green, Edward Hamilton 79, 85–90, 92

Greenwich Street, Manhattan 49, 230, 283

Gutman, John R , Commissioner 279, 294, 299, 306

Hall, Edward alias Hills 225, 244

Hamburg 96, 133–4, 151, 153, 155–6

Hamilton, Emily and also Bessie 98–9, 107

'Harry' (See George Macdonnell)

Hartford, Connecticut 25, 28, 63, 64, 322

Haydon, Sergeant Michael 297, 298, 318

Haymarket, London 174, 175, 253

Hibbey, Captain alias of Austin Bidwell 103, 104

Hills, Edwin Noyes 14–16, 33, 35–8, 40–1, 49, 62–4, 119, 139, 165–8, 171–3, 176, 181–2, 184–5, 193–204, 206, 209–213, 225, 233–4, 237––9, 241–6, 253, 258, 266, 271, 278–9, 304–5, 308, 314, 316, 325–6, 331

Howe, Mr (See Edwin Hills)

Howell QC, David 197, 207, 209, 234, 241

Illness 118 134, 152, 217, 320

Irving, Jimmy Captain 275–6, 283–6, 303, 318–9

Jarvis, Judson, Deputy Sherriff 274–6

Justice Room, Mansion House 35–7, 39–41, 160

'Kamchatka defence' (Giffard) 182–3, 281

Kellogg Samuel R (See Hills)

Kenealy, Dr Edward 36, 37, 41, 258

Kibbe Frank 17, 18, 20, 44

Langham Hotel, London 66, 101, 103, 114, 117, 119, 166, 173

Laverock, Ann 263–5

Lidington, Alfred 211, 266

Liverpool 15, 66, 72, 76, 79, 87, 96, 99, 107, 162–3, 166, 168, 171–2, 208, 231, 254–6, 278, 310, 324–5

Lombard Street 10, 13, 78–9, 165, 197–8, 201, 202, 212, 214

London & Westminster Bank 37, 109–10, 132, 141, 143, 148, 151, 157–8, 250

London Bridge 80, 97, 196, 199, 200, 210,

Lord Mayor of London (See Sir Sydney Waterlow)

Louisville, Kentucky 55–60, 64, 67, 69, 71

Lucas, Cuban informant 268–70, 272, 281, 283, 287–8, 302

Lusitania, SS 99, 107

Lyall, Sir George (Governor of Bank of England) 36, 143, 261

Macdonnell, George 16, 28–9,

55, 57–76, 88, 97–8, 105–6, 114–5, 119, 156–60, 162–4, 173–4, 179–80, 181–92, 195, 204–5, 212, 225–6, 243, 247–250, 252–253, 256, 272–4, 279, 285–6, 299–300, 302, 306–7, 308–310, 325–9, 331

Macdonnell, Mary 325, 326, 328, 330

Macdonnell, Michael 63–4, 305

McIntyre QC, Mr 91–2, 94–5, 135–8, 140–2, 182

Mansion House 13, 35, 39–41, 81, 131–2, 138–9, 142–3, 148, 151, 159–61, 172, 193, 207, 211, 223, 228–9, 244–5, 258, 262, 299, 323

Mapelson, Colonel (See George Macdonnell)

Martinique, SS 224, 268, 269, 272

May, Frank 8–14, 37, 135, 212, 215

Metcalfe QC, Austin 105, 106, 163, 227, 229, 231, 247, 248

Meunier, Jules 226, 237, 239

Morrison, Gregory (See George Macdonnell)

Mowat, James 161, 162

Munich 97, 152, 154, 218

Nelson, J.R. (See George Bidwell)

Nelson's Portland Hotel 118, 173

Nelson & Co. printers 153, 167

New York Police Department 24, 46, 48–2, 55, 65–6, 231, 270, 273, 275, 285, 318, 322

Newgate 25, 41, 82, 190, 216, 223, 224, 233, 236, 241, 267, 299, 308, 311, 318, 319

North Atlantic Express Company 252, 257, 300

Norton, Owen, Newgate warder 232, 233, 236

Edwin Noyes (See Hills, Edwin Noyes)

Nunn, Harry 192, 221, 224, 281, 291, 302

Old Bailey 68, 89–94, 105, 108, 123, 132, 126, 136, 138, 140, 142, 144,

149–51, 156–60, 162–3, 176, 178, 180–4, 197–8, 202–3, 209, 212, 217, 219, 222, 225–9, 231–4, 237, 240, 245, 262, 279, 281, 286, 300, 312, 314–6, 330

Panic of 1873 203, 204, 214

Pacific Hotel, Greenwich Street 230, 283

Paternoster Row 146, 148, 149, 150, 151, 153, 157, 167, 211

Pentonville Prison 319, 326

Pinkerton, Allan 13, 21, 30–3, 50, 52, 56, 73, 309–10

Pinkerton 'operatives' 23, 25, 27, 30, 71–72, 74, 228, 230, 270, 272–3

Pinkerton, Robert 24, 30, 49, 51, 72, 281, 326

Pinkerton, William 22–4, 28, 32, 33, 57, 70, 72– 5, 103, 176, 201, 228, 230, 236, 270–2, 277, 280–3, 287–8, 291–6, 297–8, 300–5, 307, 309, 321, 331–2

Poland QC, Sir Harry Bodkin 122–7, 132–4, 136, 153, 176, 178, 179, 181, 183–5, 198, 199, 202–3, 210–11, 232, 239, 250, 253, 255, 312–13

Prostitutes 115, 117, 153, 175, 245, 296

Pullman carriages 123, 125, 128

Pyrenees 220, 221, 224, 269

Queen's Hotel 207–9

Queenstown 255, 256, 272

Regent Street 25, 115, 173, 176, 219, 246

Ribton, Mr. QC. Hills' attorney 139, 140, 212–3

Robinson, Jack, US Marshal 306–7, 309–10

Rothschilds 37, 41, 66, 97, 128–131, 133–4, 143–4, 160, 164, 177–8, 188

Scotland Yard 15, 67, 72, 74–5, 231, 235, 305

Sheridan, Walter (See Stuart, Stanford)

Siebert, Warren (See George Engels)

Silk Hats 48, 49, 53, 297, 307

Smith, Sergeant William 235, 250, 252, 265, 266

Spaulding, W.J. (See A. Bidwell)

Spittle, John Detective Sergeant 193, 194, 239, 265, 266

Stanton, John Thomas 14, 165, 198–9, 202, 210–3

Straker, Thomas 167, 211, 250

Swift, Edward (See George Macdonnell)

Taylor, Pastor J.B., (See George Macdonnell)

Telegrafo Hotel, Havana 268, 269, 278, 271, 281, 282, 291–294, 297

Thuringia 273–275, 285, 286, 319

Torbert, General Alfred Thomas Archimedes 269, 279, 281, 287–8, 290–1, 292

Trafford, A.H. (See Austin Bidwell)

Trouville 120, 152, 228, 229

Turkish Divan 174–6, 178

Union Bank of London 37, 96

Vernon, Nellie (Helen Ethel) 115–7, 120, 152, 154–6, 159, 160, 170–3, 197, 216–9, 222–6, 229, 234, 236–40, 242, 244, 246–7, 252, 300, 322

Wall Street 26, 45, 48, 50–1, 53–5, 65, 204

Warren, F.W., (See George Bidwell)

Waterlow, Sir Sydney 36, 38, 42, 82, 208, 223, 233, 266, 308, 316, 323

Wiesbaden 66, 155, 187, 190

Williams QC, Charles Watkin 85–7, 89, 149, 159, 247, 254

Wilkes, George 51–4, 75, 118, 270, 307, 332

Wilson, George (See George Bidwell)

Wilson, Oscar 297–9, 302, 304